Social History of Africa

PLANTING RICE
AND
HARVESTING SLAVES

D0221848

Recent Titles in
Social History of Africa Series
Allen Isaacman and Jean Allman, Series Editors

PLANTING RICE
AND
HARVESTING SLAVES

TRANSFORMATIONS ALONG THE GUINEA-BISSAU COAST, 1400–1900

Walter Hawthorne

Social History of Africa
Allen Isaacman and Jean Allman, Series Editors

HEINEMANN
Portsmouth, NH

Heinemann

361 Hanover Street
Portsmouth, NH 03801-3912
www.heinemann.com

Offices and agents throughout the world

© 2003 by Walter Hawthorne

ISBN: 0-325-07050-4 (Heinemann cloth)
ISBN: 0-325-07049-0 (Heinemann paper)
ISSN: 1099-8098

Library of Congress Cataloging-in-Publication Data

Hawthorne, Walter.
    Planting rice and harvesting slaves : transformations along the Guinea-Bissau coast, 1400–1900 / Walter Hawthorne.
        p. cm.—(Social history of Africa, ISSN 1099-8098)
    Includes bibliographical references and index.
    ISBN 0-325-07050-4 (alk. paper)—ISBN 0-325-07049-0 (pbk. : alk. paper)
    1. Slave trade—Guinea-Bissau—Atlantic Coast—History.   2. Balanta (African people)—History.   3. Balanta (African people)—Social conditions.   4. Balanta (African people)—Agriculture.   5. Oral tradition—Guinea-Bissau—Atlantic Coast—History.   6. Rice trade—Guinea-Bissau—Atlantic Coast—History.   7. Atlantic Coast (Guinea-Bissau)—History.   I. Title.   II. Series.
HT1419.G93H39   2003
306.3′62′096657—dc22   2003056670

British Library Cataloguing in Publication Data is available.

Printed in the United States of America on acid-free paper

Copyright Acknowledgment

T&C Digital

For Jackie

CONTENTS

ILLUSTRATIONS

MAPS

PHOTOGRAPHS

TABLES

FIGURES

ACKNOWLEDGMENTS

This book explores the resiliency of small-scale communities in the Guinea-Bissau region of West Africa. As I reflect on the many years that I spent researching and writing it, I am struck by the incredible amount of support that I have received from the communities of which I am a part. It is a great pleasure to have an opportunity to thank the scholars, friends, and family members who comprise those communities for all that they have contributed to this book.

I owe my greatest intellectual debt to my adviser and friend Richard Roberts. At Stanford University, where I did my graduate work, Richard taught me how to ask important questions, research them, and write about them. Both in and out of the classroom he challenged me and the close community of students who he assembled to make the most that we could of our abilities. He has read countless drafts of this book, which is as much a product of his dedication to the craft as it is mine.

Others from the Stanford community have also offered me their support and friendship over the years. In seminars and long telephone and electronic mail exchanges, they helped me conceptualize parts of this study. Many thanks to Emily Osborn, Lynn Schler, Benjamin Lawrance, Wilmetta Toliver, Tim Lane, Kathryn Barrett-Gaines, Thom McClendon, Meredith McKittrick, Steven Gish, Andrew Hubbell, and Jim Lance. At Heinemann, Jim also helped me a great deal with the editing and publishing of my manuscript.

While a student at Stanford, I received the first of many grants and fellowships that made the research and writing of this book possible. There generous financial support came from the History Department, the Foreign Language Area Studies Title VI program, Fulbright IIE, and the Andrew W. Mellon Foundation. At Ohio University, where I now teach, the History Department, African Studies program, and Ohio University Research Committee gave funding to me.

I conducted research for this book in Guinea-Bissau, Cape Verde, Portugal, and Senegal. In each of these places I was welcomed by people who made my stays comfortable and who did all that they could to meet my requests for interviews, books, and manuscripts. In Portugal, my friend Joaquin Almeida was a wonderful host and teacher. In Guinea-Bissau, Agostinho Clodé Suba Nania and his family made me feel particularly welcome. They fed me wonderful meals, gave me support and encouragement, and taught me Graça, the Balanta language. My good friend Carlos Intigue shared his knowledge of Balanta history with me and introduced me to my informants. He also helped with the translation and transcription of my interviews and looked out for me in countless ways in Catio. Domingos Nagague, known affectionately as Tita, helped me hone my card playing skills , dropped by in the evenings to chat, and did me the greatest of services by repairing and re-repairing my Renault 4. Also in Guinea-Bissau, Peter Karibe Mendy and Carlos Cardoso helped facilitate my archival and field research. During my first trips to Guinea-Bissau, I was graciously received by Ambassador Roger McGuire, Harriet McGuire, and all who staffed the U.S. Embassy. Rodney McMillian and others in the U.S. Peace Corps shared their knowledge of the country with me. In addition, I was greatly assisted by two friends who were conducting their own research in the country, Antonio Tomás and Thomas Micholitsch. They both exchanged many ideas with me. I would like to offer special recognition to Mam Nambatcha, a dear departed friend who spent hours and hours discussing history with me in Cufar. Above all, I am forever indebted to my informants, the Guinean women and men who had knowledge of the past that I set out to explore. I was constantly amazed by the willingness of the people of Guinea-Bissau to share their memories with me. They welcomed me into their homes, applauded my project, and offered me food and shelter.

None of my documentary research would have been possible without the help of an enormous and dedicated community of archivists and librarians. Special thanks to Karen Fung at the Hoover Institute and to all who assisted me at the Arquivos Históricos do Instituto Nacional de Estudos e Pesquisa in Bissau, Archives Nationales de Sénégal in Dakar, Arquivo Histórico Nacional in Praia, and Arquivo Histórico Ultramarino, Arquivo Nacional da Torre do Tombo, Biblioteca Nacional, and Sociedade de Geografia in Lisbon.

While researching and writing this book, I also relied on a community of Africanist scholars for both their knowledge and support. Marie Perinbam sparked my interest in African history. She pressed me to pursue a Ph.D. and helped me during the early stages of this project. I, like many others, miss her greatly. Pier Larson gave me considerable advice when I was both crafting my dissertation and rewriting it as a book manuscript. He greatly influenced my thinking on slavery and the slave trade. Joshua Forrest also offered me endless encouragement while I labored to transform my dissertation into this book. His comments on several drafts helped me recast some of my central arguments. Martin Klein provided important criticisms of a draft and of several articles in which I tested ideas. He has been extremely supportive of this project for many years. Series editors Allen Isaacman and Jean Allman saw promise in my manuscript and helped me better explain core ideas and rewrite the text so that it was more readable. Two anonymous readers also gave me much to think about. Thanks as well to Peter Mark, Philip Havik, Mustafah Dhada, John Thornton, Tom Spear, and Judith Carney for taking time to read and critique parts of this study in draft and article form.

A close community of scholars in the Department of History at Ohio University also influenced my thinking as I wrote this book. Special thanks to Steven Miner for sharing ideas with me and for structuring my schedule so that I would have time for research and writing, and to Patrick Griffin for closely reading parts of this study and offering terrific suggestions for ways to improve it. At Ohio University, I have found a home in the incredible African Studies community that Stephen Howard has brought together. While I was researching some finer points of this study, Stephen helped me find funding and put me in touch with a world of Africanists outside my field of history. Thanks also to Jason Cook of House of Equations, Inc. for his incredible attention to copyediting and to Joanna Tague for assisting with table calculations.

I also owe a tremendous debt to my family. My mother and father, Judy and Walter Hawthorne, have been amazingly enthusiastic about this project and contributed to it in more ways than they will ever know. Each read drafts, highlighted errors, and underlined passages that needed rewriting. In addition to them, I relied on my sister and brother-in-law, Sarah and Steve Covert, and their children, Paul and Benjamin, for their support.

Last but certainly not least, I thank my dog Bella for pulling me away from my work for some much needed fun and, most of all, for introducing me to Jackie one morning during a break from typing. Since we met, Jackie Belden Hawthorne, now my wife, has been a constant source of love, encouragement, and understanding. She spent hours making maps for me, shared ideas about this study with me, and pressed me to see this book through to its conclusion no matter how long it kept me from home. I can't find words to express just how important she is to me and how central she has been to this project, so I hope the dedication will serve as an indication.

Table 0.1 Translation of a Page of the 1856 Bissau Registry of Slaves

Names of the Owners and Their Residences	Name of the Slave	Sex		Nationality	Age	Signs	Professions	Observations
		Male	Female					
João Marques Barros of Bissau in name of his children Honorio and Clara	Paulo	134		Bissau	15	Long face, large eyes	Carpenter's apprentice	Died
	Leão	135		Nalu	28	Dumb	Carpenter	
	Andre Gomes	136		Thoma	49	Short, full face, short brow, large mouth, full lips	Rower	Fled
João Marques Barros of Bissau for Domingos Alves Branco	Umbellina		111	Floup	44	Regular stature, long face, irritable scars on back, left shoulder, and arms		Died
	Maria Lirá		112	Mandinka	34	Regular stature, round face, scars on face and belly		
	Antonia		113	Bijago	33	Regular stature, long face, crossed left eye, marked belly		Freed herself
	Luerecia		114	Mandinka	28	Regular stature, short face, pointed beard, right eye half-shut		
	Germania		115	Bissau	15	Regular stature, long face, eyes not very open	Dressmaker	
	Domingas Nhengo		116	Geba	9	Long face	Dressmaker's apprentice	Freed by his uncle on October 30, 1858

Source: AHU, AUL, GG, Lv. 0010, "Livro dos escravos do concelho de Bissau e ilheu do Rei," 1856, 29.

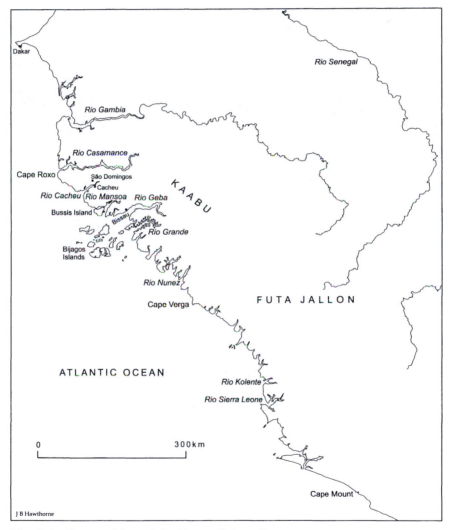

Rio Senegal

Dakar

Rio Gambia

Rio Casamance

Cape Roxo

São Domingos

Cacheu

K A A B U

Rio Cacheu

Rio Mansoa

Rio Geba

Bussis Island

Bissau

Rio Grande

Bijagos
Islands

Rio Nunez

FUTA JALLON

Cape Verga

ATLANTIC OCEAN

Rio Kolente

Rio Sierra Leone

0

300 km

Cape Mount

J B Hawthorne

Map 0.1   Senegambia and the Upper Guinea Coast

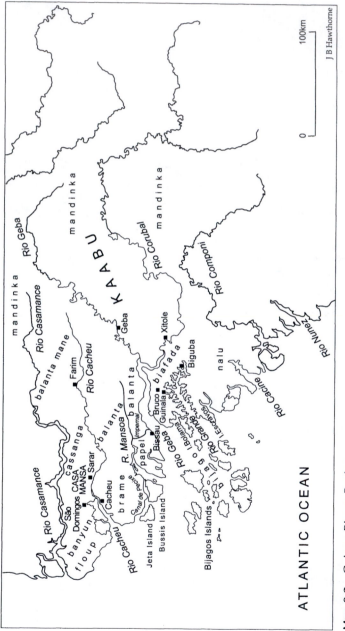

Map 0.2 Guinea-Bissau Region

INTRODUCTION

The West African coast is home to a species of vicious ants that sometimes attack *bagabaga,* or termite, mounds and carry away as many victims as possible. When collecting oral histories among people from an ethnic group known as Balanta in a rural region of Guinea-Bissau in 1994 and 1995, I happened to observe just such an attack. Ants, moving rapidly in long and orderly lines, entered a *bagabaga* mound and exited a short while later, their booty tightly held in their pincers. While I was watching, a Balanta friend explained that these were the "ants of Filim." Not coincidentally, Filim has long been a large and powerful village. Later that afternoon, I mentioned the "ants of Filim" to N'terra Siga, an elderly man, and inquired as to the origin of the name. Siga replied:

> In times long past, there were abuses by some larger groups of other smaller groups. They could attack the small groups and carry away the people and all of their belongings. For example, the group Filim was very large and very bad. Thus, they practiced many abuses. This group was the largest. Any other group that the people of Filim encountered was attacked. They stole all of their goods, and they carried away some of the people to their *moranças* [households]. This conflict of *morê* [organized raids] today is exemplified by the ants, which attack and kill the *bagabaga.* Thus, these ants are called the "ants of Filim."[1]

In the pages that follow, I argue that Siga's narrative speaks broadly of a time when Balanta communities conducted raids on distant strangers for captives, many of whom they traded to area merchants who exported them to the Americas as slaves. Only after months of talking with Balanta about their history did I conclude that Balanta participated in the Atlantic slave trade. Indeed, on the warm January afternoon that N'terra Siga spoke with me about the "ants of Filim," I was struck by his narrative's improbability. I knew that from the sixteenth through the mid-nineteenth century, Atlantic merchants had exported slaves from the ports of Bissau and Cacheu, which were less than a day's journey from Filim. But according to scholarship on the region, Balanta should not have produced any of those slave exports. In his watershed study of the Upper Guinea Coast (the section of West Africa between the Gambia and Cape Mount, of which Guinea-Bissau is a part), Walter Rodney claimed Balanta "were hostile to the slave trade" and did not participate in it.[2] Other historians described the slave trade from the region as a "royal monopoly."[3] But Balanta never had royalty, so how could they have entered the trade in human beings?

Like most in the coastal reaches of Guinea-Bissau, Balanta society was politically decentralized. In such societies, the village or a confederation of villages was the largest political unit. Though a range of positions of authority often existed within villages and confederations, no one person or group claimed prerogatives over the legitimate use of coercive force. In face-to-face meetings involving many people, representatives from multiple households sat as councils threshing out decisions affecting the whole. At times, particularly influential people emerged, sometimes wielding more power than others and becoming "big men" or "chiefs." However, no ascriptive authority positions existed. Consensus was king. Whereas state-based systems concentrated power narrowly in a single ruler or small group of power brokers, in decentralized systems power was more diffuse. Decentralized systems relied on unofficial *leaders,* but they lacked *rulers.*[4]

According to Rodney and others, the politically decentralized Balanta, who were situated on the coastal frontiers of Kaabu, one of West Africa's largest centralized slave-producing states, should have been victims of the slave trade. Lacking large-scale standing armies, Balanta should not have had the ability to organize against stronger captor states, particularly Kaabu. However, the more I talked with Balanta about the past, the more I discovered that they did not consider theirs to be a history of victimization. They did not see the era of the Atlantic slave trade as having "decimated" their society.[5] Most Balanta were proud of the challenges they said their ancestors had overcome. They found ways to stage attacks on distant strangers and established connections with area merchants. To merchants, Balanta traded captives, for which they received valuable imports, especially iron, deposits of which were lacking on the coast. Iron gave Balanta the ability to forge strong defensive weapons and to step up agricultural production. With iron-reinforced tools, Balanta adopted and developed sophisticated paddy rice farming techniques, producing surpluses of food that fed not shrinking but growing populations. By planting rice and harvesting slaves, politically decentralized Balanta defended and provided for their communities.

After more than a year living in Balanta villages and talking with Balanta about history, I turned my attention to written European and Afro-European archival records compiled by merchants, explorers, and administrators who visited the Guinea-Bissau region. My knowledge of Balanta oral narratives informed my reading of those documents and sharpened questions that I hoped to have answered by them. What I present here, then, draws from two sets of sources: oral and written.

I weave these sources together to tell a story about the social, political, and economic transformations that occurred in the politically decentralized Guinea-Bissau area as the result of interactions among coastal farmers, hinterland merchants, and Atlantic sailors between 1400 and 1900. The story begins just before coastal Africans and Atlantic merchants came into direct contact with one another and ends when Portugal and France were attempting to force people of the Guinea-Bissau area to pay taxes to their colonial regimes. Within these 500 years, the Atlantic slave trade rose and gradually came to an end, influencing transformations that occurred at two levels: the regional and the local. I explore these transformations in two contexts. Part I of this book employs a wide-angle lens to focus broadly on the coast. Through this lens, I examine how the Atlantic slave trade affected decentralized Guinea-Bissau area systems and societal interactions. Because the region is pictured broadly, Balanta do not appear in the foreground, but occupy a place next to Bijago, Biafada, Papel, Mandinka, Brame, and Floup, who composed the social patchwork that was Guinea-Bissau. Part II looks more narrowly at Balanta communities. Here I tighten my focus to view the dynamics of historical change within societies, processes that are not visible with a wide-angle lens.

The transformations I chart with these two lenses allow me to make several arguments. First, though Balanta, like many people living in decentralized societies, have not recorded their history on paper, and have few formalized and structured oral narratives, they nonetheless share memories of the past.[6] As in other societies, Balanta relate these memories through everyday interactions—during ceremonies, in songs and jokes, through farming and food preparation techniques, and even in discussions of things as seemingly insignificant as ants. Hence it is local vernaculars that professional historians of Africa, who seek to construct studies on an evidentiary base composed of more than culturally biased European sources, must find a way to tap. Second, I argue that, in the era of the Atlantic slave trade, decentralized societies were not necessarily the passive victims of their state-based neighbors. Relative to states, the communities that composed decentralized societies may have appeared as small as ants, but like ants they achieved great strength in numbers. They discovered ways to defend themselves and to engage with the Atlantic market. Third, I argue that within communities themselves, the changes that accompanied the rise of the Atlantic slave trade resulted from struggles among "insiders." Though the elder tellers of Balanta oral narratives may today depict the past as a time of great unity, when village members marched unquestionably together in long lines to prey on weaker enemies, Balanta communities were divided along faults that separated young and old, and men and women. The era of the Atlantic slave trade held great dangers for their communities, but it also held great opportunities for some individuals—opportunities that could lure them away to distant places. When young men and women moved to exploit those opportunities, older men sought ways to keep their communities whole. European expansion into the Atlantic did not determine how Balanta ultimately restructured local institutions to defend, retain, and provide for their members. Rather, Balanta, struggling among themselves and across community divides, shaped their own history, though not under conditions of their choosing.

ORAL NARRATIVES AND WRITTEN SOURCES

I constructed the evidentiary base for this study from both Balanta oral narratives and European and Afro-European written documents. Both sets of sources present problems. Indeed, a relative dearth of evidence is a major obstacle confronting those who wish to examine the histories of decentralized societies. In many cases, detailed written sources simply do not exist. Arab and European contemporaries were most concerned with commerce, and most commerce flowed to and was largely controlled by states. Hence, chroniclers wrote about states and left few accounts of the happenings in decentralized societies.[7]

Not possessing a solid body of written accounts of decentralized societies, many historians have also been confounded by the problem of collecting oral historical narratives in such societies. As African nationalists forced the dismantling of European colonial regimes in the 1950s and 1960s, a new generation of professional Africanist historians sought ways to reconstruct Africa's past without having to rely on written accounts left by "outsiders"—Europeans whose views were tainted by cultural biases and racism. They wanted to push the field in a different direction by telling African history from an "insider" or African perspective. At the time, most historians of the West thought written archival documents were the only reliable sources upon which to base scholarship. However, new Africanist historians could not draw on a large body of written insider sources since most indigenous African languages historically had no written form. Undaunted, they turned to a different sort of source: oral traditions, unwritten accounts dependent on the memories of successive generations. For decades, scholars have developed methodologies for collecting and analyzing oral traditions. In so doing, they have directed most of their efforts toward state-based groups, many of which have rich historical narratives that served to justify differences in power and wealth and to lend legitimacy to hierarchies. Many states employ a special class of indigenous historian—"men of memory" or "griots"—trained in the art of preserving traditions.

But what of societies lacking hierarchical political structures and specialists trained to retell historical narratives? What of decentralized societies? Many of the earliest and most influential scholars of oral traditions thought such societies have no need or means to disseminate and preserve historical information.[8] "In certain cases," Jan Vansina wrote in 1964, "oral traditions are very numerous and provide a framework solid enough for the reconstruction of history; this is true generally of societies with state structures. In other instances, on the contrary, they are scanty and vague; this is typical for uncentralized segmentary societies, for societies dominated by age organization or composed of bands, or with a simple and relatively 'anarchic' village structure."[9] Conducting research among the decentralized Langi of Uganda, John Tosh noted just such "vague" traditions. "Lango culture itself," he wrote, "is very poorly endowed with oral literature." This is largely because the chain of transmission of oral traditions among Langi—and in other decentralized societies—is weak:

> The handing-down of traditions from one generation to the next is seldom controlled by any set procedures; it does not have to coincide with specific rituals, nor is it done in secret. In Lango within the setting of the clan section there are—and were—no ceremonies during which traditions are passed on by the elders, nor is knowledge of the past restricted to a small number of people. . . . Traditions are transmitted piecemeal in any domestic setting which brings people together.[10]

Balanta also present oral narratives in an informal and piecemeal fashion.[11] That is, elders tell them during meals, over drink, or in the fields. In such settings, the conveyers of traditions might encounter some controls on accuracy or style, with others listening to make sure stories they know are told correctly. However, the informal manner in which Balanta relate narratives does restrict how much of the content of a message is handed down from generation to generation. Frequently only select segments or the general outline of stories parents or grandparents told decades earlier are remembered. Hence narratives simply do not survive "intact" or in detail for long.[12]

Another problem is that social organization places spatial limits on the information contained in oral narratives. As Vansina notes, "large-scale societies" possess histories that deal with large territories, often coextensive with the area of the state. The histories of "small-scale societies," on the other hand, are typically spatially limited to the area controlled by the largest political unit.[13] Tosh notes the spatial limitations of Langi traditions,[14] and I found similar limitations among Balanta, whose narratives often pertain only to the village. With the exceptions of narratives of early migrations and myths of creation, there are simply no widely accepted Balanta oral narratives; that is, there are no narratives that every Balanta community shares, agrees upon, and recounts. Narratives speak to very local concerns and local patterns of change, frequently accounting for or legitimizing the realities of the distribution of power and wealth at the village level but not beyond. In sum, historians studying the societies of decentralized regions face the problem of identifying what sorts of trends affected broad areas encompassing many villages or communities.[15]

I employ a variety of methodologies to address these evidentiary limitations. I call upon a wide range of written sources—the accounts of outside observers that, though scanty, do allow me to draw conclusions about historical change. This is particularly true when a reading of written outsider accounts is informed by a strong knowledge of insider oral narratives. When conducting field research, I had to accept that Balanta society is poorly endowed with oral traditions. However, I discovered that the very informal manner in which Balanta transmit traditions does serve to capture "culturally encoded" clues to the distant past. Hence my challenge was identifying the places where bits of historical information could be found, recognizing them, and then asking the right questions about them.

The informal discourse of everyday life was the "place" I found clues to the Balanta past and the "place" to which I attempted to anchor my questions during discussions with Balanta. As the story of the "ants of Filim" serves to illustrate, buried in everyday conversation are culturally encoded clues to Balanta history. Such clues can be applied as evidence in the studies of professional historians. Further, such clues can serve as starting points for framing meaningful questions during oral interviews with local people. By inquiring about Balanta names, the words that they use to identify animals and types of rice, the songs that they sing, and many other things, I was often able to frame my questions in a culturally relevant manner and to jar memories of cogent, if vague, narratives of the precolonial period. I did just that with N'terra Siga by asking about the "ants of Filim." Siga's narrative spoke broadly of a time when powerful Balanta villages staged raids on the weak, capturing people and claiming booty. He provided no names or specifics, but his narrative does evidence one of the ways that local people shaped and channeled the large forces set in motion by the rise of the Atlantic slave trade.

I could not access such narratives by asking about something as culturally irrelevant as "the time of the Atlantic slave trade." Indeed, Balanta narratives do not conform to a Western notion of historical periodization. Further, to the extent that they address world systemic process, they do so from a very local vantage point. In their oral narratives, Balanta understand large movements such as the Atlantic slave trade in terms of local struggles. Thus, Balanta narratives can only be accessed by historians who have some understanding of the very local ways that narratives are encoded and transmitted informally; they can only be understood by historians who have some understanding of Balanta language and culture; and they can only be recorded by historians who find ways to gain extensive access to the most local, sometimes secret, places where Africans spin narratives of enslavement.[16] The story of the "ants of Filim" is only one example of the manner in which Balanta informally transmit history. I raise it here to demonstrate that "the problem" of collecting oral traditions in decentralized regions might reside less in the weakness of chains of transmission than in the inability of historians to identify how traditions are captured in local vernaculars. In looking for structured and formalized ways that traditions are handed down, historians risk missing the everyday manner that common people preserve and tell *their* histories. In addition, by failing to comprehend the popular ways that history is circulated and remembered in any cultural setting, historians risk not being able to ask questions that reverberate with interviewees.[17]

Having found that Balanta possess oral narratives of the precolonial period, I still faced the problem of overcoming the narratives' limited spatial horizon. I wanted to write a history of the coastal region that Balanta occupy, but my sources spoke of very localized processes. To address this problem, I collected narratives in select sets of villages spread out over a large swath of territory stretching from northern Guinea-Bissau near the Senegal border to the southernmost region of Catio, and I attempted to identify the ways that multiple narratives encapsulate the local manifestations of larger pressures that I knew from written archival sources were exerting themselves at various times as the result of shifts in a dynamic Atlantic economic system. That is, I have linked narratives addressing village-level processes to larger regional and global processes. In many instances, I have noted similarities in the ways Balanta throughout Guinea-Bissau reacted to and channeled broad forces. In other cases, I have discovered that particular Balanta villages and individuals reacted quite differently.

STATES, DECENTRALIZED SOCIETIES, AND THE SLAVE TRADE

The oral traditions that new Africanist historians focused attention on in the 1950s and 1960s served as the evidentiary base to push the study of Africa in a new direction. Liberation from European colonialism, achieved by Ghana in 1957 and by other sub-Saharan African colonies shortly thereafter, brought great challenges to the continent, one of which was the debunking of racist colonial interpretations of history that had painted Africans as "savages," "children," and "inferiors" incapable of running their own affairs. As Africans looked for proud histories to serve as the foundations of new national identities, new historians sought to use oral traditions to demonstrate that Africans had historical "agency," that they had played a central role in shaping not only their own pasts but also those of Europe and the Americas. Through the 1960s and into the 1970s, the new Africanist historians pressed forward against the opposition of well-known scholars such as H. R. Trevor-Roper who said they were looking for the "unrewarding gyrations of barbarous tribes in picturesque but irrelevant corners of the globe."[18]

A focal point of the new Africanists' studies became the Atlantic slave trade. Their interest in the subject was encouraged by a growing scholarly commitment to African American history that accompanied the rise of the civil rights movement in the United States. Revisionist historians of the United States were churning out studies that, for the first time, focused not on white slave holders but on black slaves. They demonstrated that despite the horrors of slavery and the burden of racism, people of African descent in the Americas did not passively accept slavery in the manner of the "Sambo" of white stereotypes. Black slaves resisted oppression and exercised initiative, shaping their own lives and the world we know today. However, when it came to the African dimensions of the slave trade, a focus on African agency had problems. According to the racist narrative of earlier decades, Africa had been a "savage continent," made that way before the nineteenth century largely because of the ravages of the trade in human beings. As "savages," Africans had never commanded their own destinies; they had no serious role to play in their own history; they were victims, children rescued from evil slave traders by good Europeans. New Africanists set their sites on reinterpreting this culturally arrogant narrative. Yet as Philip Curtin explained in 1975, "If they said that African states had had real and legitimate interests, which they pursued through diplomacy and wars—that they were not mere puppets in the hands of the slave traders—the new Africanists could be accused of trying to shift the burden of guilt for the horrors of the trade from European to African heads."[19]

Hence, many new Africanists proceeded cautiously. That some Africans produced and traded slaves was indisputable. Why they did so became the focus of debate. Ironically, many new Africanists clung to the notion of African passivity. This was particularly true of "dependency school" scholars, who argued that Africa was economically and militarily weak vis-à-vis Europe and was therefore "forced" to trade human beings and raw materials for manufactured goods.[20] More recent studies of economies, military technology, and warfare have often rejected the notion of African weakness. The best have argued that Europe did not "impose" the slave trade on Africa, but that Atlantic merchants along with some African entrepreneurs introduced new political and economic opportunities to various parts of a politically divided continent. People "chose" to engage those opportunities differently, some in positions of power exploiting others and enslaving them.[21]

Power, indeed, lies at the heart of any exploration of slave production. Since enslavement most often involved violence or coercion, it was necessarily those holding power (be it political, judicial, economic, military, religious, or physical) who traded slaves. Recognizing this, many new Africanist historians identified the perpetrators of the slave trade in Africa as the political or military elite who controlled the machinery of any number of states and through it exploited commoners to augment their own strength. For example, Walter Rodney saw the slave trade as a product of class exploitation. "The responsibility for the slave trade," he wrote, "as far as Africans themselves bear a part of this responsibility, lies squarely upon the shoulders of the tribal rulers and elites. They were in alliance with the European slave merchants and it was upon the mass of people that they jointly preyed."[22] More recently, Boubacar Barry put forward a similar argument. "To satisfy its 'hunger for Negroes,' Europe imposed the slave trade as a permanent reality, with the complicity of the region's reigning aristocracies."[23] In time, slave "trading became a royal monopoly based on violence."[24]

Though they might be divided about Barry's notion that Europe "imposed the slave trade," most historians would agree that Africa's "aristocracies" perpetuated the trade and that successful aristocracies necessarily commanded "predatory states."[25] These highly militarized states reproduced themselves through large-scale warfare conducted on their peripheries or "slaving frontiers."[26] According to the "predatory state thesis," the rulers of such states had to conduct warfare in order to accumulate or capture the resources—slaves— that were needed for the reproduction of the state itself. Slaves served this purpose as agricultural laborers, as wives or concubines, and as commodities that could be traded abroad for imported goods. For the rulers of predatory states, then, slave production was crucial. The sale of some slaves brought income for state coffers, and the retention of others brought labor for a host of endeavors. Examples of these states include the Segu Bambara and Umarian state of the middle Niger valley, Damel Lat Sukaabe's Wolof Kajoor state, the Wattara state of Kong, and Samori's empire.[27]

Though the predatory state thesis helps explain how and why some slaves who entered the Atlantic trade were produced in Africa, its depiction of the common folk who lived within states' borders and those who occupied states' "slaving frontiers" has been problematic. In essence, the thesis illustrated the agency of some Africans but not of others. That is, it replaced the dichotomous vision of passive Africans and active slavers with one of passive African subjects and active African elites, and of active state core and passive frontier. These dichotomies obscure the ways that power was employed and contested in Africa. Within states themselves, leaders, after all, did not have absolute power. They lived in moral communities, acknowledging responsibilities and obligations to their subjects and expecting loyalty in return. When leaders attempted to breach their social contract—to perform immoral or illegitimate acts—their actions were sometimes checked or challenged. In some instances, common folk rejected the legitimacy of kings' slaving practices and attempted to stop them, their actions sometimes taking the form of popular revolts or civil wars that tore states apart. Some of the best recent studies of the slave trade in Africa have identified popular discontent with the trade as an explanation for the Islamic reform movements in Senegambia between the seventeenth and nineteenth centuries,[28] the rise of Kimpa Vita's Antonian movement in Kongo in the early eighteenth century,[29] and the Ravoandriana revolt in Madagascar in the late eighteenth century.[30] Recent scholarship has also explored how commoners living in states sometimes encouraged the slave trade, providing captives to Atlantic merchants for sale abroad. When warfare, drought, disease, political instability, or economic decline placed strains on societies, the slave trade offered opportunities that some common folk exploited. Out of greed or as a desperate attempt to aid kin or community, some kidnapped strangers and others organized small-scale raids, selling their captives to merchants for valuable imported goods.[31]

Though new scholarship has begun to grapple with the complexities of power relations in the core of predatory states, very little attention has been given to power relations on states' frontiers.[32] People living there were often members of small-scale or decentralized societies. Lacking large standing armies and, presumably, the ability to organize large-scale resistance, such societies have been depicted as the passive frontier victims of powerful predatory states. Ultimately, scholars argue, the slave trade must have led to their demise as localized institutions failed when attacked by predators' armies. Patrick Manning, for example, has depicted decentralized societies as the slave "sources" of state "captors." "Crudely, these were the Raided and the Raiders, the losers and the winners in the grim game of enslavement."[33] Similarly, Joseph Miller argues that in West Central Africa, the slaving frontier of powerful coastal states "dragged some of its victims out to sea in the undertow of slave exports that flowed from it, but it set most of the people over whom it washed down again in Africa, human flotsam and jetsam exposed to slavers combing the sands of the African mercantile realm."[34] But were those living outside predatory states mere jetsam? Were they unable to act, to defend themselves and their communities?

In this study, I argue that few societies were "sources" composed of "the raided." Few were "reservoirs" of potential captives. In very few instances can we point to people who were passively tossed in the currents of change or who allowed themselves to be plucked from the sands of Africa's shores.[35] Those living in decentralized societies and on the frontiers of predatory states adopted strategies through which to cope with the broad structural changes unfolding around them. In the Guinea-Bissau region, communities uprooted themselves from difficult-to-defend upland regions and settled in isolated, marshy, and riverine coastal zones. These zones provided natural hiding places for small groups and barriers inhibiting the movement of large slaving armies. Here coastal residents adopted new architectural designs for houses so slave raiders would have a difficult time snatching victims, and they concentrated these houses into fortified villages, or *tabancas,* in which they organized young men to combat external threats. Through these and other strategies many decentralized societies successfully resisted predatory states' slaving armies, forcing them to look elsewhere for captives and to go farther and farther afield. Since such strategies increased the cost of slaving and therefore the cost of the resource (slaves) that predatory states needed to reproduce themselves, the actions of decentralized societies certainly affected the stability of states themselves.[36]

However, it would be an exaggeration to say that the goal of individuals living on states' slaving frontiers was to fight back against the Atlantic slave trade itself. Most individuals—farmers, fishermen, salt producers, and traders—did not aim to bring about a revolutionary change in the Atlantic economy. Rather, they struggled to defend kin and community and to make the best of the opportunities presented to them. Thus, those who perceived themselves to be in a powerful enough position to do so, sometimes took advantage of the opportunity to enslave others. Some engaged with the slave trade out of greed and others to get much needed imports.[37] Residing in terribly dangerous places, farmers needed weapons for protection. Because they were inaccurate, cumbersome, and difficult to repair, European guns were not of much use. Lacking ore deposits of their own, coastal farmers desired iron, from which they themselves could forge spears, swords, knives, and arrows made entirely of or tipped with iron. Before the arrival of Atlantic sailors, iron-bearing merchants from the eastern interior who desired salt, dried fish, mollusks, and other goods had supplied the coast with some quantities of iron. However, with the rise of the Atlantic slave trade, regional trade patterns shifted. The most important traders no longer came from the east. They came from the west, from the ocean. They were not interested in salt or other coastal products. They demanded slaves. So to obtain iron from which to forge weapons to defend communities, many coastal people produced slaves.

To state that Africans living in decentralized societies produced and traded captives is not to say that common folk were "guilty" of perpetuating the slave trade. It is to recognize that as broad economic and political structures change, people are presented with limited sets of strategies that they can pursue. Individuals themselves could not hope to alter the structural realities of the Atlantic system; they could only seek to make the best of the options presented to them at the most local of levels. One of the cruel ironies of the Atlantic slave trade was that, in desperate times, individuals living on the frontiers of powerful regional states might one day have feared being swept up in an attack by a large army but on the next day might have used the power that they wielded locally to participate in the kidnapping of a stranger for sale abroad. To divide the Atlantic world into fixed sets of "victims" and "victimizers" or into "sources" and "captors" is, then, to obscure the realities of power in Africa and to render passive those who found ways to shape their own lives.

GENERATIONAL AND GENDERED STRUGGLES WITHIN COMMUNITIES

If the communities that composed decentralized societies defended themselves and sometimes produced slave exports, how did they do so? How were community institutions fashioned and refashioned to respond to the challenges presented by a dynamic Atlantic economic system? To answer these questions, I shift analytical lenses, from one capable of viewing broad regional interactions among societies in the Guinea-Bissau area to one powerful enough to explore local interactions among people within Balanta *tabancas*.

Throughout this study, I refer to *tabancas* as "communities," in the sense that they were composed of people who engaged in daily, face-to-face interactions with one another.[38] The *tabanca* is today the central social, political, and economic unit for Balanta. The most important rituals, proceedings of the largest decisionmaking bodies, and major agricultural activities are all organized and directed at the *tabanca* level. Balanta formed these communities in response to the intensification of slaving in the Guinea-Bissau area in the late seventeenth century. It was then that dispersed households, or *moranças,* came together to form *tabancas* on isolated and difficult-to-access lowlands, where together they could more easily defend themselves from powerful and threatening neighbors. In new and densely populated villages, strangers had to become neighbors; they had to find ways to overcome *morança* divides and to forge a sense of *tabanca* unity or community. Doing this required the fashioning of new local institutions through which *tabanca*-wide activities could be organized and predictability could be added to daily interactions.[39]

The *tabanca*-based institutions that I examine are marriages, age grades and councils of elders. Through marriages, Balanta facilitated cooperation with community members by forging enduring familial ties—*morança* to *morança* and also *tabanca* to *tabanca*. By fashioning an age-grade system that placed members of independent *moranças* into common "grades" or "groups" based on age and gender, Balanta further reinforced these ties. Brought together from different *moranças,* males in their grades and females in theirs grew up together, enduring common ordeals and performing common tasks. By fashioning councils of elders composed of older male members from all of the *moranças* in a *tabanca,* who sat together to hash out disputes and to make community-wide decisions through consensus, Balanta further strengthened community bonds.

However, no matter how firm these bonds became, as Balanta moved to meet the challenges presented by a dynamic Atlantic economic system, they did not always respond in unison. Neighbors did not always rise up together to thwart a common aggressor or to exploit a perceived opportunity. More often than not, Balanta responded to regional challenges *as individuals* who sometimes saw themselves sharing common interests and at other times clashed bitterly with those living in their midst. These clashes were not over whether or not communities should exist, but were over what the nature of community ideals and institutions should be.[40] Since older men, who sat on councils of elders, held considerable power over *tabancas,* community conflicts frequently took place across lines of gender and generation, with women and youths challenging older male attempts to control them. By reading as deeply into my sources as I can, I explore these sorts of conflicts. That is, I attempt to depict Balanta communities for what they were: individuals and groups of individuals—youths, women, and older men who often differed with one another and frequently struggled among themselves.[41]

In so doing, I follow a course charted by a large number of Africanist historians who have described communities and households as fractious places where women and men engaged one another over issues of production, consumption, and resource distribution.[42] Marcia Wright was particularly influential in demonstrating that African women had historical agency, that they had "strategies" that they pursued to shape their own lives.[43] Following Wright, others explored how women flexed political and economic muscle in a variety of societies through associations,[44] and how they challenged patriarchal power by running away, becoming prostitutes, expressing dissatisfaction through spiritual possession, and pursuing various other means of resistance.[45] Since written sources for the precolonial period often do not reveal much about individual experiences or the gendered dimensions of particular events, much of what we know of the dynamics of gender relations in Africa is derived from research about the colonial period.[46] As a result, the historiography generally gives the impression that the early twentieth century was unique or unusually transformative.

The relatively small number of studies exploring the dynamics of gender in precolonial Africa typically counters that impression, illustrating that the Atlantic slave trade was also an important catalyst for gendered struggles, particularly over how certain aspects of production were allocated to males and females in a variety of places. However, these studies have tended to adopt an unidirectional model of change. That model is built on the knowledge that over the course of the Atlantic slave trade more males than females were exported from the whole of western Africa. Thus, the ratio of men to women declined in many places on the continent. As the males who remained sought to maintain levels of agricultural production, "the shortage of men pushed women into taking up new areas of work. In areas where women had traditionally participated in agriculture, their role expanded to that of near total domination of agricultural labor."[47] In the eighteenth century, the kingdom of Kongo, then, experienced "a trend toward a predominance of females in the work force and a fairly strict division of labor by gender."[48] In the Anlo area of the Slave Coast, "male-dominated patrilineages exercised increasing control over the productive and reproductive capacities of women."[49] In the highlands of central Madagascar, the slave trade "feminized agricultural labor and impoverished households."[50]

Can we safely conclude, then, that across Africa the Atlantic slave trade created conditions whereby women performed "most of the agricultural work"?[51] Can we accept that in the precolonial period "the work of women was closer to the core of the African economy than was its English counterpart"?[52] In short, my answer is no. In some parts of Africa, women performed the bulk of agricultural work, but in others they did not. The impact of the Atlantic slave trade on the gendered division of labor differed from place to place. It is only by amassing more studies that we can understand the multiple ways Africans coped with the forces of a dynamic Atlantic system. Simply put, a trend away from performing the very difficult fieldwork necessary to identify local, insider sources that speak of change *within* precolonial communities and toward research based on relatively abundant written sources found in colonial archives has meant that scholars have too few local studies from which to discern broad precolonial patterns.[53] In finding ways to examine the interior structures of one decentralized society, I attempt to add to the precolonial story by demonstrating that localized struggles over resources led to the emergence of a gendered division of labor in Guinea-Bissau that was very different from what accepted historical models would have predicted.

In Guinea-Bissau, where some societies marketed more female than male captives to Atlantic merchants, the demography of the slave trade diverged from western African patterns. The reasons for this can be found by looking at how local people organized slave raids and agricultural production. Balanta slave raids were necessarily small affairs, bands of men drawn from the ranks of *tabanca* age grades made up quasi-military units that quickly struck unsuspecting strangers. Few in number, Balanta slave raiders generally avoided targeting men who might be trained in combat. Instead, they typically overpowered women and children, who were safer to transport over long distances, trading most of them for iron and integrating some into communities as wives or adoptees. But no matter how they were introduced into *tabanca* communities, women were never the centerpiece of agricultural production.

It was male labor that became crucial for the subsistence of Balanta society. Male labor was particularly important in the production of a new crop—paddy rice. As they settled in *tabancas* on isolated lowlands in the seventeenth and eighteenth centuries, Balanta slowly turned to this crop because it could be efficiently produced in their new environment. However, paddy rice required the input of large amounts of well-organized group labor. Hence, communities came to rely on the strongest and most cohesive group in their midst—young males whose ranks were divided into age grades. When Balanta stepped up rice production in the eighteenth century to feed growing populations and to meet regional demands for the crop, young males' work loads increased dramatically relative to what they had been before the intensification of slaving.

However, young males were reluctant to accept the implementation of this work regimen and therefore began seeking employment outside the communities of their birth. Some turned to "illegitimate" pursuits, enriching themselves personally by kidnapping victims for sale to area merchants. Others sought employment with area merchants in coastal entrepôts. Hence, struggles ensued between young male opportunists and older men who sought to retain the labor of their sons. Older men found some success in preventing young males from leaving by denying them the ability to make contact with outsiders offering alternatives to *tabanca* life. They did this by pressing women to carry out trade with area merchants, a strategy that had the unforeseen consequence of opening up new opportunities for some women to accumulate personal wealth and escape patriarchal village demands. Old men also offered young males a compromise: those who remained in the *tabancas* of their birth received the promise of power over their communities in the future as they passed through the ranks of the age-grade structure. In some parts of Guinea-Bissau, then, the impact of the slave trade was just the opposite of what many historians' models would have predicted. In Balanta areas, the slave trade masculinized agricultural labor.

New scholarship looking into the internal structures of Igbo communities in the decentralized Bight of Benin region has also challenged some of the prevailing assumptions about the Atlantic slave trade. Most significantly, G. Ugo Nwokeji's innovative approaches to the study of a region that, like Guinea-Bissau, at times produced a higher ratio of female slave exports than most of western Africa, have allowed him to peer deeply into local community structures and argue that the demands of the Atlantic and trans-Saharan slave trades cannot fully account for why Africans made the choices they did about who was sold to merchants for shipment abroad. Rather, decisions were rooted in "the character of African warfare and the role of women in the indigenous economy and social institutions."[54] A focus on communities in both the Guinea-Bissau and Bight of Benin regions forces us, then, to recognize that the slave trade took the shape it did as the result of the intersecting of local and global processes. Shifts in a broad Atlantic system placed pressures on communities, but the local struggles that ensued determined how myriad African political and social institutions were refashioned, how crops were produced, and how people were enslaved.

SUMMARY OF THE CHAPTERS

To explore shifts in both broad societal and local intracommunity inter-actions, I have divided this book into two parts. Part I looks at the larger Guinea-Bissau region. In Chapter 1, I begin my examination of societal in-teractions by focusing on how, prior to the mid-sixteenth century, the decen-tralized nature of Balanta society shaped its relationship with a West African economic and political system. During this period, Balanta *moranças* were dispersed across uplands, cultivating principally yams, which provided a means of subsistence but did not command high prices in regional markets. Lacking a valuable trade item, *moranças* were unable to acquire large amounts of imported iron and could not, therefore, forge the strong implements needed to produce the crops that farmers in the Gambia area specialized in, princi-pally paddy rice.

With a focus on how slaves were shipped from this particular politically decentralized region, Chapter 2 turns to the impact of European mercantile capitalism on systems and societies in the Guinea-Bissau area. Here I argue that Atlantic merchants and African communities forged lasting commercial ties with one another by working through the predominant African mode of social and economic interaction—the extended family. Thus, women became the nexus of coastal-Atlantic exchange as foreign male merchants who settled on the coast married locals, creating familial bonds with their relatives, the potential suppliers of exports. The chapter also explores the volume and de-mography of the slave trade from the Guinea-Bissau region. I argue that, un-til the mid-eighteenth century, most slaves exported from the region had their origins near the coast. The eighteenth century saw an important demographic shift, with supply lines from the interior bringing increasing numbers of slaves to Guinea-Bissau's coastal entrepôts.

Chapter 3 examines how the bulk of the slaves who left Guinea-Bissau before the mid-eighteenth century were made captive. Because the coast was decentralized, there were few broad-based institutions through which people in distant lands could establish predictable and ordered relationships. Uncer-tainty fostered mistrust, which in turn became the foundation for the slave trade. That is, the lack of a coastal institutional framework made far-off people strangers who posed potential military threats or who could be captured and traded for valuable imports. The most important of these imports was iron, which could be forged into weapons to defend communities from regional threats.

In Part II of the book, beginning with Chapter 4, I narrow the focus of the study to explore transformations within Balanta communities. Faced with heightened levels of regional violence, dispersed Balanta *moranças* sought ways to protect themselves by banding together into large *tabancas* on isolated lowlands for defensive purposes. To facilitate *tabanca*-wide cooperation, Balanta created new institutions that fostered a sense of village unity. During this period, older Balanta men manipulated community structures so that they could ensure their control over women and youths. Through these structures they directed young male age grades to stage raids on distant communities for the purpose of producing captives who could be traded for iron. Because raiding parties were relatively small, they did not generally have the necessary physical force to subdue large numbers of strong men. Hence they minimized risks by targeting females and children.

Chapter 5 continues an exploration of transformations in Balanta communities by demonstrating how older men directed male age grades to do much more than defend *tabancas* and raid for captives. In the late seventeenth and eighteenth centuries, male age grades also became a means for communities to organize young males into large work groups for undertaking new and labor-intensive agricultural pursuits, specifically the production of paddy rice. Since paddy farming became centered on young male labor, the period saw the masculinization of agricultural work. However, in coastal societies that were not swept up in the paddy rice revolution, agricultural labor was feminized, with males dedicating themselves more to slaving than to food production.

Turning to the nineteenth century, Chapter 6 examines how Balanta produced increasing volumes of paddy rice for domestic consumption and export. As the slave trade slowly died, the export of nonslave goods from the region grew. Given that coastal Guinea-Bissau was not controlled by a strong, centralized state, this chapter probes how Africans at the most local of levels adjusted to radical transformations in regional markets. It also explores the roles various actors—Balanta, other Africans, official Portuguese, European merchants, Cape Verdeans, and Luso Africans—played in the development of a system for producing and transporting nonslave goods.

At the end of the nineteenth and start of the twentieth century, the Portuguese, French, and British governments competed for monopoly control over that system. This competition led to a "scramble" for territory and the division of the Upper Guinea Coast and the rest of Africa into a series of European colonies. I end this study in the midst of that scramble, when coastal farmers in the Guinea-Bissau region were grappling with new challenges and different sets of options that they could pursue to overcome them.

NOTES

1. Interview with N'tera Siga, Patche Ialá, January 25, 1995.

2. Walter Rodney, *A History of the Upper Guinea Coast, 1545 to 1800* (New York: Monthly Review Press, 1970), 109.

3. Boubacar Barry, *Senegambia and the Atlantic Slave Trade* (Cambridge: Cambridge University Press, 1998), 107. A great number of studies focus on the role of the state and of state elites in directing the slave trade. See J. D. Fage, "Slavery and the Slave Trade in the Context of West African History," *Journal of African History* 10, no. 3 (1969): 393–404; Martin A. Klein and Paul E. Lovejoy, "Slavery in West Africa," in *The Uncommon Market: Essays in the Economic History of the Atlantic Slave Trade,* eds. H. A. Gemery and J. S. Hogendorn (New York: Academic Press, 1979), 181–212; Richard L. Roberts, *Warriors, Merchants, and Slaves* (Stanford: Stanford University Press, 1987); A. Adu Boahen, "New Trends and Processes in Africa in the Nineteenth Century," in *General History of Africa,* vol. 6, *Africa in the Nineteenth Century Until 1880s,* ed. J. F. Ade Ajayi (Oxford : Heinemann International, 1989), 40–63; Patrick Manning, *Slavery and African Life: Occidental, Oriental, and African Slave Trades* (Cambridge: Cambridge University Press, 1990); Martin A. Klein, "The Impact of the Atlantic Slave Trade on the Societies of Western Sudan," in *The Atlantic Slave Trade: Effects on Economies, Societies, and Peoples in Africa, the Americas, and Europe,* eds. Joseph E. Inikori and Stanley L. Engerman (Durham: Duke University Press, 1992), 25–48; Ivor Wilks, "The Mossi and Akan States," in *History of West Africa,* vol. 1, eds. J. F. Ade Ajayi and Michael Crowder (New York: Columbia University Press, 1972), 344–486; I. A. Akinjogbin, *Dahomey and Its Neighbors, 1708–1818* (Cambridge: Cambridge University Press, 1967); and Robin Law, *The Oyo Empire, c. 1600–1836: A West African Imperialism in the Era of the Atlantic Slave Trade* (Oxford: Oxford University Press, 1977).

4. David Northrup, *Trade Without Rulers: Pre-Colonial Economic Development in South-Eastern Nigeria* (Oxford: Clarendon Press, 1978), 92–93. Some, including myself elsewhere, have used the term "stateless" instead of "decentralized" to describe very similar political systems. Martin Klein makes a forceful argument for the use of "decentralized," since "stateless," in some scholarship, refers to societies with no leadership positions whatsoever. Though Balanta communities come close to this characterization of stateless societies, at times powerful and influential men did emerge in villages. See Martin A. Klein, "The Slave Trade and Decentralized Societies," *Journal of African History* 42, no. 1 (2000): 52; Andrew Hubbell, "A View of the Slave Trade from the Margin: Souroudougou in the Late Nineteenth-Century Slave Trade of the Niger Bend," *Journal of African History* 42, no. 1 (2000): 25–27; Andrew Hubbell, "Patronage and Predation: A Social History of Colonial Chieftaincies in a Chiefless Region—Sourdoudougou (Burkina Faso), 1850–1946" (Ph.D. diss., Stanford University, 1997); Walter Hawthorne, "The Production of Slaves Where There Was No State: The Guinea-Bissau Region, 1450–1815," *Slavery and Abolition* 20, no. 2 (August 1999): 97–124; Walter Hawthorne, "Nourishing a Stateless Society During the Slave Trade: The Rise of Balanta Paddy-Rice Production in Guinea-Bissau," *Journal of African History* 42, no. 1 (2001): 1–24; and Robin Horton, "Stateless Societies in the History of West Africa," in *History of West Africa,* vol. 1, eds. J. F. A. Ajayi and M. Crowder (New York: Columbia University Press, 1972), 78-119. Michael Taylor chooses the term "organized anarchy." Michael Taylor, *Community, Anarchy, Liberty* (Cambridge: Cambridge University Press, 1982), 5–7. "Acephalous society" also appears in scholarly work. "Acephalous" is derived from the

Greek *a,* meaning "without," and *kephale,* meaning "head." Thus, an acephalous society lacks an elevated ruler or head. "Segmentary lineage societies" are sometimes defined similarly. See Marshall D. Sahlins, "The Segmentary Lineage: An Organization of Predatory Expansion," *American Anthropologist* 63, no. 2(1961): 332–345; and Taylor, *Community, Anarchy, Liberty,* 73–75.

5. Barry, *Senegambia,* 81.

6. Graça, the Balanta language, has no written form. However, several Graça word lists have been published. See Fernando R. Quintino, *Algumas notas sobre a gramática balanta* (Bissau: Centro de Estudos da Guiné, 1951); Fernando R. Quintino, *Conhecimento da língua balanta através da sua estrutura* (Bissau: Centro de Estudos da Guiné, 1961); and W. W. Wilson, *Outline of the Balanta Language* (London: University School of Oriental and African Studies, 1961).

7. Horton, "Stateless Societies," 78–80; Northrup, *Trade Without Rulers,* 3–5; and Philip D. Curtin, "Africa North of the Forest in the Early Islamic Age," in *African History: From Earliest Times to Independence,* 2nd ed., eds. Curtin et al. (London: Longman, 1995), 71. In Guinea-Bissau, European and Afro-European merchants were certainly attracted to large coastal and inland trade entrepôts. See André Álvares de Almada, *Tratado breve dos rios de Guiné,* trans. P.E.H. Hair (Liverpool: University of Liverpool, Department of History, 1984), 92; André de Faro, "Relaçam (1663–4)," in *André de Faro's Missionary Journey to Sierra Leone in 1663–1664,* trans. P.E.H. Hair, Occasional Paper no. 5 (Sierra Leone: University of Sierra Leone, Institute of African Studies, 1982), 69; and P.E.H. Hair, Adam Jones, and Robin Law, eds., *Barbot on Guinea: The Writing of Jean Barbot on West Africa, 1678–1712* (London: Hakluyt Society, 1992), 170.

8. J. D. Fage, "Some Notes on a Scheme for the Investigation of Oral Tradition in the Northern Territories of the Gold Coast," *Journal of the Historical Society of Nigeria* 1, no. 1 (1956): 15–19. Also see Jan Vansina, *Oral Tradition: A Study in Historical Methodology* (Chicago: Aldine, 1965), 31, 170–172; Meyer Fortes, *The Dynamics of Clanship Among the Tallensi* (London: Oxford University Press, 1945), 26.

9. J. Vansina, R. Mauny, and L. V. Thomas, "Introductory Summary," in *The Historian in Tropical Africa: Studies Presented and Discussed at the Fourth International African Seminar at the University of Dakar, Senegal, 1961* (London: Oxford University Press, 1964), 64.

10. John Tosh, *Clan Leaders and Colonial Chiefs: The Political History of an East African Stateless Society, c. 1800–1939* (Oxford: Clarendon Press, 1978), 10–11. Also see Robert W. Harms, *River of Wealth, River of Sorrow: The Central Zaire Basin in the Era of the Slave and Ivory Trade, 1500–1891* (New Haven: Yale University Press, 1981), 8–12. Among decentralized Bobangi traders in Zaire, Harms found that "oral traditions known in the area were very few and very short (8)."

11. Balanta villages do have one location—the confines of village-based circumcision compounds where Balanta men gather every three or so years—in which elders pass on more formalized narratives. I have never attended a *fanado* (circumcision ceremony), nor do Balanta typically allow anyone from outside the *tabanca* into the circumcision compound. A few elders did discuss the circumcision process with me, but all of the discussions were "off tape," and I was always asked not to share what I was told. I will honor these wishes. It is generally known that, since independence, the state has attempted to regulate the timing and hygienic conditions of the ceremonies. Hence the nature of the *fanado* has at times been a national issue. Further, Balanta scholars have published some

information about the *fanado* for a Centro de Educação Popular Integrada project. Agostinho Clode Suba et al., "As estruturas sociais balantas," *Bombolom* 1 (no date).

12. Tosh, *Clan Leaders,* 11–12.

13. Vansina, *Oral Tradition: A Study,* 116–117. This is not to imply that only centrally controlled traditions exist within the confines of a state. Indeed, David Cohen found that the "unofficial" locally situated traditions of the Busoga were of particular value in historical reconstruction. David William Cohen, *The Historical Tradition of Busoga, Mukama, and Kintu* (Oxford: Clarendon Press, 1972).

14. Tosh, *Clan Leaders,* 8–9.

15. Vansina, *Oral Tradition as History* (Madison: University of Wisconsin Press, 1985), 116–117.

16. For discussions of the secretive memories of enslavement, see Martin A. Klein, "Studying the History of Those Who Would Rather Forget: Oral History and the Experience of Slavery," *History in Africa* 16 (1989): 209–217; Martin A. Klein, *Slavery and Colonial Rule in French West Africa* (Cambridge: Cambridge University Press, 1998), 238–239, 245, 251; and Susan J. Rasmussen, "The Slave Narrative in Life History and Myth, and Problems of Ethnographic Representation of the Tuareg Cultural Predicament," *Ethnohistory* 46, no. 1 (1999): 67–108. See also Pier M. Larson, *History and Memory in the Age of Enslavement: Becoming Merina in Highland Madagascar, 1770–1822* (Portsmouth, N.H.: Heinemann, 2000), 32.

17. Some scholars see a "growing new orthodoxy against oral tradition" among Africanists. See David Newbury, "Africanist Historical Studies in the United States: Metamorphosis or Metastasis?" in *African Historiographies: What History for Which Africans?* eds. Bogumil Jewsiewicki and David Newbury (Beverly Hills: Sage, 1986), 161. Pier Larson makes a particularly forceful argument that "serious work in vernacular languages and cultures" is needed to advance our knowledge of the impact of the slave trade on Africa. My work is informed by his. See Larson, *History and Memory,* 277–282. Taking an opposing view, Ralph Austen writes, "Most of the oral traditions concerning the slave trade that have survived among African and African-American communities cannot be used as empirical evidence because their narrative content is, by any modern standards, patently implausible." This is certainly not the case with many Balanta traditions. At times, however, assessing their plausibility does entail penetrating the metaphorical language in which they are often told or understanding the cultural context of the message. See Ralph A. Austen, "The Slave Trade as History and Memory: Confrontations of Slaving Voyage Documents and Communal Traditions," *William and Mary Quarterly* 58, no. 1 (January 2001): 237–238.

18. H. R. Trevor Roper, "The Rise of Christian Europe," *The Listener* 70 (November 28, 1963): 871; Jan Vansina, *Living with Africa* (Madison: University of Wisconsin Press, 1994), 123; Philip D. Curtin, *Economic Change in Precolonial Africa: Senegambia in the Era of the Slave Trade* (Madison: University of Wisconsin Press, 1975), 153–154; Patrick Manning, "Contours of Slavery and Social Change in Africa," *American Historical Review* 88, no. 4 (October 1983): 835.

19. Curtin, *Economic Change,* 153–154; Steven Feierman, "African Histories and the Dissolution of World History," in *Africa and the Disciplines: The Contributions of Research in Africa to the Social Sciences and Humanities,* eds. Robert H. Bates et al. (Chicago: University of Chicago Press, 1993), 167–212.

20. John K. Thornton, *Africa and Africans in the Making of the Atlantic World, 1400–1680* (Cambridge: Cambridge University Press, 1992), 1–9.

21. Ibid., 125. About the decentralized area of southwest Nigeria, David Northrup wrote, "It must be emphasized . . . that there was nothing inevitable or coerced about the role of this region in the slave trade." Northrup, *Trade Without Rulers,* 85–86. See also Larson, *History and Memory,* 83; Curtin, *Economic Change,* 153; and Joseph C. Miller, *Way of Death: Merchant Capitalism and the Angolan Salve Trade, 1730–1830* (Madison: University of Wisconsin Press, 1988), 105.

22. Rodney, *A History,* 114. See also Joye L. Bowman, "'Legitimate Commerce' and Peanut Production in Portuguese Guinea, 1840s–1880s," *Journal of African History* 28, no. 1 (1987): 87. Like Rodney, Bowman argues that it was the "African ruling and merchant classes in Portuguese Guinea" who were "active in the Atlantic Ocean trading network from the late fifteenth century, exchanging slaves, gum, ivory, dyes and hides for European imports." For a similar argument, see Rosemary E. Galli and Jocelyn Jones, *Guinea-Bissau: Politics, Economics, and Society* (London: Frances Pinter, 1987), 17–18.

23. Barry, *Senegambia,* 61.

24. Ibid., 107.

25. For an analysis, see Hubbell, "A View of the Slave Trade," 25–27; and Klein, "The Slave Trade and Decentralized Societies," 49–65.

26. On "slaving frontiers" see Paul Lovejoy, *Transformations in Slavery: A History of Slavery in Africa* (Cambridge: Cambridge University Press, 1983), 80, 83–87; Robin Law, *The Slave Coast of West Africa, 1550–1750* (Oxford: Oxford University Press, 1991), 188; Miller, *Way of Death,* 140–153; Steven Feierman, "A Century of Ironies in East Africa," in *African History,* eds. Philip Curtin et al. (New York: Longman, 1995), 358–359; Larson, *History and Memory,* 11; and Walter Hawthorne, "The Interior Past of an Acephalous Society: Institutional Change among the Balanta of Guinea-Bissau, c. 1450–1950" (Ph.D. diss., Stanford University, 1998), 171–176. Basil Davidson uses "slave watershed" in *Black Mother: The Years of the African Slave Trade* (Boston: Little, Brown, 1961), 197. On warfare and the production of slaves, see Larson, *History and Memory,* 12–13; Barry, *Senegambia;* Thornton, *Africa and Africans,* 99; Miller, *Way of Death,* 115–122, 122–159; Roberts, *Warriors;* and Lovejoy, *Transformations,* 66–78, 135–158.

27. Hubbell, "A View of the Slave Trade," 27; Richard L. Roberts, "Production and Reproduction of Warrior States: Segu Bambara and Segu Tokolor, c. 1712–1890," *International Journal of African Historical Studies* 13, no. 3 (1980): 389–413; Claude Meillassoux, *The Anthropology of Slavery: The Womb of Iron and Gold,* trans. Alide Dasnois (Chicago: University of Chicago Press, 1991); Klein, "The Slave Trade and Decentralized Societies"; and Klein, "The Impact of the Atlantic Slave Trade."

28. Martin A. Klein, "Social and Economic Factors in the Muslim Revolution in Senegambia," *Journal of African History* 13, no. 3 (1972): 419–441; Klein, "The Impact of the Atlantic Slave Trade;" Klein, *Slavery and Colonial Rule,* 1998, 44–45; and David Robinson, "The Islamic Revolution in Futa Toro," *International Journal of African Historical Studies* 8, no. 2 (1975): 185–221.

29. John K. Thornton, *The Kongolese Saint Anthony: Dona Beatriz Kimpa Vita and the Antonian Movement, 1684–1706* (Cambridge: Cambridge University Press, 1998).

30. Larson, *History and Memory,* 107–115.

31. Lovejoy, *Transformations,* 84–85; Hawthorne, "Production of Slaves"; Larson, *History and Memory,* 102–107. And see especially P.E.H. Hair, "The Enslavement of Koelle's Informants," *Journal of African History* 6, no. 2 (1965): 193–203.

32. Charles Piot has produced a wonderful study: "Of Slaves and the Gift: Kabre Sale of Kin During the Era of the Slave Trade," *Journal of African History* 37, no. 1 (1996): 31–49. See also the review in Klein, "The Slave Trade and Decentralized Societies."

33. Manning, *Slavery and African Life,* 39.

34. Miller, *Way of Death,* 149.

35. In West Africa, a few areas were "decimated" by slaving states. The Tanda of Senegal saw severe population decreases, people in the Birim valley of Ghana dispersed when threatened by slavers, and Samori "stripped Wasuli clean." However, as Klein emphasizes, "many areas were regularly raided but survived." Klein, "The Slave Trade and Decentralized Societies," 53.

36. Manning writes, "The cost of obtaining slaves rose as prospective captives learned to defend themselves better." Manning, "Contours of Slavery," 845.

37. Hawthorne, "Production of Slaves."

38. Jonathon Glassman, *Feasts and Riot: Revelry, Rebellion, and Popular Consciousness on the Swahili Coast, 1856–1888* (Portsmouth, N.H.: Heinemann, 1995), 20.

39. On institutions, see Michael Hechter, "The Emergence of Cooperative Social Institutions," in *Social Institutions: Their Emergence, Maintenance, and Effects,* eds. Michael Hechter, Karl-Dieter Opp, and Reinhard Wippler (New York: Walter de Gruyter, 1990), 14; and Jean Ensminger, *Making a Market: The Institutional Transformation of an African Society* (Cambridge: Cambridge University Press, 1992), 5. In her first chapter, Ensminger presents an excellent critical analysis of the literature on institutions. See also Douglas C. North, *Institutions, Institutional Change, and Economic Performance* (Cambridge: Cambridge University Press, 1990), 3–4.

40. See especially Glassman, *Feasts and Riot,* 8–25.

41. To the extent that I can, I attempt, then, to avoid the shortcomings of studies that underestimate the importance of intracommunity struggles in shaping institutions. For example, in his study of the Xhosa cattle killing of 1857, J. B. Peires argues that the event united "the major social classes of the precolonial social order in a communal defense of their way of life." J. B. Peires, *The Dead Will Arises: Nongqawuse and the Great Xhosa Cattle-Killing Movement of 1856–7* (Bloomington: Indiana University Press, 1989). Other works take a similar approach: Tabitha Kanogo, *Squatters and the Roots of Mau Mau* (Athens: Ohio University Press, 1987); Frank Furedi, *The Mau Mau War in Perspective* (Athens: Ohio University Press, 1989). As Larson notes, "for at least two decades scholars have been disaggregating and elaborating simplistic ideas about mutuality in communities." Larson, *History and Memory,* 34, 1–7. Similarly, Bill Bravman argues that community is not "shorthand for a harmonious group effect." Bill Bravman, *Making Ethnic Ways: Communities and Their Transformations in Taita, Kenya, 1800–1950* (Portsmouth, N.H.: Heinemann, 1998), 5.

42. See especially Dorthy L. Hodgson and Sheryl A. McCurdy, eds., *"Wicked Women" and the Reconfiguration of Gender in Africa* (Portsmouth, N.H.: Heinemann, 2001), 2–5.

43. Marcia Wright, "Women in Peril: A Commentary on the Life Stories of Captives in Nineteenth Century East-Central Africa," *African Social Research* 20 (1975): 800–819. Also see Marcia Wright, *Strategies of Slaves and Women: Life-Stories from East/Central Africa* (New York: Lilian Barber, 1993).

44. See Judith van Allen, "'Aba Riots' or Igbo 'Women's War'? Ideology, Stratification, and the Invisibility of Women," in *Women in Africa: Studies in Social and Economic Change,* eds. Nancy J. Hafkin and Edna G. Bay (Stanford: Stanford University Press, 1976), 59–86; Margaret Stroble, *Muslim Women in Mombasa: 1890–1975* (New Haven, Conn.: Yale University Press, 1979); and Iris Berger, *Religion and Resistance: East African Kingdoms in the Precolonial Period* (Tervuren, Belgium: Musee Royal de l'Afrique Centrale, 1981).

45. Marjorie Mbilinyi, "Runaway Wives in Colonial Tanganyika: Forced Labour and Forced Marriage in Colonial Rungwe District, 1919–1961," *International Journal of Sociology of Law* 16, no. 1 (1988): 1–29; Luise White, *The Comforts of Home: Prostitution in Colonial Nairobi* (Chicago: University of Chicago Press, 1990); Elizabeth Schmidt, *Peasants, Traders, and Wives: Shona Women in the History of Zimbabwe, 1870–1939* (Portsmouth, N.H.: Heineman, 1992); Patrick Harries, *Work, Culture, and Identity: Migrant Laborers in Mozambique and South Africa, c. 1860–1910* (Portsmouth, N.H.: Heinemann, 1994), 154–166.

46. Hodgson and McCurdy, *"Wicked Women,"* 3; Sandra Greene, *Gender, Ethnicity, and Social Change on the Upper Slave Coast: A History of the Anlo-Ewe* (Portsmouth, N.H.: Heinemann, 1996), 9.

47. Manning, *Slavery and African Life,* 132.

48. Susan Herlin Broadhead, "Slave Wives, Free Sisters: Bakongo Women and Slavery, c. 1700–1850," in *Women and Slavery in Africa,* eds. Claire C. Robertson and Martin A. Klein (Madison: University of Wisconsin Press, 1983), 171.

49. Greene, *Gender, Ethnicity, and Social Change,* 11.

50. Larson, *History and Memory,* 131. There are many other works that embrace a similar model. See Susan Martin, "Slaves, Igbo Women, and Palm Oil in the Nineteenth Century," in *From Slave Trade to "Legitimate" Commerce: The Commercial Transition in Nineteenth-Century West Africa,* ed. Robin Law (Cambridge: Cambridge University Press, 1995), 57–78. See also John K. Thorton, "Sexual Demography: The Impact of the Slave Trade on Family Structure," in Robertson and Klein, *Women and Slavery in Africa,* 44. According to Thornton, in the Guinea-Bissau area in the seventeenth century, an "unbalanced age and sex structure may also account for the very large share of work done by women." My findings contradict this.

51. Robertson and Klein, *Women and Slavery,* 9.

52. David Eltis, *The Rise of African Slavery in the Americas* (Cambridge: Cambridge University Press, 2000), 92.

53. See especially Larson, *History and Memory,* 280. In the 1960s and 1970s, oral histories were instrumental parts of the evidentiary base of studies of the slave trade. However, most recent studies have been based almost exclusively on written archival sources produced by outsiders, principally Europeans. See also Eltis, *The Rise of African Slavery,* 92. "Detailed studies of the role of women in seventeenth- and eighteenth-century Africa," Eltis complains, "are rare."

54. G. Ugo Nwokeji, "African Conceptions of Gender and the Slave Traffic," *William and Mary Quarterly* 58, no. 1 (January 2001): 47–66.

Part I

THE DYNAMICS OF REGIONAL INTERACTIONS

1

Political, Economic, and Agricultural Patterns Before the Mid-Sixteenth Century

From about the mid-sixteenth century, people living in coastal Guinea-Bissau reacted to the violence associated with the Atlantic slave trade and opportunities derived from contact with Atlantic merchants. In these uncertain times, they struggled to defend themselves and garner a share of the new and valuable merchandise being shipped to the coast. The social, political, and economic institutions of old were not up to the task. Coastal residents had to fashion new institutions through which to cope with the powerful forces affecting their daily lives. Though the transformations that ensued marked a radical departure from the past, change in and of itself was not something new to any of the complex and varied decentralized societies of the region. Like societies everywhere, these had never been static. Coastal dwellers were not a people without history. They had long found ways to meet new challenges. They had long adapted as ecological conditions altered, strangers introduced new ideas, and merchants brought new products and expanded trading opportunities.

By weaving Balanta oral narratives with narratives from neighboring state-based societies and the written observations of early Atlantic merchants, this chapter explores changes in the patterns of the tapestry of daily life in coastal Guinea-Bissau in the period before the intensification of the Atlantic slave trade. I focus primarily on Balanta communities before the mid-sixteenth century, examining the shifting nature of their relationships with other groups in the region.

Both exchange and resistance characterized these relationships. Balanta frequently exchanged ideas and material goods with people with whom they came into contact. Such exchanges often took place in regional markets where Balanta yam, salt, and cattle producers met and mingled with merchants, some of whom offered expensive items not found locally but carried from other ecological zones. Competing for these items with other coastal dwellers, most of whom produced the same mix of goods, Balanta purchasing power was weak. Their ability to accumulate long-distance trade items, particularly iron, which was valuable for reinforcing agricultural implements needed in the production of particular crops, was very limited.

Regularly meeting with others to trade, Balanta just as frequently resisted attempts by area groups, most importantly Mandinka from the powerful state of Kaabu, to dominate them politically. The decentralized nature of Balanta political and social structures and the physical environment that they inhabited facilitated this defense. Balanta, then, never became, as some scholars have argued, "layers within the large section of the population which laboured for the benefit of the [Mandinka] nobility."[1] They struggled, often successfully, to maintain the independence of their households.

BALANTA NARRATIVES OF "MIGRATION" AND THE MANDINKA EXPANSION TOWARD THE COAST

Early written and oral narratives indicate that Balanta have long inhabited a swath of territory near Guinea's coastline between the northern bank of the lower Rio Geba and the lower Rio Casamance. Balanta claim that the heart of this region is their "homeland." They say that they "migrated" there "in times long past" from somewhere in the east. In addition, Balanta migration narratives have two other common threads: Balanta left the east because of conflicts with either Mandinka or Fula, and these conflicts resulted from a Balanta propensity for stealing cattle. Having done research on Balanta-Bejaa near the Rio Casamance, Cornélia Giesing came to a similar conclusion: "In all of the known legends about their origin, Bejaa . . . define their relations with the symbolic figures of Mandinka and Fula domination as a relationship between *senhores* and escaped slaves or resistant warriors, those who, wanting to free themselves from their domination, fight for autonomy and succeed as farmers."[2]

The "migration" and "homeland" narratives that I collected range from the very simple to the somewhat more elaborate. For example, elder Mbunh Nanful gave a very brief answer when asked about Balanta origins: "It is said that Balanta have their origin in part of eastern Guinea-Bissau."[3] In more detail, elder Estanislau Correia Landim said, "The origin of Balanta was in Mali. For reasons involving Balanta thefts, *Malianos* [Mande-speakers or

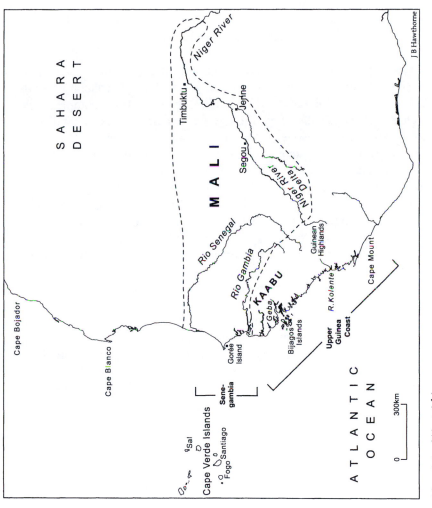

Map 1.1 West Africa

J B Hawthorne

Mandinka] revolted against Balanta. For this reason, Balanta left there. That is, some Balanta were stealing some things. When a thief was discovered, he resolved to kill the person who had discovered him. For this reason, *Malianos* chased after Balanta. . . . When Balanta left Mali, they went to Nhacra and then to Mansoa [on the Rio Mansoa]."[4] Speaking of early conflicts and the reasons Balanta occupy the shores of the Rio Geba and the Rio Mansoa, Fô Kidum told a similar story: "Balanta and other ethnic groups," Kidum said, "did not have good relations. There were always wars with other ethnic groups over land and theft. I can say that *B'minde* [Muslims in the east] always emerged victorious and pushed Balanta to littoral regions that Balanta discovered later were good for agriculture."[5]

Whether or not these narratives reveal information about an actual occurrence is a matter about which we can only speculate. Corroborating evidence is lacking. Hence, narratives of migration might conflate a complex series of events (such as a gradual expansion over the course of an extended period of time) into a single episode (such as a "migration," "flight," or "exodus"). Or they might be attempts to root the Balanta past in historic centers of power— Mali and the Futa Jallon. Or they might be ways to explain historical and present-day conflicts between Balanta and area state-based groups by fixing them in the distant past.[6] Though oral narratives often relate "factual" data in a manner similar to written narratives, they are also historical interpretations. In other words, oral narratives, like all knowledge of the past, are not inherited. They are actively made, actively interpreted and reinterpreted; they are struggled over as people seek to explain the present.[7]

What is clear is that Balanta narratives of "migration" fit well with recent studies purporting that many of the peoples of the Upper Guinea Coast are *refoulés;* that is, they were slowly pushed from the hinterlands to the coast probably as the result of expansions by Mandinka and other Mande-speaking groups. This expansion saw the absorption of some into a greater Mandinka world as myriad groups adopted Mandinka social, cultural, and political practices, though continuing to embrace many of their own. Indeed, many states that have been labeled "Mandinka," such as the Guinea-Bissau region's Kaabu, arose from a blending of many traditions rather than the imposition of a few.[8]

However, the Mandinka expansion and the control that Mandinka-influenced states attempted to exercise over populations in the Upper Guinea Coast region likely displaced many groups.[9] During a period from approximately 1100 to 1500, Mande-speaking people gradually spread from the prosperous and gold-rich Niger River basin toward the Atlantic in a movement led by merchants and smiths. Merchants exchanged iron, gold, and cloth (items that they had in abundance) for kola, salt, and *malagueta* pepper (items plentiful on the coast). Mandinka settlers who were looking for new areas to hunt and farm probably slowly followed these merchants.[10] As these Mandinka settled among coastal farmers, they linked oceanside and interior commercial networks. Interior networks were in turn linked across the Sahara to a vast trading complex stretching from North Africa to the Middle East and Europe.

The gradual expansion of Mandinka toward the coast was probably encouraged by the onset of a period of decreasing rainfall, forcing farmers and herders to move southward in search of better-watered lands. At the same time, the dry period saw the dying off of thick plant cover that harbored tsetse flies, allowing Mande-speakers around the upper Niger to breed horses and begin to perfect their skills at cavalry warfare.[11] Skillfully commanding these warriors, the Mandinka ruler, Sunjata, expanded his sovereignty over the interior savanna and upper Niger between 1230 and 1255, thereby creating the empire of Mali. His horse warriors followed established commercial routes toward the south and west, eventually reaching the Atlantic Ocean. These warriors gradually conquered vast areas as they moved through Senegambia. During Mansa Musa's reign, which lasted from 1336 to 1353, Islam spread widely throughout Mali, and the empire's economy expanded greatly as coastal salt-producing regions were integrated into broad West African trade networks. However, in time, the empire proved to be too large to hold together. Toward the end of the fifteenth century, Mali began to crumble as its distant provinces split away. Hence, Kaabu emerged as an independent state. Located to the east of coastal Guinea-Bissau, it straddled important trade routes that moved goods along the Gambia, Cacheu, Geba, and Corubal Rivers as well as between northern states and the prosperous southern Futa Jallon plateau. It was therefore well positioned to exploit new commercial ties with Atlantic merchants in the centuries to come.[12]

The Mandinka expansion greatly affected Senegambia and large parts of the Upper Guinea Coast. George Brooks writes that the Mande language became "diffused among conquered groups" and that Mande-speakers instituted "tripartite hierarchical social structures comprised of ruling elites and free people, endogamous occupational groups, and domestic slaves."[13] Similarly, Boubacar Barry emphasizes that "Kaabu, unlike the original societies of the Southern Rivers area [coastal Guinea-Bissau to Sierra Leone], was highly hierarchical." Ruled by a *mansa* chosen from one of its three most important provinces, Kaabu was a confederation that eventually encompassed a vast amount of territory and threatened the security of coastal societies in the Guinea-Bissau region. Supporting the *mansa* was the military aristocracy, or *nyaanco*. Below them came the nobility, or *korin,* who ruled over free peasant producers, and the castes of craftspeople, or *namaalo,* who made leather products and iron and kept traditional histories. Below these groups were slaves, some of whom were attached to the royal court and others of whom were bought and sold in markets.[14]

Whether or not Balanta and other groups "fled" to the coast to escape Mandinka advances or were already situated near the coast when Mandinka merchants and horse warriors slowly encroached on the region, oral narratives clearly indicate that Balanta perceive their ancestors as having been resistant to Mandinka and Mandinka-influenced state attempts at domination. Further evidence for Balanta recalcitrance might be found in the Mandinka word *balanto*, which means "those who resist." It is likely that Mandinka heard the word frequently in places harboring "resisters" and therefore incorporated it into their everyday speech.[15] Resisters, then, refused to recognize Mandinka authority, uprooting their communities and taking refuge on the coast. In this riverine area, large armies could not easily maneuver and horses could not be used effectively since they were susceptible to the *Trypanosoma rhodesiense* parasite, which was transmitted by tsetse flies found throughout the zone.

That Mandinka-influenced states had a difficult time establishing suzerainty over the coastal region in which Balanta resided is also apparent from André Donelha's 1625 description of Guinea. Discussing Mandinka *farims,* or regional leaders, he wrote, "In our Guinea there are four chief Farims, for though the kings who are kings over kings take the title of Faran, they are not as powerful (as Farims), and they each obey one of the Farims." Listing the names of the *farims* who ruled from the northernmost point, the Gambia River, to the southernmost point, the "hinterland of Serra Lioa," Donelha said that Farim Brasó ruled "over the Rio Grande de Bonabo," which is now known as the Rio Geba. Farim Brasó was a Mandinka and the head of "different nations—Cassangas, Banhus, Bramos, Balantas, Beafares and other nations— although some do not obey him because he is far away."[16] Donelha's observation that on the Rio Geba some did not obey the Farim Brasó makes clear that centralized Mandinka kingdoms found it difficult to conquer and rule coastal regions.[17]

If some Balanta resisted Mandinka suzerainty, refusing to assimilate into a greater Mandinka world, other Balanta became *mandinguizada.* That is, some Balanta did assimilate, to one degree or another, into Mandinka society. There can be little doubt that over time many Balanta intermarried with Mandinka, their children and children's children considering themselves more Mandinka than Balanta. Further, many Balanta, though not actually adopting a Mandinka identity, were greatly influenced by Mandinka social and cultural norms. Historically, foreign observers, coastal dwellers, scholars, and Balanta themselves have recognized a variety of Balanta "subgroups," distinguished by differences in linguistic, cultural, and social characteristics.[18] Among these is a group known as Bejaa or *Balanta-mané* ("Balanta-Mandinka" or Balanta who resemble Mandinka). Bejaa are situated in the northern part of Guinea-Bissau, where they have clearly been affected by centuries of contact with Mandinka states. The political structures of Bejaa communities are more hierarchical than those of other Balanta communities, Bejaa have oral narratives that link them directly to the interior Mandinka state of Kaabu, their houses are built in a Mandinka fashion, and in certain aspects of their dress and religion they resemble Mandinka.[19] At times, Bejaa traded with the Mandinka-controlled state of Casa Mansa on the Rio Casamance and paid tribute to Mandinka rulers. As a result, Bejaa created and fostered an identity that is unique—neither Balanta nor Mandinka.[20]

BALANTA POLITICAL STRUCTURES

Written accounts also tell us a bit about the political structures of Balanta society before the rise of the Atlantic slave trade. The earliest European observers indicated that Balanta governed themselves through institutions controlled at a very local level. That is, they made clear that these coastal farmers were not organized into states or chieftaincies. Politically, they were decentralized. At the beginning of the sixteenth century, Valentim Fernandes noted that there was very little stratification in Balanta society. Everyone worked in the fields, with no ruling class or families managing to exclude themselves from daily labor.[21] In 1615, Manuel Álvares commented, "They have no principle king. Whoever has more power is king, and every quarter of a league there are many of this kind."[22] In 1627, Alonso de Sandoval wrote that Balanta were "a cruel people, [a] race without a king."[23] And later that same century, Francisco de Lemos Coelho confirmed this, saying that much of the territory of the Balanta "has not been navigated, nor does it have kings of consideration."[24]

These descriptions make clear that, like many coastal societies of the region, Balanta did not recognize status groupings. Or, as one elderly Balanta explained about "times long past," "Balanta did not have a chief. It was Fula and Mandinka who had chiefs."[25] At times, particularly strong, knowledgeable, or talented people might have differentiated themselves from their neighbors and achieved positions of some prominence, but no family or class emerged as rulers among Balanta. In face-to-face meetings, community members sought consensus when threshing out decisions. Such was probably the norm in many societies on the Upper Guinea Coast and Senegambia before Mandinka influences were felt and state hierarchies emerged in some places.[26]

Though the earliest written texts do not describe how Balanta organized their politically decentralized society, linguistic evidence provides some clues. Today an *alante ndang,* or respected male elder, heads each Balanta household, or *morança.* In Graça, the Balanta language, *alante* means "man," and *b'alante* is the plural form; *ndang* means "big," and *b'ndang* is the plural form. Hence, *b'alante b'ndang* translates as "big men." A male Balanta is not recognized as an *alante ndang* and cannot head a household until he is circumcised, which usually happens sometime around or after the age of thirty, depending on the region. It is evident that the ethnic group name "Balanta" was derived from the word *b'alante*. As a show of respect—an acknowledgment of social position and authority—*b'alante* is part of most greetings and comes up repeatedly in conversations among "big men." For example, today, any group of men entering a Balanta household's compound is generally welcomed with some expression beginning with the word *B'alante,* such as *B'alante, abala lité utchole?* or "Men, how are you?"[27] Hence it is likely that Europeans, Mandinka, and other visitors to the coastal territories in the Guinea-Bissau region heard the word *b'alante* frequently and dubbed those using it "Balanta" (Portuguese), "Balante" (French), or "Balanto" (Mandinka). Significantly, Balanta do not typically refer to themselves by any of these names but by the term *B'urassa,* or *Urassa* in the singular. For our purposes, this linguistic confusion is important for one reason: the fact that the earliest written records make frequent reference to a group called "Balanta" and "Balante" and emphasize that this group did not have "kings of any consideration," indicates that *b'alante b'ndang* have long occupied prominent positions within Balanta political and social structures. Early Balanta communities, then, were decentralized and gerontocratic. Male elders held power, but regionally and within communities this power was not concentrated in a single household or ruling class.

Male elders passed this power to male heirs. "Sons," Álvares emphasized in 1615, "are the legitimate heirs to their fathers, and are their successors." That is, at some point in their lives, sons became *b'alante b'ndang,* assuming the prominent positions within Balanta political structures that their fathers had occupied. One important step toward becoming a respected elder was marrying. Before they married, young men had to obtain some number of cattle from their fathers and then had to present these to the father-in-law in exchange for his daughter.[28] Cattle, then, were commonly accepted as bridewealth, or the socially recognized valuable that formally symbolized marriage and served as a tie between two families. Since young men obtained cattle from their fathers and expected one day to inherit land and other possessions from them, they were bound to their fathers in a relationship of dependence. Within this decentralized gerontocracy, young men labored for their elders, waiting for the day that they would become *b'alante b'ndang.*

One of the earliest records that we have of the word *b'alante* comes from André Álvares de Almada. Having observed the Upper Guinea Coast in the 1560s and 1570s, he wrote, "The Creek of the Balantas penetrates inland at the furthest point of the land of the Buramos [Brame]. The Balantas are fairly savage blacks."[29] From this account, then, we can surmise that since at least the sixteenth century, and likely earlier, *b'lante b'ndang* held power within a highly decentralized Balanta political and social organization comprising independent *moranças,* perhaps linked to one another by familial and marriage ties facilitated by the exchange of bridewealth.

The decentralized nature of Balanta society is probably what made it so resistant to what Avelino Teixeira da Mota called *mandinguização,* or the process by which many peoples of the Upper Guinea Coast gradually assimilated with Mandinka.[30] Joye Bowman writes that, when establishing Kaabu, Mandinka rulers achieved legitimacy by marrying into some ruling families and conquering others militarily. "The oldest family in any given area was entitled to rule at the village level, and the larger territorial level."[31] Mandinka rule followed this pattern throughout Biafada areas around the Rio Grande, where powerful families controlled a number of small states, and through much of Guinea.[32] After bringing a hierarchically structured society under the rule of a greater Mandinka state, Mandinka *farims* demanded tribute from and exercised control through the head of the conquered territory.

In much of coastal Guinea-Bissau, however, no large state predominated. When attempting to establish authority within such an area, Mandinka would have found it impossible to gain legitimacy through intermarriage. There were simply too many independent centers of power into which to marry. Thus, each Balanta *morança* would have had to have been subdued, one after another. And had conquest proved possible, Balanta society, like others in the region, had no "king" through whom Mandinka could have exercised any authority or collected any tribute. The region, then, remained from the time of the Mandinka expansion until the start of the European colonial period largely independent of state control.

AGRICULTURAL PATTERNS

Given what we know about the early political structure of Balanta society, what can we say about Balanta agricultural patterns? Assuming Balanta have always farmed as they do today, many scholars hold that, by directing young men to clear dense lowland mangroves and construct large earth and post dikes, Balanta produced and traded great quantities of paddy rice before the mid-fifteenth century, before the intensification of the Atlantic slave trade. Part of the reason that this view is widely accepted might be that scholars have long described decentralized societies as fixed, rigid, and unchanging— "holdovers" from some distant past.[33]

Yet evidence indicates that Balanta were not prolific producers of paddy rice until well after the arrival of Europeans in Guinea-Bissau. Indeed, Álvares emphasized in 1615 that the Balanta territory "does not lack vegetables such as beans, pumpkins, yam, and it has all the staple crops in great quantities, except for rice, of which it has little. Cows, goats and hens are raised in large numbers. The land is meadow throughout, lacking any sort of wood for burning, in place of which they use *milho* [maize] canes and cow-dung."[34] In sum, if Balanta produced rice, they produced such small quantities that they were not evident to Álvares.

Following Álvares, the mix of crops that Balanta produced in the early seventeenth century consisted of beans, pumpkins, maize, and yams. Oral narratives and contemporary observations support this conclusion, emphasizing that Balanta were, above all, *milho* and yam farmers.[35] Elder Mam Nambatcha told me, "Balanta have grown rice for a long time. When they gained knowledge of rice, they started to cultivate it principally." He said that in Anhi, the *tabanca* in the Rio Geba region where he was born, "*milho* was the first crop grown." "After sometime, Balanta in that area gained knowledge of rice."[36] Similarly, some narratives explaining how Balanta as a people emerged in the Guinea-Bissau region in a *tabanca* called Dugal speak of *milho* as their first crop. One version describes a Biafada hunter visiting the part of Oio known as Nhacra. Settling there during the rainy season, he began to farm. One day he was visited by a group of female Papel traders from Bissau who were searching for foodstuffs for their suffering island. "Seeing that the hunter had great quantities of *milho* one of the women decided to stay." The others returned to Bissau with stories of the successful hunter-farmer. Thus, many more women abandoned their houses on Bissau and went to Nhacra. "Having more women with him, he decided to go to Quinara to get some young men to marry the Papel women and thus was born the first [Balanta] population of Dugal."[37]

Other sources speak of the production of yams. Almada, for example, reported that Balanta traded yams to Biafada.[38] Moreover, in the seventeenth century, Coelho was struck by the quality and quantity of Balanta yams offered for sale to European ships on the Rio Impernal, near the island of Bissau. Coelho said that on the river, "Balantas . . . come tamely to your ship to sell what they have, namely, staple foodstuffs, which they have in large quantities. They also have a plant they cultivate called 'yams,' which grows underground like turnips. They have many of these, and those from here are the best in all Guinea, so the ships buy quantities of them, which they carry both as a regular food and as a treat."[39] With Europeans actively seeking rice to feed ship crews and human captives, it seems clear that, if Balanta had been major paddy rice producers, they would have marketed it along with yams.[40]

This is not to imply that paddy rice was not cultivated on the Upper Guinea Coast before the arrival of Europeans. Roland Portères figures that Africans have grown rice in West Africa for thousands of years. The earliest areas of cultivation of a variety of indigenous African rice, *Oryza glaberrima,* he argues, was the middle Niger delta, where today there is a concentration of wild forms possessing genetically dominant characteristics.[41] From the middle Niger, delta rice production spread to Senegambia, where farmers planted this variety of rice along the coastal reaches of the Gambia River. Farmers also

Photo 1.1   Mam Nambatcha at his *tabanca* in Cufar, March 1995. Photo by Walter Hawthorne.

cultivated rice in the highlands of Guinea. These two locations are thought to be the "second cradles" of *O. glaberrima* production. From these cradles, *O. glaberrima* spread throughout the Upper Guinea Coast and Senegambia as Africans adapted it to a variety of environmental conditions. Asiatic *O. sativa* arrived later, via East Africa, especially Madagascar. Portuguese merchant-sailors probably introduced this variety of rice to the Upper Guinea Coast in the early sixteenth century. *O. sativa* thrived in paddies in which some coastal Africans had been producing *O. glaberrima* for centuries.[42]

African farmers have long utilized varieties of both *O. glaberrima* and *O. sativa* in different types of cultivation. The first type, upland or dryland rice cultivation, was adopted in areas that lacked free-standing water but still received substantial levels of rainfall. Upland rice requires at least 1,000 millimeters of annual rainfall, and these levels are attained throughout Guinea. In the area of Guinea-Bissau, hinterland peoples, especially Mandinka, were cultivators of upland rice. After felling trees, they cleared lands by burning and then lightly hoed and seeded the soil. They planted at the start of the rainy season and harvested after the rains ended.[43]

The second type of rice cultivation—wetland or lowland cultivation—was practiced in areas where the water table was naturally higher than the land or where man-made dikes kept the ground submerged. Lowland farming can be subdivided into two categories depending on the depth of the water: deep-water cultivation and floating rice cultivation, which respectively refer to rice production in water that is 0.5 to 1 meter deep, and rice production in water deeper than 1 meter. African farmers adapted indigenous *O. glaberrima* to a variety of water depths.[44]

Farmers have utilized many types of deep-water cultivation, and the techniques that they have adapted have varied with topography and technological innovations advanced in myriad locations. First, floodwater rice cultivation involved the transplanting of seedlings into freshwater pools, which remained as rivers receded after seasonal flooding. There were many areas in Africa—such as the Senegal, Niger, Mono, Zou, and Oueme Rivers—that favored this type of rice cultivation. Second, with controlled submersion, farmers erected a series of dikes or bunds, often fitted with valves, to control the flow of the water to and from a paddy. Third, mangrove rice cultivation required the clearing of coastal mangrove forests and leaching of salt from the soil before rice could be produced. This was accomplished by introducing a large quantity of freshwater onto the soil so that salt levels could be dissipated enough to permit cultivation. Mangrove farmers typically constructed dikes and paddies to capture fresh rainwater and hold back the tidal surges of brackish rivers.[45]

There are three important differences between mangrove and upland rice farming. First, yields with mangrove cultivation are considerably higher than with upland cultivation. Mangrove paddies yield 1–3 tons per hectare.[46] Upland cultivation, on the other hand, yields only about 600–800 kilograms per hectare. Hence, in areas of paddy rice production, population densities may be higher than in areas of upland rice production.[47] Second, upland and mangrove rice cultivation required different levels of labor organization. Upland rice cultivation can be successfully undertaken by small groups of workers. However, paddy rice cultivation, particularly in mangrove swamp areas, requires very large and well-organized inputs of labor. The clearing of mangroves and building of dikes can only be accomplished with unified bands of workers capable of performing very strenuous tasks, perhaps the most arduous of any agricultural tasks performed in West Africa.[48] Third, paddy rice cultivation in mangrove swamp areas can only be undertaken with iron-edged tools.[49] Before iron was widely circulated, coastal people, using punch-hole planting techniques and clearing trees by girdling with stone tools, may have farmed some amount of upland rice. Or as Mariano Martinho Natidai explained, they may have "farmed rice on land where there were few *paus*," few sticks or little timber, that is, on clear uplands. Without iron, he said, the twisted branches and roots of mangroves could not have been cut. Iron was required for mangrove rice farming.[50]

In sum, we should find paddy rice cultivation only in areas with relatively compact settlement patterns, in societies possessing institutions capable of bringing together bodies of laborers for demanding projects, and among peoples with access to large amounts or iron. These conditions did prevail in some coastal regions before the arrival of Europeans in West Africa.[51] In one of the first descriptions of rice production on the Upper Guinea Coast, Gomes Eannes de Azurara, a Portuguese chronicler, wrote that in 1446, Stevam Alfonso, having gone ashore off "a river which was of good width" some "sixty leagues beyond Cape Verde," reported having "found much of the land sown, and also possessing many cotton trees and many fields sown with rice." And he said that all that land seemed to him "like marsh."[52] Though this account is sketchy, the fact that the land was "like marsh" indicates that some farmers were producing some sort of wetland rice at this time. However, there is no indication that they were clearing mangroves or building dikes. Further, the precise location of Alfonso's landing is unclear.[53]

It was not until the end of the sixteenth century that a traveler gave a detailed description of the methods used in rice cultivation in the Senegambia region. In 1594, Almada, reflecting on earlier voyages, wrote that the area of the Gambia River was "very abundant in provisions of *milho* and rice." Further, he noted that since the fields were so close to the river, Africans constructed *tapumes de madeira,* or wooden fences, to keep hippopotamus from eating and destroying the rice. In a short passage, Almada spoke of large earthen barriers, or *valados de terra,* that were constructed to control the surge of the river, and he said that farmers transplanted rice from one set of fields to another.[54] In 1623, Richard Jobson left a similar description of the Gambia: "But in Rice they do set it first in smal [*sic*] patches of low marsh grounds, and after it doth come up, disperse the plants, and set them in more spacious places, which they prepare for it, and it doth yeeld [*sic*] a great increase."[55]

Possessing a dense population, a hierarchical political system through which large bodies of workers could be organized, and iron purchased from interior Mandinka smiths, Gambia-area Mandinka were practicing some sort of paddy rice agriculture before the arrival of Europeans on the coast. Balanta, however, did not have access to large supplies of iron and did not have densely populated settlements. Hence, in the period before European contact, they were not proficient paddy rice farmers.

COASTAL REGION TRADE PATTERNS

How widely did iron and other goods circulate in coastal Guinea-Bissau before the sixteenth century? "One puzzle of Senegambian iron production," Philip Curtin writes of precolonial Senegambia, "is the fact that smelting seems to have been confined to the interior. Many visitors described the high furnaces of Bambuhu, Gajaaga, Fuuta Tooro, and Bundu, but the reports of smithing nearer the coast are either silent about the sources of iron or say explicitly that it was imported." Curtin continues, "By the sixteenth century, the coastal states imported iron from their own hinterland as well as buying it from the Europeans."[56] From Almada's description, it is evident that iron was also scarce just to the south in the Guinea-Bissau region. In fact, he reported that European or Luso African merchants shipped iron south from the Gambia to the Rio Grande and Rio Cacheu.[57] Similarly, in the early sixteenth century, the Portuguese caravel *Santiago* purchased 1,924 iron bars from the Kolente River and then bartered them for slaves and ivory on the Rio Cacheu.[58]

Before the mid-fifteenth-century arrival of these merchants, Biafada-Sapi and Biafada-Mandinka trade networks had transported some quantities of iron and other goods to the Guinea-Bissau region. In dugout canoes capable of carrying in excess of 100 people and great amounts of cargo, skilled Biafada mariners connected to a number of small Biafada states along the Rio Grande, the Rio Corubal, and the upper Rio Geba and ventured south along the Atlantic coast, where Sapi-speakers resided.[59] Aided by seasonal winds and currents that permitted well-timed voyages down the coast and back, Biafada traveled perhaps as far as the Kolente River, an important kola-producing area. Kola, a nut with high caffeine levels, was valued by Mandinka, who consumed it after meals and gave it as gifts. As they traveled along the Atlantic coast, Biafada purchased kola, *malagueta* pepper, iron, and cloth. Mariners transported these items northward, when seasonal winds permitted, toward the area of Guinea-Bissau and Senegambia, where they were in great demand.[60]

Biafada likely discontinued their ocean travels at the Rio Geba. Strong coastal winds and currents beyond this point made seafaring very difficult. But this did not mean that the north-south flow of trade goods ended there. On the Geba, Biafada met Papel sailors, who resided on the islands of Bissau and Bussis (Peixe) and who were masters at navigating north to the Rio Cacheu by way of a circumlocutory route from the Rio Impernal to the Rio Mansoa to the Canal de Pecixe to the Canal de Jeta to the Rio Cacheu. This route allowed Papel sailors largely to avoid the strong Atlantic winds and currents that made coastal travel between the Geba and Cacheu difficult and to link the Rio Geba and the Rio Grande to the Banyun-Bak trading network that moved goods between the Rio Cacheu and the Rio Senegambia.[61]

Continuing their journeys past Bissau and up the Rio Geba, Biafada mariners met and traded with riverside dwellers—Balanta, Papel, and Biafada farmers.[62] Those residing on the lower Geba produced great quantities of salt, which Biafada traded upriver to Mandinka, who used it to preserve and flavor foods. Noting the ubiquitousness of salt manufacture by Africans on the Upper Guinea Coast from the time of the arrival of the first European merchant-sailors, Walter Rodney said that salt was "the most important item fostering contacts between the littoral and the hinterland."[63] In the area of Guinea-Bissau, Africans made salt by collecting it from the sun-dried soil of tidal flats and then purifying it through a boiling process. Coastal people also produced and traded smoked and dried fish, as well as other products from the sea, especially mollusks. Further, when venturing inland, merchants may have filled empty space in their boats with yams and other agricultural products.[64]

With their vessels loaded with kola from the area of Sierra Leone and an array of products from Guinea-Bissau's coastal zone, Biafada mariners continued their journey upriver, where they finally met and traded with Mandinka merchants at ports on the *ria,* or sunken coastline's edge. "The most distinctive feature of the Upper Guinea Coast," George Brooks writes, "is its *ria* . . . coastline (the Portuguese word *ria* means estuary or inlet). Geologic activity submerged the coast from the Saloum River to northern Liberia, enabling the ocean to flood coastal areas and make water brackish for tens of kilometers up rivers and tributary streams."[65] In the area of Guinea-Bissau, the end of the *ria* coastline approximately marks the start of the savanna-woodland region.

Rainfall differentials between coastal and savanna-woodland areas are significant. In Guinea-Bissau, for example, Bafata, which is situated in the interior, receives about 1,500 millimeters of rainfall annually, and Bissau, which is situated only about 100 kilometers to the west, receives 2,000 millimeters— a difference of 25 percent. There are also great variations in humidity. Harmattan winds blowing hot air to the south from the Sahara parch interior forests and grasslands, especially between December and February. Closer to the coast, where ocean breezes lower temperatures, water tables are high year-round, and rivers and swamps keep humidity levels elevated.[66] It is no coincidence that major trading centers have long been located at the *ria* coastline's edge. Where the sunken coastline gives way to an elevated plateau marks the farthest point to which large water-going transport vessels can venture. Hence, towns located on this ecological border have long served as transshipping points for goods being moved between the interior and Atlantic.[67]

But navigational limitations are not all that account for the successes of trade centers located at the edge of the *ria* coastline. Indeed, at the borderline between two ecological zones, Geba, Farim, Bafata, and Xitole were important entrepôts where coastal people or their "middleman" buyers met and traded with savanna-woodland peoples and their commercial representatives. Biafada merchants traded kola, fish, mollusks, salt, and other products

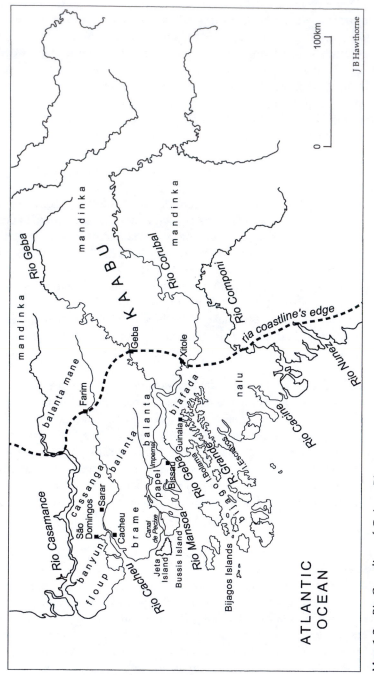

Map 1.2 *Ria* Coastline of Guinea-Bissau

J B Hawthorne

found plentifully or produced easily near the sea, and Mandinka merchants traded domestic animal products (such as meat and hides), cotton, cloth, gold, metals (especially iron), and myriad other items found or produced in the interior. In sum, ecological variations encouraged the trade of items that were of great value to people in both regions.[68]

It was in coastal markets that Biafada and other merchants sold many of the goods that they obtained in inter–ecological zone exchanges. Rich in goods from connections to coastal and inland long-distance trade routes, Biafada attracted large numbers of people to their markets. In the later part of the sixteenth century, the largest Biafada market was in Guinala and was called the "Bijorrei Fair." It may have drawn an astounding 12,000 people each time it was staged.[69] Markets of varying sizes were held in many locations in coastal Guinea-Bissau. They were scheduled periodically, according to a timetable that varied from place to place. Brame markets, for example, were held on a six-day rotation, Biafada markets occurred once every six or eight days, and on other parts of the coast, merchants sold their wares on Wednesdays and Fridays.[70] On the island of Bissau, Papel also hosted markets. Linking Biafada-Sapi and Banyun-Bak trade networks, Papel appear to have accumulated a wide range of goods that they traded among themselves and with others. "On the island," Manuel Álvares wrote in 1615, "they have many markets to which the Balantas come with cows, goats, varieties of food crops, which the Papels here buy from them for iron, cloths from the Island of Santiago and palm oil."[71]

THE WEAKNESS OF BALANTA PURCHASING POWER

Though Balanta traded with various groups in the region, the goods that Balanta offered, yams, cows, staple foods, and other provisions, did not bring very high prices. Hence, Balanta households could not afford to purchase many of the expensive goods brought to the coast by Mandinka, Biafada, and Papel merchants. Balanta participation in regional markets was limited because of the nature of inter–ecological zone trade. Richard Roberts notes three effects that ecological variations have had on commercial activity in West Africa. First, they fostered regional occupational specialization as people adapted to their unique ecological zones. Second, they encouraged trade along the divisions between broad ecological zones as well as those between microenvironments. People met at these borders to exchange goods produced more efficiently in their respective zones. Finally, ecological variations fostered a "continental division of labour," since producers within the same climatic regions produced the same goods.[72]

With people in the same regions producing the same goods and laboring in more or less the same manner, the development of local markets and short distance trade was discouraged. Put simply, the sorts of products that farmers in a given area could produce and trade most efficiently could be produced and traded just as efficiently by potential customers. As a result of this, "the scope for exchange was limited and per capita incomes remained low."[73]

Long-distance trade developed as a way to overcome the problems inherent in local trade. On the supply side, producers experienced the same cost constraints whether they produced for a local or long-distance market. But on the demand side, long-distance trade gave merchants the opportunity to connect what Anthony Hopkins called "social islands of purchasing power" or "consumers who, though only a small proportion of the total population, had sufficient wealth between them to support a market which was greater than that available to local traders in any one area." This is not to imply that "the less affluent majority" did not participate in or benefit from some degree from long-distance trade. Common people, Hopkins states, "participated in this commerce to a certain extent by using profits accumulated from local trading activities to purchase cheaper types of cloth and small quantities of essential items." But generally speaking, "long distance trade tended to cater for the needs of relatively high income groups because only prosperous consumers could afford to pay prices which took handling costs and risks of carrying goods beyond the area of production."[74]

In sum, the yams, cattle, salt, and other coastal products that a given Balanta *morança* might have traded brought very low prices because they could be and were produced efficiently by countless other households. That is, the scope of short-distance trade was limited because all households in Guinea-Bissau's coastal zone tended to produce the same mix of crops and goods. A Balanta household could not expect that any mix of the goods that it attempted to sell in markets or to merchants plying long-distance routes would garner many imports since merchants could find more or less the same mix of goods being offered for sale by competing household in the same ecological zone. Thus, Balanta accumulated only a very limited amount of the expensive items shipped over long-distance routes.

One item that should have been in particularly high demand in Balanta territories was iron, which would have been extremely valuable in the manufacture of the cutting edges of tools. As we have seen, for certain types of agriculture iron was necessary. It would have been valuable, as well, in the manufacture of weapons for hunting or warring. However, oral narratives give the impression that, before the arrival of Europeans in Guinea-Bissau, iron from the interior did not widely circulate among Balanta. While conducting some of my first oral interviews, I typically started with as broad a question as possible and then narrowed the scope of my questions to focus more tightly on issues in which I was particularly interested. Pursuing this strategy with elder Mam Nambatcha, I asked, "Are there common histories that you tell your family?" Without pausing, Nambatcha pointed to his *kebinde,* a shovel-type plow that is ubiquitous in Balanta regions, and said:

> With respect to the instruments we utilize in production . . . there are his-
> tories. Before the arrival of the first Portuguese in this land, Balanta did
> not have an iron *kebinde* since we did not have iron. Thus, our *kebinde* was
> made completely of wood, the cutting edge being burned with fire to make
> it more durable. The work of the farmer was very difficult considering how
> rudimentary the *kebinde* was. Balanta society only gained knowledge of iron
> after the arrival of the first Portuguese traders.[75]

Doubting that Balanta possessed such detailed narratives of the very distant past, I was tempted to dismiss Nambatcha's response. But in other interviews, I recorded similar information. For example, in a *morança* not far from
Nambatcha's, I asked, "Are there any histories related to Balanta farming
implements?" N'Dafa Na Combé answered, "The first Balanta *kebinde* was
made without an iron end. Thus the end of the *kebinde* was burned with fire
to make it more durable and usable in farming. The machete was attained after
smiths obtained bits of iron. Also the hatchet was first acquired from reshap-
ing the *arco de barris* [the iron ring around barrels of wine]."[76] Mariano
Martinho Natidai also noted the importance of the *arco de barris:* "Balanta
farmed with a *kebinde* without iron. These smiths got iron from the binding
of *barris de vinho* that Portuguese merchants brought."[77] And in other regions
of Guinea-Bissau, I collected similar narratives. "The first *kebinde* of Balanta,"
Tchuta Mbali stated, "did not have iron but was burned in the fire at the final
part to make it more durable. Balanta, above all at Patch, learned of iron from
Papel blacksmiths."[78] In Binar a group of five Balanta elders told a similar
story: "In times past, Balanta did not know iron. For agriculture Balanta used
a *kebinde* without iron. The Portuguese later brought iron. When whites
brought iron, Balanta learned to shape it so that it could be used on the
kebinde."[79] In over a dozen interviews, Balanta elders told me that their distant

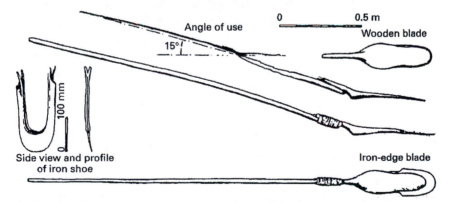

Figure 1.1 The Balanta plow, or *kebinde*. Derived from images in J. Espírito Santo,
"Notas sobre a cultura do arroz entre os balantas," *Boletim Cultural da Guiné
Portuguesa* 4 (April 1949): 197–233.

ancestors farmed the land without iron-edged tools, and in some of those interviews they indicated that it was only after contact with whites that Balanta gained knowledge of iron.[80]

This evidence fits well with the findings of Joseph Jerome Lauer. In tracing the spread of rice cultivation among the Manjaco (Brame), who like the Balanta occupied lands between the lower Rio Geba and the lower Rio Cacheu, Lauer emphasizes that a "metal cap on the blade of the *kadyendo* [digging tool very similar to the Balanta *kebinde*] is important in rice cultivation." Based on oral narratives, Lauer speculates that Manjaco probably started affixing metal tips to their digging tools sometime after 1450 when, as the result of European merchants meeting the demands of coastal Africans, there was an "increased abundance of iron."[81]

That Balanta and other coastal groups produced little or no iron and utilized only small amounts of it before about the mid-fifteenth century may seem surprising. However, as Philip de Barros and others have argued, this was not uncommon among African societies. Despite the fact that smiths across the continent have been mining iron ore, smelting it, and working the metal into various objects for about 2,000 years, some African societies either failed to adopt iron technologies or rejected them until very recent times. The reasons for this varied. Some groups lacked technologies, others access to ores, and others goods valuable enough to trade for iron produced elsewhere.[82] Another reason iron technologies were slow to spread to some regions might be that iron production was frequently accompanied by the formation of social and political hierarchies. Barros explains, "The ironworker, with his specialized knowledge and skills, was in the position to become wealthier than his non-ironworker counterparts, and those clans or lineages with access to the better ores and/or clays would be in an even better position to accumulate wealth." However, the accumulation of wealth by a particular class of specialists was sometimes seen as anathema to particular values. Following Claude Meillassoux and M. C. Dupré, Barros argues that the "potential for increased production levels leading to export through trade, the concurrent development of a class of 'big men' ironworkers, and ultimately the rise of a more centralized political authority seeking to control this production were resisted by some societies." Hence, Tio and Tsaayi of Congo rejected iron production other than what was needed for subsistence. And in the Liberia and Sierra Leone region, forest dwellers obtained iron technologies in the eighth century, but did not make much use of them, utilizing wooden tools for farming as late as the nineteenth century.[83]

BALANTA SETTLEMENT PATTERNS

A scarcity of iron partly accounts for why Balanta produced yams and not paddy rice before Europeans arrived in the Guinea-Bissau region. Balanta settlement patterns were also a factor. Because Balanta did not concentrate into villages, it would have been difficult for them to organize adequate numbers of workers for tasks as labor-intensive as paddy rice production. Populations were too dispersed, population densities too low.

With respect to decentralized societies, Robin Horton speculates that "in precolonial times, the dispersed settlement pattern was characteristic of peoples who were expanding or maintaining themselves territorially against negligible or relatively uncoordinated resistance."[84] Dispersion was the result of "fission," a strategy that involved the splitting of households or settlements—some members moving elsewhere when resources were insufficient or when intragroup rivalries could not be resolved. Fission was possible only when virgin farmlands were available and when people felt some assurance that a powerful enemy would not attack an isolated and relatively weak household. By dispersing settlements, people maximized efficiency. They did not have to travel far to reach the fields that they tended, and they could protect their crops from hungry animals or humans.

In the period before the rise of the Atlantic slave trade, Balanta exhibited a dispersed settlement pattern. Clearly, at times, Balanta *moranças* came together for defensive purposes. And there may have been ceremonies—marriages, funerals, and rites of passage—that brought the members of scattered *moranças* together for some period of time. But when relative peace prevailed and when populations were expanding, sons likely sought to establish their own *moranças,* probably at some distance from those of their fathers. After all, every Balanta man could become an *alante n'dang,* "king" of his own politically independent household. Though some number of *moranças* may have concentrated in given locations, the need to travel to distant fields likely discouraged the concentration of many, keeping village formations rare.[85]

Who moved away from a household or *morança* was likely determined by the particularities of Balanta social structures during this period. Meyer Fortes points out that whether a son "moves out of the parental home altogether to farm on his own or remains residentially attached to his father's homestead depends on factors internal to the domestic group. If he is the only son he will be less likely to move away than if he has brothers."[86] Among Balanta today, fathers give farmland to their sons when they marry. A first marriage typically occurs when a man is in his late twenties or early thirties. Upon receiving land, he sets up a separate household. If possible, fathers give one plot of land to each son. However, when land is scarce it is more likely that firstborn sons will receive land, with little being left for younger sons. Land scarcity also presents a problem for men who want to take on more than one wife, since they are expected to provide each wife with a separate field for planting. Dissatisfied wives frequently leave their husbands, taking up residence with a "lover" who can provide a plot. If there is little land for younger brothers to inherit, their chances of building a large and productive household are diminished.[87] In sum, since rules of inheritance favor older brothers, younger brothers tend to migrate to distant underpopulated territories, areas where fields abound. If fields are abundant near their birth village, they remain. "In times long past," rules of inheritance may have played an important role in determining which Balanta left their fathers' *moranças* and which remained. It is also likely that small communities of *moranças* or *moranças* themselves fissioned when disputes could not be settled by consensus. Since vacant farmable land was abundant, Balanta unwilling to accept community decisions could migrate.[88]

Early written sources certainly point to a pattern of migration and household dispersion. Though he was speaking broadly about coastal peoples and not specifically about Balanta, Balthasar Barreira noted in 1606 that households were typically established close to the lands that household members farmed. It was very difficult to spread the "Holy Faith," Barreira complained, in part because

> in only one quarter of the year are they [Africans] engaged in their villages; and for three-quarters they are engaged in cutting the bush in the lands they are going to sow that year, because they always cut the bush anew, and in sowing the lands and weeding and harvesting the crops. For this reason they make thatched huts there, in which they spend this period, and they leave empty the houses they have in the villages, which they generally build anew each year after they have finished harvesting the rice and other staple foods.[89]

CONCLUSION

In sum, before the rise of the Atlantic slave trade, the decentralized nature of Balanta society shaped the interactions of Balanta and a broad West African economic and political system. The efficiency of living as close as possible to fields encouraged the dispersion of politically independent Balanta *moranças* as sons sought to become *b'alante b'ndang,* respected male elders or heads of households. Since *moranças* produced and marketed the same mix of crops, prices for Balanta goods and Balanta purchasing power remained low. Thus, though Balanta traded yams, salt, and other commodities in Biafada, Brame, and Papel markets and to Biafada merchants who plied coastal waterways, they could not attract great quantities of expensive long-distance trade items. Balanta found it particularly difficult to accumulate iron, which could not be produced locally but was valued for reinforcing the cutting edges of agricultural implements. Lacking iron, Balanta could not engage in the production of some high-yield crops, particularly paddy rice, which was grown by Mandinka farmers on the Gambia.

The decentralized nature of Balanta society also meant that the group was difficult to assimilate into an expanding Mandinka sphere of influence. Before the rise of the Atlantic slave trade, Mandinka states rose to the interior of Guinea-Bissau. The rulers of these states found it relatively easy to gain legitimacy over vast territories through intermarriage with existing ruling families. But in Guinea-Bissau's coastal zone, where political power was diffuse and where there were no ruling families who had large followings, Mandinka could not establish suzerainty. Most Balanta households remained relatively independent of Mandinka influence.

NOTES

1. Walter Rodney, "The Guinea Coast," in *The Cambridge History of Africa*, vol. 4, *From c. 1600 to c. 1790,* ed. Richard Gray (Cambridge: Cambridge University Press, 1975), 280–283. See also Carlos Lopes, *Kaabunké, espaço, território e poder na Guiné-Bissau, Gâmbia e Casamance pré-coloniais* (Lisbon: Commissão Nacional para as Comemorações dos Descobrimentos Portugueses, 1999).

2. Cornélia Giesing, "Agricultura e resistência na história dos Balanta-Bejaa," *Soronda* 16 (July 1993): 128.

3. Interview with Mbunh Nanful, Mato-Farroba, December 6, 1994. Also interviews with Tchuta Mbali, Patche Ialá, January 8, 1995; Bisi Binhaga and José Gomes, Patche Ialá, January 31, 1995; and Cubumba Sangê, Bletê, and Chefe Lima, N'Tin, April 5, 1995.

4. Interview with Estanislau Correia Landim, João Landim, February 2, 1995.

5. Interview with Fô Kidum, Quinhaque, January 7, 1995. See also Giesing, "Agricultura," 127.

6. Personal communication, Peter Mark, December 11, 2000.

7. See Pier M. Larson, *History and Memory in the Age of Enslavement: Becoming Merina in Highland Madagascar, 1770–1822* (Portsmouth, N.H.: Heinemann, 2000), 38–44.

8. See especially Mamadou Mané, "Contribuition á l'histoire du Kaabu, des origins au XIXe siécle," *Bulletin de l'IFAN* 40, ser. B, no. 1 (January 1978): 96–101; Joye Bowman Hawkins, "Conflict, Interaction, and Change in Guinea-Bissau: Fulbe Expansion and Its Impact, 1850–1900" (Ph.D. diss., University of California–Los Angeles, 1980), 65–66; Joye L. Bowman, *Ominous Transition: Commerce and Colonial Expansion in the Senegambia and Guinea, 1857–1919* (Brookfield, Vt.: Avebury, 1997), 13; and Lopes, *Kaabunké.*

9. For a summary, see Walter Rodney, *A History of the Upper Guinea Coast, 1545 to 1800* (New York: Monthly Review Press, 1970), 6; Boubacar Barry, *Senegambia and the Atlantic Slave Trade* (Cambridge: Cambridge University Press, 1998), 7; and Lopes, *Kaabunké,* 90.

10. Bowman Hawkins, "Conflict," 53; Antonio Carreira, *Mandingas da Guiné portuguesa,* Publicação Comemerativa do Centenário de Descoberta da Guiné no. 4 (Bissau: Centro de Estudos da Guiné Portuguesa, 1947), 9–12; D. T. Niane, "Mali and the Second Mandingo Expansion," in *General History of Africa: Africa from the Twelfth to the Sixteenth Century,* vol. 4, ed. D. T. Niane (London: Heinemann, 1984), 117–171; M. Lytall, "The Decline of the Mali Empire," in Niane, *General History of Africa,* vol. 4, 172–186; Y. Pearson, "The Coastal Peoples: From Casamace to the Ivory Coast Lagoons," in Niane, *General History of Africa,* vol. 4, 301–323; C. Wondji, "The States and Cultures of the Upper Guinea Coast," in *General History of Africa: Africa from the Sixteenth*

Century to the Eighteenth Century, vol. 5, ed. B. A. Ogot (London: Heinemann, 1992), 368–398.

11. Donald R. Wright, *The World and a Very Small Place in Africa* (Armonk, N.Y.: M. E. Sharpe, 1997), 34.

12. Lopes, *Kaabunké,* 79; Barry, *Senegambia,* 8, 21. Kaabu may have been founded by one of Sundiata's military commanders, Tiramagan Traore, though some narratives purport that he was merely a key participant. Nonetheless, in oral narratives his four sons are depicted as provincial rulers. See Mané, "Contribuition," 98; Mamadou Mané, "Les origins et la formation du Kaabú," *Éthiopiques* 28 (October 1981): 96; and Sékéné Mody Cissoko, "De l'origanisation politique du Kaabu," *Éthiopiques* 28 (October 1981): 199.

13. George E. Brooks, *Landlords and Strangers: Ecology, Society, and Trade in Western Africa, 1000–1630* (Boulder, Colo.: Westview Press, 1993), 46.

14. Barry, *Senegambia,* 21–22, 40.

15. A. J. Dias Dinis, "As tribos da Guiné portuguesa na história," in *Congresso comemorativo do quinto centenário do descobrimento da Guiné* (Lisbon: Sociedade de Geografia de Lisboa, 1946), 252; Diane Lima Handem, *Nature et fonctionnement du pouvoir chez les Balanta Brassa* (Bissau: Arquivo Histórico do Instituto Nacional de Estudos e Pesquisa, 1986), 10.

16. André Donelha, *Descrição da Serra Leoa e dos rios de Guiné do Cabo Verde (1625),* ed. Avelino Teixeira da Mota, trans. P.E.H. Hair, Centro de Estudos de Cartografia Antiga no. 19 (Lisbon: Junta de Investigações Científicas do Ultramar, 1977), 121.

17. One scholar who argues that Mandinka controlled the entire coast concedes "that certain Balanta clans were fiercely independent." Lopes, *Kaabunké,* 64.

18. Among the "subgroup," names that have appeared are B'nhacra (or Bunge), Baitche (or Patch), Kuntoé (or B'sofa), Bejaa, Monsoanca, and Bnaga. Early Portuguese observers called Baitche and Kuntoé *Balanta brabo* (wild Balanta) or *Balanta de dentro* (Balanta of the interior). They referred to the B'nhacra as *Balanta manso* (docile Balanta) or *Balanta de fora* (Balanta of the exterior). And they dubbed the Bejaa "Balanta-Mané." These distinctions are made clear in many Portuguese documents. See Handem, *Nature et fonctionnement,* 10, 241 ff. Handem provides a slightly different classification and further explanation on pp. 10–19.

19. Avelino Teixeira da Mota, *Guiné portuguesa,* vol. 1 (Lisbon: Agência Geral do Ultramar, 1954), 141, 290; Avelino Teixeira da Mota, *A habitação indígena na Guiné portuguesa* (Bissau: Centro de Estudos da Guiné Portuguesa, 1948), 52; Giesing, "Agricultura," 125–176; Handem, *Nature et fonctionnement,* 10–19.

20. Giesing, "Agricultura," 125–134. Monsoanca also had close contact with Mandinka. See Gaspard Mollien, *Travels in the Interior of Africa to the Sources of the Senegal and Gambia Performed by the Command of the French Government in the Year 1818,* ed. T. E. Bowdich (London: Frank Cass, 1967), 329.

21. Rodney, "The Guinea Coast," 223–324, 292; Dinis, "As tribos," 250.

22. Manuel Álvares, *Ethiopia Minor and a Geographical Account of the Province of Sierra Leone,* trans. P.E.H. Hair (Liverpool: University of Liverpool, Department of History, September 30, 1990), chap. 12.

23. Alonso de Sandoval, *Natvraleza, policia, sagrada i profana, costvmbres i ritos, disciplina i catechismo evangelico de todos etiopes* (Seville: Francisco de Lira, 1627), 39.

24. Francisco de Lemos Coelho, "Descrião da costa da Guiné desde o Cabo Verde athe Serra Lioa com todas as ilhas e rios que os Brancos Navegam," in *Duas descrições seiscentistas da Guiné,* ed. Damião Peres (Lisbon: Academia Portuguesa da História, 1953), 81.

25. Interview with Mariano Martinho Natidai, N'Fotot or Quidet, July 15, 2000.

26. See, for example, Wright's description of the Niumi region near the Gambia. Wright, *The World,* 45–53.

27. Literally, "Men, are your bodies cold?" Unfortunately, we have no records that specifically describe very early Balanta greeting practices. Álvares left this: "Their greeting when they meet is to sniff at the right hand of the other, taking and raising it to the nose three times." Álvares, *Ethiopia Minor,* chap. 12.

28. Ibid.

29. André Álvares de Almada, *Tratado breve dos rios de Guiné,* trans. P.E.H. Hair (Liverpool: University of Liverpool, Department of History, 1984), 92. Fernandes (fifteenth century) provides an earlier account of what were probably Balanta in the area of the Casamance, but he refers to them as *Balangas.* Dinis, "As tribos," 250.

30. Mota, *Guiné portuguesa,* 141, 155.

31. Bowman Hawkins, "Conflict," 65–66.

32. See Donelha, *Descrição,* 121.

33. Avelino Teixeira da Mota, "A agricultura dos Brames e Balantas vista através da fotografia aérea," *Boletim Cultural da Guiné Portuguesa* 5 (1950): 154–155; Rosemary E. Galli and Jocelyn Jones, *Guinea-Bissau: Politics, Economics and Society* (London: Frances Pinter, 1987), 12; Olga F. Linares, "From Tidal Swamp to Inland Valley: On the Social Organization of Wet Rice Cultivation Among the Diola of Senegal," *Africa* 5, no. 2 (1981): 579; Brooks, *Landlords,* 118; Rodney, "The Guinea Coast," 290; J. Espírito Santo, "Notas sobre a cultura do arroz etre os balantas," *Boletim Cultural da Guiné Portuguesa* 4 (April 1949): 197–233; Antonio Carreira and A. Martins de Meireles, "Quelques notes sur les mouvements migratories des populations de la province portugaise da Guinée," *Bulletin de l'IFAN* 22 (1960): 379–392; Antonio Carreira, "A organização social e ecónomica dos povos da Guiné portuguesa," *Boletim Cultural da Guiné Portuguesa* 16 (1961): 641–736.

34. Álvares, *Ethiopia Minor,* chap. 12. In medieval Portuguese, *milho* meant "millet" or "grain." In modern Portuguese it means "maize." Since Álvares is describing "*milho* cane," it is likely he is referring to maize. See P.E.H. Hair's comments in Donelha, *Descrição,* 180 ff.

35. Balanta were also among the most prolific coastal livestock tenders and salt producers. Balanta tended a West African shorthorn cattle breed that is resistant to *Trypanosoma rhodesiense,* "sleeping sickness." *Trypanosoma rhodesiense* is carried by several types of flies, *Glossina palpalis* being the most widespread. The flies are found in thick brush where cattle graze. Goats and pigs also are resistant to the sickness, but horses, camels, sheep, donkeys, and zebu cattle are all susceptible to it. The clearing of land around villages and households can protect humans, who also are susceptible. See Brooks, *Landlords,* 12–13; and Philip D. Curtin, *Economic Change in Precolonial Africa: Senegambia in the Era of the Slave Trade* (Madison: University of Wisconsin Press, 1975), 218–219.

36. Interview with Mam Nambatcha, Cufar, December 2, 1994.

37. *Anuário da Guiné portuguesa* (Lisbon: 1946), 435.

38. Almada, *Tratado breve,* 92. Hair translates this passage as follows: "These blacks [Balanta] provide the land of the Beafares with some provisions in the form of rice and yams." However, there is no reference to rice in the António Brásio's 1964 edition, which is in Portuguese and reads: "*destes Balantas se provê a terra dos Beafares de inhames e outros mantimentos.*" See André Álvares de Almada, *Tratado breve dos rios de Guiné do Cabo Verde dês do Rio de Sanagá até os Baixios de Santa Ana de todas as nações*

que há na dita costa e de seus costumes, armas, trajos, juramentos, guerras, ano 1594, ed. António Brásio (Lisbon: Editorial LIAM, 1964), 81.

39. Francisco de Lemos Coelho, *Description of the Coast of Guinea (1684),* trans. P.E.H. Hair (Liverpool: University of Liverpool, Department of History, 1985), chaps. 5, 8.

40. On European rice purchases, see Joseph Jerome Lauer, "Rice in the History of the Lower Gambia-Geba Area" (M.A. thesis, University of Wisconsin, 1969), 42, 48.

41. Portères figures that *Oryza glaberrima* was cultivated in the central Niger delta as early as 1500 B.C. From the genetic analysis of approximately 1,500 varieties of *O. glaberrima,* he concludes that it must have spread from the central Niger delta to other parts of Africa. In Senegambia, *O. glaberrima* probably dates from 800 B.C. Portères emphasizes that *O. sativa* became an important variety of rice in the eighteenth century due to increasing levels of trade. Roland Portères, "Vieilles agricultures africaines avant le XVIe siecle," *L'Agranomie Tropicale* 5 (1950): 489–507; Roland Portères, "Taxonomie agrobotanique des riz cultivés," *Journal d'Agriculture Tropicale et de Botanique* 3 (1956): 341–384, 541–580, 629–700, 821–856; Roland Portères, "Berceaux agricoles primaires sur le continent africain" *Journal of African History* 3, no. 2 (1962): 195–210; Roland Portères, "African Cereals: Eleusine, Fonio, Black Fonio, Teff, Brachiaria, Paspalum, Pennisetum, and African Rice," in *Origins of African Plant Domestication,* eds. Jack R. Harlan et al. (Paris: Mouton, 1976), 409–452. A. Chevalier's theories oppose those of Portères, and Robert McIntosh builds on Chevalier's work. See Robert J. McIntosh, *The Peoples of the Middle Niger* (Oxford: Blackwell, 1988), 150–154. For a world history of rice, see D. H. Grist, *Rice* (New York: Longman, Green, 1953). For more on the history of rice in Africa, see A. J. Carpenter, "The History of Rice in Africa," in *Rice in Africa,* eds. I. W. Buddenhagen and G. J. Persley (New York: Academic Press, 1978), 3–10; I. W. Buddenhagen, "Rice Ecosystems in Africa," in Buddenhagen and Persley, *Rice in Africa,* 11–27; and Jack R. Harlan, "Wild-Grass Seed Harvesting in the Sahara and Sub-Sahara of Africa," in *Foraging and Farming,* eds. David R. Harris and Godon C. Hillman (London: Unwin Hyman, 1989), 79–98.

42. Portères, "African Cereals"; Carpenter, "The History of Rice." For contrasting views on how *O. sativa* arrived on the Upper Guinea Coast, see N. M. Nayar, "Origin and Cytogenetics of Rice," *Advances in Genetics* 17 (1974): 153–292.

43. R. Chabolin, "Rice in West Africa," in *Food Crops of the Lowland Tropics,* eds. C. L. A. Leakey and J. B. Willis. (Oxford: Oxford University Press, 1977), 9–15. See also António Castro, "Notas sobre algumas variedades de arroz em cultura na Guiné portuguesa," *Boletim Cultural da Guiné Portugueza* 5, no. 19 (July 1950): 347–350. On upland rice production without iron implements, see Olga F. Linares, "Shell Middens of the Lower Casamance and Problems of Diola Protohistory," *West African Journal of Archaeology* 1 (1971): 22–54.

44. Chabolin, "Rice in West Africa," 9–10, 15–24.

45. Ibid.

46. Castro, "Notas," 350.

47. Chabolin, "Rice in West Africa," 9–15; Mota, *Guiné portuguesa,* 208; Curtin, *Economic Change,* 28–29.

48. See Brooks, *Landlords,* 89, 118. Olga F. Linares demonstrates the ways that a variety of societies in coastal West Africa achieve great levels of labor organization. Linares, "From Tidal Swamp."

49. Brooks, *Landlords,* 89; Linares, "Shell Middens," 49.

50. Interview with Mariano Martinho Natidia, N'Fotot or Quidet, July 15, 2000. See also Linares, "Shell Middens," 49.

51. Wet rice may have been cultivated by Diola (Floup) in the Casamance region as early as A.D. 300. See Linares, "Shell Middens," 48. However, abundant evidence exists that intensive farming of lowlands here did not begin until the late sixteenth and seventeenth centuries, when Diola had access to iron brought by Atlantic merchants.

52. Gomes Eannes de Azurara, *The Chronicle of the Discovery and Conquest of Guinea,* vol. 2, trans. Charles Raymond Beazely and Edgar Prestage (London: Hakluyt Society, 1899), 263–264.

53. Ibid. The footnote to this passage (no. 208) says that this was "Undoubtedly the Rio Grande." However, there is really not sufficient evidence to draw a conclusion. See Mota, *Guiné portuguesa,* 369.

54. Almada, *Tratado breve* (Brásio's ed.), 54, 57.

55. Richard Jobson, *The Golden Trade* (London: Nicholas Okes, 1623), 125.

56. Curtin, *Economic Change,* 210. In a more recent study, Wright agreed, arguing that before Europeans arrived, blacksmiths in the Niumi region of the Gambia "worked iron rather than produced it." Wright, *The World,* 120. See especially Jobson's description of the Gambia region in *The Golden Trade,* 125, 158.

57. Almada, *Tratado breve* (Hair's ed.), chap. 6.

58. Brooks, *Landlords,* 155.

59. Note Almada's sixteenth-century observation about the Biafada: "The canoes in which they traveled the river are large ones, and many of them carry more than one hundred people, as well as cows and other goods." Almada, *Tratado breve* (Hair's ed.), 89.

60. Brooks, *Landlords,* 80–87.

61. Ibid.; Rodney, *A History of the Upper Guinea Coast,* 149.

62. Almada, *Tratado breve* (Hair's ed.), 89.

63. Rodney, *A History of the Upper Guinea Coast,* 19. See also Lauer, "Rice," 26; Brooks, *Landlords,* 260; P.E.H. Hair and Avelino Teixeira da Mota, eds., *Jesuit Documents on the Guinea of Cape Verde and the Cape Verde Islands, 1585–1617* (Liverpool: University of Liverpool, Department of History, 1989), doc. 13; and Coelho, "Descrição," chap. 5.

64. Lauer, "Rice," 26; Brooks, *Landlords,* 96; Donald R. Wright, *The Early History of Niumi: Settlement and Foundation of a Mandinka State on the Gambia River* (Athens, OH.: Ohio University, Center for International Studies 1977), 7–40.

65. Brooks, *Landlords,* 21.

66. Ibid., 21–22.

67. See Coelho, *Description,* chap. 6; Mollien, *Travels,* 316–318; and Francisco Travassos Valdez, *Six Years of a Traveller's Life in Western Africa,* vol. 1 (London: Hurst and Blackett, 1861), 241.

68. Anthony G. Hopkins, *An Economic History of West Africa* (New York: Columbia University Press, 1973), chap. 2; Philip D. Curtin, *Cross-Cultural Trade in World History* (Cambridge: Cambridge University Press, 1984), chap. 2; Richard L. Roberts, "Linkages and Multiplier Effects in the Ecologically Specialized Trade of Precolonial West Africa," *Cahiers d'Études Africaines* 20, nos. 77–78 (1980): 135–148.

69. Almada, *Tratado breve* (Hair's ed.), 110; Rodney, *A History of the Upper Guinea Coast,* 32.

70. Almada, *Tratado breve* (Hair's ed.), 87, 110.

71. Quoted in Avelino Teixeira da Mota, ed., *As viagens do Bispo D. Frei Vitoriano Portuense à Guiné e a cristianização dos reis de Bissau* (Lisbon: Junta de Investigações Científicas do Ultramar, 1974), 60.

72. Roberts, "Linkages," 137.

73. Hopkins, *An Economic History,* 53–58. When local trade was carried out, it resulted

from differences among local households' production strategies and "variations in the natural and human resource endowment of the micro-environment."

74. Ibid., 57–58; Roberts, "Linkages," 140.

75. Interview with Mam Nambatcha, Cufar, December 2, 1994.

76. Interview with N'Dafa Na Combé, Mato-Farroba, December 12, 1994.

77. Interview with Mariano Martinho Natidai, N'Fotot or Quidet, July 15, 2000.

78. Interview with Tchuta Mbali, Patche Ialá, January 8, 1995.

79. Interview with Batcha Bedocur, Barbosa Indani, João Imbali, Sobré Betura, and Agostinho Elsabai, Binar, July 15, 2000.

80. Interviews with Mam NamBatcha, Cufar, December 2, 1994, and March 3, 1995, N'Raba Na Bedanh and Imbunh Na Bedanh, Cufar, December 18, 1995; N'Dafa Na Combé, Mato-Farroba, December 12, 1994; Isnaba Nambatcha, Cufar, March 3, 1995; Tona Na Isna and Suna Na Isna, Cantoné, March 5, 1995; Adelino Bidenga Sanha, Quinhaque, January 7, 1995; Tchong Binhom and Wangna Sanhá, N'talod, January 25, 1995; Bitar Nabidé, Thamba Nanghasen, and Cumé Nanghasen, Oko, February 18, 1995; Tchuta Mbali, Patche Ialá, January 8, 1995; Estanislau Correia Landim, João Landim, February 2, 1995; João Bafã, Patche Ialá, January 8, 1995; Nhafede Sambe and Abna Dafa, Blimat, January 28, 1995; Frós Intchalá and Ndum Mhana, Ilonde, January 28, 1995; N'tera Siga, Patche Ialá, January 25, 1995; Alfrede Neves, Chiguna Clusse, and Bcolof Sukna, Patche Ialá, January 31, 1995; and Fona Benuma, Encheia, January 13, 1995; Batcha Bedocua, João Imbali, Sobré Betura, and Agostinho Elsabai, Binar, July 15, 2000.

81. Lauer, "Rice," 18–19.

82. Philip de Barros, "Iron Metallurgy: Sociocultural Context," in *Ancient African Metallurgy: The Sociocultural Context,* ed. Joseph O. Vogel (Walnut Creek, Calif.: Altamira Press, 2000), 147–198.

83. Ibid.; Claude Meillassoux, "The Economy in Agricultural Self-Sustaining Societies: A Preliminary Analysis," in *Relations of Production: Marxist Approaches to Economic Anthropology,* ed. D. Sheldon (London: Frank Cass, 1978), 127–156; M. C. Dupré, "Pour une histoire des productions: La métalurgie du fer chez les Téké— Ngungulu, Tio, Tsaayi," *Cahiers del'ORSTOM, Série Sciences Humaines* 18 (1981–1982): 195–223.

84. Robin Horton, "Stateless Societies in the history of West Africa," in *History of West Africa,* vol. 1, eds. J. F. A. Ajayi and M. Crowder (London: Longman, 1976), 91–92. See also Marshall Sahlins, "The Segmentary Lineage: An Organization of Predatory Expansion" *American Anthropologist* 63, no. 2, part 1 (Apr. 1961): 326–327; and P. Bohannan, "The Migration and Expansion of the Tiv," *Africa* 24 (January 1954): 79–80.

85. To concentrate populations in villages, Allen Johnson and Timothy Earle point out in a study of the present-day settlement patterns of Central Enga of Papua New Guinea, "is to increase the distance to agricultural fields and thus the costs of farming." Allen W. Johnson and Timothy Earle, *The Evolution of Human Societies: From Foraging Group to Agrarian State* (Stanford: Stanford University Press, 1987), 177.

86. Meyer Fortes, introduction to *African Political Systems,* eds. Meyer Fortes and E. E. Evans Pritchard (London: Oxford University Press, 1966), 13.

87. See Ursula Funk, "Land Tenure, Agriculture, and Gender in Guinea-Bissau," in *Agriculture, Women, and Land: The African Experience,* ed. Jean Davison (Boulder, Colo.: Westview Press, 1988), 42.

88. Ronald Cohen, "Evolution, Fission, and the Early State," in *The Study of the State,* eds. Henri J. M. Claessen and Peter Skalník (The Hague: Mouton, 1981), 94–95.

89. Quoted in Hair and Mota, *Jesuit Documents,* doc. 13.

2

SHIPPING SLAVES FROM A DECENTRALIZED REGION

It is not they [the ship owners] themselves who usually buy the slaves for the ships from the natives, but Portuguese men who can speak the language and live in the land and who go further inland taking the goods with which they buy them.

—Balthasar Barreira, 1606[1]

Relations among the people of the Upper Guinea Coast would radically change after 1441, the year that Nuno Tristão sailed from Portugal to Cape Blanco on West Africa's coast. His was one of many voyages made during the golden age of Portuguese seaward exploration, a steady push south at first motivated by a desire to bypass Arab overland trade routes that supplied Europe with African gold and Asian spices and silks. Though they found Africans willing to trade gold, this was not enough to quench the Portuguese thirst for riches. In the early 1440s, Atlantic merchants took captives from Morocco, and between 1441 and 1447 Captain Antão Gonçalves, the first Portuguese slave trader of record, made regular journeys to Cape Bojador. Slaves, often Slavs exported from Black Sea trading posts, had long been used on Mediterranean sugar plantations. If captives could be had from sub-Saharan Africa, sugar production might be stepped up. Thus Tristão, like his counterparts, saw the possibility of profiting from the trade in human beings. However, these were the early years of the Atlantic slave trade, a time when relations between Africans and Europeans were very uncertain. Overestimating the strength of his position in 1446, Tristão was killed on a foray onto the coast. He and his men had attempted to seize captives by force of arms, but a powerful African opponent outmatched them militarily.[2]

Over the next four centuries, other Portuguese as well as Cape Verdean, Spanish, English, French, Dutch, Dane, Brazilian, and American slave traders would perish on failed slaving voyages. Dealing in human captives was, after all, a dangerous business for everyone involved. However, as Atlantic merchants changed their tactics from raiding to establishing regular, ongoing trade relationships, they found Africans who were willing to produce and sell captives so that they could gain access to valuable goods. "When you have settled your trading-place," the captain of the Portuguese caravel *Santiago* was instructed in 1526, "then forbid all your ship's company to do anything un-reasonable/wrongful affecting the blacks. Instead you and your men should establish as good a relationship with them as possible." For the next several hundred years, Atlantic merchants continued to recognize the need to main-tain this sort of relationship.[3]

As the nature of interactions between ship crews and people in the Guinea-Bissau region improved, Kaabu turned its powerful state institutions toward harvesting captives, and smaller states and decentralized societies on Kaabu's frontiers refashioned very local-level institutions for the same end. As this happened, the commercial, political, and agricultural relationships of old were radically altered.

One of the most important changes that took place in the decades follow-ing Tristão's voyages was the reorientation of networks of exchange. In the Guinea-Bissau region, a new class of commercial intermediaries emerged, pushing Biafada and Papel out of their place as middlemen in trade between coastal and interior peoples. These new merchants were better able to facili-tate transactions between Africans and the captains of Atlantic-traveling ships. That is, they were better able to serve as "cross-cultural brokers." Most were Portuguese and Cape Verdean transplants who settled on the coast and inte-grated themselves into local communities, often by taking African brides or by entering into sexual relationships with African women. These relationships produced a new population of Luso Africans, or "Portuguese Africans," people referred to as *filhos de terra,* or "children of the land." With firm bonds of kinship in local communities, these settlers and their descendants were well placed to mediate the unpredictability and danger of cross-cultural exchanges between European and African strangers who had very different ways of life and whose actions could easily be misinterpreted without a broker to bring about trust and common understanding.

A focus on Portuguese and Luso African brokers reveals a great deal about how the slave trade operated in decentralized regions, and it shows that some of the assumptions that historians have made about the trade need to be modi-fied. Theorizing that very large capital outlays were needed to equip caravans, scholars generally argue that "by its nature" the slave trade tended to be "domi-nated by the political and military leaders of African societies, who controlled the process and the product of military enslavement."[4] However, in Guinea-Bissau, a new group of commercial intermediaries found ways to organize networks of exchange where no single state and no single group of political and military leaders existed. They did so by working through the predominant mode of African social and economic interaction—the extended family. By forging ties of kinship with local women and through them local communities, Portuguese and Luso African merchants linked local systems of production with a broad Atlantic economy and orchestrated the shipment of slaves from Guinea-Bissau. At coastal ports, their knowledge of European cultures and languages ensured the relative ease of commercial transactions with ship captains, meaning that Tristão's fate would not be that of most who followed him.

It is partly due to the success of Portuguese and Luso African brokers that the volume of the slave trade from Guinea-Bissau's shores grew, particularly in the years after Christopher Columbus's first voyage to the New World in 1492. By the seventeenth century, Guinea-Bissau's ports of Cacheu and Bissau had emerged as the most important commercial centers on the Upper Guinea Coast. The slaves departing from these points found themselves forced to labor beside Africans from elsewhere on the continent on plantations, in mines, and in cities across the New World.[5] In this chapter, I explore the ways African producers, a new class of "cross-cultural brokers," and ship captains organized the movement of captives through and from Guinea-Bissau, and assess the changing volume and demography of the trade from the region over a period of several hundred years.

THE RISE OF A NEW CLASS OF COASTAL MERCHANTS

The Portuguese and Cape Verdean "cross-cultural brokers" who settled in the Guinea-Bissau region were adventurers, merchants, Christian outcasts, and Jews fleeing religious persecution. The Cape Verdeans came from an archipelago situated between about 280 and 450 miles west of the coast of Senegal and discovered in either 1455 or 1456 by sailors sailing under the Portuguese flag. The colonization of the then uninhabited islands was begun in the 1460s by imported Portuguese farmers, as well as exiles and criminals. The rainfed lands of the islands of Santiago (São Tiago) and Fogo, two of the larger in the chain, could support agriculture, so slaves from the Upper Guinea Coast were employed cultivating sugar, cotton, and indigo. They also tended livestock on islands too rocky or dry to farm and labored in salt flats on the island of Sal. Skilled in spinning, weaving, and dying cloth, West African slaves of Wolof and Mandinka descent developed a thriving cloth-producing industry. Cape Verdean sailors exported *panos*—cloths—to the coast, where they were exchanged for more captives.[6]

On Cape Verde, the African slave population quickly eclipsed the European free population, and a new, distinct culture emerged, one that melded a variety of West African traditions with those of Portugal. Further, as Portuguese masters engaged in sexual relationships with their slaves, the islands saw the birth of a new population, one referred to as Crioulo. Often calling themselves "Portuguese," some of these Crioulos became merchants and made regular trips to the coast. There they had distinct advantages over their European counterparts. They spoke Crioulo, a language being developed on the archipelago and coast that blended Portuguese and African grammar and vocabulary. Further, through their parents or slaves coming from the coast, they had knowledge of African cultural practices. Finally, they possessed some immunity to diseases that plagued Europeans in Africa, in particular malaria and yellow fever.

When they settled on the coast in areas from Gambia to Sierra Leone, Cape Verdean and Portuguese merchants were referred to as *lançados* or *tangomaos* in the written sources of the day. The name *lançado* is derived from the Portuguese word *lançar,* which means "to throw," implying that these settlers either "threw themselves" or "were thrown" onto Africa's shores. The term *tangomaos* (also *Tanguomãaos, Tango maos, tangomao, tango-mão, tangosmaus,* and *tangomagos*) passed from use near the end of the seventeenth century. The derivation of the word is unknown, but it tended to have a negative connotation.[7] Take Manuel Álvares's description: "These are truly *tangos maos.* . . . They are evil itself, they are idolaters, perjurers, defiers of God, homicides, libertines, thieves who steal reputations, credit and good names from innocents as well as property, and also traitors—for they run away in order to help pirates, leading their ships to those places where our vessels are in the habit of anchoring and trading."[8]

Here Álvares was reflecting the Portuguese government's view of these settlers: they were Godless and would stand in the way of a Portuguese monopoly on trade from the region. Indeed, the government so feared this group, that at the start of the sixteenth century it declared trading in Guinea without a license a capital offense. No person "irrespective of rank or station, should throw himself with the Negroes, nor, under any circumstances, remain with the said Negroes, on pain of death."[9] Later, legislation was passed that outlawed Cape Verdean trade with the mainland. Walter Rodney speculates that the reason for this was "the *lançado* problem." "If Cape Verde ships no longer went to the Upper Guinea Coast, then the opportunities for private traders 'lancing' themselves on to the mainland would be considerably reduced." Nonetheless, Cape Verdean trade continued and the numbers of settlers increased.[10] By the end of the sixteenth century, *lançados* were no longer considered outlaws. However, they continued to present problems for Portugal. On the one hand, they served as brokers for Portuguese and Cape Verdean ship captains. On the other hand, they were unconstrained by legislation prohibiting "interlopers"—principally French and British ships—from trading in the region. Feeling no particular loyalty to Portugal, *lançados* traded with whomever they pleased, seeking the best price for their slaves and goods.[11]

In a recent study of *lançados* and Luso Africans, Peter Mark argues that this community defined itself as "Portuguese," an identity that, though fluid, had several characteristics. "To be 'Portuguese' was to be a trader, much as to be 'Juula' in Senegambia implied being a long-distance merchant." "Portuguese" houses were even constructed for trade. They had vestibules in which commercial partners could be greeted and verandahs or porches, known as an *alpainters,* on which they could conduct business on hot days. The community also defined itself by language. Initially they spoke Portuguese, but gradually this developed into Crioulo, the language becoming widely used by the beginning of the seventeenth century in both Cape Verde and on the Upper Guinea Coast. A final characteristic of Luso African identity was their religion, which mixed Jewish, Christian, and African practices.[12] Luso Africans, then, drew on different sets of traditions to place themselves in a position to serve as intermediaries between two cultures.

How *lançados* came to dominate routes that had been controlled by Biafada is a matter of speculation. Certainly the sail-driven caravels of the *lançados* outpaced Biafada dugout canoes. *Lançados* could carry a larger volume of goods and move their cargoes at a faster clip than Biafada merchants. Further, when threatened by slave-raiding neighbors, Biafada saw *lançados* and Europeans as valuable allies who could supply weapons or direct military assistance. Allowing *lançados* to trade in the region may simply have been the price that Biafada had to pay for some modicum of security, or for the hope of it.[13] Finally, *lançados* were clearly more acceptable trading partners for ship captains who docked at Guinea-Bissau's many ports. *Lançados* and ship captains often spoke the same language and shared the same customs, their cultural ties enhancing their commercial relationship.

LANÇADO CONNECTIONS TO COASTAL COMMUNITIES

To facilitate exchange in an area that lacked the broad-based institutions that policed markets, protected trade routes, and regulated exchange within states' borders,[14] *lançados* forged kinship or fictive kinship ties with people in coastal communities. That is, *lançados* worked within the predominant mode of social interaction—the extended family—to intensify relations between themselves and coastal peoples. Such ties were not established quickly or easily. Indeed, many *lançados* lived for decades in coastal villages. They participated in coastal ceremonies and rites of passage and married coastal women. In so doing, *lançados* fostered bonds of trust upon which they could base trade negotiations and through which they could gain access to exchange goods. Further, kinship or fictive kinship ties between *lançados* and coastal people at the very least lessened the chance that *lançados* would be robbed or killed while trading.[15] In a long passage, Balthasar Barreira described how these merchants lived among Africans, as Africans, and conducted business:

> The *tangosmaus* are those who throw themselves among the blacks and who travel about in the interior to conduct this trade, and they are a sort of people who, although Portuguese by nation and Christian by religion and baptism, nevertheless live as if they were neither Portuguese nor Christian. For many of them go naked, and in order to get on better with the heathen of the land where they trade by appearing like them, they sore the whole body with an iron blade, cutting until they draw blood and making many marks which, after they have been anointed with the juice of certain plants, come to re-semble various designs, such as figures of lizards, snakes or any creatures they care to depict. The *tangosmaus* make their way through the whole of Guinea in this way, trading in slaves and buying them wherever they can obtain them. . . . The *tangosmaus* live so forgetful of God and their salva-tion that they might be blacks themselves and the heathen of the land, for they spend 20 or 30 years of their lives without making a confession or bearing in mind any other form of life or any world other than this one.[16]

Familial ties to coastal communities and a knowledge of indigenous lan-guages were not all that protected *lançados* as they plied coastal waterways conducting trade. They also traveled in well-armed and well-manned vessels.[17] *Lançados* obtained arms from ship captains or trading houses, which were established at coastal ports. With firm connections to captains, they could also get expensive arms to give as gifts to valued African partners in the slave trade. For example, one well-connected *lançado* called on Captain S. B. Fernandes to help him arrange two cannons to protect the port of a renowned slave-trading king of the island of Bussis. Further, *lançados* and Luso Africans gained access to capital for equipment through diaspora credit arrangements or through diaspora links to commercial houses.[18]

In sum, the slave trade was not necessarily "dominated by the political and military leaders of African societies" on all parts of the continent, nor was it always dependent on a "state trading system."[19] Through familial ties to a number of dispersed and politically independent African communities and through cultural and linguistic ties to ship captains, a new commercial com-munity successfully overcame barriers to trade in decentralized regions of the Upper Guinea Coast. Operating principally within the *ria,* or sunken coast-line, *lançados* facilitated trade between a diverse collection of ethnic groups and Atlantic merchant-sailors. However, *lançados* appear to have been barred from operating very far into the savannah-woodland interior, where stratified Mandinka and Fula societies were located. It is likely that entrenched Mandinka and Fula merchants, who shared Muslim religious affiliations, erected barriers to competition from white and mulatto Christian traders. Hence *lançados* and merchants from the interior met and traded at entrepôts such as Farim and Geba, which sat on the *ria* coastline's edge.[20]

Throughout the area of Guinea-Bissau, *lançados,* as well as European merchants who settled only temporarily on the coast, employed native workers called *grumetes* in Crioulo, *gourmet* in French, and *grumetta* in English. Each of these words derived from various European words for "ship's boy" or "cabin boy."[21] Interacting daily with *lançados* and Europeans, most embraced Christianity, thereby transforming the religious character of the entrepôts in which they lived. Drawn from the ranks of coastal ethnic groups, *grumetes* were valued as much for their skills in navigating coastal rivers and streams as for their ability to speak local languages and negotiate commercial transactions. *Grumetes* manned trading craft or served as intermediaries in African communities and at trading establishments in the interior.[22]

Coastal youths became *grumetes* for a number of reasons. George Brooks speculates that Luso Africans—people with *lançado* fathers and African mothers—inherited their mothers' social rankings. Since land was passed from father to son, Luso Africans had no claims to agricultural plots. Lacking land and many of the prerogatives of rural African men, Luso Africans must have viewed employment as *grumetes* as an attractive alternative to village life.[23] Other *grumetes* (those not of mixed parentage) probably bonded with *lançados* in fictive kinship relations and became trusted workers. The social dislocation brought about by the rise of the slave trade, which wrought wars and devastated many coastal villages, must have pushed some Africans toward seeking such employment. Further, the demands of patriarchal households may have made the profession appealing to others.

Discussing the area of the Rio Cacheu, André Álvares de Almada said, "Both men and women work for our people, and they travel with them to the other rivers as *grumetes,* to earn money, as confidently as if they had been born and brought up among us in full security (of life and liberty)."[24] About two centuries later, Captain Philip Beaver, who had established a short-lived colony on the island of Bolama, compiled a list of the names of the *grumetes* who worked as his laborers. Among a large number of masculine names were the feminine names *Christiana, Esperanza, Maria, Dominga, Mara,* and *Joan.*[25] Obviously, the tasks of *grumetes* were not gendered. Women were important employees of European and *lançado* merchants since they had long been, as Brooks notes, "important traders in their own right and exercised leadership roles in their communities, sometimes ruling their own trading settlements."[26] Álvares emphasized this: "As well as carrying out normal duties in the upkeep of the family, such as spinning and so on, these women are keen traders and travel from fair to fair to gain a livelihood."[27] Further, some Biafada women, "known as *tangomas,*" were said to have dressed in European fashions and served "the adventurers" who traveled throughout the Rio Grande region. They even traveled with merchants to Santiago Island, of the Cape Verde Islands.[28]

As connections between Africa and the Atlantic world became more regularized in the decades and centuries after Tristão's voyage to the Upper Guinea Coast, women, then, served as a critical link between African communities and *lançado* merchants. Marriages to area women provided *lançados* a way to integrate themselves into local kinship networks and to use them to facilitate trade. Further, such marriages gave women the opportunity to expand their own as well as their families' social and economic opportunities. As women traveled about port towns in their roles as *grumetas* and *tangomas,* they likely struck advantageous deals for themselves and their kinfolk back home for much desired imported goods, and they probably gathered important "intelligence" information, such as where cattle were being stockpiled—perfect targets for thieves or raiders. Women also had important personal motivations for pursuing relationships with *lançados.* Marriages to "Portuguese" merchants released them from the mundane tasks of everyday life—planting, weeding, fertilizing, catching fish, and doing countless tasks around the household.[29]

Many of these women's children—Luso Africans, or both *"filhos da terra"* and "Portuguese" in the written sources of the day—became very successful traders in their own right.[30] Francisco de Lemos Coelho, the ship's captain who recorded many of the observations that I have drawn on in this study, may have been born in the Balola in the Rio Grande region. He certainly had strong familial connections in the region.[31] Similarly, Captain Francisco Correia, who purchased "what goods he thinks proper on the account of the Portuguese governor of Bissau," was described by Philip Beaver as a Mandinka born in the Geba area. He had been to Lisbon, made many trips to Cape Verde, spoke "very good Portuguese," read and wrote, dressed like a European, held "considerable property," and appeared to be "a very intelligent man."[32] Other *filhos da terra* were granted positions in the Portuguese administration on the coast. They commanded posts at Ziguinchor and Geba, often held lower positions in Bissau and Cacheu, and in some cases elevated themselves to higher positions. Such was the case with Sebastião da Cunha Souto Maior, who was the captain-major (the highest ranking official) in Bissau between 1766 and 1775. Though it often distrusted Luso Africans, the Portuguese government also benefited from their blood connections to local communities and rulers.[33]

LANÇADOS ON THE RIO CACHEU TO THE LATE SEVENTEENTH CENTURY

Integrating themselves into myriad coastal communities through marriages, *lançados* funneled goods from them into commercial networks that poured into the region's many coastal ports. The most important of these networks stretched along the Rio Cacheu and through a region that possessed great ethnic and political diversity. Here, there were no broad-based institutions through which people in different localities could establish predictable and ordered relations. Diversity and unpredictability fueled the wars and encouraged the raids that produced thousands of captives. "On this Rio de São Domingos [a small tributary of the Cacheu]," Almada wrote in the late sixteenth century, "there are more slaves than in all the rest of Guinea since they take them [from] these nations—Banhuns, Buramos, Cassangas, Jabundos, Falupos, Arriatas and Balantas."[34] Each of these groups was located within the *ria* coastline and close to the frontier of the powerful and expanding interior state of Kaabu.[35]

In the sixteenth century, trade from the Atlantic up the Cacheu came to be dominated by Cape Verdeans, Portuguese merchants leaving few descriptions of it, possibly because they considered the area unhealthy. Having entered the river by bypassing some dangerous shoals, Cape Verdeans generally went first to one of the São Domingos tributaries, where they visited any number of the scattered trading villages collectively called São Domingos. Found there in great numbers, *lançados* facilitated exchanges between Cape Verdean captains and local African rulers.[36]

In the closing years of the century, Cacheu replaced São Domingos as the most important entrepôt on the Rio Cacheu. Cacheu was well situated between two tributaries, the Rio Grande de São Domingos and Rio Pequeno de São Domingos, along which navigation was possible to the north, and it sat on high ground that had natural freshwater supplies.[37] Location was not all that made Cacheu attractive for trade. The town began to attract increasing numbers of *lançados* in large part because area Papel recognized the advantages of allying themselves with them. Thus, Papel did all they could to make *lançados* feel welcome and comfortable. Brooks describes how Papel success in wooing these influential trading partners forced others to become more accommodating in order to get a share of the goods arriving from the Atlantic: "The Banyun, for instance, opened their overland and riverine trade routes and markets to lançados and allowed them to settle in Banyun communities."[38]

Further up the Rio Cacheu, the port of Sarar, on the Sapateiro/Buache marigot, attracted *lançados* seeking trade with the state of Casa Mansa, a tributary of the powerful interior Mandinka state of Kaabu. To better facilitate exchanges with *lançados,* the Casa Mansa king, Masatamba, captured Sarar in the 1560s. Masatamba then went to great lengths to attract *lançados* to his land. In one notable case, he had a man who found and remitted to the royal court a dagger dropped by a "Portuguese" put to death because he had failed to act quickly, holding the lost item overnight. André Donelha said that foreign merchants could move through Casa Mansa more securely than on Cape Verde or in "any other Christian place."[39]

However, along the Cacheu, relations between *lançados* and local African rulers were not always peaceful. For example, *lançados* at Cacheu tried in the 1580s to erect a fortification and assert their independence from local Papel. After *lançados* had mounted canons on the stockade and retreated inside with their *grumetes,* Papel leaders ordered that the site be seized. Three days of fighting resulted in a *lançado* victory, but Papel rulers still had the upper hand. They cut off water supplies to the fort and ordered that their followers not trade with it. Eventually, the *lançados* agreed to a payment of tribute, a clear recognition of Papel authority. Despite such disputes, Cacheu flourished. By the 1590s, 700–800 "Christians" lived there. Many were from Cape Verde. Others were coastal refugees and their descendants who had embraced Christianity.[40]

About 135 kilometers upriver from Cacheu, Farim was also an important port on the Cacheu. Farim sat at the *ria* coastline's edge and attracted a great number of Mandinka merchants, who dubbed the town Tubabodaga, or "White Man's Village." There *lançados* met with Mande-speaking traders, most of whom were from Kaabu. Connections to Mandinka at Farim were crucial to the success of *lançado* merchants, particularly in the seventeenth century. This was a period of expansion of both the Kaabu empire and the Atlantic slave trade. Slaves taken in Kaabu's wars were sold to *lançados* at Farim and then shipped west to Cacheu, where they were put aboard vessels bound for the Cape Verde Islands and points beyond. Indicating the ability of *lançados* to orchestrate the movement of slaves through the decentralized region surrounding the Rio Cacheu, shipping records for the island of Santiago in 1609 and 1610 show that fourteen of sixteen vessels coming from the mainland had departed from the port of Cacheu with 1,264 slaves and some beeswax the only commodities that filled their hulls and those of the two other vessels, one from the Gambia and one from "Guinea." Successful as a slave trading entrepôt, Cacheu saw increases in its population by the second half of the seventeenth century, when some 1,500 people were said to reside there, 500 of whom were "white."[41]

LANÇADOS ON THE RIO GEBA AND RIO GRANDE TO THE LATE SEVENTEENTH CENTURY

Located near the sea on the Rio Geba and possessing a port large enough for oceangoing craft, Bissau, like Cacheu, was well situated to become an important commercial entrepôt in the era of the Atlantic slave trade. It is not known when *lançados* first settled on the island. In the early seventeenth century, Barreira wrote the first description of them, saying that there were white men on Bissau in need of a priest for confession. With *lançado* journeys up the Rio Geba to the important inland entrepôt of Geba catching the attention of even earlier observers, it is likely that they had been on the island for at least some decades.[42]

On Bissau, *lançados* tapped into the lucrative trade routes that had long been dominated by Papel and Biafada sailors. These stretched from the island to Cacheu, Geba, and as far south as Sierra Leone. Eventually, with better sailing vessels and connections to Atlantic merchants, *lançados* themselves began to monopolize these routes. Thus they exploited the Cacheu-Bissau route by purchasing wax in the Cacheu region and selling it at Bissau.[43] Further, as Jean Barbot noted in the late seventeenth century, members of the 150 *lançado* families residing on Bissau sailed south along the coast to the area of the Rio Nunez and Sierra Leone, where they garnered a great variety of valued exports, mainly "slaves, ivory and some gold-dust."[44]

Despite the fact that they had taken over trade routes once controlled by Papel, *lançados* and European merchant-sailors were warmly welcomed by the Papel chiefs who ruled the island. Barreira noted in 1605 that the ruler of Bissau was "a great friend of the Portuguese."[45] In 1684, Coelho said, "The people are very well-behaved and very friendly towards the white man, and there are many Christians here."[46] Addressing the hospitableness of the islanders, Barbot described how Bissau's leaders welcomed foreign merchants by making a sacrifice to one of the island's important *chinas*. "The blacks of the island on which stands the town of Bissos [Bissau] . . . have the custom of killing an ox or several hens, in honor of the idol China, whenever European traders arrive, to assure them that they are welcome and safe and that they will not be cheated." He continued, "The whites for whom the sacrifice is made have to be present at the ceremony, and the priest in charge throws drops of blood from the sacrifice over their shoes."[47]

It is likely that Atlantic merchants and *lançados* received such a warm welcome because for Papel rulers and common people, trade with them was very lucrative. In their markets, Papel were able to offer an array of imported items that attracted people from neighboring communities. By the first quarter of the seventeenth century, Balanta were visiting Bissau regularly, trading cattle and agricultural products for imported iron and cloth from Santiago.[48] Further, the chief of Bissau received "an anchorage tax on all vessels which lie in his roads, and also no-one can take water or wood from here without paying the customary due."[49] By 1630, the influence of *lançado* settlers was obvious to a Dutchman who reported that many of the Papel had adopted Portuguese clothing fashions.[50] Papel also began to convert in large numbers to Christianity. By 1694 there were 700 Christians in Bissau, "almost all from the Papel race."[51]

The allure of European imports also drew the Papel of Bissau into the trade in slaves. By the beginning of the seventeenth century, Papel found guilty of various crimes, especially adultery, were subject to being sold to ship captains.[52] Papel found other ways to profit from the New World's demand for laborers. In 1605, Barreira said that a Papel chief's son on Bissau was loath to become Christian "because, if he did so, he would have to give up 'roping them in,' that is, attacking and enslaving blacks."[53] In 1686, Spanish Capuchins described how bands of Papel left the island and raided coastal communities, bringing captives back. "Usually," a Capuchin said, "the Papel depart in their canoes and plunder and pirate men on the shores of the sea and inland." Papel slavers explained that "they abduct men because the whites buy them."[54]

Purchasing some slaves on Bissau and others from neighboring communities, *lançados* and their *grumete* mariners also obtained slaves from suppliers in the interior. Taking advantage of a powerful tidal bore, *lançado* boats sped inland up the Rio Geba.[55] On the river, *lançados* sought to maintain friendly relations with riverside dwellers, particularly Biafada, who sometimes offered valuable trade goods from a number of small kingdoms.[56] Of these, Guinala was the most important. With its capital at Bruco, it was well positioned to control trade routes that stretched between the Rio Grande, the Rio Geba, and the Rio Corubal. Bruco was only 15 kilometers from the Geba estuary, an easy overland crossing.[57] Further, ships could reach it by navigating the Rio Grande, a difficult but often lucrative approach to a kingdom renowned for its supplies of slaves. With so many *lançados* circulating in the region, Biafada learned Criolo and, like Papel, adopted Portuguese fashions.

Further up the Rio Geba, *lançados* and *grumetes* were attracted to the entrepôts of Geba and Malampanha, which were situated in the Biafada state of Degola.[58] This state was "in the land of the Mandingas." That is, it was a province of the powerful state of Kaabu. Having paid taxes to the local king, *lançados* were free to tap the rich merchandise available in the region.[59] Almada described this trade as it stood in the mid-sixteenth century: "From the Gambia, which is another land of the Mandingas, much black and white cotton cloth, many strips of cotton cloth, and many slaves come here. But the most important of the trade-goods brought here is cola . . . a fruit which comes from Serra Leoa to the Rio Grande."[60] In addition to purchasing cloth and slaves in Degola, *lançados* purchased other items as well. In 1625 at the port of Malampanha, Donelha reported "whites and some quite rich settlers" hosting a great trade in ivory.[61] Later that century, Coelho said that "wax and many blacks" were sold there.[62]

Because *lançados* were barred by Muslim merchants from trading much farther into the interior, *grumetes,* one observer noted in the late eighteenth century, were the ones who traveled further inland, bringing Atlantic imports to exchange for an array of other items, especially captives from Kaabu (Cabo): "The Portuguese concern themselves with only one thing, commerce, especially the trade in captives and in the beeswax that the *gourmettes* find in the Mandinka villages. There is a king four or five days journey on the road to Gambia who is called the king of Cabe or the king of Cabo. He provides them with a lot of captives."[63] With the trade in slaves booming, so many *lançados* and their *grumete* employees were attracted to Geba that it developed into a Christian town. By the end of the seventeenth century, Bispo Vitoriano Portuense could boast that 1,200 Christians were resident there.[64]

THE VOLUME AND DEMOGRAPHY OF THE SLAVE TRADE FROM THE GUINEA-BISSAU REGION TO THE LATE SEVENTEENTH CENTURY

Though observers left accounts of a "booming" trade in slaves from the Guinea-Bissau region, arriving at an accurate estimate of the number of slaves exported from the coast before the eighteenth century and determining their origins is a difficult task. Records have been destroyed, and those that remain are incomplete, sometimes inaccurate, and scattered in archives throughout Europe and the Americas. We know that from their earliest voyages to Africa, sailors purchased and seized captives.[65] Gomes Eannes de Azurara, a fifteenth-century chronicler, reported that up to 1448 some 927 "infidels" had been brought from the continent to Portugal.[66] According to Alvise Cadamosto, a sailor employed by Portugal between 1458 and 1460, 700–800 slaves were exported annually to Europe.[67] Most of these had been shipped from the Portuguese trading post in Arguim and shores of Senegambia.

The focus began to shift south to the Upper Guinea Coast in 1466, when the Portuguese crown granted trading rights to the area between the Rio Senegal and Sierra Leone to the residence of Cape Verde.[68] In the early years of their trade with the coast, Cape Verdeans took untold numbers of captives to their archipelago, where they were employed in agriculture and cloth production. Slaves from the Upper Guinea Coast were also shipped to Lisbon.[69] In a detailed study of previously known and newly uncovered records, Ivana Elbl estimates that the closing decade of the fifteenth century saw an annual average of 1,070 slaves being exported from the region. Commercial exchanges with the Gulf of Guinea were also expanding as Portugal steadily monopolized trade farther and farther to the south.[70]

Though sixteenth-century exports never attained the volume that they would in the seventeenth and eighteenth centuries, they did show dramatic increases over fifteenth-century levels. In 1505 and 1506, Duarte Pacheco Pereira said that 3,500 slaves were produced annually in the Upper Guinea Coast "when commerce of this land was well ordered."[71] However, Elbl argues that this figure was a sizable overestimation. Drawing on a variety of sources, she puts total exports from the Upper Guinea Coast at 1,600 annually between 1500 and 1509 and 2,000 annually between 1510 and 1515.[72] Because the Portuguese government sought to restrict Cape Verdean trade with the Upper Guinea

Coast in a futile effort to prevent the islanders from adding to the numbers of disloyal *lançados* who were settling there, the volume of slave exports decreased significantly between 1516 and 1521, standing at about 280 annually.[73] However, as Portuguese restrictions were lifted, exports picked up after 1521, with many slaves being taken directly from the Guinea-Bissau region. Indeed, Philip Curtin estimates that between 1526 and 1550, 543 slaves were exported annually from Guinea-Bissau, 25.6 percent of the total exports for the whole of Africa.[74]

Throughout the late sixteenth and early seventeenth centuries, slave exports from the region of Guinea-Bissau continued to increase. Demand explains a large part of this. In 1518 a royal contract established the sugar trade from Brazil. As sugar became the colony's export crop of choice, tremendous amounts of slave labor were needed to plant, cut, and process the cane. Using contemporary estimates of the volume of the slave trade from Guinea-Bissau's ports, Stephen Bühnen notes that, from the late sixteenth to the middle of the seventeenth century, various ports on the Upper Guinea Coast were said to export between 1,800 and 3,000 slaves annually. The lowest of these estimates was recorded in 1616 by Álvares for the Rio Cacheu. Less than a decade later, Donelha said that the Rio Grande exported 3,000 slaves each year.[75] Taking Álvares's lower figure of 1,800 slaves per year leaving the Rio Cacheu and Donelha's figure of 3,000 slaves leaving the Rio Grande, and considering the fact that there are no estimates for slave exports from the Bijagos Islands or the Rio Geba, it is conceivable that in the seventeenth century in excess of 4,800 slaves annually were exported through Guinea-Bissau's ports alone. This figure is close to Rodney's estimate of the slave trade from the whole of the Upper Guinea Coast during about the same period.[76] Curtin is more conservative with his estimates. Using Spanish licenses, which were first published by Pier and Huguette Chaunu, for ships permitted to supply slaves, he notes that figures for the Upper Guinea Coast as a whole vary widely—from 4,370 slave exports between the years 1591 and 1595 to 140 slave exports between the years 1631 and 1635. "It is tempting," Bühnen writes, "to use these official figures to arrive at absolute export figures. . . . The figures of Chaunu/ Curtin, if processed, lead to an *annual* average of only 421 slaves exported from Upper Guinea in the period 1551–1595 and of only 181 slaves in the period 1596–1640." However, to rely solely on these figures is to ignore the observations of contemporaries who visited ports. Hence Bühnen dismisses Curtin's estimates as entirely too low, and he dismisses the highest contemporary estimates as "optimistic" or "exaggerated to illustrate the region's riches." He arrives at an average of 2,000 or 3,000 slaves exported annually for the whole of the Upper Guinea Coast between 1596 and 1640.[77]

Whether we accept Curtin's, Bühnen's, or Rodney's figures for the period, what can we say about the origins of slaves exported from the Guinea-

Bissau region? In short, demographic data from Latin America indicate that, before the eighteenth century, most slaves had their origins in small-scale and politically decentralized coastal communities (that is, among Brame, Banyun, Cassanga, Floup, Balanta, Bijago, Biafada, and Nalu who resided within the *ria* coastline) than in interior state-based communities (that is, among Mandinka and other groups that resided beyond the *ria* coastline's edge). First, James Lockhart, who bases his work on surveys of the Afro-Peruvian population taken between 1548 and 1560, finds that of the 207 African slaves whose identities were revealed in the surveys, 154 (74 percent) had come from the whole of the Upper Guinea Coast and 71 (34 percent) from coastal communities in Guinea-Bissau. There were 8 Banyun, 23 Brame, and 40 Biafada.[78] Second, using studies of the ethnic origins of Afro-Mexicans in 1549, Curtin demonstrates that 73 of 83 slaves (or 88 percent) whose origins could be identified had been born in the regions of Senegambia and Guinea-Bissau. Of those from Guinea-Bissau, 1 was Cassanga, 5 were Banyun, 14 were Biafada, and 23 were Brame.[79] Third, using "scattered data from Peruvian notorial records," Frederick Bowser indicates that the Upper Guinea Coast supplied about 56 percent of the slaves exported to Peru between 1560 and 1650. Moreover, his data show that the overwhelming majority of the slaves from Senegambia and the Upper Guinea Coast had their origins in the coastal reaches of Guinea-Bissau (see Table 2.1).[80] Finally, drawing on Peruvian baptism, confirmation, and marriage records for the period 1583–1702, Jean-Pierre Tardieu presents data that complement those of Bowser (see Tables 2.2–2.5).[81] More than any other numerical data, Bowser's and Tardieu's figures demonstrate the extent to which politically decentralized populations *within* the *ria* coastline of Guinea-Bissau produced slaves. Clearly, during this period the interior state-based populations of the Senegambia and Guinea-Bissau region were not producing slave exports at the same rate that coastal populations were.[82]

A survey presented by Curtin of the ethnic origins of Afro-Mexicans at the end of the seventeenth century shows that, relative to Angola, Guinea-Bissau had become a relatively unimportant supplier of slaves to the Americas. Less than 4 percent of the slaves in the survey had their origins in Guinea-Bissau. However, the survey also reveals that Brame, Biafada, and Banyun populations were still the most preyed upon in the Guinea-Bissau region.[83] All of these groups resided within the sunken *ria* coastline.

THE FRENCH AND PORTUGUESE IN BISSAU AND CACHEU FROM THE LATE SEVENTEENTH CENTURY

The demographic makeup of slaves leaving the Guinea-Bissau region began to change in the eighteenth century. The reasons for this lay partly with

Table 2.1 Ethnicities of Afro-Peruvians from Senegambia and the Upper Guinea Coast in Peruvian Notorial Records, 1560–1650

From Guinea-Bissau's Coastal Zone	Number in Survey	From Senegambia, Guinea or the Interior	Number in Survey	From Guinea, Unspecified Location	Number in Survey
Brame	849	Wolof	128	"Guinea"	22
Banyun	316	Mandinka	284		
Cassanga	49	Serer	45		
Floup	237	Fula	8		
Balanta	75	Soso	18		
Bijago	180	Sape	214		
Biafada	594				
Nalu	103				
Total	2,403		697		22

Source: Adapted from Frederick P. Bowser, *The African Slave in Colonial Peru, 1524–1650* (Stanford: Stanford University Press, 1974), 39–41.

Table 2.2 Ethnicities of Afro-Peruvians from Senegambia and the Upper Guinea Coast in the Parish of San Marcelo de Lima, Peru (libros de bautismos), 1583–1589

From Guinea-Bissau's Coastal Zone	Number in Survey	From Senegambia, Guinea or the Interior	Number in Survey
Brame	98	Wolof	11
Banyun	38	Mandinka	19
Cassanga	24	Sape	9
Bijago	4		
Biafada	10		
Nalu	4		
Total	178		39

Source: Derived from Jean-Pierre Tardieu, "Origins of the Slaves in the Lima Region in Peru (Sixteenth and Seventeenth Centuries)," in *From Chains to Bonds: The Slave Trade Revisited,* ed. Doudou Diène (Paris: UNESCO, 2001), 43–54.

Portuguese and French competition for slaves on the coast. From the end of the sixteenth century, the Portuguese monopoly on trade on the Upper Guinea Coast had been challenged more and more frequently by its European competitors. Portugal's fragile position would erode quickly after the mid-

Table 2.3 Ethnicities of Afro-Peruvians from Senegambia and the Upper Guinea Coast in Hernay, Chincha, Pisco, Caucato, and Cóndor, Peru (parishioners confirmed), 1632

From Guinea-Bissau's Coastal Zone	Number in Survey	From Senegambia, Guinea or the Interior	Number in Survey
Brame	39	Wolof	4
Banyun	17	Mandinka	22
Cassanga	4	Sape	5
Floup	20		
Balanta	3		
Bijago	6		
Biafada	1		
Cacheu	1		
Nalu	7		
Total	98		31

Source: Derived from Jean-Pierre Tardieu, "Origins of the Slaves in the Lima Region in Peru (Sixteenth and Seventeenth Centuries)," in *From Chains to Bonds: The Slave Trade Revisited,* ed. Doudou Diène (Paris: UNESCO, 2001), 43–54.

Table 2.4 Ethnicities of Afro-Peruvians from Senegambia and the Upper Guinea Coast in the Parish of San Marcelo de Lima, Peru (libros de matrimonies), 1640–1680

From Guinea-Bissau's Coastal Zone	Number in Survey	From Senegambia, Guinea or the Interior	Number in Survey
Brame	81	Wolof	7
Banyun	28	Mandinka	8
Cassanga	2	Sape	9
Floup	36		
Balanta	4		
Bijago	21		
Biafada	20		
Nalu	20		
Total	212		24

Source: Derived from Jean-Pierre Tardieu, "Origins of the Slaves in the Lima Region in Peru (Sixteenth and Seventeenth Centuries)," in *From Chains to Bonds: The Slave Trade Revisited,* ed. Doudou Diène (Paris: UNESCO, 2001), 43–54.

seventeenth century as the result of British, French, and Dutch efforts to establish regular trade relationships with African rulers and *lançados*.[84]

Seeking to strengthen their claims to at least one port, the Portuguese government allowed the creation of the Company of Cacheu in 1676. The indi-

Table 2.5 Ethnicities of Afro-Peruvians from Senegambia and the Upper Guinea Coast in the Parish of San Marcelo de Lima, Peru (causas de negros), 1630–1702

From Guinea-Bissau's Coastal Zone	Number in Survey	From Senegambia, Guinea or the Interior	Number in Survey
Brame	33	Wolof	3
Banyun	12	Mandinka	15
Cassanga	1	Sape	9
Floup	21	Soso	2
Bijago	8		
Biafada	18		
Cacheu	1		
Nalu	6		
Total	100		29

Source: Derived from Jean-Pierre Tardieu, "Origins of the Slaves in the Lima Region in Peru (Sixteenth and Seventeenth Centuries)," in *From Chains to Bonds: The Slave Trade Revisited,* ed. Doudou Diène (Paris: UNESCO, 2001), 43–54.

viduals from Santiago and Cacheu who formed it were to reinforce Cacheu's stockade and man it with soldiers. Duties collected on local trade and a portion of tax revenues on slave exports were to accrue to the company. However, the company was poorly capitalized, lacking the financial support of interests in Lisbon. Thus it floundered. As bureaucrats and officials sought answers to the company's problems, they decided that Cacheu was too difficult to control. Their focus then shifted south, to the island of Bissau.[85] This is not to imply that Cacheu was abandoned. In 1690, a second Company of Cacheu was incorporated, and the Portuguese government negotiated an agreement to supply slaves to Spanish America. However, this company also struggled financially, the captain-major complaining in 1707 that the Portuguese could barely finance one slaving voyage a year from the region.[86]

Portuguese efforts at Bissau would not, in the short term, yield greater dividends. Because it offered a large and deep port and was centrally located in relation to Geba, the Rio Cacheu, the Rio Grande, and the Bijagos Islands, Bissau was especially alluring to the Portuguese. Unfortunately for this weak European country, the French were also attracted to Bissau. Thus both France and Portugal attempted to fortify their positions there starting at the end of the seventeenth century. It was then that French official La Courbe approached Papel chief Bacompolo Có with inquires about building a fort on Bissau. Bacompolo Có refused this request but did grant the French permission to establish a trading factory. From Bissau, French factor Jean de la Fond dispatched 1,800 slaves and almost 400 quintals of wax in 1685 and 1686. Bourguignon exported 700 slaves in 1687 and 1688, and Fond, returning to Bissau in 1689, managed to amass a shipment of 300 slaves in three months time. As the century progressed, the French continued their activities on Bissau. French ships loaded some 300 slaves and 200 quintals of ivory in 1694.[87]

Disturbed by this, Portuguese officials and missionaries stepped up activity on Bissau. In 1692, Portugal's government sent thirty exiles to serve as a garrison on the island. Lavishing Bacompolo Có with gifts, the Portuguese crown gained permission to build a fort in 1694. Enthusiastic about an alliance with Portugal, Bacompolo Có "with all of his vassals" adopted Christianity and sent his eldest son, Batonto, to Europe, where he was baptized, the king of Portugal serving as his godfather.[88] In 1696, Bissau became a Portuguese captaincy, answering to the captain-major of Cacheu, and José Pinheiro accepted the task of supervising construction of a fort. Unfortunately for Pinheiro, Bacompolo Có died in February of that same year. Though the new Papel chief, Incinha Te, acceded to the commencement of construction of the fort, he refused to recognize Portugal's claim to a monopoly on trade in the area. However, Pinheiro was persistent in his demands. He instructed Incinha Te that the islanders would not conduct business with "foreigners" while he was alive to stop it, and he directly challenged Incinha Te's authority by first turning two English vessels away from Bissau's principal port and then insisting on the expulsion of a Dutch ship. Tensions between the chief and Pinheiro escalated to a tense standoff. Pinheiro at first appeared to have the upper hand when a large force of *grumetes* from Geba arrived in Bissau to support the Portuguese representative. However, once the *grumetes* had returned upriver, Pinheiro again found himself in dire straits. Held up in his fort and surrounded by Incinha Te's followers, Pinheiro finally relented, reluctantly recognizing Incinha Te's authority as *Senhor da Terra*. But that was not good enough for the Papel leader, who took Pinheiro into custody and had him beaten to death.[89]

By 1700 the situation on the island had not improved for the Portuguese. Papel refused to recognize Portuguese claims to monopoly trade, and they thwarted Portuguese efforts to claim a 10 percent tax on goods bought and sold by "foreign" vessels at Bissau. Portugal was simply in no position to put up a challenge to the powerful Papel. Free trade continued, unabated by a weak and ineffectual Portuguese garrison. Realizing the futility of attempting to establish a regional trade monopoly, the Portuguese ended their official presence on Bissau in 1707. Troops were withdrawn and the fort was destroyed.[90]

Throughout the century that followed, Portugal continued to hold out hope that it would someday dominate trade on the Rio Geba and collect duties at Bissau. However, during the first half of the eighteenth century, "foreigners" were the principal European traders on the Rio Geba. French merchants were particularly active, dispatching a ship and a sloop from Gorée to ply the southern rivers from November to May between 1736 and 1744. The French also sought to entrench themselves militarily on Bissau, eventually placing sixteen pieces of artillery there. As for the British, by sea and land routes they managed to exploit trade at Geba. Indeed, Portuguese officials at midcentury lamented that trade there was "passing to the English of Gambia."[91]

Though the Portuguese crown was not able to realize duties from trade at Bissau, Portuguese merchants did find ways to trade there. In 1746, at least five European vessels visited Bissau in search of slaves and other items. Three were Portuguese and two English, "all conducting trade, loading slaves, ivory and wax."[92] By 1755 the unregulated trade in slaves from Bissau was booming. That year, Portuguese officials in Cacheu reported that Portuguese and French ships were leaving the island with "substantial cargoes of captives." The official mentioned that he knew that a number of ships had visited the island that year: a French vessel left with more than 260 slaves, a Portuguese vessel sailed with about 200 slaves, and another French ship was loading in the port and already had 240 slaves aboard.[93]

If Portugal was looking for an opportune time to venture another attempt at establishing a permanent and official presence on Bissau, it found it when

France became involved in European wars at midcentury. Lavishing another Papel chief with gifts, the Portuguese gained permission to build a new fort on the island. By 1752, construction had begun, but the rise of Papel opposition coupled with the problem of finding people to man the Bissau post meant that little was accomplished during the first few years of halfhearted effort.[94] Eventually the Portuguese crown turned the project over to the Company of Grão Pará e Maranhão, which was accorded monopoly trading privileges for the Guinea-Bissau region beginning in 1755. The company had been created to supply the Brazilian states of Pará and Maranhão with slave laborers. These were the most underdeveloped states in the Portuguese colony, and attempts to use indigenous Indian laborers had consistently met with failure. By 1775 the company had completed a fort, the Praça de José de Bissau. During its construction, deaths were high—about ten people per day—due to diseases, epidemics, and attacks launched by Papel communities.[95] The fort had strong 40-foot-high stone walls that formed a square, at the corners of which were four bulwarks. Trenches surrounded all of this.[96] And the company had an enormous holding pen for slaves.[97]

Like the Portuguese government had on many occasions before, the Company of Grão Pará e Maranhão sought to undercut the power of Luso African traders who lived in the region. The company was especially keen on defending its monopoly trading rights, and it feared Luso Africans would not recognize these. With British vessels regularly purchasing slaves in Bissau and Geba from "Portuguese" in the 1760s, the company's fears were well grounded.[98] Complaints were also aired in the 1770s, when "residents of Cacheu" were venturing to the Bijagos Islands to trade in slaves.[99] Company disdain for Luso Africans is revealed in the words they sometimes chose for them in official reports: "poor whites," "so-called Portuguese," and even "monkeys."[100] Attempting to do away with their competition in 1766, Sebastião da Cunha Souto-Mayor, the captain-major of Bissau, took the drastic step of prohibiting the circulation of "white residents" in the region "in their canoes" and the trading of slaves at the fort by their *grumetes*. This prohibition reveals as much about company attitudes toward Luso Africans as it does about their reliance on them, the captain-major himself being a Luso African.[101] Hence, Cunha Souto-Mayor may well have been defending his own interests (attempting to undercut the strength of local rivals), and not necessarily those of the company. Luso Africans did not, then, work in concert. Their ranks frequently divided, probably along familial lines, as the descendants of various *lançados* competed with one another for control of the slave trade passing through the region.

Despite this intrigue, the company managed to export large numbers of slaves from the Guinea-Bissau region. Between 1756 and 1788, it purchased 22,404 slaves on the Upper Guinea Coast, exporting the vast majority of them

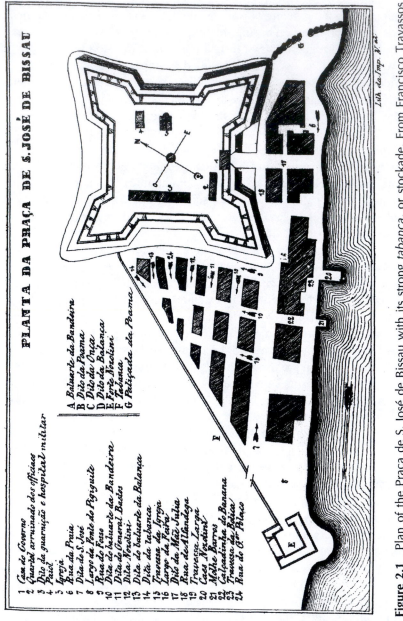

Figure 2.1 Plan of the Praça de S. José de Bissau with its strong *tabanca*, or stockade. From Francisco Travassos Valdez, *Africa occidental: Noticias e considerações* (Lisbon: Imprensa Nacional, 1864), 316.

Table 2.6   Exports of the Company of Grão Pará e Maranhão from the Ports of Bissau and Cacheu, 1756–December 1777

Export, Unit of Measurement	Quantity	Value in Réis	%
Wax, in arrobas	21,916	183,200$000	10.3
Ivory, in arrobas	712	5,507$000	
Campecha wood, in logs	79	767$000	
Hippo Teeth, number	207	9$000	
Gazelle Skins, number	210	9$000	
Slaves, number	20,338	1,592,623$000	89.4

Note: 1$000 = 1,000 réis.
Source: António Carreira, *Os Portuguêses nos rios de Guiné (1500–1900)* (Lisbon: 1984), 71.

from Bissau and Cacheu. Almost 9 percent (1,920) of those died awaiting shipment, and almost 10 percent (2,116) died aboard company vessels bound for Brazil or in holding pens before they could be sold after arrival.[102] For the period 1788 to 1793, official tax records indicate that 4,049 slaves were embarked at Bissau and Cacheu.[103] To be sure, such "official" records do not account for all of the slaves shipped from Rio Geba region. Indeed, "smugglers," exporting slaves not only from the Bijagos Islands but from Bissau itself, regularly eluded Portuguese and company officials.[104] Perhaps the captain-major of Bissau, José António Pinto, was not far off the mark when he estimated that from year to year, 1,600 slaves left from Bissau and Cacheu. Though the company purchased many products for export from Guinea-Bissau, the life of Grão Pará e Maranhão was sustained with the blood of the slave trade. Slaves accounted for almost 90 percent of the value of all exports for Cacheu and Bissau (see Table 2.6). As Pinto commented, "The Portuguese trade is made in hardly more than slaves."[105]

THE DEMOGRAPHY OF THE SLAVE TRADE FROM THE GUINEA-BISSAU REGION FROM THE LATE SEVENTEENTH CENTURY

The reestablishment of an entrenched, if weak and ineffectual, Portuguese administration and military in Bissau corresponded with the rise of Rio Geba as one of the most important corridors for slave traffic on the Upper Guinea Coast. However, the reasons for the growth of the Rio Geba slave trade were rooted less in Portuguese actions on the coast than in occurrences in the interior of the continent, where a state-directed jihad, which was begun in 1725 by Muslim Fulbe and later spread from the Futa Jallon into Kaabu and other interior regions, produced large numbers of captives.

At the beginning of the eighteenth century most of the slaves exported from the Rio Geba region continued to have their origins in Guinea-Bissau's coastal zone. A French slave trader's log dated November 30, 1718, indicates that he purchased 32 captives on Bissau. Of those whose ethnicity was indicated, 11 were Bijago, 4 were Papel, 3 were Nalu, 3 were Biafada, 2 were Balanta, and 2 were Mandinka.[106] Of these, only the Mandinka (composing 8 percent of those whose ethnicity is known) had their origins in the interior. However, as the eighteenth century progressed, slaves exported from Guinea-Bissau increasingly had their origins beyond the *ria* coastline's edge, having arrived at the coast via long-distance trade routes that moved goods between the Futa Jallon and Bissau.[107] As the Fula-led jihad that produced these slaves spread into areas of Kaabu and Sierra Leone, it became what Rodney called "the greatest recruiter of slaves in the latter part of the eighteenth century."[108]

In the interior, merchants transported captives along a well-trodden route that ran from deep in the Futa, over the Rio Grande, through Kaabu, and to Geba. French explorer Gaspard Mollien traveled this route in the early nineteenth century. Having proceeded through Kaabu from Sumakonda to Seraconda, Gaspard Mollien noted that even at the height of the rainy season, when the roads were "almost impassable," the route to Geba was "covered with slave-dealers and salt-merchants; the latter came from Geba, and were going into the countries situated to the east: the former, on the contrary, were going towards the sea-coast to the west; they drove their slaves, who were fastened together by the neck, with long sticks."[109]

In Geba, merchants from the Futa met and traded with *lançados, grumetes,* Luso Africans, and Africans from many points on the coast and in the interior. Indicative of the importance of Geba as a trade entrepôt is the fact that even Wolof from the region of Senegal traveled there.[110] Mollien described a population "which amounts to seven hundred and fifty individuals, comprised of blacks or mulattos, who are nevertheless called whites, because all who are free claim that distinction." "The commerce of this factory," he continued, "consists in hides, wax, ivory and slaves, which are sent to Bissao, whither the Europeans formerly came to traffic for them."[111] Having established themselves in the Praça de José de Bissau, Portuguese officials also noted the importance of Geba and the Rio Geba trade route for supplying Bissau with slaves and other exports from savannah-woodland regions. In 1776 the captain of Bissau said that "from Geba there comes the better part of the Captives, wax, ivory, and some gold."[112]

If in the eighteenth century the interior had become the most important source for slave exports from Guinea-Bissau's ports, slaves continued to be exported from coastal regions as well. Indeed, in 1778 an official noted that Bissau was "well located for trade with the Bijago from whom they [merchants] buy many slaves. . . . On this Island of Bissau, one can purchase from one year to the next 1,200 slaves, and 1,800 arrobas of wax, and 200 quintals of ivory."[113]

A look at S. W. Koelle's linguistic inventory of the population of Sierra Leone in the 1840s indicates that, for some decades, slaves were being

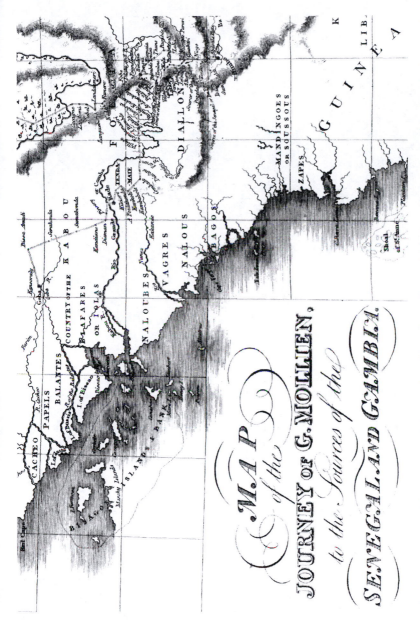

Figure 2.2 Map of the journey of Gaspard Mollien. From Gaspard Mollien, *Travels in the Interior of Africa to the Sources of the Senegal and Gambia Performed by Command of the French Government of the Year 1818* (London: Henry Colburn, 1820), xii.

Figure 2.3   Gaspard Mollien in Bissau. From Gaspard Mollien, *Travels in the Interior of Africa to the Sources of the Senegal and Gambia Performed by Command of the French Government of the Year 1818* (London: Henry Colburn, 1820), 324.

harvested in both coastal and interior zones. In the mid-nineteenth century, Koelle set as his task composing a list of vocabularies of African languages. By this time the British navy was attempting to bring the slave trade to an end by stopping slaving vessels at sea and releasing their human cargoes at Sierra Leone. Hence the colony became populated with people from across West Africa, making it an ideal sight for Koelle's research. For the purposes of this book, his efforts are important because he recorded from where his informants, known as recaptives, originated.[114] A list of recaptives from Guinea-Bissau and the surrounding region is provided in Table 2.7. Since Koelle did not indicate the ports at which those who had been enslaved were embarked, we cannot be certain that those from interior populations were put on ships in Guinea-Bissau. Indeed, they could have been embarked at any number of coastal locations. This limitation aside, Koelle's inventory indicates that people from Guinea-Bissau's coastal and interior populations suffered enslavement in the early nineteenth century, but that most of the slaves exported from Guinea-Bissau probably came from interior locations via long-distance trade routes such as the one Mollien traveled from the Futa Jallon to Geba.

Table 2.7 People from Guinea-Bissau and Surrounding Region in Koelle's Linguistic Inventory, Sierra Leone, 1840s

	From Coastal Populations (Within the Ria Coastline)		From Interior Populations (Beyond the Ria Coastline)	
Modern Ethnic Group	Number Present in Sierra Leone	Date of Capture or Start of Residence	Modern Ethnic Group	Number Present in Sierra Leone	Date of Capture or Start of Residence
Floup (Diola)	4	1839/36	Mande or Mandinka	56	1820-42
Brame	2	1813/33			
Papel	1	1831			
Biafada	6	1829			
Bijago	3	1834			
Nalu	4	1824			
Balanta	7	1835			
Total	27			56	

Source: Adapted from Philip Curtin, The Atlantic Slave Trade: A Census (Madison: University of Wisconsin Press, 1969), 289–298.

Slave censuses taken in Bissau and Cape Verde in 1856 provide comple-
mentary evidence (see Appendices 1 and 2). Book 1 of the Bissau census lists
1,107 slaves.[115] Of those, 240 had been born slaves in places such as Bissau
and Bolama or had failed to provide information about their origins. Of the
remaining 867 slaves, 472 (54 percent) had their origins in the interior. Another 91 (10 percent) had their origins in coastal Sierra Leone. The remaining 304 (35 percent) had their origins in Guinea-Bissau's coastal zone. Since
it fails to list the "nationality" of most of the slaves, the Cape Verde census
provides a much smaller sample size (see Appendix 2). Of the 130 slaves who
are identified by ethnicity, 67 (52 percent) were from the interior, and 60
(46 percent) were from Guinea-Bissau's coastal zone.

CONCLUSION

When taken together, Koelle's linguistic inventory and the censuses from
Bissau and Cape Verde reveal the flexibility of *lançado* commercial networks.
In sixteenth century, *lançados* and their Luso African descendants, working
through partnerships with area women, successfully established lasting relationships in communities in the Guinea-Bissau area. At the same time, they
spoke the languages and shared the customs of the Atlantic merchants who
sailed to Guinea-Bissau's bustling ports. They were therefore well placed to
serve as brokers between two very different groups of people, African producers and European consumers of slaves. In the sixteenth, seventeenth, and
early eighteenth centuries, most of the slaves these brokers purchased and sold
for export had their origins in the decentralized lowland coastal zone. When
interior state-based groups stepped up production of slaves in the eighteenth
century, *lançados* and Luso Africans found ways to orchestrate the shipment
of increasingly large numbers of captives from entrepôts on the *ria* coastline's
edge, the approximate line of division between the lowland coastal and upland savannah-woodland ecological zones. Though a clear demographic shift
had taken place in the slave trade, *lançados* had managed to respond.

That *lançados* and Luso Africans established such a lasting and flexible
commercial network in a decentralized region challenges the generally held
proposition that the elites who controlled powerful state-based political,
military, and commercial institutions tended to dominate the shipment of
slaves within Africa. In the Guinea-Bissau region, a group of "cross-cultural
brokers" organized commercial networks where no single state existed.

NOTES

1. Quoted in P.E.H. Hair and Avelino Teixeira da Mota, eds., *Jesuit Documents on
the Guinea of Cape Verde and the Cape Verde Islands, 1585–1617* (Liverpool: University
of Liverpool, Department of History, 1989), doc. 16.

2. Richard A. Lobban Jr., *Cape Verde: Creole Colony to Independent Nation* (Boulder, Colo.: Westview Press, 1995), 13–16; John K. Thornton, *Africa and Africans in the Making of the Atlantic World, 1400–1680* (Cambridge: Cambridge University Press, 1992), 13–42; Philip Curtin, *The Rise and Fall of the Plantation Complex* (New York: Cambridge University Press, 1990).

3. George E. Brooks, *Landlords and Strangers: Ecology, Society, and Trade in Western Africa, 1000–1630* (Boulder, Colo.: Westview Press, 1993), 154, 168–169.

4. Robin Law, "Slave-Raiders and Middlemen, Monopolists and Free-Traders: The Supply of Slaves for the Atlantic Trade in Dahomey, c. 1715–1850," *Journal of African History* 30, no. 1 (1989): 45. See also Paul E. Lovejoy and Jan S. Hogendorn, "Slave Marketing in West Africa," in *The Uncommon Market: Essays in the Economic History of the Atlantic Slave Trade*, eds. H. A. Gemery and J. S. Hogendorn (New York: Academic Press, 1979), 213–232; and Richard L. Roberts, *Warriors, Merchants, and Slaves* (Stanford: Stanford University Press, 1987), 13. An exception is David Northrup, who argues that in decentralized regions of southwestern Nigeria the slave trade "was not conducted through institutions as centralized as those at the coast." David Northrup, *Trade Without Rulers: Pre-Colonial Economic Development in South-Eastern Nigeria* (Oxford: Clarendon Press, 1978), 93–94. Another exception is Robert W. Harms, *River of Wealth: The Central Zaire Basin in the Era of the Slave and Ivory Trade, 1500–1891* (New Haven: Yale University Press, 1981). Harms describes decentralized Bobangi slave-trading networks on the Congo. However, both Northrup and Harms see these trading systems as extensions of earlier trade systems. In the Guinea-Bissau area, the slave trade was carried out by new, not existing, trading communities. Further, unlike in southwest Nigeria, in Guinea-Bissau the slave trade brought about a radical reorientation of trade routes.

5. Walter Rodney, *A History of the Upper Guinea Coast, 1545 to 1800* (New York: Monthly Review Press, 1970), 128. Ultimately, the slave trade witnessed the movement of about 11.4 million captives from Africa's shores. David Eltis, Stephen D. Behrendt, David Richardson, and Herbert S. Klein, eds., *The Trans-Atlantic Slave Trade: A Database on CD-ROM* (Cambridge: Cambridge University Press, 1999). I have utilized the database to the extent that I can. Unfortunately, the Portuguese trade has the largest gaps in the database and the seventeenth-century French trade is missing. See also David Eltis, "The Volume and Structure of the Transatlantic Slave Trade: A Reassessment," *William and Mary Quarterly* 58, no. 1 (January 2001): 17–45.

6. António Carreira, *Panaria Cabo-Verdiano-Guineense: Aspectos históricos e sócioeconomicos* (Lisbon: Junta de Investigações Científicas do Ultramar, 1968).

7. António Carreira, *Cabo Verde: Formação e extinção de uma sociedade escravocrata (1460–1878)* (Praia, Cape Verde: Instituto Caboverdeano de Livro, 1983), 58; see pp. 53–92 for an informative discussion of *lançados*. See also George E. Brooks, *Perspectives on Luso-African Commerce and Settlement in the Gambia and Guinea-Bissau Region, Sixteenth–Nineteenth Centuries,* Boston University African Studies Center Working Papers no. 24 (Boston: Boston University Press, 1980), 2–3; Jean Boulègue, *Les Luso-Africains de Sénégambie* (Lisbon: Instituto de Investigação Cinetífica Tropical, 1989); Maria da Graça Garcia Nolasco da Silva, "Subsídios para o estudo dos 'lançados' na Guiné," *Boletim Cultural da Guiné Portuguesa* 25, nos. 97–100 (1970): 25–40, 217–232, 397–420, 513–560; Rodney, *A History,* chap. 3, 8; and Peter Kaibe Mendy, *Colonialismo português em África: A tradição de resistência na Guiné-Bissau (1879–*

1959) (Bissau: Arquivo Histórico do Instituto Nacional de Estudos e Pesquisa, 1991), 109–110. For a look at relationships between African women and *lançados* in two coastal commercial entrepôts in Senegal, see George E. Brooks, "The *Signares* of Saint-Louis and Goreé: Women Entrepreneurs in Eighteenth-Century Senegal," in *Women in Africa: Studies in Social and Economic Change,* eds. Nancy J. Hafkin and Edna G. Bay (Stanford: Stanford University Press, 1976), 19–44.

    8. Manuel Álvares, *Ethiopia Minor and a Geographical Account of the Province of Sierra Leone,* trans. P.E.H. Hair (Liverpool: University of Liverpool, Department of History, September 30, 1990), chap. 4.

    9. Rodney, *A History,* 75.

    10. Ibid., 75–76.

    11. Ibid., 123; Hair and Mota, *Jesuit Documents,* doc. 9.

    12. Peter Mark, "The Evolution of 'Portuguese' Identity: Luso-Africans on the Upper Guinea Coast from the Sixteenth to the Early Nineteenth Century," *Journal of African History* 40, no. 2 (1999): 174–175. Mark argues that in the eighteenth and nineteenth centuries, Luso Africans were increasingly drawn into a European discourse on race and, consequently, increasingly defined themselves by skin color. For more on Luso African architecture, see Peter Mark, "Constructing Identity: Sixteenth- and Seventeenth-Century Architecture in the Gambia-Geba Region and the Articulation of Luso-African Ethnicity," *History in Africa* 22 (1995): 307–337; Peter Mark, "'Portuguese' Architecture and Luso-African Identity in Senegambia and Guinea, 1730–1890," *History in Africa* 23 (1996): 176–196; and Peter Mark, *"Portuguese" Style and Luso-African Identity: Precolonial Senegambia, Sixteenth–Nineteenth Centuries* (Bloomington: Indiana University Press, 2002).

    13. Brooks, *Landlords,* 270–271.

    14. Much has been written about how states facilitate trade through broad-based institutions. For example, see Jean Ensminger, *Making a Market: The Insitutional Transformation of an African Society* (Cambridge: Cambridge University Press, 1992); and Roberts, *Warriors,* 13.

    15. For an example of this, see Eve Lakshmi Crowley, "Contracts with the Spirits: Religion, Asylum, and Ethnic Identity in the Cacheu Region of Guinea-Bissau," (Ph.D. diss., Yale University, 1990), 240.

    16. Quoted in Hair and Mota, *Jesuit Documents,* doc. 4.

    17. Mateo de Anguiano, *Misiones Capuchinas en África,* vol. 2 (Madrid: Instituto Santo Toribio de Mogrovejo, 1950), 141–144.

    18. The best description of these ties was given by Francisco Travassos Valdez in the nineteenth century. Francisco Travassos Valdez, *Africa occidental: Noticias e considerações* (Lisbon: Imprensa Nacional, 1864), 340–342.

    19. Law, "Slave-Raiders"; Lovejoy and Hogendorn, "Slave Marketing."

    20. Brooks, "Perspectives," 6–7. For more on interior trade organizations and how they excluded competitors, see Lovejoy and Hogendorn, "Slave Marketing."

    21. Brooks, "The *Signares,*" 27.

    22. See George E. Brooks, "A Nhara of the Guinea-Bissau Region: Mãe Aurélia Correia," in *Women and Slavery in Africa,* eds. Claire C. Robertson and Martin A. Klein (Madison: University of Wisconsin Press, 1983), 309; and Mendy, *Colonialismo,* 111–112.

23. Brooks, "Perspectives," 7–8. See also Rodney, *A History,* 204.

24. André Álvares de Almada, *Tratado breve dos rios de Guiné,* trans. by P.E.H. Hair (Liverpool: University of Liverpool, Department of History, 1984), 88.

25. Philip Beaver, *African Memoranda* (London: Dawsons of Pall Mall, 1968), 490–493. The majority of the *grumetes* in his list were male.

26. Brooks, "Perspectives," 8–9.

27. Álvares, *Ethiopia Minor,* chap. 7.

28. Almada, *Tratado breve,* 107.

29. For the importance of marriage bonds between communities and traders in another decentralized region, see Northrup, *Trade Without Rulers,* 94–100.

30. For the names of Luso Africans and Portuguese traders in Bissau, Geba, and Cacheu in the 1640s, see J. Faro, "A aclamação de D. João IV na Guiné," *Boletim Cultural da Guiné Portuguesa* 13, no. 52 (1958): 490–515. Faro examines petitions signed by local merchants.

31. Rodney, *A History,* 204; P.E.H. Hair, introduction to Francisco de Lemos Coelho, *Description of the Coast of Guinea (1684),* trans. P.E.H. Hair (Liverpool: University of Liverpool, Department of History, 1985).

32. Beaver, *Africa Memoranda,* 275. See also Rodney, *A History,* 204.

33. Rodney, *A History,* 203–205; Joel Frederico Silveira, "Guiné," in *O Império Africano 1825–1890,* eds. Valentim Alexandre and Jill Dias (Lisbon: Editorial Estampa, 1998), 222.

34. André Álvares de Almada, *Tratado breve dos rios de Guiné do Cabo Verde dês do Rio de Sanagá até os Baixios de Santa Ana de todas as nações que há na dita costa e de seus costumes, armas, trajos, juramentos, guerras, ano 1594,* ed. António Brásio (Lisbon: Editorial LIAM, 1964), 9; see also Hair's edition, 86. Here I have translated from Brásio's edition. Hair's translation differs in some important ways. See also Rodney, *A History,* 103.

35. Almada, *Tratado breve* (Hair's ed.), 106; Hair and Mota, *Jesuit Documents,* doc. 4.

36. Brooks, *Landlords,* 226–232; Almada, *Tratado breve* (Hair's ed.), 89.

37. Brooks, *Landlords,* 91–93.

38. Ibid., 237.

39. Quoted in ibid., 233–237.

40. Ibid., 237–244.

41. Ibid.

42. Ibid., 271–272.

43. P.E.H. Hair, Adam Jones, and Robin Law, eds., *Barbot on Guinea: The Writing of Jean Barbot on West Africa, 1678–1712* (London: Hakluyt Society, 1992), 321.

44. Quoted in ibid., 319 .

45. Quoted in Hair and Mota, *Jesuit Documents,* doc. 13.

46. Coelho, *Description,* chap. 5.

47. Quoted in Hair, Jones, and Law, *Barbot on Guinea,* 320.

48. Avelino Teixeira da Mota, ed., *As viagens do Bispo D. Frei Vitoriano Portuense à Guiné e a cristianização dos reis de Bissau* (Lisbon: Junta de Investigações Científicas do Ultramar, 1974), 59.

49. Hair, Jones, and Law, *Barbot on Guinea,* 321.

50. Brooks, *Landlords,* 272. See also Hair, Jones, and Law, *Barbot on Guinea,* 320. Barbot noted that the "king of Bissos . . . dresses in Portuguese fashion."

51. Quoted in Mota, *As viagens,* 69.

52. Álvares, *Ethiopia Minor,* chap. 11.

53. Quoted in Hair and Mota, *Jesuit Documents,* doc. 9.

54. Quoted in Anguiano, *Misiones Capuchinas,* 141.

55. Brooks, *Landlords,* 264; Almada, *Tratado breve* (Hair's ed.), 93.

56. Brooks, *Landlords,* 270–271. However, relations between *lançados* and Biafada sometimes became strained. See Coelho, *Description,* chap. 6.

57. Brooks, *Landlords,* 261.

58. The name *Degola* was derived for the word *kola,* indicating the region's centrality in the ancient trade of kola between Sierra Leone and Guinea-Bissau. This trade was exploited by *lançados.* See Arquivo Histórico Ultramarino (AHU) (Lisbon, Portugal), Guiné, cx. 10, doc. 6-A. See also Mota, *As viagens,* 71. On other trade items, see AHU, Guiné, cx. 9, doc. 55.

59. AHU, Guiné, cx. 10, doc. 6-A. According to Brooks, Mandinka renamed the state "Badour." Brooks, *Landlords,* 85–86.

60. Almada, *Tratado breve* (Hair's ed.), 93.

61. André Donelha, *Descrição da Serra Leoa e dos rios De Guiné do Cabo Verde (1625),* ed. Avelino Teixeira da Mota, trans. P.E.H. Hair, Centro de Estudos de Cartografia Antiga no. 19 (Lisbon: Junta de Investigações Científicas do Ultramar, 1977), 163.

62. Coelho, *Description,* chap. 6.

63. Quoted in Sieur Michel Jajolet de La Courbe, *Premier voyage du Sieur de la Courbe fait à la coste de l'Afrique en 1685,* ed. Prosper Cultru (Paris: E. Champion, 1913), 251–252.

64. Mota, *As viagens,* 71.

65. For a study of the reasons for Portugal's participation in the slave trade, see Françoise Latour da Veiga Pinto and António Carreira, "Portuguese Participation in the Slave Trade: Opposing Forces, Trends of Opinion Within Portuguese Society—Effects on Portugal's Socio-Economic Development," in *The African Slave Trade from the Fifteenth to the Nineteenth Century* (Paris: UNESCO, 1979), 119–149.

66. Gomes Eanes de Zurara, *Chrónica de Guiné,* ed. José de Bragança (Lisbon: Biblioteca Histórica, n.d.), chap. 96; Anthony Luttrell, "Slavery and Slaving in the Portuguese Atlantic (to About 1500)," in *The Transatlantic Slave Trade From West Africa* (Edinburgh: University of Edinburgh, Center of African Studies, 1965), 61–79.

67. Philip D. Curtin, *The Atlantic Slave Trade: A Census* (Madison: University of Wisconsin Press, 1969), 17.

68. See António Carreira, *As companhias pombalinas de navegação comércio e tráfico de escravos entre Africana e o nordeste Brasileiro* (Bissau: Centro de Estudos da Guiné Portuguesa, 1969), chap. 1. The crown soon became cold to the idea of a Cape Verdean monopoly and settlement of *lançados* on the Guinea Coast. See Walter Rodney, "Portuguese Attempts at Monopoly on the Upper Guinea Coast, 1580–1650," *Journal of African History* 6, no. 3 (1965): 307–322. See also Ivana Elbl, "The Volume of the Early Atlantic Slave Trade, 1450–1521," *Journal of African History* 38, no. 1 (1997): 62.

69. Curtin, *The Atlantic Slave Trade,* 18; Luttrell, "Slavery and slaving," 77.

70. Elbl, "The Volume," 62–63.

71. Quoted in ibid., 67; Luttrell, "Slavery and Slaving," 77.

72. Elbl, "The Volume," 73.

73. Ibid., 69.

74. Curtin, *The Atlantic Slave Trade,* 101.

75. Stephan Bühnen, "Ethnic Origins of Peruvian Slaves (1548–1650): Figures for Upper Guinea," *Paideuma* 39 (1993): 82.

76. Rodney, *A History,* 98.

77. Bühnen, "Ethnic Origins," 82. Estimates put the number of slaves in Brazil in 1600 at 7,000. Most of them were from the Guinea Coast. See Pierre Verger, *Trade Relations Between the Bight of Benin and Bahia from the Seventeenth to the Nineteenth Century* (Ibadan, Nigeria: Ibadan University Press, 1976), 2.

78. James Lockhart, *Spanish Peru, 1532–1560: A Colonial Society* (Madison: University of Wisconsin Press, 1968), 173; Curtin, *The Atlantic Slave Trade,* 96.

79. Curtin, *The Atlantic Slave Trade,* 98–99.

80. Frederick P. Bowser, *The African Slave in Colonial Peru, 1524–1650* (Stanford: Stanford University Press, 1974), 39–41.

81. Jean-Pierre Tardieu, "Origins of the Slaves in the Lima Region in Peru (Sixteenth and Seventeenth Centuries)," in *From Chains to Bonds: The Slave Trade Revisited,* ed. Doudou Diène (Paris: UNESCO, 2001), 43–54. See also David Pavy, "The Provenience of Colombian Negroes," *Journal of Negro History* 52, no. 1 (January 1967): 35–80. Pavy taps records for criminal court proceedings in an effort to determine the origins of Peruvian slaves. A 1589 case, "Criminal contra Gonzalo Ortiz contrabanda de negros," lists five Biafada and three Brame from coastal Guinea-Bissau but no slaves from the interior of the Upper Guinea Coast region. A 1607 case, "Andres Garces residente de la cuidad de los Remedios contral el capitán Alonzo Velasquez Xaramillo," lists three Brame, two Biafada, and one Bijago from the coastal reaches of Guinea Bissau. Only one slave from the interior (a Mandinka) appeared in this case.

82. John Thornton's data derived from inventories of slave holdings in Hispaniola in 1547, 1549, 1606, and 1656 dovetail nicely with the data I have presented here. Thornton, *Africa and Africans,* 198–199.

83. Curtin, *The Atlantic Slave Trade,* 113.

84. See AHU, Guiné, cx. 1, doc. 44; cx. 2, doc. 48; cx. 3, doc. 8; cx. 3, doc. 48; cx. 3, doc. 89; and Rodney, *A History,* 122–151.

85. Rodney, *A History,* 141–142; João Barreto, *História da Guiné, 1418–1918* (Lisbon: J. Barreto, 1938), 108–109.

86. Rodney, *A History,* 240–1; Barreto, *História,* 127–129.

87. Rodney, *A History,* 143–144; Christiano José de Senna Barcellos, *Subsidios para a história de Cabo Verde e Guiné,* vol. 1 (Lisbon: Academia Real das Sciencias, 1900), 113. A quintal is equal to 100 kilograms or 220.46 pounds.

88. AHU, Guiné, cx. 3, doc. 95. For more on the baptism, see Rodney, *A History,* 144–147; and Mendy, *Colonialismo,* 121–122. See also Mota, *As viagens,* 137–140.

89. Rodney, *A History,* 144–147; Mendy, *Colonialismo,* 123–125.

90. Rodney, *A History,* 151, 241; Mendy, *Colonialismo,* 123–136.

91. For complaints that British and French ships were not paying duties to the Portuguese crown, see AHU, Guiné, cx. 7, doc. 11; and cx. 6, docs. 8, 11. See also Barreto, *História da Guiné,* 26–27. Jean Mettas presents information about French activity in

Bissau in "La traite portugaise en haute Guinée," *Journal of African History* 16, no. 3 (1975): 343–363. See also Rodney, *A History,* 244.

92. AHU, Guiné, cx. 7, docs. 5, 19.

93. Ibid., cx. 9, doc. 11.

94. Rodney, *A History,* 244–245.

95. Mendy, *Colonialismo,* 131–132; Rodney, *A History,* 246; Avelino Teixeira da Mota, *Guiné portuguesa,* vol. 2 (Lisbon: Agência Geral do Ultramar, 1954), 27; Richard A. Lobban Jr., *Historical Dictionary of the Republics of Guinea-Bissau and Cape Verde* (Metuchen, N.J.: Londres, 1979), 25–26; Bernardino António Álvares de Andrade, *Planta da praça de Bissau e suas adjacentes,* ed. Damião Peres (Lisbon: Academia Portuguesa da História, 1952).

96. Francisco Travassos Valdez, *Six Years of a Traveller's Life in Western Africa* (London: Hurst and Blackett, 1861), 238.

97. Carreira, *As companhias,* 77.

98. Ibid., 80.

99. AHU, Guiné, cx. 11, doc. 7.

100. Ibid.; Rodney, *A History,* 246.

101. Carreira, *As companhias,* 82–83; Silveira, "Guiné," 222.

102. Carreira, *As companhias,* 96–97. Also see Mettas, "La traite portugaise," 346. Mettas presents slightly different figures for the same period.

103. António Carreira, *O tráfico de escravos nos rios de Guiné e ilhas de Cabo Verde (1810–1850): Subsídios para o seu estudo* (Lisbon: Junta de Investigações Científicas do Ultramar, 1981), 15.

104. João Barreto estimated exports from Guinea-Bissau at 1,500 per year in the eighteenth century. Barreto, *História,* 287.

105. Quoted in António Carreira, *Os portuguêses nos rios de Guiné (1500–1900)* (Lisbon: António Carreira, 1984), 71.

106. Mettas, "La traite portugaise," 352–353; António Carreira, "As companhias pombalinas," *Boletim Cultural da Guiné Portugueza* 13, nos. 91–92 (1968): 321.

107. John Ralph Willis, "Jihad Di-Sabil Allah: Its Doctrinal Basis in Islam and Some Aspects of Its Evolution in Nineteenth-Century West Africa," *Journal of African History* 8, no. 3 (1967): 395–415; Walter Rodney, "Jihad and Social Revolution in Futa Djalon in the Eighteenth Century," *Journal of the Historical Society of Nigeria* 4 (June 1968): 269–284; Amar Samb, "L'islam et le Ngabou," *Ethiopiques* 28 (October 1981): 116–123; David Robinson, *Holy War of Umar Tal: The Western Sudan in the Mid-Nineteenth Century* (Oxford: Clarendon Press, 1985); Joye Bowman Hawkins, "Conflict, Interaction, and Change in Guinea-Bissau: Fulbe Expansion and Its Impact, 1850–1900" (Ph.D. diss., University of California–Los Angeles, 1980).

108. Rodney, *A History,* 236. See also Rodney, "Jihad and Social Revolution," 281.

109. Gaspard Mollien, *Travels in the Interior of Africa to the Sources of the Senegal and Gambia Performed by the Command of the French Government in the Year 1818,* ed. T. E. Bowdich (London: Frank Cass, 1967), 316–317.

110. Ibid., 318. One of these Wolof traders, having learned both French and Portuguese from his business dealings, assisted Mollien (a Frenchman) in communicating with a Portuguese administrator who manned the Geba post. It is ironic that at Geba only African merchants could communicate in both languages. The Wolof merchant was even able to translate a letter written by Mollien.

111. Ibid., 323.
112. AHU, Guiné, cx. 9, doc. 55; see also cx. 11, doc. 57; cx. 10, doc. 6A.
113. Ibid., cx. 11, doc. 57.
114. Curtin, *The Atlantic Slave Trade,* 251.
115. Book 2 is not listed in the AHU's inventory and could not be located by archivists during my last visit to Lisbon.

3

PRODUCING SLAVES IN A DECENTRALIZED REGION

Two brief accounts reveal a great deal about how slaves were produced and how contact with Atlantic merchants led to a series of radical transformations in the coastal reaches of the Upper Guinea Coast. The first describes happenings in Casa Mansa, a small state located in the northern part of the Guinea-Bissau region on the Rio Casamance and Rio Cacheu that was ruled by Masatamba at the start of the seventeenth century. While visiting Masatamba's kingdom, André Donelha related a story about a "skinny and shrunk" *tangomao,* or "Portuguese" merchant living on the coast. His name was Sad Life, and his general unsociability greatly angered a certain black man. Determined to do away with Sad Life, the black man attempted "to involve him in a *chai,*" a plot or trap. He "arranged with his wife that she should go to Sad Life's house and ask him for something, and if he did not give it to her, she should scream and say that Sad Life had forced her." The "well built" woman did this, and for the crime of which he was accused, Sad Life was tied up and taken to the ruler of Casa Mansa in the company of his accusers. "The husband said that he found the man in intercourse with his wife." But Sad Life repeatedly denied the accusation. Finally, the king, "after having thought a moment, called a black man, his servant, a young man, and said to him: 'Under pain of death, I order you, immediately, in front of me, to have intercourse with this woman.'" With a large crowd looking on, the youth pushed her down, but the black woman, "not wishing to be mounted in the sight of His Majesty and so many others, defended herself. The youth used all his strength to carry out the king's order, and she to defend herself, to the extent that the youth began to tire." When the king saw this, he ordered an end to the spectacle and said, "Rascally woman, if this black, who is a youth and well built, was unable to take you, after I ordered him to do so under pain of death, how could Sad Life, who is so feeble and contemptible, have forced you, considering that, as we have seen, you are such a well built woman? If he slept with you, it was by your own will; and so that no other case like this will be brought before me, you and your husband will become Sad Life's (slaves)." He told the old *tangomao,* "Sell them and benefit at their expense, since they wished to benefit at yours." Sad Life did this, disposing of the couple at Cacheu where they were probably boarded for shipment to the Americas.[1]

Manuel Álvares recorded the second account a few years earlier. He described a politically decentralized group of people living to the southwest of Casa Mansa on an archipelago called the Bijagos. Of the islanders, who were known as Bijago, Álvares said, "Excellent warriors, they have spread terror and desolation among all those to the windward." They did this during slave raids staged from enormous seagoing craft. "Whatever they come upon at sea they grab, even if it belongs to their own people; and so, once they get into their canoes, they plunder the Biafares, the Falupos, the Papels or Burames, the Balantas and the Nalus. To sum up, those not aboard the Bijagos fleet cannot escape their claws. They themselves say that the sea has no king, just as they have no king, even on land." Though lacking kings, Bijago posed a grave threat to their state-based neighbors, even those firmly attached to Kaabu. "They have destroyed the Biafares," Álvares bemoaned, "and even burnt down Our Lady of Guinela in 1610, and they have made large-scale assaults on Biguba."[2]

These two descriptions, both from the early seventeenth century, illustrate the depth of the transformation that had occurred in the economic, political, and social systems of the coastal zones of the Upper Guinea Coast since Nuno Tristão's 1441 voyage. New lines of commercial exchange had come into existence. No longer were coastal people's most important trading partners located to the east. The most powerful markets were now to the west; they stretched across the Atlantic. Merchants sailing this ocean did not desire salt, dried fish, or many of the agricultural goods that coastal people had long offered for exchange. They demanded captives. Thus it was by harvesting slaves that coastal people gained access to valuable imports.

The descriptions also illustrate that both states and decentralized societies had found ways to garner a share of the goods being brought to the region's shores from the Atlantic. How and why decentralized societies produced and marketed captives is an important focus of this chapter. I argue that the body of scholarship that sees the slave trade as contributing to the demise of decentralized societies and to the rise of politically centralized states, needs to be rethought.[3] That is, I challenge some of the assumptions underlying the "predatory state thesis."[4] Proponents of this thesis argue that large armies conducting wars on their states' "slaving frontiers" produced most of Africa's slaves. State elites either integrated captives into communities as laborers and wives or sold them for export in exchange for valuable goods that could be redistributed to clients to assure their loyalty.[5]

Though the predatory state thesis shows a clear link between the formation and reproduction of African states and the development of the Atlantic slave trade, its depiction of the societies occupying "slaving frontiers" is problematic. Such societies were often politically decentralized and have therefore been seen as lacking institutions powerful enough to ward off attacks. Hence, scholars have argued, they became human reservoirs, areas tapped by warring armies.[6] Challenging this thesis, I argue that few societies were sources composed of "the raided;" few were "reservoirs" of potential captives. Most societies very effectively protected themselves, sometimes by refashioning highly decentralized and often egalitarian political institutions so that they could better serve defensive functions.

However they restructured their societies, many residents of the coastal reaches of the Upper Guinea Coast found it necessary to produce slave exports in order to garner the imports needed for protection. What coastal people wanted most from Atlantic merchants was iron, which could be fashioned into defensive weapons. Hence, in order to obtain the iron needed to defend themselves from slavers, decentralized societies produced and marketed captives. The "iron-slave cycle" fueled the conflicts that generated slaves in this politically fractured region.

Societies in the Guinea-Bissau area produced slaves in other ways as well. Unable to generate sufficient numbers of captives through attacks on "outsiders," they often enslaved "insiders," people within their own communities. They did so by transforming judicial institutions so that those found guilty of various "crimes" could be sentenced to sale. Sad Life's story illustrates how states did this. In decentralized societies, councils of elders and others who presided over relatively egalitarian community-based institutions found ways to rid themselves of those who violated norms by convicting them and selling them for export. In the era of the slave trade, myriad societies embraced the market and produced the human exports that fed it. To focus our attention solely on the actions of states and to depict those living on states' frontiers as passive is to miss this point.

THE RIO CASAMANCE AND RIO CACHEU: A "PREDATORY STATE" AND ITS "SLAVING FRONTIERS"

The Rio Cacheu region is an ideal site to demonstrate how both states and decentralized societies participated in slaving. In the early sixteenth century, the Rio Cacheu was situated on the frontier of the Casa Mansa (or Casamance) kingdom and possessed a mixed population of Cassanga, Mandinka, Floup, Balanta, Brame, and Banyun. Some of these groups were incorporated into Casa Mansa.[7] Others operated as politically independent communities. The groups attached to Casa Mansa recognized the rule of the Cassanga king, who in turn paid tribute to the Mandinka kingdom of Kaabu.[8] Casa Mansa prospered by controlling trade between the Rio Cacheu and Rio Gambia and the interior and by manufacturing and marketing cloth. Cassanga fairs attracted as many as 8,000 people, including "Portuguese," who traded iron, horses, beads, paper, and wine.[9]

By about the mid-sixteenth century, the Cassanga king had become wealthy by directing military and judicial institutions toward producing slaves who were sold to Atlantic merchants. André Álvares de Almada noted that, with "spears, arrows, shields, knives and short swords" as well as thick clubs "of up to three hand-spans long," Casa Mansa's armies attacked Banyun, Brame, and Balanta communities between and around the Rio Casamance and Rio Cacheu, making slaves of many people.[10] Offering captives and other items for sale and providing protection for merchants who came to trade, King Masatamba had established such good trading relations with the Portuguese and Luso Africans that they could call him their "best friend" and "brother-in-arms" in the early seventeenth century.[11] Donelha said that the Cassanga king made "many wars" and conquered many Banyun. "This king gave ten or fifteen blacks for a horse, if it was a good one. He was so much a friend of the whites that they went about freely."[12]

The Cassanga king also produced slaves through judicial proceedings.[13] The slave trade provided the Casa Mansa's rulers with a way to eliminate rivals and unwanted or unruly commoners by condemning them to captivity and sale for whatever "crimes" they may have committed. Balthasar Barreira said that the king "calls to judgment those he thinks might have committed the crime and those whom he pretends to suspect. The latter are always noble and rich blacks whom for some whim he wishes to kill, or whose possessions he greedily wishes to seize." The king used a specific test to determine guilt. He ordered a basin of "red water," which contained extracts of the crushed bark of trees, to be brought before him. The accused was then forced to drink the liquid. "If they do not vomit, they are freed; if they vomit, they are immediately judged guilty." Unfortunately for those subjected to the "red water ordeal," the failure to vomit sometimes brought death by poisoning. When the victims died, their possessions were taken by the king "and all their wives, children and families become his slaves, and these he sells to the Portuguese."[14] Similarly, the Casa Mansa's king produced slaves through accusations of witchcraft. "Any person who falls from a palm tree and dies," Almada wrote, "they consider a witch. The officers of the king immediately go to his house and seize all his possessions. They even take his wives, children and other relatives, and sell them." Because palm wine was a popular drink, many people regularly climbed trees to extract the sap. "Hence, they regularly fall from them."[15]

The sale of slaves brought wealth directly in the form of revenue streams or indirectly as taxes or gifts to the rulers of the kingdom. Much of the wealth derived from the slave trade was used to equip the armies that took captives from decentralized groups on the frontier of Casa Mansa; some may have been redistributed to regional leaders or others in return for their support; and some was appropriated by the king, who "enjoyed royal state, and was served with pomp—[he possessed] a table, silk carpets, chairs, a gilded bed, curtains and canopies of silk, and a whole dinner service in silver."[16] The wealth that the king derived from the slave trade certainly elevated him well above the masses, giving him untold power over many institutions—judicial, military, and economic.[17]

It seems clear, then, that this state was similar to other "predatory states" of West Africa. Such states conducted wars against smaller-scale, often decentralized communities. The primary purpose of this warfare was to produce captives, who were vital to the functioning and reproduction of state institutions. Captives were put to use as laborers, incorporated into the households of warriors as wives, or sold for precious merchandise that was monopolized by the state and redistributed to its warriors and dependents.[18] Though Casa Mansa was small in relation to predatory states such as Segou in the Niger River valley, it did have a corps of professional soldiers and appears to have reproduced itself through slave raiding and trading.[19] Slaving strengthened Casa Mansa by providing it with valuables—weapons, horses, iron, and beads—that could be used to coerce or to reward.[20]

However loyal its warriors may have been, Casa Mansa did not establish lasting hegemony over many of the decentralized societies in the northern reaches of Guinea-Bissau or the area of the lower Rio Casamance. Further, since their resistance increased the cost of doing business in the region, some politically decentralized coastal groups jeopardized the Cassanga king's military and commercial expansion. For example, Almada reported that trade on the Rio Casamance had been brought to an end by "blacks called Jabundos, who speak the language of the Banhun." Jabundo were probably a Banyun chieftaincy. They resided near the ocean on the south side of the lower Rio Casamance and often conducted trade with Europeans in slaves and beeswax. However, at the time of Almada's visit to the coast, they had imposed a blockade and seized several European vessels on the river. Almada also gave an example of a battle in which the forces of the Cassanga chief were "routed and put to flight" after crossing the Rio Cacheu to attack the forces of "King Bambara," ruler of a Banyun chieftaincy.[21] Years later, many Banyun continued to be uncontrollable, staging frequent attacks on Portuguese vessels. "Regular losses result from this," Manuel Álvares complained, "losses greater than need be, and affecting not only those involved but also the Crown revenue."[22]

Other decentralized groups in the region added to the problems that Cassanga and Portuguese faced in orchestrating the orderly shipment of slaves. Many Floup put up fierce resistance to Cassanga threats, and they dissuaded slavers from visiting their region by attacking their vessels. They were, Álvares wrote, "the mortal enemies of all kinds of white men. If our ships touch their shores they plunder the goods and make the white crew their prisoners."[23] Further, nineteenth-century traveler M. Bertrand-Bocandé said that at an earlier time Cassanga had been defeated in battle by a northern Balanta group at "Brikam" on the Rio Casamance.[24]

Decentralized societies resisted the incursions of powerful state armies in three ways. First, they took advantage of the natural protection offered by the landscape by making their homes in the riverine, marshy, and tsetse fly–infested areas of coastal Guinea-Bissau. Large armies relying on horse warriors could not operate effectively in such places since the *Trypanosoma rhodesiense* parasite, which is carried by tsetse flies and causes sleeping sickness, took an enormous toll on horses. Further, the region's many rivers presented effective barriers to the movement of large numbers of foot soldiers. Indeed, in the battle between a Cassanga army and the followers of King Bambara, the Rio Cacheu played a key role. The Cassanga king had to call upon Portuguese allies to assist in the transportation of his troops across the river. Moreover, upon being surprised in a Banyun ambush, the Cassanga troops were massacred as they returned to the river in retreat. Almada said that as they tried in haste to board their boats, "many were drowned, for the numbers were so great that those of our men who were assisting the king [of the Cassanga to escape] had to kill many Cassangas, cutting their hands off as they clung to boats."[25]

Second, by assuming a defensive-household or fortified-village posture, decentralized coastal groups erected their own barriers to invasion.[26] Almada mentioned that in the battle that he observed, the forces of King Bambara appeared braced for an attack since they "were in fortified positions" near the Rio Cacheu. Elsewhere, he noted that in coastal Guinea-Bissau the houses "are large and well built, and have so many doors and rooms that they are more like labyrinths than houses." They made them that way, he said, because bands of raiders caused the people "so much trouble."[27]

Finally, chieftaincies and independent villages resisted large state-based armies, as well as small-scale raiding parties, by arming themselves. Arms, or the material from which to forge them, could be obtained by trading slaves. Thus, to defend against attack, decentralized groups participated in slave raids; they produced captives and traded them so that they could get arms to deter slave raiders.

THE IRON-SLAVE CYCLE

Some historians have dubbed the process through which Africans produced captives and traded them so that they could get arms to deter slave raiders the "gun-slave cycle."[28] In a thoughtful analysis, John Thornton attacks gun-slave cycle theories by refuting the notion that before the eighteenth century European arms were a decisive factor in African warfare. Imported guns were unreliable, inaccurate, difficult to repair, cumbersome, and provided only one shot before having to be reloaded. "It is unlikely," he writes, "that any European technology or assistance increased the Africans' chance of waging successful war . . . or that it made attackers suffer fewer losses. Therefore, Europeans did not bring about some sort of military revolution that forced participation in the Atlantic trade as a price for survival."[29]

The problem with the arguments of both Thornton and supporters of gun-slave cycle theories is that they consider only the trade in guns. In Guinea-Bissau, coastal people used imported guns to a limited extent. Iron knives, spears, and swords, and iron-tipped arrows were the weapons of choice. But coastal people faced an obstacle: iron ore was not found in abundance in the region. Before the rise of the Atlantic slave trade, coastal people obtained some quantities of iron through interregional exchanges orchestrated by Biafada merchants, who traded with interior smiths. However, Biafada commercial networks collapsed under the weight of competition from Luso African networks that formed in the era of the Atlantic slave trade.[30]

Coastal people, then, found themselves dealing with new trading partners—Atlantic merchants, who brought goods not from the interior but from the ocean. Atlantic merchants demanded a different mix of trade items. Not interested in salt and mollusks (the products that coastal groups had previously traded with interior peoples), they wanted slaves, ivory, and beeswax. Thus coastal people harvested these things, and for them they demanded iron.[31] In sum, the need to obtain European weapons for defensive purposes may not have compelled Africans to conduct slave raids, but the need to obtain iron from which to forge practical defensive or offensive weapons—as well as cutting edges for digging tools—did compel *coastal* Africans in Guinea-Bissau to produce and market captives.[32]

Written sources make clear that iron was in high demand in Guinea-Bissau's coastal zones.[33] Having visited the coast in the 1560s and 1570s, Almada said that "white adventurers" conducted trade in cotton, cloths, cloth strips, iron, and wine.[34] Early in the next century, Sebastian Fernandes Cacão wrote that "French, Flemish and Dutch ships are to be found laden with iron and other trade-goods, which they exchange in order to leave with heavy cargoes."[35] Similarly, Francisco de Moura noted in 1622 that in Guinea iron and other defensive merchandise were important in the trade that the French had on the coast.[36] Francisco de Lemos Coelho also carried iron to the Guinea-Bissau area when he was trading for slaves.[37] Further, shipping records from the late seventeenth century indicate that iron made up the bulk of imports into the Guinea-Bissau region.[38] Imports continued to have much the same composition in the eighteenth century, though rum and gunpowder at times filled most of ships' hulls.[39]

Throughout the era of the Atlantic slave trade, iron was in such demand that slave prices were frequently quoted in iron bars. This practice grew from a Mande practice. Mande smiths forged bars that were 9 nine inches long, with one end 2 fingers and the other 3 fingers thick. Easy to transport and convenient for use in a variety of transactions, Mande bars served as a standard in exchange. Embracing this standard, Europeans typically shipped iron in flat narrow bars weighing between 26 and 28 pounds a piece. The bars were between 13.5 and 18 feet long. Smiths on the Upper Guinea Coast cut these into "country bars," which were between 8 and 12 inches long, about the Mande standard.[40] Thus, Jean Barbot said that on Bissau, "the price for one slave is 30 bars of iron." And he noted that on the Bijagos Islands a "slave can be had for 8–10 bars of iron."[41]

That iron was valued by coastal people is also apparent from its use in religious displays. On the island of Bissau, for example, the king's wooden representation of a god was "sweated on an iron object shaped like a trivet." Propped against it was "a short, iron shafted spear, whose head, made of the same metal, resembles a scraper."[42] Further, the inhabitants of the Bijagos Islands affixed "a piece of wood, armed with two iron horns" on the sterns of their boats, "the tutelary deity to protect them from the fury of the winds."[43]

All of this is not to imply that iron was the only import valued by coastal people. They also desired other items—cloth, tobacco, beads, guns, gunpowder, wine, and rum. These things could increase the prestige of certain individuals or could make life more comfortable for many. Thus, wherever power congealed—in institutions controlled by states, chieftaincies, or independent villages—it was often turned toward producing whatever Atlantic merchants demanded. When merchants demanded slaves, small-scale and politically decentralized communities found ways to produce them.

THE RIO CASAMANCE AND RIO CACHEU: THE PRODUCTION OF SLAVES BY DECENTRALIZED SOCIETIES

Many of these communities were located on the Rio Casamance and Rio Cacheu to the south of Casa Mansa. Here, Banyun, living under a fractured political system composed of numerous chieftaincies, joined in the slave trade by directing armed units toward seizing of captives. They attacked Cassanga, Brame, and even other Banyun communities around the Rio Cacheu, and offered many slaves and other provisions to European merchants.[44]

Fighting among decentralized groups in the Rio Cacheu was a major contributor to the volume of slave exports from the region. In 1616, the Portuguese captain of the fort at Cacheu wrote that of some twenty or thirty neighboring communities, "10 or 20 are very powerful, with forces of slaves armed with spears which they release" against others. In 1617, Padre Sebastião Gomes described how the aggressiveness of the local populations and the frequency of skirmishes between them had forced merchants in the area between the Rio Cacheu and Rio Grande to constantly change business locations. Noting the ubiquity of raids in the region, Almada wrote, "From the Rio de São Domingos more slaves are obtained than from any other river in Guinea, because this river has around it the following nations: the Buramos, whose kingdom is very large, the Banhuns, the Cassangas, the Falupos, the Jabundos and the Arriatas."[45]

By the mid-seventeenth century, Floup communities were also drawn into the trade in captives. Initially, members of this decentralized group had shunned all contact with outsiders. Keeping merchants from entering their territory was perhaps a defensive strategy aimed at preventing the spread of knowledge about Floup areas. Lacking such knowledge, raiders might have been loath to enter the territory. Hence, in 1506, Fernandes noted that Floup were not welcoming. Similarly, based on observations he had made in the 1560s and 1570s, Almada said that the Floup "do not trade in slaves because they do not trade with us." However, many Floup were, by this time, becoming victims of organized raids staged by Cassanga and Mandinka, who went to Floup territories "capturing many of them along the beaches and streams, as they fished and ate oysters together." It was probably these raids that pressed Floup to establish more regularized trade relations with outsiders. Floup needed iron from which to forge strong defensive weapons. By 1594, when he was preparing his narrative, Almada was able to state that "now they know better, and defend themselves, and kill or capture their enemies." Nonetheless, Floup sold few captives directly to Atlantic merchants. Still preferring to keep strangers at bay, they ransomed captives back to the communities from which they had come or sold them to Brame, who acted as commercial intermediaries.[46]

In the years that followed, Floup communities struggled to find ways to improve their defenses against threats from slave-raiding Mandinka and Cassanga. The problem was especially acute in the decades after Almada composed his account. Rivals in the region were acquiring increasing quantities of iron. With it, they reinforced the cutting edges of weapons and stepped up attacks. Floup, then, also had to acquire more iron, and to do so they had to market increasing numbers of captives.[47] Thus, in 1669 Coelho could report captives being sold directly to Atlantic merchants in Floup territories.[48] By the late eighteenth century, Floup were traveling to the port town of Cacheu with slaves for sale.[49] It is likely that many of those sold into slavery were taken from neighboring Banyun communities. With slave traders circulating in the area and Floup advancing on their villages, many Banyun were captured and sold for export or held in domestic servitude.[50] In contrast, many Floup found ways to cope with the threats of the large slave-raiding states on whose frontiers they were situated. By acquiring European iron from which to forge weapons, they held off Mandinka and Cassanga armies. As Francis Moore remarked in the early eighteenth century, though decentralized, Floup managed to "unite so firmly that all the forces of the Mundingoes (though they are numerous) cannot get the better of them."[51]

However, participation in the slave trade came with a cost. In his study of Esulalu, a Floup subgroup, Robert Baum argues that profits from the slave trade "heightened differences in wealth between families." Those successful in the trade garnered more livestock, cloth, and most important, iron than their neighbors.[52] Wealthy slavers used their economic strength and social prestige to seize local religious and political institutions. They took control of local shrines, forcing ordinary people to call on them to perform even basic family rituals.[53] As slave raiding increased in the nineteenth century, successful warriors became even more powerful by retaining a portion of their captives and putting them to work in fields.[54] For Floup, then, the slave trade was the catalyst for a radical reorganization of local power structures. No unified Floup state emerged. However, new elites, able to refashion local institutions to defend communities and harvest captives, used the wealth that they derived from trade to elevate themselves over others.

To the south, the decentralized Brame also produced captives "in large numbers." Though Almada thought that Brame were "not very war-like," he did emphasize that some among them wielded knives, spears, and arrows. Presumably, they used these for defensive purposes or for raiding for slaves who were traded to ship captains and agents.[55] Brame may have taken some captives during "wars" with Balanta.[56] They produced others from among their own ranks. Indeed, by transforming legal institutions, Brame produced large numbers of exports. Like the Cassanga king, Brame villagers employed the "red water ordeal," which involved the drinking of a red poison to assess the guilt or innocence of those accused of crimes. The families of those found guilty were often sold to slave traders.[57]

Similar sorts of judicial enslavement appear to have been common in both hierarchical and decentralized societies across the Upper Guinea Coast. In their 1686 antislavery manifesto, the Spanish Capuchins, who belonged to a branch of the Franciscan Order that had established itself in Bissau, gave a detailed description of the way in which the legal institutions across the region had been refashioned for the production of slave exports. The first way that Africans produced slaves, the Capuchins said, was by "seizing them for some offense that they call 'chai.'" This word was Crioulo and was probably derived from the Portuguese word *achaque,* which means "ailment" or "vice," though it is sometimes best translated "trap."[58] "And they say *tem chai* [he has an ailment or vice] to make someone a slave, and this is the same as saying, speaking vulgarly, that they accuse him of some offense." An elaborate ceremony followed such an accusation. During the ceremony, guilt was assessed. "With this, the poor person starts to clamor, saying, 'Senhor, don't kill me, sell me for rum.' If there is occasion, they sell him, if not, they kill him."[59] The Capuchins mentioned that this form of enslavement was practiced in several coastal zones and on the Bijagos Islands. Other sources also mention judicial proceedings generating slaves on the Bijagos. In 1856 a Portuguese representative attempting to bring the slave trade to an end was stunned when islanders on Orango told him that if those convicted of being witches could not be sold, they would be killed "because you could not live with witches."[60]

Obviously, the machinery of a powerful state was not necessary to accuse someone of being a witch or having *chai*. Common people, working through councils of elders or other relatively egalitarian locally based institutions, could condemn those deemed socially deviant or criminal to captivity and sale. In the process of ridding their communities of what they perceived as troublesome elements, they received valuable imports, especially iron.

THE BIJAGOS ISLANDS: REFASHIONING DECENTRALIZED INSTITUTIONS TO PRODUCE SLAVES

Slave ships also went in large numbers to the Bijagos Islands at the mouth of the Rio Geba. Indeed, from the sixteenth to the nineteenth centuries Bijago were among the most important slave producers and traders in the area of Guinea-Bissau. Almada's late-sixteenth-century observations indicate that each of the Bijagos Islands was independent of the next, perhaps ruled over by a powerful elder or group of elders. "There is no king among them," Almada wrote. "They only have nobles whom they obey, the lords of the inhabited islands. In any one island there may be two or three nobles who live there and form settlements along the seashore or nearby."[61] At times, some successful warriors held positions of prestige and power. However, even the greatest among them ate with the people. "The *tagarra* or gourd, from which they eat is common to all," Álvares explained. "The man of standing, the slave, the child, all dip their hand in."[62]

Over the centuries, no man of standing forged a powerful monarchy. No entrenched ruling class emerged on the islands. At the end of the eighteenth century, Philip Beaver said that there was little difference between Bijago rulers and people. "Their government, like all others on the coast that I know any thing about, is monarchical, but the power of the sovereign seems trifling; he cannot be known from his subjects by any external mark of dress, or respect shown him; and he eats out of the same calabash with any of his people."[63] Thus there was no broad-based Bijago state. Power congealed in institutions controlled at the village or perhaps the island level.[64] And Bijago directed this power toward slave raiding.

Indeed, in the era of the Atlantic slave trade, Bijago redirected boat building and navigating skills, which they had developed for fishing and trading, toward producing captives. From huge boats manned by dozens of rowers, Bijago staged sudden and frequent hit-and-run raids on coastal and riverside villages on and between the Rio Cacheu and Rio Grande. Bijago, Barreira wrote in 1606, "make a living out of continual attacks on neighboring kingdoms, and as they are great sailors, very courageous and skilled in arms, they have ravaged and destroyed all that coast, because it is cut up by many rivers and creeks, where they enter at night." Reaching the mainland before dawn, they set fire to grass houses. "And so that those inside do not get away, they place themselves one at each door, with several poisoned spears in the left hand, and a single one in the right, and if the person that comes out does not come out with his arms crossed and throw himself at their feet, he is immediately run through, even if he offers no resistance." Bijago warriors took captives to their islands, "where they always find Portuguese ships awaiting their return to buy slaves, and this trade is one of the main trades of these parts."[65]

Such raids were so effective that by the seventeenth century, Bijago had transformed their islands into major slave-trading centers frequented by Portuguese, Dutch, French, English, and Spanish merchants.[66] On many of the islands, slave-trading ports were created to meet a growing international demand. In a harbor between the islands of Ponta and Ago, Coelho once bought fifty-four captives with "iron, lengths of red and blue cloth and some yellow . . . spirits, wine (to give away, since one cannot go there without taking some), knives, small beads (also to give away, but in part to buy food), under-garments and a number of good cloths to give one's hosts." At a port on Una, Coelho bought sixty-nine slaves. He said that the harbor on Camona Island "is the most pleasant . . . in all these islands. Moreover, the people there are very well behaved, and they sell very good blacks." Slaves could also be purchased at a harbor on Nhoco, where Coelho once sent a crew that "brought back many good cheap blacks." Finally, Coelho frequently visited Xoga Island, which was "small, but very pleasant and with a fine port." There, the "blacks are extremely good, both the natives and those which are bought, the majority being captured during wars."[67]

With ports on so many islands, a large portion of the Bijago population had easy access to European imports. According to Coelho, individuals sold slaves on their own accounts, remitting half of their profits to "the owner of the port." "Because the Bijagos have no king," Coelho continued, "each man wishes to be king in his village, and they greatly desire the ship to go to the harbour of their own village, because each black sold to a ship earns the host a gift from the seller as a tribute."[68] There can be little doubt that port owners were wealthy and respected individuals. However, others profited from the slave trade as well. Álvares noted that the booty from Bijago slaving voyages was divided relatively evenly, the captain of the boat receiving one part, the "war-captain" another, and the warriors the final third.[69] Further, Almada was struck by how goods—"red cloth, copper shaped in cauldrons, large brass basins like wash basins and barbers' basins, large pearls, cows, yearling calves, and iron"—"circulated" among islanders.[70] Access to such goods motivated a large cross section of Bijago men to participate in the slave trade.

Clearly, then, state elites were not the only Africans who benefited from the slave trade.[71] Further, it is evident that participation in the slave trade did not lead inexorably toward political centralization. Decentralized societies, villages, and households could (and did) muster the capital resources required to stage raids, to transport captives over long distances, and to market them. Decentralized Bijago were even able to mount incredibly large scale and so-phisticated attacks on powerful states that had ties to Atlantic merchants and missionaries. In a remarkable letter to the king of Portugal, King Emchabole of the Biafada state of Biguba wrote on April 24, 1607, that "because their fleets are today so powerful, the Bijagos assaulted the port [of Biguba] at dawn with thirty of their boats, and burned [houses] and killed or captured as many persons as were in the port, whites as well as blacks." Further, in a separate letter, King Bamala of the Biafada state of Guinala complained that the Bijago had "laid waste [the lands of] myself and my seven kings." And King Mangali of Bisege claimed that Bijago "have put me in such great distress that I have left my home and fled into the forest here I go about in fear lest they carry off myself and my sons."[72]

Slave raiding remained a staple of the Bijago economy through the eigh-teenth and into the nineteenth century.[73] Beaver wrote of the discipline with which heavily armed Bijago warriors carried out well-planned attacks using both European and African weapons with great mastery. "Every Bijuga," he wrote, "is a warrior; his amusement the chace, his delight war." Each typi-cally carried a long buccaneer gun in one hand and a round convex shield covered with buffalo's hide in the other. A "solingen sword, about four feet long, and as sharp as a razor" was often slung over a warrior's shoulder, and a spear, held behind the shield, completed the ensemble. "When they attack," Beaver observed, "they first discharge their guns, kneeling and supporting the left elbow on the left knee, they then throw it down, and advancing to a proper distance, covering themselves with their shield, they launch their assagaye, and then have recourse to their sword. They approach squatting, with their shield nearly covering their whole body, its convex form is admirably adapted to turn off the enemy's shot, indeed a musket ball will not penetrate it."[74]

Like they had 200 years earlier, Bijago used their mastery of the sea to harvest captives even as the Atlantic slave trade slowly ground to a halt.

THE RIO GRANDE: WEAK STATES AND SLAVE PRODUCTION

If the Biafada were among the principle victims of Bijago raids, they were also some of the most important slave dealers in the sixteenth and seventeenth centuries. Two ports, Guinala and Biguba, both on the Rio Grande, were extremely important centers for slave exports. By the beginning of the sixteenth century, ships visiting these ports were buying "six or seven slaves for a horse."[75] In 1625, from the island of Santiago, Donelha wrote that "our ancient port" of Guinala is "the best in all Guinea and the best for the slave trade." He continued, "Large ships can go up [the river] as far as the port of Guinala and the port of Biguba. Trade in these ports used to be the best of this island. I once found myself in the port of Guinala with eight ships from this island, and more than ten belonging to *tangomaos,* and two ships registered for the Indies."[76] Though Rio Geba trade would eclipse that of the Rio Grande in the following century, Biafada nonetheless continued to sell slaves to Europeans. Recalling a meeting with a Biafada chief in 1792, Beaver, an opponent of the slave trade, said that "it was very hard that we would not buy his slaves."[77]

By the time of European contact with the coast there were about ten small Biafada states along the Rio Grande, the Rio Corubal, and upper Rio Geba. The precise nature of political power in them is unclear. Some of the states had become clients of Kaabu. "Over the Beafaras," Almada wrote, "is a Farim, who is like an emperor among them and whom all the kings of the Beafares obey. His name is Farim Cabo [Kaabu], and he is also obeyed by the Mandingas of the South bank of the Gambia River." Other Biafada states, notably Degola, which was on the upper Rio Geba and Rio Corubal, were actually incorporated into Kaabu.

Within Biafada states on the Rio Grande, kings appear to have relied on regional leaders to administer smaller territories. Describing a region on the Rio Grande, Almada wrote, "These territories belong to nobles, who have as many possessions as the king himself. . . . Their status resembles that of a duke. These three nobles—[the rulers] of Balole, Mompara, and Bixiloli—are, as I say, rulers of dukedoms or earldoms." Continuing, Almada noted, "The land of the Beafares is very large, and since it is so large it has many kings, some in the hinterland, others along the river."[78] Also noting the division of Biafada lands into subterritories, Sebastian Fernandes Cacão wrote that the "King of Biguba . . . has power over four kingdoms," the "King of Guinala has seven crowned kings under his dominion," and the "King of Bisege has five kingdoms under his dominion."[79]

In Guinala, which possessed one of the most important regional ports, political power was divided between two competing "hereditary groups of people, the nobles and the plebeians. At times the nobles inherit the power and take over; at other times the plebeians, [such as] blacksmiths and shoemakers, inherit the power." To ensure that no one person became too powerful, people of Guinala elected only "very old men" as their kings. If they lived too long, they were suffocated. "As they are old and feeble," Almada continued, "it takes little time to finish them off." Further, to guarantee that no one in a king's circle sought power after a king's death, many of the king's servants and wives were killed and buried with him.[80] In his 1625 account, Donelha gave a similar description of the limitations placed on a Guinelan king's power. "In the kingdom of Guinala," he wrote, "neither a son nor a relative inherits the kingdom, nor do they proceed by election." Upon the death of a king, "the great men and those in the government" went to a road and took the oldest man who happened to pass by the arm and led him to the royal residence. Donelha claimed that they whipped him severely and then placed "as a crown a cap of red cloth" on his head. They explained "that they whipped him so that he should know what it felt like, in order that he should give justice with clemency. And having carried out other ceremonies . . . with loud cries they call him king." Such kings ruled only three years, at which time they were killed and another unfortunate man became ruler.[81]

Because a king's rule was so fleeting, political and economic power was spread throughout Guinala and was certainly not a royal monopoly. Hence, those below the king, those Almada called "lords" and "dukes," wielded considerable influence over small areas. Almada's "lords" and "dukes" probably controlled local political, military, religious, and economic institutions. And it is evident from contemporary description that they directed these institutions toward making slaves of fellow Biafada and neighboring non-Biafada people. The region of the Rio Grande, Fernão Guerreiro said, "is wholly inhabited by a nation of blacks called Beafares, who are subjects of many lords, and are very great thieves, since one group steals blacks from another in order to sell them to Portuguese vessels."[82]

The dispersed nature of power around the Rio Grande had another consequence. Those outside of the sphere of "legitimate" institutions found it relatively easy to maneuver within the region. Hence gangs of "bandits" circulated on the Rio Grande and its many tributaries, terrorizing isolated and weak communities by seizing captives for sale to merchants. "Large canoes travel along the river [Grande]," Almada wrote, "and in these go many thievish blacks, who in the language of the land are called *gampisas*. They are like bandits, for thieving is their full-time occupation. They steal slaves, which they carry off to sell to the ships, and if they cannot sell them, they kill them, so as not to be found out."[83] Álvares left a similar description. Discussing what he saw as "justifiable" methods of enslavement, he singled out kidnapping as strictly "unjust." Slaves "who have been stolen, sometimes in large numbers," he wrote, were being brought to "contractors" "by the Biafar and Banhu criminals who were responsible."[84] Some of these criminals may have been former captives or "maroons" who had escaped from merchants and owners and fled to the Ilha dos Escravos (Island of Slaves) on the south side of the Rio Grande near the coast. "So many of them [escapees] have come together in this place," Almada bemoaned, "that they have formed a settlement and live there as rebels or outlaws."[85] The threat of slave raids from Biafada "bandits" and from Bijago must have weighed heavily over the region, since Biafada generally armed themselves with swords, knives, and bows and arrows. Iron was important in forging all of these, even the arrows, which had iron tips.[86]

These were not the only ways that slaves were produced. Almada said that some households located near ports profited from the slave trade by "tricking" unsuspecting strangers and then selling them quickly to merchants. "These Beafares are so smart," he wrote, "that if a yokel arrives from the interior, they pretend that they want to give him shelter, and they receive him into their homes. After a few days have passed, they persuade him that they have friends on the ships, and that they would like to take him [there to introduce him] and have a party. But when they go to the ships, they sell him. In this way they trick many yokels."[87]

Biafada obtained slaves in other ways as well. Some were purchased from neighboring people. Almada said, "The Beafares of Bisegue are in the hinterland neighbors of the Nalus, and from this land many slaves come to Bisegue." Other slaves were obtained from Mandinka, Bijago, and Brame. Further, like many groups on the Upper Guinea Coast, Biafada refashioned local-level judicial institutions—perhaps controlled by "lords"—for the production of tradable captives. When the eldest males of households were condemned by judicial decision "to lose their goods and liberty," "the whole family" was enslaved.[88] Witchcraft and sorcery were also punished with enslavement. "Throughout this nation," Coelho said, "they hate sorcerers so much that when they learn about one, the king immediately sells him and all his family on the maternal side . . . because they say that sorcerers are a caste, and inherit (their powers), and so none (of the family) is spared."[89]

Biafada territories were administered by hierarchical political structures, and were by all accounts integrated into a larger Mandinka sphere of influence. However, one could hardly say that "the captors" were strictly "monarchies who succeeded in profiting and expanding at the expense of their neighbors."[90] Nor could one say that the slave trade "was important" simply because "it strengthened the state and shaped its nature."[91] Indeed, the Atlantic slave trade was insidious because its effects penetrated deep into the social fabric of the Upper Guinea Coast—beyond the level of the state and to the level of the village and household. The trade opened up the possibility for people holding power at all levels of society—and on the margins of society—to direct that power toward seizing captives. Hence, in many areas, the slave trade pitted neighbor against neighbor, village against village, maroon against former master.

Clearly, many people chose not to participate in the slave trade. However, some did, and not just members of an elevated ruling class. At the village or chieftaincy level, the slave trade provided local elites, who held sway over judicial institutions, with a way to profit by convicting people to sale for a variety of crimes. At the household level, the trade gave knowledgeable insiders power over lost outsiders. On the edges of society, the trade gave outcasts, maroons, and the desperately poor and greedy "illegitimate" outlets through which they could enrich themselves or reproduce their communities through raiding and kidnapping.

THE "RENOWNED ISLAND OF BUSSIS": DEFENDING AGAINST RAIDERS BY SUBMITTING TO THE RULE OF A POWERFUL MONARCH

A striking contrast to the Rio Grande region, where state leaders were unable to consolidate power in institutions they controlled, is the Papel island of Bussis, which is situated just off the coast between the Rio Cacheu and the Rio Geba and is today called Pecixe. On Bussis a powerful monarch emerged over a small, politically centralized, and militarily powerful state. The history of the island illustrates that though Guinea-Bissau's coastal zone remained generally decentralized—a patchwork of political, social, and economic systems—powerful men did, at times, use the wealth that they derived from the trade of slaves to dominate local community institutions and to separate themselves from daily face-to-face interactions with their neighbors. In some places, farmers and fishermen submitted to the tyrannical rule of monarchs because monarchs offered protection against slave raiders.

A relatively brief passage left by Almada, who traded along the West African coast in the 1560s and 1570s, is the first written description of Bussis. At this time, neither the island nor its ruler was particularly remarkable. Almada said the king was "wicked" and in possession of some fine European clothing that he did not wear. He also noted that Atlantic merchants were not always welcome, several having been killed or having had their boats seized. George Brooks speculates that this hostility may have arisen when *lançados* pushed the merchants of Bussis out of their middleman position in trade on the Rio Boboque and Rio Mansoa. As for the general population, young girls wore only a strip of cloth until they were married, at which time they came to "dress like other women." Generally, people spent their time farming, building houses, harvesting palm wine, and trading relatively freely in cows, cloth, and iron.[92]

Writing about Bussis at the start of the seventeenth century, Álvares left a lengthy description of an incredibly powerful ruler, "the richest in all this part of Ethiopia." Among Bussis islanders, there was a clear social hierarchy. The poor wore goat skins, "and if they lack even these they make use of *cibe* leaves," while the king, "in order to dress well, cuts up silks and other expensive cloths." He dined on the finest foods brought from the Canaries, lived in an enormous house, and possessed a bed that was "a paradise." He was regularly presented with gifts of gold and silver by merchants. Captain Jorge Fernandes Granjo offered him his own prized "Christian slave-woman." While admiring furniture in Lisbon, M. P. Oliveira considered shipping the king "an exotic writing-desk from China." He settled instead on a beautiful coffin, which to Oliveira's dismay was lost in transit during a raid by Floup sea robbers.[93]

How did the king of Bussis elevate himself to a position of such grandeur? Situated near slave-raiding Bijago, the people of this tiny island had, in the period from the 1570s to the 1610s, adopted a strategy of militarization to survive during very violent times. In so doing, they subordinated themselves to one powerful warrior who was very skilled in the art of negotiating with foreign merchants. These merchants could provide iron for manufacturing weapons needed to combat neighboring slave raiders.[94]

Hence, sometime around the start of the seventeenth century, the king of Bussis began to welcome Atlantic merchants. "The Portuguese," Álvares said, "come ashore in full security and they are received with all the signs of friendship, since this king is fond of saying that, without his permission, only the snakes in the forest can do anyone ill in his land." When whites cut down bananas, farmers refused to take money from them for fear of offending the king's honored guests. Atlantic merchants, after all, had turned the king "into a *lascarim*," or a shameless soldier. More accurately, the wealth that Atlantic merchants offered in exchange for captives had helped the king transform Bussis into a militarized state, the institutions of which he restructured to protect his dependents from slave raiders.[95]

With iron obtained by trading slaves, the king could "put in the field nearly 2,000 men armed with shields, spears, swords and knives." With his military, the king was able to defend himself and his people "from the inhabitants of the Bijagos Islands, 3–4 leagues out to sea." The king's soldiers kept watch by day and by night, so closely "that a bird cannot appear out at sea or cross the land without it being generally known." Soldiers were placed in treetops with drums, or *bambalous,* which they used to warn of coming raiders. Strong connections to Atlantic merchants allowed the king to place two cannons in his port and another by his house, perhaps for prestige as much as protection. He also possessed a storehouse of "muskets, swords, and daggers." Such an armory could only be acquired by engaging regularly in the slave trade Atlantic ship captains. For battles with Bijago, he had a fleet of "fine war canoes." "In fact the Bijago dare not touch his island, because the king has promulgated a law to the effect that any of his subjects who yield ground in battle will be sold, and hence out of fear they fight with total determination."[96]

The king and his army may have protected the people from raiders, but this protection came at a cost. While the masses toiled in the fields, the king expropriated large portions of what they produced. No slave, bullocks, or castrated goats could be sold without the king's permission, and he claimed "any part he fancies" of every large fish caught at sea. Further, only the king could grant permission for a marriage to take place, keeping beautiful brides that were pledged to others for himself and adding them to his retinue of over 200 wives. Thirty or forty of these were kept for sacrifice in the event of the king's death. This was no egalitarian society. Greatly feared by his people, the king dominated judicial institutions, with no laws existing "other than the king's appetites." "In material power," Álvares emphasized, "this savage is far above all the other kings and lords of this Ethiopia. As everyone concedes, he alone is king, and behaves accordingly, requiring obedience appropriate to the royal dignity."[97]

The ruler of Bussis, then, had become a great warrior king. He elevated himself above his people by proving himself a skilled slaver and trade negotiator. With goods obtained from Atlantic merchants, he built a skilled army and enriched himself. For his followers, the price of survival was subordination. They submitted to the whims of their monarch so that they could be free from the fear of capture by Bijago raiders. Unlike most people in coastal Guinea-Bissau, Papel of Bussis did not live under decentralized institutions. Decisionmaking procedures did not involve face-to-face relations; the king had the authority to coerce, and with his powerful army backing him, he did.[98]

CONCLUSION

In Guinea-Bissau, people participated in the slave trade for two main reasons. First, they needed iron to fashion weapons for both offensive and defensive purposes. Iron ore was not found in abundance on the coast, so iron had to be imported. When Atlantic merchants offered iron in exchange for slaves, decentralized populations responded. They raided distant communities for and turned judicial institutions toward producing captives. As raids intensified, coastal populations increasingly found that they had to participate in the slave trade so that they could garner the materials necessary to defend themselves against attack. Evidence for the region of coastal Guinea-Bissau indicates that European-manufactured guns were not a major trade item. However, the best material from which to forge strong weapons—swords, knives, spearheads, and arrowheads—was in very high demand. Hence, in the Guinea-

Bissau area, European technology did not increase Africans' chances of waging successful campaigns against neighbors. Indeed, coastal peoples used their own technologies to transform iron bars into weapons. Nonetheless, trade with Europeans did bring a military revolution, one that compelled participation in the slave trade as a price for survival. Thus the "iron-slave cycle" fueled regional trade.

Second, Africans living in decentralized communities in the Guinea-Bissau area participated in the slave trade because the region lacked broad-based institutions through which regular and predictable relations with those living some distance away could be established. Irregularity and unpredictability fostered mistrust that in turn became the foundation upon which the slave trade from coastal Guinea-Bissau was built. In other words, the lack of a coastalwide institutional framework made many of those residing in the region strangers who posed potential threats or who could be captured and traded to merchants for valuable imports.

A focus on one of Africa's decentralized regions challenges us to rethink many of our assumptions about the slave trade. Evidence from Guinea-Bissau suggests that slave raiding was a chaotic process, occurring for very localized reasons, and that slave trading was not limited to a few centrally controlled locations. Further, it reveals that decentralized regions were not necessarily areas acted upon by states. The residents of such regions were historical actors. Some fell victim to the violence that surrounded them, but many managed to protect their communities. Few societies crumbled during this period. Individuals fell victim to slavers, but even decentralized societies on the slaving frontiers of powerful states found ways to survive and some even to thrive.

NOTES

1. André Donelha, *Descrição da Serra Leoa e dos rios de Guiné do Cabo Verde (1625)*, ed. Avelino Teixeira da Mota, trans. P.E.H. Hair, Centro de Estudos de Cartografia Antiga no. 19 (Lisbon: Junta de Investigações Científicas do Ultramar, 1977), 165–171.

2. Manuel Álvares, *Ethiopia Minor and a Geographical Account of the Province of Sierra Leone,* trans. P.E.H. Hair (Liverpool: University of Liverpool, Department of History, September 30, 1990), chap. 9.

3. J. D. Fage, "Slavery and the Slave Trade in the Context of West African History," *Journal of African History* 10, no. 2 (1969): 289–310; Martin A. Klein and Paul E. Lovejoy, "Slavery in West Africa," in *The Uncommon Market: Essays in the Economic History of the Atlantic Slave Trade,* eds. H. A. Gemery and J. S. Hogendorn (New York: Academic Press, 1979), 181–212; Richard L. Roberts, *Warriors, Merchants, and Slaves* (Stanford: Stanford University Press, 1987); Patrick Manning, *Slavery and African Life: Occidental, Oriental, and African Slave Trades* (Cambridge: Cambridge University Press, 1990); Martin A. Klein, "The Impact of the Atlantic Slave Trade on the Societies of Western Sudan," *Social Science History* 14, no. 2 (1990): 231–53.

4. Andrew Hubbell, "A View of the Slave Trade from the Margin: Souroudougou in the Late Nineteenth-Century Slave Trade of the Niger Bend," *Journal of African History* 42, no. 1 (2000): 25–27; Martin A. Klein, "The Slave Trade and Decentralized Societies," *Journal of African History* 42, no. 1 (2000): 49–65.

5. On "slaving frontiers," see Paul E. Lovejoy, *Transformations in Slavery: A History of Slavery in Africa* (Cambridge: Cambridge University Press, 1983), 80, 83–87.

6. Manning, *Slavery and African Life*, 39. See also, Joseph C. Miller, *Way of Death: Merchant Capitalism and the Angolan Slave Trade, 1730–1830* (Madison: University of Wisconsin Press, 1988), 149.

7. See Robert Martin Baum, *Shrines of the Slave Trade: Diola Religion and Society in Precolonial Senegambia* (New York: Oxford University Press, 1999), 65.

8. André Álvares de Almada, *Tratado breve dos rios de Guiné,* trans. P.E.H. Hair (Liverpool: University of Liverpool, Department of History, 1984), 66, 73. See also Francisco de Lemos Coelho, "Descrição da costa da Guiné desde o Cabo Verde athe Serra Lioa com todas as ilhas e rios que os Brancos Navegam," in *Duas descrições seiscentistas da Guiné,* ed. Damião Peres (Lisbon: Academia Portuguesa da História, 1953), 85; P.E.H. Hair and Avelino Teixeira da Mota, eds., *Jesuit Documents on the Guinea of Cape Verde and the Cape Verde Islands, 1585–1617* (Liverpool: University of Liverpool, Department of History, 1989), doc. 4; Álvares, *Ethiopia Minor,* chap. 3; and Baum, *Shrines,* 65.

9. Baum, *Shrines,* 66.

10. Almada, *Tratado breve* (Hair's ed.), chaps. 8–9; George E. Brooks, *Landlords and Strangers: Ecology, Society, and Trade in Western Africa, 1000–1630* (Boulder, Colo.: Westview Press, 1993), 233.

11. Álvares, *Ethiopia Minor,* chap. 3.

12. Donelha, *Descrição,* 167.

13. Walter Rodney, *A History of the Upper Guinea Coast, 1545 to 1800* (New York: Monthly Review Press, 1970), 109.

14. Quoted in Hair and Mota, *Jesuit Documents,* doc. 9. See also Almada, *Tratado breve* (Hair's ed.), 68.

15. Almada, *Tratado breve* (Hair's ed.), 70.

16. Donelha, *Descrição,* 169–171.

17. The chief was clearly set apart from the people, so much so that no one was allowed to watch him eat. He was secluded behind white cloths when dining, and his wives served him huge bowls of food. Almada, *Tratado breve* (Hair's ed.), 71.

18. See Hubbell, "A View"; Klein, "The Slave Trade"; and Roberts, *Warriors.*

19. Brooks, *Landlords,* 93.

20. For models, see Klein, "The Impact," 31–32; and Roberts, *Warriors,* 39.

21. Almada, *Tratado breve* (Hair's ed.), 62–67.

22. Álvares, *Ethiopia Minor,* chap. 3.

23. Ibid.

24. M. Bertrand-Bocandé, "Notes sur la Guinée Portugaise ou Sénégambie Méridionale," *Bulletin de la Société de Géographie* 3, nos. 11–12 (1849): 312–314, 317, 336.

25. Almada, *Tratado breve* (Hair's ed.), 67.

26. Avelino Teixeira da Mota, *Guiné portuguesa,* vol. 1 (Lisbon: Agência Geral do Ultramar, 1954), 205–208; Boubacar Barry, *Senegambia and the Atlantic Slave Trade* (Cambridge: Cambridge University Press, 1998), 43.

27. Almada, *Tratado breve* (Hair's ed.), 67, 90.

28. See Joseph E. Inikori, introduction to Joseph E. Inikori, ed., *Forced Migration: The Impact of the Export Slave Trade on African Societies* (London: Hutchison University Press, 1982), 41–51; Joseph E. Inikori, "The Import of Firearms into West Africa, 1750–1807: A Quantitative Analysis," *Journal of African History* 18, no. 3 (1977): 339–368; Basil Davidson, *Black Mother: The Years of the African Slave Trade* (Boston: Little, Brown, 1961), 242–246; W. A. Richards, "The Import of Firearms into West Africa in the Eighteenth Century," *Journal of African History* 21, no. 1 (1980): 43–59; and Lovejoy, *Transformations,* 66–68, 78–87, 103–107.

29. John K. Thornton, *Africa and Africans in the Making of the Atlantic World, 1400–1680* (Cambridge: Cambridge University Press, 1992), 98–116. Allen Isaacman argues that in the Mozambique area in the mid-seventeenth century, "guns . . . probably provided little technological superiority." But unlike Thornton, he does think that they "added to the general power advantage" that Portuguese settlers had in the area. Allen F. Isaacman, *Mozambique: The Africanization of a European Institution—The Zambesi Prazos, 1750–1902* (Madison: University of Wisconsin Press, 1972), 18.

30. Brooks, *Landlords,* 80–87; George E. Brooks, *Perspectives on Luso-African Commerce and Settlement in the Gambia and Guinea-Bissau Region, Sixteenth–Nineteen Centuries,* Boston University African Studies Center Working Papers no. 24 (Boston: Boston University Press, 1980).

31. Baum argues that in the Casamance region "iron and firearms" were especially important trade items. Baum, *Shrines,* 79.

32. On iron tools, see Philip D. Curtin, *Economic Change in Precolonial Africa: Senegambia in the Era of the Slave Trade* (Madison: University of Wisconsin Press, 1975), 311–312; and Peter Mark, *A Cultural, Economic, and Religious History of the Basse Casamance Since 1500* (Stuttgart: Franz Steiner Verlag Wiesbaden GMBH, 1985), 30. Iron was also used in the manufacture of very specialized weapons for hunting animals. Emphasizing the importance of iron imports elsewhere, Patrick Manning argues, "Iron imports . . . served to constrict iron mining in Africa, although the imported iron did help expand the blacksmith trade." Patrick Manning, "Contours of Slavery and Social Change in Africa," *American Historical Review* 88, no. 4 (October 1983): 852–853. See especially Almada, *Tratado breve* (Hair's ed.), chap. 9.

33. Peter Mark argues that iron was in particularly high demand in the Casamance. He writes, "While iron would have been available long before the fifteenth century, the arrival of the Europeans on the coast provided an important and abundant source of the metal." Mark, *A Cultural, Economic, and Religious History,* 29. See also Curtin, *Economic Change,* 311–312.

34. Almada, *Tratado breve* (Hair's ed.), 82.

35. Quoted in Hair and Mota, *Jesuit Documents,* doc. 9.

36. António Brásio, *Monumenta Missionaria Africana* ser. 2a, no. 4 (Lisbon: Agência Geral do Ultramar, 1958), 699–700.

37. Francisco de Lemos Coelho, *Description of the Coast of Guinea (1684),* trans. P.E.H. Hair (Liverpool: University of Liverpool, Department of History, 1985), chap. 7. For other descriptions of the iron trade in the same century, see Arquivo Histórico Ultramarino (AHU) (Lisbon, Portugal), Guiné, cx. 3, doc. 95.

38. AHU, Guiné, cx. 3, doc. 9. See also David Eltis's calculations of imports for various regions of Africa. He figures that, between 1662 and 1703, 27 percent of goods imported into the Upper Guinea Coast as a whole were metals. Along with personal decorator

items, metals were the largest single item. The Bight of Biafra was the only region that had higher metal imports. David Eltis, *The Rise of African Slavery in the Americas* (Cambridge: Cambridge University Press, 2000), 300. Also see Kenneth Gordon Davies, *Royal Africa Company* (London: Longmans, 1957), 234. Here it is reported that in the late seventeenth century, iron bars composed one-fourth to one-half of what was shipped to the Gambia.

39. Arquivo Nacional da Torre do Tombo (ANTT) (Lisbon, Portugal), "Registo de carregações, de entradas, de extractos, e de despesas dos navios," vol. 63 (1755–1758), doc. 83; ANTT, "Borradores de enfardamento: Enfardamento de artigos para Bissau," vol. 73 (1760–1768); AHU, Guiné, cx. 9, doc. 11; cx. 12, doc. 3-A; cx. 14, doc. 7-A. See also António Carreira, *Os portuguêses nos rios de Guiné (1500–1900)* (Lisbon: António Carreira, 1984), 71; José Conrado Carlos de Chelmicki, *Corografia Cabo-Verdiana*, vol. 1 (Lisbon: Typ. de L.C. da Cunha, 1841), 105, 120; vol. 2, 67; and Luiz Frederico de Barros, *Senegambia portugueza* (Lisbon: Mattos Mareira, 1878), 46.

40. Rodney, *A History*, 194; Curtin, *Economic Change*, 240–241.

41. Quoted in P.E.H. Hair, Adam Jones, and Robin Law, eds., *Barbot on Guinea: The Writing of Jean Barbot on West Africa, 1678–1712* (London: Hakluyt Society, 1992), 168.

42. Álvares, *Ethiopia Minor*, chap. 10.

43. Gaspard Mollien, *Travels in the Interior of Africa to the Sources of the Senegal and Gambia Performed by the Command of the French Government in the Year 1818*, ed. T. E. Bowdich (London: Frank Cass, 1967), 336.

44. Almada, *Tratado breve* (Hair's ed.), 82. See also Rodney, *A History*, 103.

45. Almada, *Tratado breve* (Hair's ed.), 82, 85–87.

46. See especially Olga F. Linares, "Deferring to the Slave Trade: The Jola of Casamance, Senegal, in Historical Perspective," *History in Africa* 14 (1987): 113–118. Almada is quoted in Linares on page 116.

47. Baum, *Shrines*, 108. See also Mark, *A Cultural, Economic, and Religious History*, 29.

48. Cited in Linares, "Deferring," 113–118.

49. Bernardino António Alberto de Andrade, "Benardino Álvares de Adrade, um 'Guineense' esquecido," *Boletim Cultural da Guiné Portugueza* 98 (1970): 190–195.

50. Linares, "Deferring," 121.

51. Francis Moore, *Travels into the Inland Parts of Africa* (London: Edward Cave, 1738). Robert Baum writes, "It might be belaboring the obvious to point out that there were no formalized state structures that regulated Esulalu [a Floup group] participation in the slave trade. Diola [Floup] concerns about the problems of centralized polities . . . shaped their responses to the increasingly important Atlantic trade system." Baum, *Shrines*, 126.

52. Baum, *Shrines*, 126; Mark, *A Cultural, Economic, and Religious History*, 27–29.

53. Baum, *Shrines*, 108–117, 126–129, 158–161; Linares, "Deferring," 118–124.

54. Bertrand-Bocandé, "Notes," 91. Also see Linares, "Deferring," 124.

55. Almada, *Tratado breve* (Hair's ed.), 79, 82.

56. Alonso de Sandoval, *Natvraleza, policia, sagrada i profana, costvmbres i ritos, disciplina i catechismo evangelico de todos etiopes* (Seville: Francisco de Lira, 1627), 39.

57. Almada, *Tratado breve* (Hair's ed.), 83; Quoted in Hair and Mota, *Jesuit Documents*, doc. 4.

58. See P.E.H. Hair's comments in Donelha, *Descrição,* 313–315 ff.

59. Avelino Teixeira da Mota, ed., *As viagens do Bispo D. Frei Vitoriano Portuense à Guiné e a cristianização dos reis de Bissau* (Lisbon: Junta de Investigações Científicas do Ultramar, 1974), 120–133.

60. AHU, Cabo Verde, SENMU/DG/RC/001/cx. 73, doc. 73, pasta 21.

61. Almada, *Tratado breve* (Hair's ed.), 96.

62. Álvares, *Ethiopia Minor,* chap. 9.

63. Philip Beaver, *Africa Memoranda* (London: Dawsons of Pall Mall, 1968), 338.

64. In 1606, Barreira spoke of independent "lords" of each island. Hair and Mota, *Jesuit Documents,* doc. 16.

65. Quoted in ibid. According to Coelho, Bijago raids continued unabated in the second half of the century. Coelho, "Descrição," 42. See also António Carreira, *As companhias pombalinas de navegação comércio e tráfico de escravos entre Africana e o nordeste Brasileiro* (Lisbon: Editorial Presença, 1982), 128; and Almada, *Tratado breve* (Hair's ed.), 92.

66. Hair, Jones, and Law, *Barbot on Guinea,* 168.

67. Coelho, *Description,* chap. 7.

68. Ibid.

69. Álvares, *Ethiopia Minor,* chap. 9.

70. Almada, *Tratado breve* (Hair's ed.), 99.

71. See especially Manning, "Contours," 852. Though emphasizing a link between the slave trade and the rise of a wealthy class in Africa, he argues that "only a small portion of imported goods properly qualified as luxuries [and] all segments of society, not just an elite, were linked to the slave trade."

72. Quoted in Hair and Mota, *Jesuit Documents,* doc. 24.

73. AHU, Guiné, cx. 11, docs. 57, 37.

74. Beaver, *African Memoranda,* 335–336. See also Mollien, *Travels,* 336.

75. Duarte Pacheco Pereira, "Esmeraldo de situ orbis" (1505), in *Os mais antigos roteiros da Guiné,* ed. Damião Peres (Lisbon: Academia Portuguesa da História, 1952), 96–97.

76. Donelha, *Descrição,* 59, 177.

77. Beaver, *African Memoranda,* 299.

78. Almada, *Tratado breve* (Hair's ed.), 103–108.

79. Cação, "Letters," doc. 24.

80. Almada, *Tratado breve* (Hair's ed.), 104.

81. Donelha, *Descrição,* 178–179.

82. Quoted in Hair and Mota, *Jesuit Documents,* doc. 4.

83. Almada, *Tratado breve* (Hair's ed.), 121. James Searing noted the prevalence of "lesser pillage" in the Senegambia region. James F. Searing, *West African Slavery and Atlantic Commerce: The Senegal River Valley, 1700–1860* (Cambridge: Cambridge University Press, 1993), 35. On kidnapping as a form of slave production, see Lovejoy, *Transformations,* 84–87.

84. Álvares, *Ethiopia Minor,* chap. 5.

85. Almada, *Tratado breve* (Hair's ed.), 117.

86. Ibid., 106.

87. Ibid., 121.

88. Ibid., 115–118.

89. Coelho, *Description,* chap. 8.
90. Manning, *Slavery and African Life,* 132.
91. Klein, "The Impact," 40–41.
92. Brooks, *Landlords,* 264; Almada, *Tratado breve* (Hair's ed.), chap. 9.
93. Álvares, *Ethiopia Minor,* chap. 8.
94. Ibid.
95. Ibid.
96. Ibid.
97. Ibid.
98. Coelho, *Description,* chap. 5.

Part II

THE DYNAMICS OF INTRACOMMUNITY INTERACTIONS

4

STRUGGLES OVER NEW POLITICAL AND ECONOMIC INSTITUTIONS IN BALANTA COMMUNITIES IN THE SEVENTEENTH AND EIGHTEENTH CENTURIES

Whereas the previous chapters used a wide-angle lens to explore regional patterns of change, this chapter tightens the focus to the local, that of the Balanta "compact village," or *tabanca*, where struggles ensued among individuals and groups of individuals attempting to cope with the broad economic and political transformations sparked by the rise of the Atlantic slave trade. At the end of the sixteenth and start of the seventeenth century, the exigencies of an expanding world system brought tremendous forces to bear on Balanta. Faced with the proliferation of violence associated with slave raids, Balanta living in dispersed *moranças,* or households, began concentrating into *tabancas* in secluded areas near coastal rivers, where they could better defend themselves.

Present-day Balanta oral narratives reveal a great deal about these processes. However, they tend to emphasize *tabanca* unity in the face of adversity. This is probably because Balanta consider *tabancas* to be their most historically important social, political, and economic units and because older tellers of historical narratives have long had an interest in emphasizing the centrality of the *tabanca* to young males whose collective labor they have needed for farming rice in lowland fields. Balanta narratives, then, give one version of events, one interpretation. They depict *tabancas* as cohesive entities whose members shared common interests. But like communities everywhere, *tabancas* were often fractured, divided along lines of kin, generation, and gender. It is these divisions that oral narratives de-emphasize. In other words, they do not explore the struggles that ensued among the individuals who formed *tabancas* in the era of the Atlantic slave trade. They do not describe *tabancas* as sites of conflict between old and young, men and women, wealthy and poor.[1] Yet these struggles were profoundly important, since it was through them that the nature of community reactions to the slave trade was determined.

Undifferentiated communities did not confront a dynamic Atlantic economic system. Neither did individuals. Individuals confronted other individuals—family members, neighbors, and strangers—coping with, protecting themselves from, and exploiting opportunities opened up by the Atlantic slave trade and the regional transformations that accompanied it. The outcome of struggles among individuals and groups of individuals often determined the pace and direction of change locally. Bits and pieces of data point to those struggles, so I draw on them in this chapter to offer a look at the interior past of Balanta communities. More specifically, this chapter examines how elderly men, or *b'alante b'ndang,* who before the seventeenth century headed dispersed and independent *moranças* and directed women and youths to grow yams, sought to shore up their power within communities and to protect dependents from raiders as *moranças* concentrated into *tabancas.*

B'alante b'ndang accomplished these things in a number of ways. First, they transformed the institution of marriage so that it would unite people within *tabancas* and link *tabancas* regionally. Second, they restructured age grades to provide a means of organizing young people for labor-intensive projects. Third, they created councils of elders to serve as local decision making bodies. Finally, *b'alante b'ndang* drew on these newly crafted institutions to meet Atlantic demands for a changing mix of trade goods. The item most demanded by Atlantic merchants was slaves. The item most demanded in Balanta communities was iron, which they forged into weapons for defense against external threats and attacks on distant strangers.

To obtain the captives necessary for purchasing iron, *b'alante b'ndang* needed strong young men to stage slave raids. However, convincing young men to remain in the *tabancas* of their birth to make war for their fathers presented challenges. An expanding Atlantic market offered employment opportunities outside natal communities, principally in coastal ports or interior trade entrepôts. Hence, *b'alante b'ndang* struggled to limit the ability of young men to establish contacts with "outsiders"—*lançado* and Luso African merchants—and to structure incentives for young men to submit to their authority. The institutions that ultimately emerged, then, reflected intracommunity tensions between old and young.

The institutions that Balanta fashioned in the era of the Atlantic slave trade also reflected tensions between women and men. To keep control of young men, *b'alante b'ndang* ended up losing some control over women. Certainly women's vulnerability increased in this period of extreme violence. The nature of coastal warfare meant that strong male adversaries were often too dangerous to capture. Women and children were therefore the targets of slave raids. Captors retained some women and sold many for iron. Consequently, the percentage of female slave exports from the coastal zone was considerably higher than from most other parts of Africa. However, the period also brought gains to some women, as opportunities for personal economic and social advancement increasingly presented themselves. Because *b'alante b'ndang* were concerned with keeping young men firmly under their control, women emerged in this period as the principal brokers between *tabancas* and outsiders. Many women were able to exploit opportunities made available through contacts with *lançados* and Luso Africans to increase not only their families' wealth but their personal wealth as well.

A look at gendered and generational struggles in Balanta communities challenges us, then, to reassess some common assumptions about the social history of precolonial Africa. Though many historians have suggested that male-dominated households exercised increasing control over women in the era of the Atlantic slave trade,[2] this was not the case in Balanta regions. Here, elderly men sought to limit the mobility of young men, who were desperately needed to defend communities and produce captives. Here, women's mobility and their ability to accumulate capital increased.

FASHIONING *TABANCAS*

As the violence connected with the Atlantic slave trade proliferated on the coast at the end of the sixteenth and start of the seventeenth century, many Balanta found living in dispersed *moranças* to be very dangerous. Hence *moranças* began to "concentrate" into defensive *tabancas,* many of which were surrounded by large stockades. As settlement patterns became tighter, Balanta altered interhousehold social relations and developed new institutions through which they would interact with one another and the broader world in the centuries that followed.

Like other people in Africa, Balanta formed compact and elaborately stockaded villages for a reason.[3] They needed to defend themselves against powerful enemies determined to annex their territories, to force them to pay tribute, or to enslave them. Hence, where we can document a "compact village settlement pattern," we might reasonably expect to find people fearful of attack. On the other hand, where we can document a "dispersed settlement pattern," we should expect to find people maintaining themselves or expanding territorially in the face of negligible or uncoordinated resistance.[4] Clearly, in the era of the Atlantic slave trade, the people of the Upper Guinea Coast needed to defend themselves against any number of very powerful opponents.[5]

For evidence of the formation of compact villages on the Upper Guinea Coast, we can turn to linguistic analyses. Discussing the activities of slave raiders down the coast from Guinea-Bissau, André Álvares de Almada wrote, "These Manes were great warriors. When attempting any place, as soon as they were in position, they dug themselves in, and made fortifications of their own type, which they called *atabancar.*"[6] *Atabanca,* Almada explained in another passage, is what Mane speakers called "entrenchments."[7] Other chroniclers used a similar word to describe fortifications. Of the region of Guinea-Bissau, Francisco de Lemos Coelho said that the settlement of Cacheu was "surrounded by a stockade formed of pointed stakes with sharp tips, fastened together with crossbars, and it has two gates which are closed at night. The fence is called the *tabanca.*"[8] As late as 1888, people in the Guinea-Bissau region were protecting their villages with such walls. That year an observer noted, "The most important populations are protected by strong *tabancas.* . . . The houses or huts are arranged in a circle. Around them is constructed a type of wall, with tall and thick trunks of trees." *Tabancas,* he continued, were considered "impregnable," so much so that locals "only attack open or undefended populations."[9]

The words *atabanca* and *tabanca* were Mane in origin.[10] In the era of the Atlantic slave trade, the word *tabanca* was incorporated into the Crioulo language increasingly spoken on the coast. There it took on a slightly different meaning than it had had previously. That is, *tabanca* came to mean "village," which is its meaning in Crioulo today. The association of the word *tabanca*—"entrenchment" or "wall"—with villages supports the conclusion that compact settlements served one purpose: defense.

Turning our attention more directly to Balanta, oral narratives describe the concentrating of dispersed *moranças.* For example, Adelino Bidenga Sanha stated:

> As for the *tabanca* of Quinhaque, the founder was Nthomba Dhata, and after him the others came because of the good agricultural conditions in the zone. Little by little the *tabanca* grew to the point where it is today. The people who came did not all come from the same blood. Some were simply friends who came to procure land. On the other hand, the *tabanca* grew rapidly because of the wars of the Fula. For this, Balanta liked to agglomerate so as to make groups for war or to counter attacks of Fula and Mandinka who at times attacked Balanta. After this, Balanta began to marry among themselves. This contributed to the enlargement of this and other *tabancas.*[11]

Similarly, Fona Benuma told me, "In times long past, Balanta mistreated their fellow Balanta. They did not have a chief who could reprimand anyone who abused others. Thus, no one had the courage to build a house far from the houses of others since it could be attacked in the night and the people killed."[12] And N'terra Siga emphasized that safety and strength could be found in numbers. "In times long past," he said, "there were abuses by some larger groups of other smaller groups. They could attack the small groups carrying away the people and all of their belongings."[13] It was advantageous, then, to belong to a large group, to concentrate populations for protection on isolated lowlands.

DANGEROUS STRANGERS AND TRUSTED IN-LAWS

As Balanta sought refuge from wars and raids by concentrating into *tabancas* on lowlands, new sorts of social relations were established among people in neighboring *moranças*. Put simply, as spatial distance between people decreases, so too does social distance. This is especially true in societies with no obvious class distinctions, no permanently elevated and esteemed rulers or lineages, no groups traditionally set apart from and above others. Where everyone is relatively equal, there are more opportunities for daily interaction. Since spatial distances separating people within any village setting can be very small, social distances can be small as well. Hence the people within a given village tend to feel close to everyone else within it. In village communities, then, mutual bonds, obligations, and trust are necessary qualities for neighbors.

Concomitantly, the spatial distances separating village from village can be very great. Thus the people within a given village tend to feel distant from those outside it. This social distance can be lessened through "crosscutting institutions"—ties that link people across village divides;[14] but in cases where villages form for defensive purposes, the feeling of closeness to village-mates and distance from outsiders is reinforced. That is, a distrust of all people outside the village is typical at times when outsiders pose serious threats to the health and safety of village-mates.[15]

The distrust of outsiders is a recurring theme in Balanta oral narratives. In these narratives, strangers are generally depicted as people who could be stripped of material goods, killed, or taken captive (or who might do these things to an unsuspecting traveler). For example, in "times long past," elder Bisi Binhaga said, "There were conflicts among Balanta. Balanta were so cruel that no one had the courage to travel alone to a location where he did not know anyone. If a Balanta were encountered [by strangers] alone on the path, he would have been killed." Such conflicts, he continued, "were the result of an abuse of power."[16] Isnaba Nambatcha related a similar story:

I have heard that Balanta killed one another in times long past. These conflicts were very severe. So severe that no one had the courage to walk alone
to another *tabanca,* since, if he were discovered, he would have been apprehended and could be killed. No one had the courage to remain in his or
her *morança* alone, far from other *moranças.* When someone wanted to
travel he was always accompanied to his destination. In that time, when a
cow was robbed, the owner could not go to another *tabanca* to retrieve it
even if he knew who the thief was. Thus, he had to procure the thief se-
cretly. Or he could capture another person of the thief's *morança.* If he
succeeded in capturing someone from the thief's *morança,* he would communicate this information to the family of the thief. The family would have
to bring back the stolen cow and something else to pay as a fine. The conflicts among Balanta ended when the Portuguese arrived in Guinea and
started to attempt to dominate them.[17]

That Africans on the Upper Guinea Coast often distrusted people outside
the village unit is also evidenced by contemporary written accounts. Indeed,
if Jesuit Balthasar Barreira's 1606 generalization was correct, coastal people,
and likely Balanta, greatly feared visiting the villages of strangers:

It . . . often happens that, when a black goes from his village to another,
which is very common as they communicate with each other very much,
if any individual of the village where he is going to has had any offense
from him or from a relative of his, or from anyone else from his village,
he lays hand on the visitor and carries him off to sell to the Portuguese,
whether the offense be great or small, true or false, in order to palliate his
(or his relative's) crime.[18]

Neighboring Balanta *tabancas* were not, however, always or even usually
at odds. Through the institution of marriage, *tabancas* formed powerful alliances with one another.[19] This is certainly the case today, and appears to have
been historically.[20] Indeed, Armando Moraes e Castro mentioned the practice
in a 1925 report about Balanta: "Among them there is a very curious custom.
If two families are enemies, they make peace by exchanging their children in
marriage."[21] Similar references can be found in oral narratives. Discussing
"past" Balanta conflicts, Estanislau Correia Landim emphasized that "wars
ended when Balanta married among themselves. Thus, without problems, the
tabanca in which a father's married daughter lived could be visited by people
of the *morança* or the *tabanca* in which the girl had been born." Later in the
interview he noted, "Before colonization, Balanta resolved conflicts through
the nephews and nieces of the *tabancas.* Thus, when someone had committed an offense [against another *tabanca*], his nephew [sister's son] informed
him. The offending party then killed a pig and cooked it, and the two *tabancas*
ate together. This was a sign of peace."[22]

Upon wedding, a Balanta woman left her father's household and took up residence with her husband. The system, then, was characterized by viri-locality (women living in the domiciles of their marriage partners). Under this arrangement, the institution of marriage increased the strength Balanta *tabancas* and *moranças* in several ways. First, the father of the bride received cattle in bridewealth, thus adding to the material wealth of his *morança*.[23] Second, the strength of a groom's *morança* was augmented by increasing its wealth in people. That is, marriage brought into his lineage a woman who could work and bear children. Third, and of particular importance in the era of the Atlantic slave trade, marriage served to cement bonds of trust between neighboring *tabancas*. Those that were tied together through marriage aided one another in conflicts with people from outside the immediate area. That is, they combined forces in warding off attacks from enemies.[24]

In addition, when disputes arose between *tabancas* that had exchanged women as brides, the zeal with which rivals attempted to address claims was diminished because of their familial ties to one another.[25] In other words, Balanta men did not typically stage violent attacks on the *tabancas* in which their daughters or sisters lived. Inversely, when a man had a wife from another *tabanca,* he had an interest in being friends with the residents of that community. This incentive was grounded in more than sentiment. If a woman's husband quarreled with her kin, she could make life very unpleasant for him by refusing to fetch water, prepare meals, and keep the household.[26]

RETAINING YOUNG MEN AND MAINTAINING *TABANCA* STABILITY

As *b'alante b'ndang* sought to ensure some level of regional peace by forging ties with neighbors through the exchange of daughters as marriage partners, they were also keen to find ways to defend and retain their dependents, for without a strong and reproducing labor force the communities that they controlled would cease to exist. Hence, *b'alante b'ndang* had to find ways to keep a hold on the labor of youths and women. Women were valued as mothers, keepers of households, and field laborers, but young men were particularly important to the maintenance and reproduction of *tabancas*. The patrilineal, virilocal system, which older men controlled, depended on the retention of young males. Paddy rice production, which Balanta intensively undertook in the late seventeenth and eighteenth centuries, centered on young male labor (see Chapter 5). Further, young male fighters composed the corps who defended communities against attack and raided distant groups for captives who could be traded for valuable imports. If young men could be retained, their success in agricultural and military pursuits would enrich communities, making them stronger vis-à-vis neighboring communities. Neighbors would then be more likely to attempt to establish ties by offering

daughters as marriage partners, further increasing community size and
strength. Retaining young men, then, was the key to *tabanca* success.

But military and agricultural work for *b'alante b'ndang* was not the only
option that young men had. Indeed, an expanding Atlantic economic system
opened up new opportunities for them—opportunities outside the village. They
could join with comrades to form bandit communities—*gampisas*—for whom
"thieving" and raiding for captives became a "full-time occupation."[27] Or they
could abandon their fathers to work for *lançados* or Luso Africans, taking up
employment as *grumetes.*

B'alante b'ndang, then, did all they could to retain young males. Three
strategies were particularly important: using social ridicule, relying on women
to conduct trade with outsiders, and creating a system of incentives. In the
years of Portuguese colonization (and perhaps before), social pressure in the
form of ridicule was one way elders controlled young men. Those who left
their *tabancas* to go to urban areas to seek employment were branded with
the nickname *pmusee bele* in Graça, or *limbi prato* in Crioulo. This means
"plate licker" and was particularly salient since, João Bafã claimed, Balanta
who left home were so poor that they did not have enough money for food,
and "thus they had to lick the plates of the Portuguese after the Portuguese
had finished eating."[28]

A second way to ensure that young men would remain in the *tabancas* of
their birth was by denying them contact with outsiders, particularly merchants
who needed laborers in area ports and therefore offered youths alternatives
to village life. When contact with outsiders was necessary, *b'alante b'ndang*
worked through women. Hence, as was the case in many of the defensive
communities of Brame, Floup, and Biafada, Balanta relied on women to carry
out exchanges with area merchants.[29] Women are today the most important
links between Balanta and outsiders,[30] and oral narratives speak of the
importance of women as traders. For example, Inguesse Nhasse told me that
"in the past" women "winnowed rice and sold it in Bissau." They also prepared and sold salt, sometimes for foreign merchants residing in Nhacra.[31]
Nineteenth-century observers described similar practices. In 1841, José
Chelmicki noted that Balanta "women dress in cloths that they obtain in trade
for salt, which they make in abundance." Apparently they coveted cloth from
manufacturers on the Cape Verde Islands and in Mandinka regions in the interior. They obtained it by venturing to Bissau and by traveling about the
countryside, for it was Balanta women "who go from one village to the next"
trading and gaining great "respect."[32]

Given the nature of Balanta "crosscutting institutions," women were in the
best position to establish contacts with merchants. Thus they sometimes married regional merchants, an extension of an existing system through which
women frequently married outside their *tabancas.* Their departure from

tabancas after marriage did not challenge the patrilineal and virilocal system over which *b'alante b'ndang* held sway. To the contrary, women provided lasting ties to merchants who could provide imports that might strengthen the position of *b'alante b'ndang* within *tabancas.*

However, some women were able to exploit new opportunities opened up in the era of the Atlantic slave trade, increasing their personal wealth and autonomy beyond what *b'alante b'ndang* desired. This was especially true of some Floup women. Floup communities relied on women to conduct most of their trade at ports in the Rio Cacheu region, particularly in the late eighteenth century. Women, "who were the ones who rowed their boats," were said to "move about buying goods from port after port to bring back to theirs and there sell them." Their men were good for little more than "defending the land from invaders of other barbarians who attack it."[33] Banyun women also carried on exchanges with those outside their communities: "As well as carrying normal duties in the upkeep of the family, such as spinning and so on, these women are keen traders and travel from fair to fair to gain a livelihood. [Hence] on the number of his wives depends the greater or lesser importance of the household of each man, whatever rank he holds." Balanta women may have used similar trade opportunities to make personal economic gains. As early as the seventeenth century, whatever wealth Balanta women accumulated was their own, not controlled by their husbands but held separately, so much so that nephews and other relatives inherited it.[34]

Though opportunities to leave communities and trade probably brought most women only modest economic advances, some became very powerful commercial brokers as the result of their contacts with Atlantic merchants. For example, Mãe Aurélia Correia married a Cape Verdean trader and rose to be one of the most influential people in Guinea-Bissau in the early nineteenth century.[35] Similarly, Balanta and other coastal women often married area merchants, some elevating their social position only slightly, but a few becoming very wealthy by inheriting their husbands' businesses, ships, storehouses, and slaves.[36] In the early 1840s, José Joaquim Lopes de Lima described the central role such women played in trade. Discussing white, black, and mulatto merchants who occupied the region's important towns, he said that, "because it is convenient to their interests, they accommodate themselves to the practices and the demands of the brutal people . . . with whom they conduct exchange. This internal trade," he continued, "is more often than not directed by a *Bella de Guiné* [Beauty of Guinea], who is associated with the merchant's bed and with his office. She administers his warehouses and manages his transactions in the interior with ability and with great advantages in that she has many relations with kinsfolk and a perfect knowledge of things of the country."[37]

A final way *b'alante b'ndang* ensured the retention of young males was by creating an age-grade system that gave them incentives to remain in the *tabancas* of their birth. Age grades divided a given village's males and females into two gendered groups. The male group was divided into two main bodies: elders, or *b'alante b'ndang,* and youths, or *blufos.* Each of these bodies was subdivided into various grades, the parameters of which were roughly determined by the age of the people within them. Before passing from one grade to the next, members had to undergo a specific rite or ordeal, the most important of which was circumcision, which marked the passage into the ranks of the *b'alante b'ndang.* Among Balanta, members of male age grades could be identified by ornamentation and clothing. For example, *b'alante b'ndang* were easily distinguished by their red caps. Members of the *n'haye* grade were distinguished by white mud, which they smeared on their bodies. Further, members of each age grade had specific rights and duties.

Within village settings, then, age grades were crucial collective institutions that fostered an esprit de corps. They served to unite males irrespective of descent or *morança* affiliation so that loyalties to age-mates overlaid with loyalties to kin. Though *b'alante b'ndang* held the prerogatives of power, all male youths regardless of *morança* affiliation could attain the status of *b'alante b'ndang.* Hence they had an incentive to support the system, to submit to the authority of older men, and to remain in the *tabancas* of their birth. In time, they too would be older men, *b'alante b'ndang.* They stood to inherit their fathers' lands and prerogatives of power.[38]

Another institution that Balanta fashioned in the era of the Atlantic slave trade was the *tabanca*-based council of elders, *ko* or *beho,* on which males earned the right to sit when they became *b'alante b'ndang.* As J. B. Labat noted in the early eighteenth century, within a Balanta canton, or district, power concentrated in the hands of a council composed of the elders. Looking to European models, he dubbed the Balanta system a "republic."[39] Speaking generally of coastal societies, nineteenth-century observer Francisco Geraldes left a similar description: "Each tribe has its elders who resolve the disputes of small and large importance. The youths, or those who have not attained the age of about forty years, do not have an active voice in such meetings. The elders are the only judges, with more experience in life and therefore more knowledge of how to resolve questions." In another passage, he wrote, "The Balanta held diverse and independent possessions, one from the other, each governed by its elders, to whose decisions they are subject."[40]

BALANTA RAIDING PRACTICES

In the era of the Atlantic slave trade, *b'alante b'ndang,* working through their councils, directed the youths who composed age grades to carry out two critical large-scale projects. First, as I explain in Chapter 5, *b'alante b'ndang* relied on both male and female age grades to organize young laborers into large pools that were necessary for paddy rice cultivation, which Balanta began to undertake intensively in the late seventeenth and eighteenth centuries. Second, male age grades became institutions through which *b'alante b'ndang* could rapidly mobilize young men from different *moranças* into large quasi-military units. Age grades, then, acted as the front line of defense against enemy invaders. Balanta also utilized male age grades as offensive units in raids on distant strangers. During such raids, age-grade members seized captives, who were sold to merchants.

Slave raiding probably grew out of the ancient Balanta practice of raiding for cattle.[41] Oral narratives and early written accounts indicate that before they were circumcised, Balanta males snatched cattle from distant communities to prove themselves brave warriors and to augment herd sizes. In a region plagued with violence, demonstrating prowess as a warrior was indeed important. Quemade N'dami explained, "There were those who did not steal. They had colleagues who had many cows and therefore sat as inferiors in relation. Balanta insulted them telling them that they were not men but were women. They slept [rather than raided] every night and were cowards."[42] Illustrating the importance of cattle raiding historically, some narratives of migration center on conflicts over stolen cattle.[43] The centrality of cattle theft is also evident in rituals carried out to this day. For example, when a Balanta woman gives birth to a male child, a cord is often placed in the doorway of the house, signifying that the child will have the courage to steal many cows.[44] Finally, Portuguese and French officials on the coast left many complaints about Balanta stealing cattle at the same time they were capturing people. "They are all great thieves," Manuel Álvares noted in the early seventeenth century, "and they tunnel their way into pounds to steal the cattle. They excel at making assaults . . . taking everything they can find and capturing as many persons as possible."[45]

It is evident that as Balanta were drawn into the Atlantic economy, they adapted cattle raiding skills to slave raiding. In oral narratives, Balanta refer to "raids" broadly as *b'ostemoré* and to raids aimed specifically at taking captives as *b'kindeu,* "the hunting of people." These narratives claim that the Balanta organized *b'ostemoré* to quickly overwhelm enemies and seize as many material objects and people as possible. Elder Chefe Lima explained, "*Ostemoré* is taking something or someone by force during the day or night. Here, you attack someone or some group and take everything that he has or they have."[46] And N'Sar N'Tchala spoke of "the hunting of people":

In times long past, there were . . . people who practiced *kindeu.* When they encountered a person, they could kill him or capture him and carry him back to the *tabanca*. For this reason, no one had the courage to walk alone, to stay alone in a house, or to go get his cows or women when raiders from another *tabanca* took them. A lone person could have been attacked and killed. During that time, the Balanta taught *kindeu* to the youth.[47]

Oral narratives are not the only places we can find evidence of the prevalence of *b'ostemoré* and *b'kindeu*. The practice is sometimes reinacted. Nhafde Sambe, a Balanta of the subgroup Patche, explained:

> In times long past, the Balanta were very cruel to other Balanta. Many went to the houses of the weakest Balanta and seized all of their goods and carried the people back to their own *moranças*. The *tabanca* of Filim [the largest tabanca of the Balanta of Patche] is the group which practiced what is called *moré* [the Balanta Patche pronunciation of *ostemoré*]. Thus, today, when the Balanta of Filim play *chôro* [play drums during a funeral] for an elder, at the beginning of their playing, they seize a person who is just passing by and is not of Filim. The person is seized and held in a room in a house in a *morança* where he is given all he wants to eat and drink for some time. They do this to remember the way things were in the past. They used to seize people and possessions and carry them to their *moranças*. . . . The subgroup of Filim continues to reenact this practice; however, they do not mistreat anyone.[48]

As I argued in the introduction to this book, the practice is also remembered through the name given to particularly vicious ants—the "ants of Filim"—found throughout Guinea-Bissau.

Archival sources also speak of the Balanta practice of *ostemoré*. For example, Álvares noted in 1615 that Balanta "excel in making assaults, and from their villages they direct these against other villages of their own people, in order to plunder them by taking everything they can find and capturing as many persons as possible."[49] He went on to compare them to the infamous Bijago, who regularly raided communities from the sea. Further, in July 1777, Portuguese officials in Bissau complained that the "savages" or "*gentios* who neighbor this fort and who are called Balanta continually visit the population stealing, burning houses, stealing people. . . . They continue to be in arms as much at day as at night."[50] Months later, in January 1778, Portuguese officials in Bissau wrote of innumerable "assaults and robberies by the neighboring *gentios* (principally those called Balantas who have for honor been thieves, and there is among them the greatest authority for he who steals the most)."[51] Even after the Portuguese waged a "war," Balanta continued to venture to Bissau to steal cattle and people.[52]

The fractured nature of the region's social and political landscape, coupled with the Americas' demand for slave laborers, led to a great deal of fighting among distant communities in the Guinea-Bissau area. Fona Benuma explained this when he emphasized that "Balanta mistreated their fellow Balanta" because they "did not have a chief who could reprimand anyone who abused others."[53] In other words, within Balanta territories and across coastal Guinea-Bissau, there were no broad, overarching institutions through which *distant* groups could regulate and order their interactions. On a local or area level, institutions such as marriages did cut across village divides. But on a broader, regional level, such institutions could not ensure peace or stability. Hence to obtain captives that could be traded for iron and luxury items, such as cloth, beads, rum, and coral, Balanta seized people not from neighboring *tabancas,* but, as the Capuchins emphasized, "from foreign lands." Noting that raids were directed at "distant" groups, Mam NamBatcha told me, "People went to distant *tabancas* to conduct *ostemoré.* They carried away cows and other goods. The people who had been attacked did not have the courage to retrieve their goods. Captives could also be taken."[54] Similarly, Geraldes wrote in 1887, "The Balanta arrive on rainy nights having walked 6 and 7 leagues to seize a cow or any stray savage of a different tribe that he can seize, then he goes immediately to sell [who he has seized] in a remote territory."[55]

But Balanta did not always have to go far to find targets to raid. Occupying lands next to some of the most important interregional trade routes (the Rio Geba, Rio Cacheu, and Rio Mansoa), Balanta staged frequent attacks on merchant vessels. During such assaults, Balanta seized passengers to sell back to the communities from which they had come, to "black neighbors," who took them to Bissau or Cacheu, or to Luso Africans and their agents. Balanta also claimed all of the wares that merchants had aboard their vessels—cloth, rum, guns, powder, iron, and beads. In the late seventeenth century, Capuchins noted that "the Balanta and the Falup cause notable damages and seize everyday the vessels that pass by . . . and this even though the vessels are well armed."[56] Further, as late as 1732, European sailors were loath to venture up the Rio Geba for fear of coming in contact with Balanta age-grade warriors. Reflecting European ignorance of the Geba's course, Jean Barbot naively wrote that the river was "generally believ'd by all travellers to be one of the six known branches which convey the Niger into the Atlantick ocean, and the most southerly of them." Because it "is so little frequented by Europeans, except some few Portuguese," he continued, "there can be no particular description of it given." Concluding, Barbot left this warning:

> The main reason why so little is known [of the Geba] to sea-faring people, is its being inhabited on both sides by wild, savage Blacks, little acquainted with trade, who have often insulted such as have been forced to put in there, either for want of provisions, or some such accident. Besides, the tide runs out extremely rapid, and the entrance is much incumber'd with sands and

shoals; and there is reason to believe that some ships have perish'd there, and others been assaulted by the natives, who wear long collars of old ropes about their necks, which it is likely they have had from such vessels as have been cast away, or they have plunder'd.[57]

Based upon his geographic description, the "savage Blacks" about whom Barbot wrote were without doubt Balanta.

Staging attacks on one of the region's principal trade corridors, Balanta greatly affected the flow of commerce. To ward off attacks, merchants had to ply coastal waters in well-armed and well-manned vessels. Further, to avoid the danger of being trapped on a sandbar or a muddy riverbank, where defense against a band of determined Balanta warriors would be very difficult, merchants had to time their voyages so as to make sure that they would clear narrow straits before tides fell. Obviously, then, this decentralized society, like many in the region, greatly impacted the operation of markets in the region.

Balanta conducted attacks in two ways. On some rivers, they circulated, as Bispo Vitoriano Portuense said, "in canoes of war" while waiting for unsuspecting merchant vessels to approach.[58] Balanta canoes were dugout sections of tree trunks manned by crews of age-grade paddlers bent on capturing booty and proving their valor. However, Balanta appear to have been generally hesitant to attack the sleek, fast, and well-armed merchant vessels as they plied brackish, tidal rivers. Most often, as Barbot pointed out, Balanta preyed on the unfortunate mariners who ran their boats aground as tides fell. Tide levels vary greatly on Guinea-Bissau's coastal rivers and can challenge even the most skilled sailors.

Upon finding a stranded boat, young Balanta warriors summoned *tabanca* age-grade members with a *bombolom*. This instrument, a hollowed section of tree trunk with a horizontal slit that is struck with two sticks, is used by Balanta today to transmit detailed information over long distances. In casual conversation, one elder told me that the *bombolom* is "the Balanta telephone." Álvares described these instruments in the early seventeenth century: "*Bambalous* are also used to signal what they want announced in a very public way within districts or among neighboring village, and these serve the same purpose as do sentinels and beacons, so that as soon as the sound of the *bombalous* is heard this is the signal for all to listen. . . . When a war breaks out, within an hour it is known over a district of 20 leagues. If there are settlements all the way the information is passed along more easily, even if the houses are a league apart, since each tells the next."[59] Similarly, Spanish Capuchins specifically mentioned that Balanta "play a certain instrument that they call in their language *bombolón*" to "announce the attack."[60]

Having assembled in what the Capuchins called "a great number," Balanta warriors struck their stranded victims quickly and with overwhelming force. "Upon approaching a boat," the Capuchins said, "they attack with fury, they kill, rob, capture and make off with everything." Such attacks happened with a great deal of regularity and struck fear in the hearts of merchants and missionaries alike.[61] Others also commented on the frequency of Balanta raids on river vessels. On March 24, 1694, Bispo Portuense feared that he would fall victim to the Balanta when his boat, guided by *grumetes,* ran aground on a sandbar, probably on the Canal do Impernal, "very close to the territory of those barbarians." Portuense and his crew surmised that the Balanta did not attack since they were conducting what sounded like a funeral service. They were relieved that the Balanta "did not stage an assault like they generally do when people are similarly stranded."[62]

Faced with an impediment to the flow of trade to their ports, the Portuguese tried to bring an end to Balanta raids. But they were outclassed militarily by skilled Balanta age-grade fighters. Portuguese adjutant Amaro Rodrigues and his crew certainly discovered this. In 1696, he and a group of fourteen soldiers from a Portuguese post on Bissau anchored their craft somewhere near a Balanta village close to where Bissau's Captain José Pinheiro had ordered the men to stage an attack. However, the Portuguese strategy was ill conceived. A sizable group of Balanta struck a blow against the crew before they had even left their boat. The Balanta killed Rodrigues and two Portuguese soldiers and took twelve people captive.[63]

Decades later, on June 2, 1777, Ignacio Bayao reported from Bissau that he was furious that Balanta had been adversely affecting the regional flow of trade goods carried by boats along Guinea-Bissau's rivers. It was "not possible," he wrote, "to navigate boats for those [Balanta] parts without some fear of the continuous robbing that they have done, making captive those who navigate in the aforementioned boats." Further, he said that Balanta were almost continuously staging well-organized cattle raids in Bissau. In response, Bayao sent infantrymen in two vessels "armed for war" into Balanta territories. After these men had anchored, disembarked, and ventured some distance inland, they "destroyed some men, burning nine villages," and then made a hasty retreat to back to the river. Finding their vessels rendered "disorderly," the infantrymen were quickly surrounded by armed Balanta. Bayao lamented that "twenty men from two infantry companies" were taken captive or killed.[64] Having sent out more patrols to wage "war" against the "savage Balanta," the Portuguese found that conditions on Guinea-Bissau's rivers did not improve.[65] Balanta continued their raids on merchant vessels. Indeed, such raids would tax Portuguese patience until well into the twentieth century.[66]

SELLING, RANSOMING, AND KILLING CAPTIVES

If Balanta staged raids on villages and merchant vessels, what did they do with those they seized? Like people in other parts of Africa, Balanta exercised several options with captives. They sold, ransomed, killed, and retained them, and they did these things for reasons inexorably linked to the logic of Balanta communities.

Balanta typically divided captives into two groups: whites and Africans. Whites were often killed, dismembered, and displayed as trophies by bold young men who returned to their villages with members of their age grades to celebrate a victory. Capuchin observers noted this behavior: "The Balanta only hold the blacks to sell them, but as for the whites that they seize, unfailingly, they kill them. Immediately, they cut them to pieces, and they put them as trophies on the points of spears, and they go about making a display of them through the villages as a show of their valor, and he who has murdered some white is greatly esteemed."[67] Barbot also left a description of Balanta killing white merchants. The inhabitants of the banks of the Rio Geba, he wrote, "are more wild and cruel to strangers than themselves; for they will scarce release a white man upon any conditions whatsoever, but will sooner or later murder, and perhaps devour them."[68] La Courbe told a similar story. Balanta, he warned, "are great thieves. They pillage whites and blacks indiscriminately whenever they encounter them either on land or at sea. They have large canoes and they will strip you of everything if you do not encounter them well armed. When they capture blacks, they sell them to others, with whites they just kill them."[69]

Descriptions of the ferocity with which Balanta warriors staged raids, killed whites, and made trophies of white corpses or parts of them indicate that raids became a site for the display of the qualities that came to personify the ideal Balanta male. Among these qualities was bravery in the face of a powerful opponent. Balanta traditions are replete with stories of "men of power" or "men of confidence"—those who distinguished themselves from others in egalitarian communities by performing incredible feats. It is likely that killing whites—powerful, well-armed, and wealthy outsiders—was one way of becoming a "man of power."[70] Whites might also have been killed as a warning to slavers to stay clear of Balanta territories. That is, brutality was a defensive mechanism, a way of protecting communities in violent times. As early as the 1560s and 1570s this brutality had earned Balanta the reputation of being "savages" who "refuse to be slaves of ours."[71]

As La Courbe and the Spanish Capuchins indicated, Balanta often sold their black captives. However, it took some time for most Balanta to begin to carry out direct transactions with Atlantic merchants. Indeed, it was not until the late seventeenth and early eighteenth centuries that face-to-face dealings with white merchants became normalized. Again, this was perhaps because of a fear that outsiders posed a threat to *tabanca* communities. Thus, in the sixteenth century, an Atlantic merchant thought that Balanta would "only bring themselves to see our people reluctantly."[72] Similarly, during his journey to

Guinea in the 1660s, missionary André de Faro intended to visit Balanta to begin to convert them to Christianity. "But the Balanta," de Faro complained, "are so wicked that they will not allow any whites in their lands."[73]

Before the late seventeenth century, then, Balanta typically sold captives "to other black neighbors." Since such transactions took place in locations that Europeans did not dare visit, little has been recorded about them. Though records do not mention Balanta trading slaves to Biafada, Brame, and Papel, they may have marketed captives to merchants from these groups. Balanta, after all, had sometimes welcomed Biafada merchants into their lands and had visited Biafada, Papel, and Brame markets before the intensification of the Atlantic slave trade.[74] And if the Capuchins were correct, at least some Balanta continued to trade "with other pagans" in the seventeenth century.[75] Iron was generally available in regional markets as were cotton cloth, aguardente, tobacco, and other luxury items. Balanta also met and traded with *grumetes* employed by *lançados* or other Bissau-based merchants. Records detailing these transactions are scarce, but Francisco de la Mota did indicate that residents of Bissau—Christian Crioulos—"are the ones that usually enter [the surrounding territories] to buy the slaves."[76]

Balanta also ransomed captives back to the communities from which the people had come. In 1927, Alberto Gomes Pimentel mentioned this when he wrote that enslavement lasted until relatives paid for the freedom of kin. Cattle, he said, were often demanded as payment.[77] Oral narratives also give us a picture of what might have been a typical transaction. Speaking of Balanta raids, Cabi Na Tambá said that "prisoners were tied to the branch or trunk of a cabeceira tree for some time. Those of strength communicated to the families of the prisoners that they should pay a ransom for the prisoners if they were to be freed. Thus the families of each prisoner paid five or six cows to those of strength."[78]

There are several reasons Balanta captured people and then ransomed them for cattle. First, in raids it was often easier to grab people than cattle, especially if they were in their fields, far from their villages, and without weapons. Second, seizing people might have been a way of warning outsiders to stay away from Balanta communities—a way of demonstrating strength and discouraging slavers from attacking. Third, the raiding of distant communities for captives and trading of captives for cattle dovetailed with Balanta social and cultural norms. Balanta did not stage raids for reasons growing out of the logic of mercantile capitalism. They staged them because of the logic of their own society. For Balanta, cattle were a key indicator of success. As Mam Nambatcha stated, "Cattle were important for Balanta since the cow was the thing most highly valued by Balanta. . . . He who had no cows felt bad."[79] In a society that historically had no standardized currency, cattle were the primary store of wealth. Therefore, when iron supplies were adequate, when cattle stocks were low, or when Luso African merchants with connections to coastal slave exporters were unavailable, Balanta likely chose to ransom the victims of their raids. Fourth, Balanta captured people and then ransomed them because it might not have been possible for Luso African and *grumete* merchants to sell locally born Mandinka and Papel at ports for export. Mandinka and Papel were close partners with Luso Africans in the slave trade. Many had friends and kin in Bissau or Cacheu who would have objected forcefully to their enslavement.[80] Hence, ransoming was sometimes the only option.

Over time, ransoming served as a transition into the slave trade, a gateway into the growing Atlantic market. Thus, sometime in the late seventeenth century, when Balanta were in great need of increased quantities of iron to reinforce weapons for defense and agricultural implements for paddy rice farming (see Chapter 5), some Balanta began to meet more frequently with white and Luso African merchants to carry out transactions. In 1669, Coelho mentioned that some Balanta sold captives along the edges of Guinea-Bissau's rivers: "there is not in their [Balanta] ports more than foodstuffs, and some ivory, and *negros*."[81] Bernardino Andrade left a similar observation, saying that on the "rio called the Balanta" at the ports of the Brame and Balanta slaves could be found for sale.[82] In 1813, officials in Bissau said that slaves were being sold on the "*costa de Balanta,*" the lower Rio Mansoa.[83] Finally, by the late nineteenth century, observers noted, "Any merchant who goes to be a guest in the house of a Balanta is sacred among them. There is nothing that they won't do for the guest to make him comfortable."[84] Over the course of several hundred years, Balanta had moved from killing white and Luso African merchants, to ransoming captives or trading them to middlemen, to meeting regularly with whites and welcoming merchants into their territory. Faced with new sets of opportunities presented by an expanding world economic system, many Balanta communities chose to market captives.

Not all people, however, were worth the risk of capturing. Hence Balanta killed some number of those they encountered while staging raids. N'Sar N'Tchala noted this when he said, "In times long past, there were . . . people who practiced *kindeu*. When they encountered a person, they could kill him or capture him."[85] And Bisi Binhaga and José Gomes told me that, long ago, "If a Balanta was encountered [by strangers] alone on a path, he would have been killed."[86] Other groups in the area adopted a similar strategy. In late-nineteenth-century conflicts in the interior of Guinea-Bissau, Fula were reported to kill male captives who resisted and to take away women to hold as wives.[87] Further, the killing of potentially dangerous prisoners was common during Bijago raids.[88] Powerful opponents and resisters were killed to avoid injury or death while struggling to subdue and transport them. Balanta, after all, did not have armies of tremendous size like those of the interior state of Kaabu. They could not overwhelm opponents with mounted troops. They could not stage a siege or a campaign spanning months or even days.[89] Nor did they control secure trade routes to ports along which they could orchestrate the movement of large numbers of strong young male captives.[90] Like other coastal groups, they relied on the element of surprise, striking quickly, seizing a few people, and retreating. When the risks of a protracted battle were great, they withdrew cautiously.[91] Typically then, those killed by Balanta warriors were men, who were more difficult to subdue than women or children, since they were more likely to be armed and trained for combat and since they were more likely to pose a threat while in captivity.

If Balanta, Bijago, and other coastal groups killed some strong men rather than risk death or injury during raids, we might expect export records from the region to show higher numbers of females compared to males. At first glance, however, this is not the case. An examination of the records of twenty-one ships that left the ports of Bissau, Cacheu, or the Bijagos Islands between 1700 and 1840 and whose records show the proportions of males and females aboard, reveals that 64.9 percent were male (see Appendix 5).[92] This figure does not deviate considerably from the findings of studies of slave exports into the Atlantic for all of Africa. We might, then, be led to conclude that coastal raiders captured men with some frequency, selling them to Atlantic merchants in higher proportions than women.[93]

But if we take into account the fact that many of the slaves exported from Guinea-Bissau's ports had their origins in the interior, beyond Guinea-Bissau's coastal zone, our findings lead us to very different conclusions.[94] Slave censuses taken in Bissau, Cape Verde, and Cacheu in 1856 allow us to make distinctions between the gender ratios of slave populations produced and marketed by interior and coastal groups. Book 1 of the Bissau census (see Appendix 1) lists 1,107 slaves, 240 of whom had been born in captivity in a Portuguese enclave. Of the 867 who had been taken captive somewhere, 521, or 60 percent, were male—slightly lower than the percentage of males that made up the cargo aboard ships leaving the region. The census lists the "nationality" of each slave. Of those from Guinea-Bissau's coastal zone (Balanta, Banyun, Bijago, Brame, Papel, Manjaco, Floup, Cassanga, and Biafada), only 44 percent were male. That is to say, slaves who had a greater chance of having been seized by raiders from decentralized communities tended to be female. However, slaves from the interior, who had a great chance of having been taken captive by state-based armies, tended to be male. Indeed, 77 percent of Mandinka, 77 percent of Fula, 87 percent of Futa-Fula, 60 percent of Tilibonca,[95] and 62 percent of the Wasulunke[96] slaves were males. Strikingly, only 22 percent of Balanta, 33 percent of Brame, and 43 percent of Bijago held in captivity in Bissau were male. Since it fails to list the "nationality" of most of the slaves, the Cape Verde census (see Appendix 2) provides a much smaller sample size. Of the 130 slaves who are identified

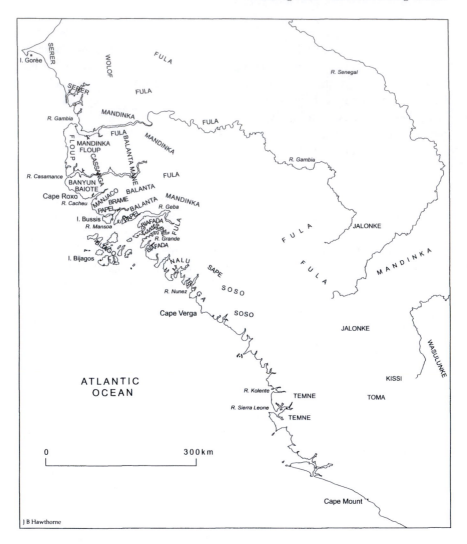

Map 4.1   Ethnic Groups of Senegambia and the Upper Guinea Coast

by ethnicity, 70 percent were male. Of those from Guinea-Bissau's coastal zone, only 57 percent were male. As in Bissau, a low percentage of Balanta held in captivity were male—only 47 percent. However, a high percentage of slaves whose origins were in the interior were male: 79 percent of Mandinka, 95 percent of Fula, 75 percent of Bambara, and 75 percent of Kissi. Finally, the Cacheu survey (see Appendix 3) lists 1,085 slaves, 467 of whom had been born in captivity or had no identifiable ethnic designation. Of the 618 who had been taken captive somewhere, only 249, or 40 percent, were male. This figure is well below that of Bissau in large part because Cacheu possessed a much higher proportion of slaves from Guinea Bissau's coastal zone. That is, 479 of the slaves in the Cacheu survey were from a coastal ethnic group, and of those 479 only 183, or 38 percent, were male. Figures from all three surveys have been combined in Appendix 4. They further illustrate that slaves from beyond Guinea-Bissau's *ria* coastline (many of whom had been taken captive during wars staged by interior states) were overwhelmingly male, while slaves from within the *ria* coastline (many of whom had been made captive by small, village-based raiding parties) were overwhelmingly female.

Further evidence that Balanta and other coastal groups in the Guinea-Bissau region sometimes avoided capturing and often killed men during raids can be found by examining the average ages of slaves in the Bissau slave census. The average age of 298 slaves whose origins were in the coastal zone (that is, all of the slaves identified as Balanta, Biafada, Bijago, Brame, Floup, Manjaco, and Papel) was twenty-seven years. The average age of 505 slaves whose origins were in the interior (that is, all of the slaves identified as Fula, Futa-Fula, Mandinka, Toma, Tilibonca, and Wasulunke) was thirty-five years. Unfortunately, the census does not indicate how long each slave had been held in captivity, so with this information alone we cannot state definitively that decentralized and coastal societies typically seized children during raids. Nonetheless, if we assume that the average time in captivity was the same both for slaves from coastal areas and for slaves from interior areas, then the data indicate that individuals with a high probability of having been enslaved by raiders from decentralized societies tended to be younger than individuals with a high probability of having been enslaved by the armies of state-based interior groups. That is, the census indicates that Balanta and other coastal groups tended to seize younger victims, who were less likely to resist than older, stronger people. Written and oral accounts of "slaves" being retained by Balanta and incorporated into their communities lend further weight to this argument.[97]

"INCORPORATING" CAPTIVES INTO COMMUNITIES

Balanta could exercise one other option with their captives: they could retain them and attempt to incorporate them into their *moranças*. In the Guinea-Bissau region, "incorporated captives" should not be seen as "slaves" in the Western or plantation sense of the word. Their primary function was not to produce commodities for export. It is likely that many were given menial or labor-intensive tasks within *moranças* and *tabancas,* living beside community members but having something of a lower status. In the late nineteenth and early twentieth centuries, "slaves" (*escravos* in Portuguese) of other decentralized groups in the area were said to live "with the families of their owners." Some observers were struck by the nature of the "master-slave" relationship: "We spoke with some female slaves of Nalu origin, who reported how they were captured and treated: well [like] people of the family!" Similarly the slaves of Floup were said to have been "purchased when they were young and became house slaves, treated as members of the family and quickly enjoying the same privileges, and able to marry free women, and only sold in cases of absolute necessity." This is not to imply that the conditions under which those incorporated into communities lived were pleasant. Other observers reported that within households *escravos* "were perfect animals of work, only lessening their hard condition through their owners. Only death, however, ended their social inferiority." In some communities, the children of *escravos* inherited the status of their parents. With the death of the "head of the household," *escravos* "constituted part of the inheritance" of his children. In other communities, however, slaves belonging to a man with few heirs could inherit possessions and religious shrines. The promise of inheritance probably kept some Floup slaves from fleeing or shirking responsibilities.[98]

Discussing Balanta raiding practices, Mam Nambatcha noted how some captives were incorporated into the Balanta communities:

> People went to distant *tabancas* to conduct *ostemoré*. They carried away cows and other goods. . . . Captives could also be taken. Their families could pay something and in the end could gain the liberty of the captured people. If the families could not pay, the captives stayed in the houses of their captors. For example, in the *tabanca* of Cumbumba, there once was an old man called Mpas Na Uale who was said to be of the subgroup Mansoanca. He had been captured in *ostemoré*. Since his family did not have the courage to pay a ransom and retrieve him from the tabanca of Cumbumba, Mpas Na Uale stayed there until he died. At that point he was not a Balanta Mansoanca but a Balanta Nhacra. The practice of *ostemoré* was one of the things that led to the mixing of the Balanta with other ethnic groups.[99]

It is likely that Uale had been seized as a child. Indeed, elder Tona Na Isna gave the clear impression that children were the principal victims of *kindeu*. "At times," he said, "someone would take a child from such a house and remain with him or her forever." Further, speaking of the ancient Balanta practice of raiding cattle, Mariano Martinho Natiori said, "At times, children were sequestered together with cattle. *Ostemoré* was the robbing of cattle and children."[100] Archival sources also speak of the seizing of children. In a general statement about Guinea, one priest wrote in 1731 that those "hunted and kidnapped" were usually children.[101] Children were considerably easier to overpower and transport than full-grown men. Hence, to avert casualties when staging *b'ostemoré* or *b'kindeu,* Balanta raiders and kidnappers often nabbed youths.[102]

Child captives held another advantage over adult male captives: they were more easily integrated into Balanta age grades.[103] Since members of male age grades were bound together throughout the course of their lives, passing as a group from one social rank to the next after carrying out certain duties and undergoing specific and at times extremely painful ordeals, captured grown men (or even adolescents) could not be incorporated into *tabanca* life. Age-grade members, after all, had rights and privileges by virtue of having "paid their dues" in previous years. Outsiders, men who had neither contributed to the *tabanca* nor subjected themselves to any of the ordeals that other village men had endured, were simply not acceptable as full age-grade members. Older male outsiders—"slaves"—had no place in a community that lacked a social hierarchy and relied on strong bonds and trust between male equals to ensure unity and a common defense. Captured male or female children, on the other hand, could have been brought into age grades at an early stage, as boys and girls were beginning to form lifelong bonds and beginning to learn about the duties and privileges associated with the age-grade system.

In addition, Balanta incorporated some women captives into *tabanca* settings as wives.[104] Balanta women have today—and, in the era of the Atlantic slave trade, probably had—their own age-grade system. But this system was not as "closed" as that of Balanta men. Indeed, the Balanta patrilineal and virilocal social scheme complicated female age grades. That is, women did not spend their entire lives in the same *tabanca.* Upon marrying, a Balanta woman left the *tabanca* of her birth and took up a new residence in her husband's *tabanca.* This took place after the potential husband gave the father of the bride a number of cattle as bridewealth.[105] Hence, the female age-grade system did not serve to unite a body of women throughout their lives. Rather, it united women within a *tabanca* until marriage, at which time a woman's place in her new family and village unit was marked not by specific age-grade ordeals but by her ability to conduct affairs within her new *morança.* The "opening"—marriage—in the female age-grade system provided a point of entry through which captured female outsiders could be incorporated into Balanta *tabancas* and *moranças.* The incorporation of a female captive into a household through marriage may have been desired since she would not have had a family demanding a bridewealth payment.[106] Also, she would not have had a family to whom to flee if conditions were unacceptable, work loads were too heavy, or a husband was abusive.

Both oral and written sources reveal that women were the targets of many raids and that captors held some women. As quoted above, N'Sar N'Tchala said that in times long past "no one had the courage . . . to go get his cows or women when raiders from another *tabanca* took them."[107] Lending credence to this narrative, E. J. da Costa Oliveira wrote of frequent raids for women in the Guinea-Bissau region. When an enemy was particularly threatening, women fled to the bush to hide.[108] Further, Portuguese administrator Alberto Gomes Pimentel wrote in a 1927 report, "Many wars have been conducted among them [Balanta] for the motive of the theft of cows and women." He also noted, "The men captured in war were immediately killed, but the women and children were saved."[109] Another administrator said that Balanta frequently kidnapped Brame women or children when staging raids.[110]

That decentralized coastal groups preferred women and children captives over men is also reflected in area price differentials.[111] In an 1858 discussion of the problems of liberating the slaves of Portuguese and Luso African masters, the Portuguese governor of Bissau explained that in the region slave values differed according to age and employment. For the residents of Bissau, children of one to five years were particularly valuable since they could be "sold to the Natives for good prices."[112] Other sources indicate that in the early twentieth century Balanta sold captured youths for six cows, while for adults the price was less. Young women with children were also valued, being sold for ten cows.[113]

We should not, however, make the mistake of thinking that differences between the prices of female and child captives compared to male captives reflect the value that Balanta placed on female and male labor. Female and child captives fetched a higher price than male captives because they could be integrated into *tabanca* structures and not because women performed more labor than men. *B'alante b'ndang* struggled to control their sons, but they had little use for enslaved male strangers.

CONCLUSION

Toward the end of the sixteenth and start of the seventeenth century, the exigencies of an expanding Atlantic market forced Balanta to alter their settlement patterns and to forge new community-based institutions through which to interact both with one another and with the broader world. In the struggles that ensued, older Balanta men crafted institutions through which they could continue to control the labor of youths and women. Through councils of elders, they devised a way to make decisions on a local level while ensuring that no one household would rise to dominate others. Further, through marriages, older Balanta men created the conditions necessary to ensure some level of peace among neighboring *tabancas* and to establish links to valuable trading partners. These marriages opened up possibilities for social and economic advancement for some women who were encouraged to leave their communities and spin webs of connections linking locals to "outsiders." The use of women in this manner ensured that young men, whose military might was needed to defend communities and attack strangers, would have few contacts with outsiders and would be more likely, therefore, to remain under the control of their fathers.

Older Balanta men organized young men into age grades for raiding vessels and distant communities. Such raids were conducted because Balanta wanted a share of the imported goods that Atlantic merchants brought to coastal ports. One of the most important was iron. During the period of the Atlantic slave trade, Balanta, like other coastal people, used iron to forge both weapons and, as we shall see in the next chapter, farming implements. Further, Balanta, like other coastal people, wanted cloth, rum, beads, and other goods traded at Bissau and Cacheu. Finally, Balanta seized and ransomed strangers for cattle, which augmented herd sizes.

Balanta warriors sought to avoid injury or death when conducting raids and when transporting captives. Therefore, they often killed males they encountered during raids and captured women and children, who were less likely to be armed and trained in combat. Women and children were also favored because the nature of *tabanca*-based institutions directly impacted the options that Balanta had in dealing with captives. Balanta found it difficult to incorporate male captives into age grades. However, because the age-grade system provided a point of entry for children and women captives, Balanta retained some of the females and younger males they seized in raids, trading others for imports or cattle.

For women in coastal Guinea-Bissau, the period of the Atlantic slave trade, then, was one of great ambiguity. They were vulnerable to slave raiders' attacks and therefore depended on men for protection. However, men depended on women for their contacts with the world outside the *tabanca*. Women established lasting relationships with neighbors, who might provide assistance in times of war, and with traders, who carried much needed supplies of iron throughout the region.

NOTES

1. Jonathon Glassman, *Feasts and Riot: Revelry, Rebellion, and Popular Consciousness on the Swahili Coast, 1856–1888* (Portsmouth, N.H.: Heinemann, 1994), 19–21. I agree with Glassman that many studies "underestimate conflict within the community—conflict between men and women, old and young, rich and poor." The challenge is to demonstrate this conflict for periods and places where sources are scarce, such as in decentralized communities in the period before the nineteenth century.

2. See, for example, Susan Herlin Broadhead, "Slave Wives, Free Sisters: Bakongo Women and Slavery, c. 1700–1850," in *Women and Slavery in Africa*, eds. Claire C. Robertson and Martin A. Klein (Madison: University of Wisconsin Press, 1983), 171; Sandra Greene, *Gender, Ethnicity, and Social Change on the Upper Slave Coast: A History of the Anlo-Ewe* (Portsmouth, N.H.: Heinemann, 1996), 11; Pier M. Larson, *History and Memory in the Age of Enslavement: Becoming Merina in Highland Madagascar,*

1770–1822 (Portsmouth, N.H.: Heinemann, 2000), 131; and John K. Thornton, "Sexual Demography: The Impact of the Slave Trade on Family Structure," in Robertson and Klein, *Women and Slavery,* 44.

3. For similar responses in other parts of Africa, see Charles Piot, "Of Slaves and the Gift: Kabre Sale of Kin During the Era of the Slave Trade," *Journal of African History* 37, no. 1 (1996): 33–34; Denis D. Cordell, "The Myth of Inevitability and Invincibility: Resistance to Slavers and the Slave Trade in Central Africa in the Late Nineteenth and Early Twentieth Centuries," paper presented at the conference "Fighting Back: African Strategies Against the Slave Trade," Rutgers University, February 16–17, 2001; Gustav Nachtigal, *Sahara and Sudan,* trans. Allan G. B. Fisher and Humphery J. Fisher (London: C. Hurst, 1987), 340–343; Martin A. Klein, "The Slave Trade and Decentralized Societies," *Journal of African History* 42, no. 1 (2000): 53–55; Andrew Hubbell, "A View of the Slave Trade from the Margin: Souroudougou in the Late Nineteenth-Century Slave Trade of the Niger Bend," *Journal of African History* 42, no. 1 (2000): 32; Richard Fardon, *Raiders and Refugees: Trends in Chamba Political Development, 1750–1950* (Washington, D.C.: Smithsonian Institution Press, 1988), chap. 5; and Peter Mark, "Constructing Identity: Sixteenth- and Seventeenth-Century Architecture in the Gambia-Geba Region and the Articulation of Luso-African Ethnicity," *History in Africa* 22 (1995): 308–310. For a wonderful study of how the slave trade shaped African architecture, see Thierno Mouctar Bah, *Architecture militaire traditionnelle et poliorcétique dans le Soudan occidental du XVIIe à la fin du XIXe siècle* (Yaounde: Editions Cle, 1985). For a narrative of populations concentrating in reaction to the violence associated with slaving, see George Schwab, *Tribes of the Liberian Hinterland,* papers of the Peabody Museum of American Archaeology and Ethnology, Harvard University, vol. 31 (Cambridge: Peabody Museum, 1947), 29.

4. Robin Horton, "Stateless Societies in the History of West Africa," in *History of West Africa,* vol. 1, eds. J. F. A. Ajayi and M. Crowder (London: Longman, 1976), 91–92.

5. For Guinea-Bissau, see Avelino Teixeira da Mota, *Guiné portuguesa,* vol. 1 (Lisbon: Agência Geral do Ultramar, 1954), 205–218.

6. André Álvares de Almada, *Tratado breve dos rios de Guiné,* trans. P.E.H. Hair (Liverpool: University of Liverpool, Department of History, 1984), chap. 17.

7. Ibid., chap. 18.

8. Francisco de Lemos Coelho, *Description of the Coast of Guinea (1684),* trans. P.E.H. Hair (Liverpool: University of Liverpool, Department of History, 1985), chap. 3. See also André Donelha, *Descrição da Serra Leoa e dos rios De Guiné do Cabo Verde (1625),* ed. Avelino Teixeira da Mota, trans. P.E.H. Hair, Centro de Estudos de Cartografia Antiga no. 19 (Lisbon: Junta de Investigações Científicas do Ultramar, 1977), 151.

9. E. J. da Costa Oliveira, "Guiné portugueza," *Boletim da Sociedade de Geografia de Lisboa* (1888–1889): 307.

10. Almada, *Tratado breve* (Hair's ed.), chap. 18. Also comments of Avelino Teixeira da Mota in Donelha, *Descrição,* 251 ff.

11. Interview with Adelino Bidenga Sanha, Quinhaque, January 7, 1995.

12. Interview with Fona Benuma, Encheia, January 13, 1995.

13. Interview with N'tera Siga, Patche Ialá, January 25, 1995. Also interviews with Cubumba Sangê, Bletê, and Chefe Lima, N'Tin, April 5, 1995; Isnaba Nambatcha, Cufar, March 3, 1995; Cabi Na Tambá, Mato-Farroba, December 6, 1996; Mam NamBatcha,

Cufar, March 3, 1995; and Tona Na Isna and Suna Na Isna, Cantoné, March 5, 1995. Also see Oliveira, "Guiné portugueza," 307.

14. Max Gluckman, *Custom and Conflict in Africa* (Oxford: Basil Blackwell, 1960), chap. 1; Elizabeth Colson, "Social Control and Vengeance in Plateau Tonga Society," in Elizabeth Colson, *The Plateau Tonga of Northern Rhodesia (Zambia): Social and Religious Studies* (Manchester: University of Zambia, Institute for Social Research, 1970); Meyer Fortes, *The Dynamics of Clanship Among the Tallensi* (London: Oxford University Press, 1945), 108–115.

15. Horton, "Stateless Societies," 92. Across West Africa, examples of this can be found among groups threatened by slave raiders. Olga Linares, "Deferring to Trade in Slaves: The Jola of Casamance, Senegal, in Historical Perspective," *History in Africa* 14 (1987): 113–139; Klein, "The Slave Trade," 55–56.

16. Interview with Bisi Binhaga and José Gomes, Patche Ialá, January 31, 1995. Also interviews with Cabi Na Tambá, Mato-Farroba, December 6, 1996; Mam NamBatcha, Cufar, March 3, 1995; and Fona Benuma, Encheia, January 13, 1995.

17. Interview with Isnaba Nambatcha, Cufar, March 3, 1995. Also interview with Quemade N'dami and Armando Dias, N'tatelai, February 2, 1995.

18. Quoted in P.E.H. Hair and Avelino Teixeira da Mota, eds., *Jesuit Documents on the Guinea of Cape Verde and the Cape Verde Islands, 1585–1617* (Liverpool: University of Liverpool, Department of History, 1989), doc. 16. Also see Almada's description of the way that Biafada treated unknowing "yokels" from the interior (Chapter 3 of this book). Almada, *Tratado breve* (Hair's ed.), 121. It was perhaps the fear of coming into contact with outsiders that compelled many Africans in Guinea-Bissau to carry arms with them wherever they went. Philip Beaver, *African Memoranda* (London: Dawsons of Pall Mall, 1968), 327; Robert Martin Baum, *Shrines of the Slave Trade: Diola Religion and Society in Precolonial Senegambia* (Oxford: Oxford University Press, 1999), 27, 120–121; interview with N'Sar N'Tchala, Bera, April 5, 1995; interview with Quemade N'dami and Armando Dias, N'tatelai, February 2, 1995.

19. Decentralized groups elsewhere used marriage to unite villages into confederations. See Hubbell, "A View," 36–37; Martin Klein, "Ethnic Pluralism and Homogeneity in the Western Sudan: Saalum, Segu, Wasulu," *Mande Studies* 1 (1999): 113–119; Klein, "The Slave Trade," 56; Timothy Weiskel, *French Colonial Rule and the Baule Peoples: Resistance and Collaboration, 1889–1911* (Oxford: Clarendon Press, 1980), 222; and Marshall Sahlins, "Patterns of Marital Alliance," in Marshall Sahlins, *Tribesmen* (Englewood Cliffs, N.J.: Prentice Hall, 1968), 56–63.

20. Such alliances were apparent to Europeans. For example, Coelho listed nine "*Reynos dos Balantas.*" These realms were probably composed of *tabancas* that were linked through a variety of crosscutting institutions. Coelho, *Descrição,* 86.

21. Armando Augusto Gonçalves de Moraes e Castro, *Annuario da provincia da Guiné do anno de 1925* (Bolama: Imprensa Nacional, 1925), 192.

22. Interview with Estanislau Correia Landim, João Landim, February 2, 1995. Also interviews with N'Dafa Na Combé, Mato-Farroba, December 12, 1994; Frós Intchalá and Ndum Mhana, Ilonde, January 28, 1995; and N'Sar N'Tchala, Bera, April 5, 1995.

23. Manuel Álvares, *Ethiopia Minor and a Geographical Account of the Province of Sierra Leone,* trans. P.E.H. Hair (Liverpool: University of Liverpool, Department of History, September 30, 1990), chap. 12.

24. Arquivo Histórico Ultramarino (AHU) (Lisbon, Portugal), Guiné, cx. 4, doc. 18;

João Teixeira Pinto, *Teixeira Pinto: A ocupação militar da Guiné* (Lisbon: Divisão de Publicações e Biblioteca, 1936), 126–127; interview with Alfrede Neves, Chiguna Clusse, and Bcolof Sukna, Patche Ialá, January 31, 1995.

25. Michael Taylor, *Community, Anarchy, Liberty* (Cambridge: Cambridge University Press, 1982), 70; Elizabeth Colson, *The Plateau Tonga of Northern Rhodesia (Zambia): Social and Religious Studies* (Manchester: Institute for Social Research, University of Zambia, Institute for Social Research, 1970), 102–121.

26. Gluckman, *Custom and Conflict,* 13.

27. Almada, *Tratado breve* (Hair's ed.), 121. On "lesser pillage" in Senegambia, see James F. Searing, *West African Slavery and Atlantic Commerce: The Senegal River Valley, 1700–1860* (Cambridge: Cambridge University Press, 1993), 35. On kidnapping, see Paul E. Lovejoy, *Transformations in Slavery: A History of Slavery in Africa* (Cambridge: Cambridge University Press, 1983), 84–87.

28. Interview with João Bafã, Patch Ialá, January 8, 1995.

29. Philip J. Havik, "Women and Trade in the Guinea-Bissau Region," *Stvdia* 52 (1994): 83–120; A. Teixeira da Mota, *Some Aspects of Portuguese Colonisation and Sea Trade in West Africa in the Fifteenth and Sixteenth Centuries* (Bloomington: Indiana University Press, 1978), 15; António Carreira, *Os portuguêses nos rios de Guiné (1500–1900)* (Lisbon: António Carreira, 1984), 27–28. See especially André Donelha's 1635 observation of trade in the Guinea-Bissau region in Judith Carney, *Black Rice: The African Origins of Rice Cultivation in the Americas* (Cambridge: Harvard University Press, 2001).

30. It is striking the role that women play in economic exchanges with outsiders today. When I attempted to purchase rice in rural areas, it was always women who negotiated a price with me. It is also women who line up to have their *morança*'s rice processed by European merchants who visit *tabancas* with portable gas-powered mills, and women who negotiate the price of gaining access to the mills of these outsiders.

31. Interview with Inguessa Nhasse, Oko, February 18, 1995. Quidama Kabi said that women "cut line, cooked salt, and gathered cabeciera," selling these things in Bissau. Interview with Quidama Kabi, Oko, February 18, 1995. See also Arquivo Histórico do Instituto Nacional de Estudos e Pesquisa, Bissau, "Panorama da história da etnia Balanta—Quinara," cassette no. 241.

32. José Conrado Carlos de Chelmicki, *Corografia Cabo Verdiana* (Lisbon: Typ. de L.C. da Cunha, 1841), 343, 348.

33. Quoted in António Alberto de Andrade, "Benardino Álvares de Adrade, um 'Guineense' esquecido." *Boletim Cultural da Guiné Portugueza* 98 (1970): 190–195.

34. Álvares, *Ethiopia Minor,* chap. 7.

35. George E. Brooks, "A Nhara of the Guinea-Bissau Region: Mãe Aurélia Correia," in Robertson and Klein, *Women and Slavery.* One my also look at the example of Rosa de Cacheu who married into the powerful Carvalho Alvarenga family to become a powerful trade broker in her own right. See Jaime Walter, *Honório Pereira Barreto* (Lisbon: Centro de Estodos da Guiné Portuguesa, 1947), 11.

36. Havik, "Women and Trade."

37. José Joaquim Lopes de Lima, *Ensaios sobre a statistica das possessões portuguezas no Ultramar,* vol. 1, *Das ilhas de Cabo Verde e suas dependências* (Lisbon: Imprensa Nacional, 1844), 125–126.

38. E. E. Evans-Pritchard, "The Nuer of the Southern Sudan," in *African Political Systems,* eds. Meyer Fortes and E. E. Evans-Pritchard (London: Oxford University Press, 1940), 288–290; Jan Vansina, *Paths in the Rainforest: Toward a History of Political*

Tradition in Equatorial Africa (Madison: University of Wisconsin Press, 1990), 79; Taylor, *Community, Anarchy, Liberty,* 71–72; Horton, "Stateless Societies," 93.

39. J. B. Labat, *Nouvelle relation de l'Afrique occidentale* (Paris: Cavelier, 1728), 189.

40. Francisco Antonio Marques Geraldes, "Guiné portugueza, communicação á sociedade de geographia sobre esta provincia e suas condições actuaes," *Boletim da Sociedade de Geografia de Lisboa* ser. 7a, no. 8 (1887): 517–518. Balanta narratives also speak of councils of elders. Interviews with Alfrede Neves, Chiguna Clusse, and Bcolof Sukna, Patche Ialá, January 31, 1995; João Bafã, Patche Ialá, January 8, 1995; and Nhafede Sambe and Abna Dafa, Blimat, January 28, 1995.

41. This also was the case among Floup. See Baum, *Shrines,* 110–111.

42. Interview with Quemade N'dami and Armando Dias, N'tatelai, February 2, 1995. Also interview with Cabi Na Tambá, Mato-Farroba, December 6, 1996.

43. Interviews with Adelino Bidenga Sanha, Quinhaque, January 7, 1995; and Estanislau Correia Landim, João Landim, February 2, 1995.

44. In addition, Balanta place a wooden paddle in the doorway to signify a local god, and an old *kebinde,* or shovel-type plow, in hopes that the boy will be a good farmer.

45. Álvares, *Ethiopia Minor,* chap. 12. Also, AHU, Guiné, cx. 11, doc. 57.

46. Interview with Cubumba Sangê, Bletê, and Chefe Lima, N'Tin, April 5, 1995.

47. Interview with N'Sar N'Tchala, Bera, April 5, 1995.

48. Interview with Nhafede Sambe and Abna Dafa, Blimat, January 28, 1995.

49. Álvares, *Ethiopia Minor,* chap. 12. See also Alonso de Sandoval, *Natvraleza, policia, sagrada i profana, costvmbres i ritos, disciplina i catechismo evangelico de todos etiopes* (Seville: Francisco de Lira, 1627), 39; and Mota, *Guiné portuguesa,* 218.

50. AHU, Guiné, cx. 11, doc. 43.

51. Ibid., cx. 12, doc. 3A.

52. Ibid., cx. 14, doc. 31.

53. Interview with Fona Benuma, Encheia, January 13, 1995.

54. Interview with Mam NamBatcha, Cufar, March 3, 1995.

55. Geraldes, "Guiné portugueza," 517.

56. P. Mateo de Anguiano, *Misiones Capuchinas en Africa,* vol. 2 (Madrid: Instituto Santo Toribio de Mogrovejo, 1950), 141.

57. Quoted in P.E.H. Hair, Adam Jones, and Robin Law, eds., *Barbot on Guinea: The Writing of Jean Barbot on West Africa, 1678–1712* (London: Hakluyt Society, 1992), 170–171.

58. Quoted in Avelino Teixeira da Mota, *As viagens do Bispo D. Frei Vitoriano Portuense à Guiné e a cristianização dos reis de Bissau* (Lisbon: Junta de Investigações Científicas do Ultramar, 1974), 75.

59. Álvares, *Ethiopia Minor,* chap. 7.

60. Anguiano, *Misiones Capuchinas,* 143.

61. Ibid.

62. Mota, *As viagens,* 86.

63. Quotes in ibid., 31, 171.

64. AHU, Guiné, cx. 11, doc. 30.

65. Ibid., cx. 11, doc. 7; cx. 12, doc. 3.

66. Ibid., cx. 14, doc. 62; AHU, Cabo Verde, SENMU/DGU/RC/001/cx. 73, doc. 429; SENMU/DGU/RC/001/cx. 89, doc. 298; SGG/A1/A6.9/cx. 347, February 7, 1865, March 3, 1865, March 4, 1865, April 24, 1865, May 29, 1865, August 26, 1865; Joaquim da

Graça Correia e Lança, *Relatório da provincia da Guiné portugueza: Referido ao anno economico de 1888–1889* (Lisbon: Imprensa Nacional, 1890), 50–51.

67. Anguiano, *Misiones Capuchinas,* 143.

68. Quoted in Hair, Jones, and Law, *Barbot on Guinea,* 172. Barbot did not mention Balanta by name, but he located the group that "murdered" whites on the Rio Geba (he writes "Rio Grande," a name commonly used for the Geba at the time. See the editors' note, p. 174.

69. Sieur Michel Jajolet de La Courbe, *Premier voyage du Sieur de la Courbe fait à la coste de l'Afrique en 1685,* ed. Prosper Cultru (Paris: E. Champion, 1913), 257–8. Also 247.

70. For a similar practice in Biafran warfare, see G. Ugo. Nwokeji, "African Conceptions of Gender and the Slave Traffic," *William and Mary Quarterly* 58, no. 1 (January 2001): 47–69.

71. Almada, *Tratado breve* (Hair's ed.), 92.

72. Ibid.

73. André de Faro, "Relaçam (1663–4)," in *André de Faro's Missionary Journey to Sierra Leone in 1663–1664,* trans. P.E.H. Hair, Occasional Paper no. 5 (Sierra Leone: University of Sierra Leone, Institute of African Studies, 1982), 69. See also Coelho, *Description,* chap. 5; Anguiano, *Misiones Capuchinas,* 116; and Cultru, *Premier voyage,* 257.

74. Almada, *Tratado breve* (Hair's ed.), 118.

75. Anguiano, *Misiones Capuchinas,* 116, 143.

76. Quoted in ibid., 121–133.

77. Alberto Gomes Pimentel, "Circumscrição civil de Mansôa: Etnografia," *Boletim Official da Guiné Portuguesa* 50 (December 10, 1927): 1–26.

78. Interview with Cabi Na Tambá, Mato-Farroba, December 6, 1996. Also interviews with Mam NamBatcha, Cufar, March 3, 1995; Tona Na Isna and Suna Na Isna, Cantoné, March 5, 1995; Alfrede Neves, Chiguna Clusse, and Bcolof Sukna, Patche Ialá, January 31, 1995; and Basca Fonre, Pam Bighate, Bwasat Basca, and Bian Bekle, Nhacra, January 1, 1995.

79. Interview with Mam Nambatcha, Cufar, March 3, 1995.

80. For a similar analysis, see Linares, "Deferring," 118.

81. Francisco de Lemos Coelho, "Descrição da costa da Guiné desde o Cabo Verde athe Serra Lioa com todas as ilhas e rios que os Brancos Navegam," in *Duas descrições seiscentistas da Guiné,* ed. Damião Peres (Lisbon: Academia Portuguesa da História, 1953), 36 (emphasis his).

82. Andrade, "Benardino Álvares de Andrade," 190.

83. AHU Guiné, cx. 21, doc. 23.

84. Geraldes, "Guiné portugueza," 517.

85. Interview with N'Sar N'Tchala, Bera, April 5, 1995.

86. Interview with Bisi Binhaga and José Gomes, Cafa, January, 31 1995.

87. Geraldes, "Guiné portugueza," 472.

88. Hair and Mota, *Jesuit Documents,* doc. 9. Almada, *Tratado breve* (Hair's ed.), 90.

89. Geraldes reported that wars between coastal groups were "short in duration," unlike those of Mandinka. Geraldes, "Guiné portugueza," 501.

90. Paul E. Lovejoy and Jan S. Hogendorn, "Slave Marketing in West Africa," in *The Uncommon Market: Essays in the Economic History of the Atlantic Slave Trade,* eds. H. A.

Gemery and J. S. Hogendorn (New York: Academic Press, 1979), 213–232. Also Lovejoy, *Transformations,* 88–107.

91. Álvares said Bijago attacks ended when resistance was fierce. Álvares, *Ethiopia Minor,* chap. 9.

92. Calculated from David Eltis, Stephen D. Behrendt, David Richardson, and Herbert S. Klein, eds., *The Trans-Atlantic Slave Trade: A Database on CD-ROM* (Cambridge: Cambridge University Press, 1999). The unique identification numbers of the ships are 9067, 9069, 9070, 31533, 9071, 9072, 9073, 9073, 9079, 9077, 7613, 2898, 3013, 1213, 1860.

93. David Eltis and Stanley L. Engerman, "Was the Slave Trade Dominated by Men?" *Journal of Interdisciplinary History* 23, no. 2 (Autumn 1992): 241; David Eltis and Stanley L. Engerman, "Fluctuations in Age and Sex Ratios in the Transatlantic Slave Trade, 1663–1864," *Economic History Review* 46, no. 2 (1993): 308–323; David Eltis and David Richardson, "West African and the Transatlantic Slave Trade: New Evidence of Long-Run Trends," *Slavery and Abolition* 18, 1 (1997): 31.

94. In an often-cited study of the impact of the slave trade on the gendered division of labor in Guinea-Bissau, John Thornton does not do this. Hence, he calculates that most of those exported from coastal communities were men. Thornton, "Sexual Demography."

95. Also known as Talabonca and Talibonca. António Carreira writes that these were terms used by Mandinka to designate any group of people who lived to the east. António Carreira, *Cabo Verde: Formação e extinção de uma sociedade escravocrata (1460–1878)* (Praia, Cape Verde: Instituto Caboverdeano de Livro, 1983), 432.

96. Known as Uassolonca in Portuguese. The term was applied to people from Wasulu.

97. Diola integrated male and female slaves into communities. Baum, *Shrines,* 158–161.

98. Vítor Hugo de Menezes, "Respota ao questionário de inquérito sôbre as raças da Guiné e seus caracteres étnicos, formulado pelo governo da colónia em portoria provincial no. 70, de 12 Abril de 1927," *Boletim Official da Colónia da Guiné* no. 3, apenso (January 21, 1928): 15; E. J. da Costa Oliveira, "Viagem á Guiné," *Boletim da Sociedade de Geografia de Lisboa* ser. 8a, nos. 11–12 (1888–1889): 123. The quotation about Floup slaves is from Baum, *Shrines,* 159. For look at the incorporation of outsiders into kin groups, see Igor Kopytoff and Suzanne Miers, "African 'Slavery' as an Institution of Marginality," in *Slavery in Africa,* eds. Suzanne Miers and Igor Kopytoff (Madison: University of Wisconsin Press, 1977), 3–84.

99. Interview with Mam NamBatcha, Cufar, March 3, 1995.

100. Interviews with Tona Na Isna and Suna Na Isna, Cantoné, March 5, 1995; and Mariano Martinho Natiori, N'foto or Quidet, July 17, 2000.

101. AHU, Cabo Verde, cx. 14, doc 31.

102. See also the description of Olaudah Equiano's enslavement as a youth in Olaudah Equiano, *The Interesting Narrative and Other Writings* (New York: Penguin Books, 1995), 46–61. See also Marcia Wright, *Strategies of Slaves and Women: Life-Stories from East/Central Africa* (New York: Lilian Barber, 1993); and Nwokeji, "African Conceptions."

103. Kopytoff and Miers, "African 'Slavery,'" 53; Carol P. MacCormack, "Wono: Institutionalized Dependence in Sherbro Descent Groups," in Miers and Kopytoff, *Slavery in Africa,* 181–204.

104. For a look at the incorporation of female slaves into other West African communities, see Martin A. Klein and Claire C. Robertson. "Women's Importance in

African Slave Systems," in Robertson and Klein, *Women and Slavery,* 3–28; and Claude Meillassoux, "Female Slavery," in Robertson and Klein, *Women and Slavery,* 67–88.

105. Álvares, *Ethiopia Minor,* chap. 12.

106. James Caughan, "Mafakur: A Limbic Institution of the Margi," in Miers and Kopytoff, *Slavery in Africa,* 85–103. See also Curtis Keim, "Women in Slavery Among the Mangbetu, c. 1800–1910," in Robertson and Klein, *Women in Slavery,* 144; and Wright, *Strategies.*

107. Interview with N'Sar N'Tchala, Bera, April 5, 1995.

108. Oliveira, *Viagem á Guiné,* 29.

109. Pimentel, "Circumscrição," 14–15.

110. Vítor Hugo de Menezes, "Etnografia, Manjacos e Brames, povoadores da circunscrição civil da Costa de Baixo," *Boletim Oficial da Colónia da Guiné* no. 3, apenso (Jan., 3 1928), 5–6.

111. This was generally the case across Africa. See Robertson and Klein, *Women and Slavery;* Patrick Manning, *Slavery and African Life: Occidental, Oriental, and African Slave Trades* (Cambridge: Cambridge University Press, 1990), 42; and Paul E. Lovejoy and David Richardson, "Competing Markets for Male and Female Slaves: Prices in the Interior of West Africa, 1750–1850," *International Journal of African Historical Studies* 28, 2 (1995): 261–293.

112. AHU, AUL, GG, Lv. 50, "Livro de registo de correspondência expedida pelo governador da Guiné para as diversas autoridades da mesma provincial," January 1856–August 1861.

113. Pimentel, "Circumscrição," 11.

5

THE RISE OF BALANTA PADDY RICE PRODUCTION AND MASCULINIZATION OF AGRICULTURAL LABOR IN THE SEVENTEENTH AND EIGHTEENTH CENTURIES

Serving as the front line of defense against slave raiders and as offensive units in attacks on distant villages or stranded merchant vessels, Balanta age grades also proved valuable for organizing men and women for agricultural production. This was particularly true in the late seventeenth and early eighteenth centuries, when Balanta were beginning to regularize contacts with area slave traders and to produce paddy, or "wetland," rice.

A close examination of the rise of a Balanta paddy rice monoculture is important for several reasons. First, because paddy rice is central to human existence in coastal Guinea-Bissau, a study of Balanta history must focus on the relationship between Balanta and rice. The paddy rice cycle lends a rhythm to Balanta life, its production dominating the working lives of rural Balanta men, women, and children. For Balanta, rice is the principal staple food, a store of wealth, a trade good in bartering arrangements, and a treasure offered to local gods. Rice is *the* sustenance of Balanta.[1] A Balanta proverb sums this up well: "There isn't a meal without rice." It is consumed two or three times a day, with fish, when fish is available, occasionally with chicken, or just with a sauce.[2] Some Balanta myths of creation even claim that God (Hala in Graça) created Balanta to farm paddy rice.[3]

Second, the study of the rise of Balanta paddy rice production challenges the widely held assumption that the rise of the Atlantic slave trade led to a general decline in the agricultural productivity of decentralized regions.[4] The notion that the violence associated with the slave trade limited the ability of decentralized societies to produce food crops is summed up by Albert van Dantzig, who writes that "the often mentioned negative effects of the slave trade, such as depopulation, decay of agricultural and general civilization and general insecurity must have been felt chiefly in those areas which were regularly the object of slave raids." That is, famine must have been common in areas that failed to develop "elaborate and highly centralized" systems of government.[5] Undoubtedly, some of the decentralized "slaving frontiers" of Africa's great states suffered severe agricultural declines as a result of population decreases and dislocations.[6] However, famine and sterility did not plague all decentralized regions. Indeed, the slave trade did not bring "decay" to Balanta society. Rather, it brought great challenges. By working through their own unique and very local institutions, Balanta met those challenges.

Third, a focus on the development of a Balanta paddy rice monoculture demonstrates that precolonial African labor regimes were multiple and varied, and that generalizations about them are difficult to derive. Offering an alternative to an unidirectional model for change that historians have drawn on to demonstrate that the era of the Atlantic slave trade necessarily saw an increase in African women's labor, this chapter presents an example of a society in which the sexual division of labor dictated that young men perform the most labor-intensive tasks.[7] This masculinized labor system emerged during an agricultural revolution, the catalyst for which was the Atlantic slave trade. Studies of other decentralized regions, particularly the Bight of Biafra, have also illustrated the centrality of male agricultural labor in the precolonial period. Like this chapter, they offer an explanation for why the percentage of female slave exports was higher from some ports than from most others.[8] The reasons can be found not in broad market forces but in local social processes.

IRON, VIOLENCE, AND CROP YIELD

In Chapter 1, I argued that before the rise of the Atlantic slave trade, Balanta farmers, living in households, or *moranças,* that were dispersed across uplands, produced yams and raised cattle for sustenance and trade. An obvious question arises: Why, in the era of the Atlantic slave trade, did these politically decentralized farmers, particularly Balanta on the Rio Geba, Rio Cacheu, and Rio Mansoa, largely abandon yam production in favor of paddy rice? They did so for three reasons: they had access to increasing amounts of iron, the coast was experiencing a general rise in violence, and paddy rice provided superior yields.

In part, Balanta farmers turned to paddy rice cultivation because of the availability of greater quantities of iron, which was brought in large quantities to the Upper Guinea Coast by Atlantic merchants who traded it for slaves, wax, and other goods. Before the arrival of these merchants, farmers in the Guinea-Bissau region could not afford great amounts of the expensive imported iron that was supplied via the Biafada-Sapi trade network and by Mandinka, who traded at the *ria* coastline's edge. Thus they planted and harvested yams and other crops with wooden or stone tools.[9] But the clearing of coastal lowlands, where paddy rice was eventually cultivated, required iron implements for digging and cutting. Indeed, lowland areas were covered with mangroves, the strong limbs and twisted roots of which could not have been cut with wood or stone tools. Iron cutting edges were a necessity.[10] Indicating this, one group of elders told me, "Since Balanta did not know iron, the *kebinde* did not have an iron end. Thus, the cutting end was burned in fire to make it become strong enough to perform all of the work required in farming. Later, Balanta attained iron. The *kebinde* without iron was for farming the earth. The *kebinde* with iron was for farming the *bolanha* [wet lowland areas where Balanta cultivate paddy rice]."[11] Because iron was in high demand in the Guinea-Bissau region, Atlantic merchants carried large quantities of it to regional ports, trading it to Balanta and other coastal people for captives.

If increased access to iron made farming mangrove areas possible, the proliferation of the violence associated with the Atlantic slave trade gave Balanta reason to contemplate changing their agricultural practices. That is, as slave raiding in the Guinea-Bissau region intensified, particularly in the seventeenth century, Balanta farmers decided to abandon difficult-to-defend upland areas, which were favorable to yam production, for isolated lowlands, where rice could be productively cultivated. Because they were difficult to access and maneuver in, lowlands were ideal places to establish defensive settlements, or *tabancas*. Mangrove swamps and dense riverside brush offered perfect hiding places, and creeks and marshes hindered the movement of large raiding parties. Fô Kidum clearly indicated this when he said, "Balanta and other ethnic groups did not have good relations. There were always wars with other ethnic groups." These wars, he continued, "pushed Balanta to littoral regions that Balanta discovered later were good for agriculture."[12]

Written sources also indicate that lowland regions, or *bolanhas,* provided safety to *tabanca* populations. Indeed, in the early twentieth century, Portuguese administrator Alberto Gomes Pimentel explained how Balanta utilized the natural protection of wet lowland areas when they were confronted with an attack from a well-organized and well-armed enemy:

> Armed with guns and large swords, the Balanta, who did not generally employ any resistance on these occasions . . . pretended to flee (it was and

is their tactic), suffering a withdrawal and going to hide in the *"terrafe"* [mangrove areas] on the margins of the rivers and lagoons, spreading out in the *bolanhas* some distance so as not to be shot by their enemies. The attackers, judging themselves victorious, then began to return for their lands with all of the spoils of war.

Organizing rapidly and allying themselves with others in the area, Balanta typically followed their enemies through the densely forested coastal region. At times, Balanta waited until their attackers had almost reached their home-lands before giving "a few shots and making considerable noise so as to cause a panic." Balanta then engaged their enemies in combat, "many times *corpo a corpo*."[13] Lowland areas, then, not only provided excellent cover but were conducive to organizing counterattacks.

Lowland paddy rice had another advantage over upland yams: paddy rice produces high yields and is very nutritious and can therefore sustain large, dense populations.[14] Examining Diola paddy rice farming practices, Olga Linares estimates that a hectare of land produces about 2,000 to 2,500 kilo-grams of unmilled rice. After milling, the yield would be about 1,500 to 2,100 kilograms. A household composed of a man and a woman can farm about 1.5 to 2 hectares of paddies per season, yielding between 3,000 and 5,000 kilo-grams. On average, an adult consumes 125 kilograms of rice per year and a child 75 kilograms. Using similar farming techniques, Balanta obtain even higher yields since their paddies receive more annual rainfall. In the Geba region, yields vary between 2,500 and 3,500 kilograms of unmilled rice per hectare.[15] Hence paddy rice provided more than adequate food supplies for large, compact, and growing *tabancas*.[16]

Balanta turned to paddy rice cultivation for other reasons as well. The har-vest could be stored easily without fear of spoilage.[17] Moreover, as European vessels began to visit Guinea-Bissau's shores in increasing numbers and as merchant communities proliferated in coastal ports, rice became a lucrative trade item, with captains of slave vessels purchasing large quantities of it to sustain their cargos during the Atlantic crossing.[18] Finally, the riverine and forested lowlands in which paddy rice was cultivated offered an abundance of items that could supplement diets, make life more comfortable, or be ex-ploited for economic gain. Fish taken from rivers became an important source of protein, as did shellfish found in estuaries and swamps. Moreover, game could be hunted not far from villages, providing meat for diets and skins for protection and trade. Medicinal herbs and fruits abounded in lowland forests. Plentiful quantities of wood could be obtained for cooking, and in clearings, grasses for use in thatching roofs were available. Living on the banks of brackish rivers, Balanta also developed a thriving salt industry. Salt was traded and used to flavor and preserve meats. In addition, lowlands provided food supplies for cattle, pigs, goats, and chickens.

THE RISE OF PADDY RICE CULTIVATION AMONG BALANTA

The dissemination of mangrove rice cultivation among dispersed and politically independent Balanta *tabancas* was a long and slow process. As discussed in Chapter 1, Mande-speakers in the Gambia region developed coastal paddy rice techniques before the arrival of Atlantic merchants. However, populations to the south did not begin to implement these techniques on a large scale until around the mid-seventeenth century. At that time, Kaabu was at the peak of its power, slave exports from the region numbered in the thousands each year, and Atlantic merchants were supplying the coast with increasing amounts of iron.

Indicating that Balanta grew other crops before they adopted a rice monoculture, Mam Nambatcha stated, "Balanta have grown rice for a long time. When they gained knowledge of rice, they started to cultivate it principally." He said that in Anhi, the *tabanca* in the Rio Geba region where he was born, "maize was the first crop grown." "After some time, Balanta in that area gained knowledge of rice."[19] This oral narrative dovetails well with Manuel Álvares's early-seventeenth-century observation that Balanta grew "*fundes* and *milho*" and other vegetables "except for rice, of which there is little."[20] *Fundes (fundo* in Graça) is "hungry rice" *(Digitaria exilis),* a grain common to the region. In medieval Portuguese, *milho* means "grain" or "millet," but in modern Portuguese it means "maize." Here it is likely that Álvares is describing maize, since he talks of "*milho* cane" in another passage.[21] In Biafada territories to the south, *milho* was also a staple, there being "little rice."[22] As in other parts of Africa, in Guinea-Bissau maize and other plants introduced by Atlantic merchants gradually became part of the mix of crops that farmers produced, in some cases replacing indigenous crops like yams that had been grown for generations. As yams became less important in the Balanta diet, histories about them appear to have faded from the oral record. In any case, by themselves traditions like Nambatcha's provide us with no dates or means to derive dates.

For a more detailed picture, we have to turn to written sources. The earliest Atlantic merchants to arrive in the region observed paddy rice agriculture in the Gambia region. Since it was commonly used in rituals, some amounts of rice were probably cultivated farther south as well. However, it is not until the seventeenth century that written records make clear that paddy rice (and not simply a less labor-intensive dryland or upland type) was being produced in Guinea-Bissau. In 1685, La Courbe noted that the land around the Rio Cacheu "resembles prairies; I see some lagoons of rice all along the side of the river. The fields are traversed by little causeways, from space to space, to prevent the running off of the water; in the first place, after it rains they sow the rice that grows in the water."[23] Here La Courbe might have been observing Balanta fields. However, Joseph Lauer argues that he was observing Brame (or Manjaco) fields. Drawing on other data, Lauer surmises that these fields were of a poor quality compared to those of Floup (or Diola) to the north. "This suggestion of mediocre rice agriculture and the fact that the Portuguese more commonly bought their rice from the Diola indicate," he argues, "that [paddy] rice cultivation was not well established among fifteenth century Manjaco."[24] That is, it is evident that only in the seventeenth century were Brame, neighbors to Balanta who also occupied the Rio Cacheu region, starting to perfect paddy rice techniques, probably learning them from Floup. This seems a reasonable assertion since, in the seventeenth century, the Crioulo name *Baiotes* or "men of the rice nursery" was used to designate a large number of Floup who farmed near the Rio Casamance.[25]

Whether or not La Courbe was describing Brame or Balanta fields, it is clear that Balanta in the region had also developed *bolanha* cultivation techniques during the same period. Indeed, in 1725, J. B. Labat, who was drawing on observations from the late seventeenth and early eighteenth centuries, reported that Balanta were marketing rice along with other commodities.[26] Nonetheless, the principal staple of whites who lived on the Cacheu during this period was maize and not rice, and local communities traded maize.[27] Area farmers, then, were slowly adopting paddy rice techniques.

To the south of the Cacheu, on the Geba, it appears as if paddy rice was not being cultivated at this time. While traveling along the Geba, La Courbe wrote nothing of paddy rice. And having arrived at Geba, on the upper Rio Geba, he noted that the country was "replete with lagoons appropriate for the planting of rice, but the people do not cultivate it."[28] Further, in the 1770s Portuguese observers in Bissau, which is on the Rio Geba, described Sierra Leone as "very fertile in rice" and Floup near the Casamance as "the best farmers of rice that there are in all of Guinea," but they said nothing about Balanta, who resided nearby, being significant paddy rice producers, though they took time to explore other aspects of Balanta society.[29] As late as 1796, Bernardino António Álvares Andrade could write that on the Rio Mansoa Balanta had "an abundance of all qualities of maize, beans and sesame from which they make oil with which they season [food]; and lately [*ultimamente*] they cultivate rice, cotton, and indigo, they raise much livestock and chickens."[30] Here he indicated that, in the late eighteenth century, rice cultivation was a relatively recent endeavor for southern Balanta. Andrade's observation fits well with Nambatcha's story of Balanta in the Rio Geba area switching from the cultivation of maize to the production of paddy rice "in times long past." Indeed, Andrade makes clear that, at the end of the eighteenth century, maize was still an important crop since Balanta had "an abundance" of the grain.

During this same period, paddy rice cultivation may have been a recent endeavor for the Papel of the island of Bissau as well. Descriptions of the island from previous centuries report the cultivation of rice along with a great mix of other crops. However, no early observers wrote of paddy cultivation, leaving open the possibility that Papel had long cultivated *arroz secca,* or dryland rice. One of the first accounts of Papel paddy cultivation is that of Philip Beaver, who said of his 1792 trip to the island:

> I had an opportunity when at Bissao, of once seeing the Papels prepare the ground for the lowland rice, in the beginning of August. With an instrument, something like that with which we cut turf, thrust about three inches under the soil, they first turned to the right, and then to the left; the soil thus turned up formed a little ridge on each side of the trench whence it was taken, and the trench was about a foot wide; when it rained, the water was retained in these trenches, and the rice sown in them; when the plants had attained a proper height, they were taken out, and transplanted in rows on the adjoining low lands.[31]

Decades later, Manuel António Martins reported the transplantation of rice into "artificial lagoons, which they call bulamhas" on Bissau.[32] And in 1841, José Conrad Carlos de Chelmicki noted that Papel transplanted rice into "bolanhas, natural or artificial wet areas, that they make with earthen barriers that conserve the water for a long time." He emphasized that this was not the only type of rice that Papel produced. They also cultivated *arroz secca.*[33] Papel, then, practiced a mixture of upland and lowland rice cultivation, perhaps because they were still perfecting wetland rice techniques.

In sum, Mande-speakers had developed paddy rice farming techniques in the coastal regions of the Upper Guinea Coast before the mid-fifteenth-century arrival of Atlantic merchants. However, Balanta began to cultivate large quantities of rice in *bolanha* areas only well after coastal populations in the Guinea-Bissau region began to bear the brunt of the slave raids that fed an expanding Atlantic economy and Atlantic merchants began to supply the Guinea-Bissau region with iron. Contemporary written sources indicate that for northern Balanta a paddy rice monoculture had begun to emerge by the mid-seventeenth century. However, southern Balanta in the Rio Geba area did not begin the large-scale clearing of mangroves and cultivating of paddy rice until the eighteenth century, after they had learned the techniques from their northern neighbors.

THE SPREAD OF *O. GLABERRIMA* AND *O. SATIVA* VARIETIES OF RICE

Balanta oral narratives state, "The first type of rice that Balanta knew was *n'contu;* after that *yaka, sila, thom,* and *eatanhã* were cultivated."[34] Also called *malu raça* (Balanta rice) and *malu mon* (black rice), *n'contu* is a type of *Oryza glaberrima,* a rice indigenous to Africa and cultivated long before the arrival of Atlantic merchants in the fifteenth century. The others are types of *Oryza sativa,* a rice indigenous to Asia and introduced to West Africa by Atlantic merchants in the sixteenth century.[35] Balanta farmers first planted *N'contu* in large part because it is a relatively easy rice to grow. *N'contu* is, as one Balanta explained, "resistant to salt water" and therefore can be planted on the least-fertile land and with relatively unsophisticated agricultural techniques.[36] It thrives where *O. sativa* varieties will not—on the edges of *bolanhas,* where soils are poor and fresh water is not very abundant.

There are other important differences between *O. glaberrima* and *O. sativa.* To the casual observer, the most striking difference is the color. *O. glaberrima* varieties are dark, and *O. sativa* varieties are white. Thinking dark rice was of poor quality, European and Cape Verdean merchants encouraged production of *O. sativa.* Further, Europeans preferred *O. sativa* varieties because they are not as brittle as *O. glaberrima,* which tends to break into small pieces when milled. Hence, in part because it was more marketable, *O. sativa* has today largely replaced *O. glaberrima* throughout Guinea-Bissau and the continent. Finally, on fertile lands most *O. sativa* varieties yield better and scatter considerably less seed on the ground than *O. glaberrima* varieties.[37] Thus the spread of *O. sativa* across the Guinea-Bissau region must have encouraged Balanta to step up the cultivation of *bolanhas* and would have enabled Balanta to sustain growing *tabanca* populations.

This is not to imply that *O. glaberrima* production has fallen off completely. Indeed, today in Guinea-Bissau many farmers plant indigenous rice for their own consumption, preferring its stronger flavor to that of the bland *O. sativa.* Further, varieties of *O. glaberrima* continue to be planted because they reach maturity more quickly than varieties of *O. sativa.* This ensures that stomachs will not go empty in October, when rice stores from the previous growing season may be running low. Finally, *O. glaberrima* varieties have broad canopies, which tend to suppress weed growth.[38] Emphasizing many of these points, Nambatcha explained:

> The first type of rice that Balanta knew was *n'contu.* . . . Today Balanta farm, in great quantities, other varieties of rice. This is not because they are more productive or resistant to salt than *n'contu* but because they are more profitable and are good food; however, they provide very little fodder for the pigs. *N'contu,* on the other hand, has a great deal of fodder for the pigs, but [the rice itself] is yellow when pounded. . . . *N'contu* has another importance in Balanta society: it has a short growing season. Because of this, today we cultivate *n'contu* to remedy the situation of hunger in the months of October, November, and December. It is important to emphasize that we cultivate *n'contu* only in small quantities so as to alleviate hunger in the most critical periods.[39]

Though *O. sativa* was introduced to the West African coast as early as the sixteenth century, local populations did not immediately cultivate it in the Guinea-Bissau region. In fact, Olga Linares found that among Diola in the Casamance region *O. sativa* was not planted until fairly recently.[40] Carlos de Chelmicki's 1841 statements confirm this. He noted that the Diola between the Cacheu and Casamance grew only "an ordinary rice, very small, but with a good taste." Its color, he reported, was dark. The planting of a whiter rice was being undertaken only in scattered locations on the edges of the Rio Cacheu.[41] The Gambia, Chelmicki emphasized, was the center for cultivation of *O. sativa*.[42] Thus it is likely that *O. sativa* spread south from the Gambia to the Casamance and then to the Cacheu. By the middle to late nineteenth century it was being planted in the Rio Geba area. It was then that officials, speaking of the Papel of Bissau, said, "The favorite work of the savages is the growing of rice *(oryza sativa, L.)* that constitutes their principal source of nutrition. The first sowing is done in May on the land made damp by the rains, and they transplant it later to the *bolanhas,* that is, dammed areas where rain water sits stagnant."[43] As late as the 1830s, Portuguese observers on Bissau complained that the rice produced there had a dark color.[44]

PADDY RICE AND ITS LABOR DEMANDS

Balanta may have transitioned to a paddy rice monoculture only very slowly, because doing so required the restructuring of community-based institutions so that workers could be organized for large-scale and labor-intensive projects, such as the clearing of mangroves and building of dikes. Mangrove rice cultivation required a greater amount of labor and greater level of social organization than perhaps any crop produced in precolonial West Africa. Indeed, the preparation of a rice paddy area was and still is a very laborious and time-consuming task. Among Balanta, work is allocated at the *tabanca* level, where age grades composed of members from multiple *moranças* are assigned specific tasks; at the *morança* level, where household members have certain tasks; and along gender lines.[45]

Residing on West Africa's *ria,* or sunken coast, Balanta grow paddy rice on the flats of rivers, such as the Cacheu, Mansoa, Geba, and Tombali. Due to its low elevation, the region's rivers are subjected to tidal surges of brackish waters for tens of miles inland. When tides rise, rivers swell and lowland areas (*thambe* in Graça, *bolanha* in Crioulo) flood. This creates a perfect environment for mangrove (*Rhizophora racemosa* and *Avicennia nitida*) forests.[46] It also creates ideal conditions for paddy rice to thrive, with rich silts providing nutrients and low elevations lending themselves to the accumulation of fresh rainwater as well as facilitating drainage when necessary. But

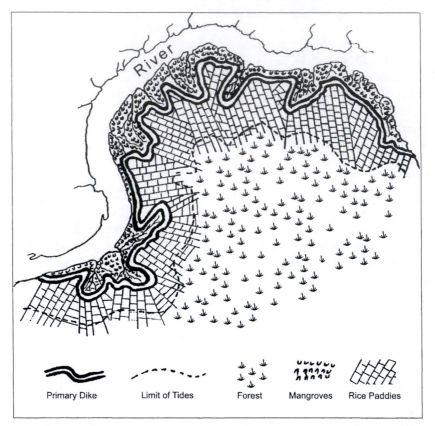

Figure 5.1   A *bolanha* with rice paddies. Adapted from an image in F. Rogado Quintino, *Prática e utensilagem agrícolas na Guiné* (Lisbon: Junta de Investigações do Ultramar, 1971), 52.

before paddies can be constructed, Balanta have to cut mangroves and desalinate the soil.

On the *tabanca* level, the eldest man of the founding *morança* has the power to allocate unclaimed land—both in *bolanhas* and on uplands areas (*lugars* in Crioulo)—to the *b'alante b'ndang* who head other *moranças* in a *tabanca*. Once a section of land has been designated for a household, the members of that household have rights to it. Sons inherit their fathers' lands, so paddies, nurseries, and other fields stay with the same family for generations, especially since the selling of *bolanhas* is taboo. Once lands are allocated, the eldest man of the founding *morança* has no control over how they are used.

However, through his connections with the spirit of the founder of the *tabanca,* he does decide when the households of the *tabanca* should begin to plant rice.

Before plots on *bolanhas* are allocated, *tabanca* councils meet to determine what sections should be cleared and delineated. Councils direct male age grades to delineate paddies first by constructing a primary dike (*quididê* in Graça, *orique centura* in Crioulo).[47] Because rice will not grow in saltwater, this dike is crucial for holding back tides. Age-grade-based work parties build a primary dike by cutting a path through mangroves and piling up mud to form a large bund, which is reinforced with posts. A typical dike is about 2.5 meters high and 3.5 meters wide at the base, but sometimes dikes are considerably larger, especially in places where the pressure of the tides is great.

Building a primary dike is incredibly labor-intensive, so much so that the workers from any one *morança* could not complete the task by themselves. Cooperation between *moranças* is absolutely necessary and is facilitated through age grades. Age grades have thus long linked the members of the independent households who form a *tabanca* into an organic whole and

Photo 5.1   Male age grades building a primary dike, date unknown. From the rare photo collection of Walter Hawthorne, date unknown.

allowed Balanta to undertake large and complex water management projects. For the most arduous task, Balanta have traditionally utilized young men in their teens and early twenties who form *nhaye* grades. A recent study called *nhaye* "the motor of Balanta society. It is *nhaye* who do the most work. . . . A youth in this phase should be able to endure any type of physical labor, from the working of the *bolanha* to the harvesting of rice."[48] For digging, male dike-builders use a long-handled wooden plow (*kebinde* in Graça) with a paddlelike end that is reinforced with an iron cutting edge. The *kebinde* is sometimes called a "fulcrum shovel" and is very similar to the Diola *cadyendo*, which is used to farm rice in the Casamance.[49]

The next step involves cutting mangroves and desalinating the soil. Once the primary dike is completed, mangroves are isolated from the river and begin to die. The ground is burned, removing some growth, but tough mangroves and their roots still have to be cut. Men do this work, using metal tools—machetes and axes. Because mangrove wood is dense and does not rot as rapidly other varieties, it is used in the construction of internal supporting structures for dikes. It is also an important fuel for cooking fires. Hence women often bundle what has been cut and carry it back to their *moranças*. After it is cleared of mangroves, the area is desalinated with freshwater brought by rains and trapped by the primary dike. The water leaches salt from the soil and is then discharged through the primary dike and into the river.

Photo 5.2   Balanta plowing fields with their *b'kebinde*, date unknown. From F. Rogado Quintino, *Prática e utensilagem agrícolas na Guiné* (Lisbon: Junta de Investigações do Ultramar, 1971), 65.

Since most rices will not grow well in salty soils, the leaching process is extremely important. It can take several rainy seasons—several years—to trap and discharge enough water to adequately desalinate a *bolanha* for planting.

Once the head of the founding *morança* has allocated parcels (what will soon be paddies) of newly claimed and desalinated *bolanhas* to *morança* heads (that is, to *b'alante b'ndang*), young male workers are directed to create paddies by constructing smaller, secondary dikes. These dikes separate one paddy from the next. Workers create these by piling mud into long mounds, which are reinforced with posts. The construction of secondary dikes is also very labor-intensive. The *alante ndang* who heads the *morança* that has claim to a certain parcel might direct his sons to carry out the work. However, he often attempts to contract the work out to male age-grade-based labor parties. Since these parties have no obligation to work for individual *moranças,* paddy owners compensate them with gifts of alcohol or pigs, which are saved for a celebration at the end of the agricultural season. *Moranças* might also contract males from particular age grades to assist in the harvesting and threshing of rice. Any inequalities among *moranças* are revealed during field preparation, harvesting, and threshing. A *morança* that has the ability to offer more gifts to age grades is often more successful in its requests for work groups.[50]

After paddies are constructed, their walls trap the fresh rainwater in which rice will grow. The level of the water has to be kept relatively constant, so many Balanta construct automatic water dischargers out of hollow logs into which are set stoppers on cords. They fit these into the outermost dike. These dischargers shut automatically with the rising of the tide, keeping saltwater out of paddies. They open when tides fall below the level of the stoppers and excess water brought by rains into the paddies flows through the water dischargers into the river. In the southern regions of Guinea-Bissau, Balanta tend not to construct water discharges, preferring to dig out a section of the dike at low tide to release water from paddies.

Throughout the rainy season, male and female farmers labor in their rice fields. Before the coming of the first rains in June, young men from an individual *morança* or male age grades contracted by an individual *morança* prepare nurseries on *lugars* situated near the *morança*. This work involves turning over soil to create long ridges. With the first rains, women from the *morança* sow rice in these nurseries. When the crop reaches a sufficient height, the same women transplant rice into paddies that have filled with fresh rainwater. If men have no other work to perform, they sometimes help with this painstaking task: each rice plant has to be pushed into the earth, one after the next by hand. The rice then matures in the paddies. But as it matures, paddies have to be monitored. Periodic weeding is necessary, and dikes have to be reinforced. Further, birds, monkeys, and other animals have to be kept away. Typically, young boys from the ages of about six to fourteen, who compose the first of the age grades, are allocated this task. Young girls are also sent to the fields, venturing there in their grades like the boys. They watch the rice by day, often with slings for whipping stones in the direction of offensive creatures.

Individual _moranças_ contract male age grades to harvest rice when it has matured. Often young men divide into teams so that they can compete to see who can harvest the most in a given day. _N'contu_, a type of _O. glaberrima_, may be ready for harvest as early as October. Other rices, particularly _O. sativa_ varieties, cannot be cut until December or later. Men harvest rice by hand by cutting it midway down the culm, or stem, with a curved iron knife made by blacksmiths. They then bundle what has been cut, and women transport the bundles to a cleared patch of land (_kindante_ in Graça) in the _bolanha_. There, men, sometimes in age-grade work groups, thresh the rice to remove the grain from the stem.

Women, children, and the elderly gather the grain from the ground, and women then carry it to the _morança_. Later, women and girls pound or mill

Photo 5.3 Rice paddies ready for harvest in Cufar, 1995. Photo by Walter Hawthorne.

the grain to remove the hulls (chaff) from the starchy endosperm. This is accomplished by placing rice in a mortar, which is fashioned from a hollowed-out section of a tree trunk, and striking it with a wooden pestle. Milling rice by hand with a mortar and pestle requires a good deal of skill. Women do not simply "pound" rice, since the application of too much force can break grains into small pieces. For sale and for domestic consumption, whole grains are preferable to broken ones. Judith Carney describes the milling process as involving a "tapping and rolling motion, where loosening the pestle grip at the right moment prior to striking the rice minimizes grain breakage."[51] Once they have milled the rice, women winnow it by pouring the grains and empty hulls into a shallow circular straw basket and then tossing the contents into the air. On a breezy day, the light hulls blow away while the heavier grains fall back into the basket. The milling and winnowing of rice may last until May, although January and February witness the greatest amount of these activities. Women place processed rice into enormous clay storage containers (*bafuul* in Graça), and the *alante ndang* of the *morança* decides how it will be allocated—some for consumption and some for sale by women who carry the crop to market or meet with merchants who visit the *tabanca*. Prior to milling, some rice is set aside for the planting of the next year's crop.

Once rice is harvested, processed, and stored, fields have to be prepared for the coming rainy season. Male youths heard cattle to the paddies to graze

Photo 5.4 Women milling rice in Cufar, 1995. Photo by Walter Hawthorne.

on the cut rice stalks, their dung providing fertilizer. Later, farmers flood their fields by opening dikes to bring in brackish water and the nutrients that they carry. Temporary submersion impedes soil oxidation and the subsequent development of acid sulfates, which are a significant problem for mangrove rice farmers. Acidic soils will not yield a crop, so *b'alante b'ndang* need to be highly skilled in soil management. They discharge the brackish water before commencing hoeing for the next season and rely on the first rains to leach salt from paddies.[52] In addition, dikes have to be reinforced and nurseries prepared. Moreover, as populations and markets expand, workers expand the production of rice commensurably. Hence they constantly have to claim new fields, push primary dikes closer to rivers' edges, and clear dense mangroves. In sum, paddy rice agriculture requires intense, organized, and yearlong inputs of labor from individuals acting in the interest of their *moranças* and from individuals acting in the interest of a *tabanca* as a whole.

THE CENTRALITY OF MALE LABOR TO PADDY RICE

At every stage of the paddy rice cycle, tasks are clearly gendered. Men build dikes, prepare fields, harvest the crop, and thresh it. Women's labor complements that of men: they sow seeds, transplant young rice plants, weed, transport the harvest, and mill, winnow, store, and market it. A similar gendered division of labor exists among other coastal mangrove rice producers. However, to the east on the freshwater floodplains of the Sahel and to the north on the Gambia, women perform almost all the labor (hoeing, harvesting, and processing) required for rice production; men contribute very little. Comparing coastal mangrove rice farming with interior freshwater-floodplain rice farming, Carney explains, "The role of female labor in each system varies in relationship to the significance of rice in the farming system, with male participation in cultivation more marked in cultures dependent on rice as the dietary staple. When rice assumes a less central role in the regional food system, the crop is often farmed solely by women."[53] That is, where rice is important for the sustenance of communities, men assume the most important roles in its production and are therefore highly valued as laborers.

Ursula Funk's observations dovetail nicely with Carney's. "Overall," she writes of Balanta communities, "men spend more days and more hours per day in field labour." Women do make a significant contribution to rice production and processing. Counting the total work hours, including food gathering, processing, and cooking, along with domestic work such as fetching water, cleaning, and child rearing, women work more hours per day than men. This makes women desirable in marriage.[54] But the tasks that men perform make them crucial to the entire paddy rice process. Without dikes, there would be no paddies; without paddies, Balanta could not produce enough food to sustain the populations of compact settlements.

In many ways, Balanta paddy rice production is centered on young male labor. Men's field tasks—especially the building of primary dikes—are highly gender specific; women do not undertake them. However, women's field tasks are not viewed the same way; if women are not available, men perform their tasks.[55] (The same cannot be said of women's domestic work, which men are loath to perform since it brings considerable shame upon them.) Noting the centrality of male labor, Funk writes that she heard many stories of worried husbands whose wives had not returned from trading ventures. Personal distress surely accounts for a good part of this worry. Further, the loss of their labor, especially around the household, would be dearly missed. But the loss of male labor was even more distressing to *tabanca* residents. "A shortage of male labour," she explains, "can have a negative impact on the production of staple crops because high yields, especially in wet rice production, are largely dependent on the intensification of men's tasks in the Brassa [Balanta] division of labour. As a consequence, elders apply social pressure to discourage young men from migrating during the peak agricultural season by citing their responsibilities to their elders."[56] As was demonstrated in Chapter 4, in the era of the Atlantic slave trade the pressure on young men to stay in the *tabancas* of their birth was tremendous. They were critical for defending communities, raiding for captives, and farming wetland rice.

The institutions that Balanta fashioned in the era of the Atlantic slave trade, then, took the form that they did largely as the result of intracommunity tensions—struggles along lines of generation and gender. *B'alante b'ndang* sought a means of controlling young men. The result was an age-grade system that placed great social pressure on young men to perform burdensome agricultural and military tasks, that offered them rewards (both material and psychological) if they stayed and worked with neighboring youths, and that held out to them the promise that they would one day inherit the power that their fathers wielded.

A MODIFICATION OF THE GENDERED DIVISION OF LABOR

What implications did the spread of paddy rice production have for the gendered division of labor in the Guinea-Bissau region? In many parts of Africa, the fact that men both performed military functions and were exported as slaves into the Atlantic in greater numbers than women meant that the demands placed on women to labor in fields producing sustenance for their communities increased, sometimes dramatically. Often existing patterns of labor organization by gender, in which women did most of the agricultural labor anyway, were reinforced.[57] In other cases, patterns of labor were modified, with women being forced to assume new productive roles with the loss of males.[58] Was this also the case in the Guinea-Bissau region? Given that women (and children) in coastal Guinea-Bissau were the principal victims of raids, that they were easier to incorporate into communities, and that they were sold to local and Atlantic merchants in greater numbers than were men, did the manner in which labor was allocated along lines of gender change, and if so, how? In what ways did the intensification of paddy rice production in the late seventeenth and eighteenth centuries affect patterns of labor organization in this politically decentralized area?

The problem we face in attempting to answer these questions is that we know very little about the gendered division of labor in the Guinea-Bissau region before the rise of the Atlantic slave trade and before the intensification of paddy rice production.[59] Only a very few vague descriptions exist. For example, speaking generally of the Upper Guinea Coast at the start of the seventeenth century, Balthasar Barreira wrote, "Agriculture is the main occupation of the people, and the women do the greater part of it."[60] Writing at about the same time, Manuel Álvares described the duties of Banyun women. Along with conducting trade for their husbands, "These women manure the land with the mud or dung they throw on it and they weed and harvest the staple crops and pound them in mortars."[61] Among Papel on the island of Bussis, women were "employed in the usual tasks, and they weed the fields in the appropriate seasons."[62]

If Balanta women performed the same tasks (conducting trade, planting, weeding, fertilizing, and pounding harvests) that Banyun and Papel women performed before the late seventeenth century, then the intensification of slaving and rise of a paddy rice monoculture after the late seventeenth century did not greatly affect Balanta women's working lives. These tasks were, after all, the ones Balanta women would perform after Balanta transitioned to a paddy rice monoculture.

However, if prior to the late seventeenth century women conducted the "greater part" of agricultural labor in Balanta communities, then the intensification of the slave trade and rise of a paddy rice monoculture brought about a revolutionary change in the working lives of young men as they assumed responsibility for most of the fieldwork for their communities. No longer would women be central to agricultural production. Young men became the most important producers of food, and the workloads of young men increased considerably.

On balance, then, the slave trade masculinized agriculture in Balanta regions. Does this mean that Balanta women's workloads were lightened? The short answer to this question is no. The tasks they performed did not radically change. However, the demands of paddy rice were much greater than those of yams and *milho,* which had been grown in earlier centuries, and the added demands were assumed by young men. Hence the value of young men in communities was great, so community leaders—*b'alante b'ndang*—searched for ways to retain them.

Young men also assumed a greater military role during this period (as discussed in Chapter 4). However, this did not significantly distract them from their agricultural duties. Across coastal Guinea-Bissau, most slave raids occurred in the months when the lowest inputs of male labor were needed in paddy rice production. According to figures presented by Jean Mettas, ships faced great difficulties in purchasing captives at Bissau and Cacheu between the months of August and October. Between 1758 and 1780, 94 percent of the ships that left Bissau and Cacheu did so between the months of December and July. Looking at Bissau alone between 1788 and 1794, Mettas notes that April, May, and June witnessed the greatest number of departures, an astonishing 65 percent. Mettas argues that this is because the rainy season made the shipment of slaves from the interior very difficult.[63] Further, the frequency of storms (with intense winds and rainfalls) probably effected Bijago raids as well, with seafaring voyages becoming dangerous during this season. But this is only a partial explanation for the cyclical decline in the number of slaves available for shipment from Bissau and Cacheu. Not all captives exported from Bissau and Cacheu, after all, came from deep in the interior or from suppliers on the Bijagos Islands.

Along with being the period of heaviest rains, August to October was the period of most intensive activity in *bolanhas,* not only for Balanta, but also for other rice-growing peoples such as Floup, Brame, and Papel. During these months, men and women were engaged in the work of reinforcing dikes, transplanting rice, and beginning preparations for the harvest. Raids, then, were curtailed when young male labor was needed most. Young males certainly worked in paddies in the months of April, May, and June, when new dikes were built. Further, plowing commenced with the coming of rains. But to do these things iron was needed, so the period of greatest slave exports corresponded with the period of greatest iron demand. This is likely the reason that a notable series of reports about Balanta raids for cattle and captives on Bissau in 1777 begin in June and July, end in August, and resume again in January 1778.[64] Both the cyclical pattern of the seasons and the cyclical demands on young male labor in coastal communities, then, determined the rhythms of the slave trade from the region.

If the intensification of slave raiding and the rise of a Balanta paddy rice monoculture in the late seventeenth and early eighteenth centuries brought revolutionary change to the working lives of young Balanta men, it had a very different effect in Bijago communities. The topography of the Bijagos Islands does not permit people to engage in paddy rice agriculture. The banks of the islands are very steep, providing few flat, marshy places for paddies. Hence, dryland rice and milho have long been the important staples. The islands, then, did not witness a great agricultural revolution in the seventeenth and eighteenth centuries. During this period, Bijago men dedicated themselves not to crop production but to "only three things: They make war, they build boats, and they draw wine from palm-trees."[65] At least two of those three tasks (warring and boatbuilding) were labor-intensive. Indeed, before they could conduct raids, Bijago men had to invest a great deal of time and energy into the construction of large oceangoing vessels, some of which were manned by dozens of rowers.[66]

As war became the principal occupation of Bijago men, agriculture became the principal occupation of Bijago women. On the islands, Francisco de Lemos Coelho wrote in the second half of the seventeenth century, "It is the women who work the land, sow the seed, and build the houses in which the Bijagos live . . . . In addition to all this work, the women go daily down to the sea to collect shellfish . . . in order to feed their husbands, their brothers and the remainder of their family." [67] Others made similar observations about Bijago. André Álvares de Almada, for example, said, "The women build the houses and work the fields, and they fish and gather shell-fish, doing all that men do elsewhere."[68] Manuel Álvares wrote, "It is on the women that everything depends. They are the ones who work the land, after cutting down and burning the bush; and they build the houses. In general, in the same way as slaves do for us, the women look after the men, and when the latter are on land they have nothing to do except tap wine and have a good time."[69] Similarly, Beaver said that Bijago women "seemed to perform all the menial domestic duties."[70]

Because they were crucial to the maintenance of island communities and because they were easier to capture than men, mainland women became the principal targets of Bijago raids. Evidently many raids were successful. Some Bijago men were said to "have twenty or thirty wives, and no one has only one." Bijago raiders also seized children. Like women, they were not as dangerous to capture as men and could be integrated into island social structures. Thus, in Bijago villages, children were said to be as numerous as in "a beehive."[71]

With Bijago men fully dedicating themselves to raiding and trading captives, the demands on women's agricultural labor increased dramatically in the period of the Atlantic slave trade. To the contrary, in Balanta communities that dedicated themselves partly to raiding and trading captives and partly to the undertaking of new and very complex agricultural pursuits, the demands on women's agricultural labor did not change dramatically. The Atlantic slave trade, then, did not necessarily intensify gender inequality everywhere, leading to greater demands being placed on women in domestic economies.[72] The impact of the slave trade on Africa was varied. Communities and the individuals who composed them reacted differently to the pressures brought to bear by an expanding Atlantic system. Across Africa people shaped local institutions in myriad ways. They placed new demands on youths, women, and men, but these demands were not the same in all places.

CONCLUSION

As the frequency of violent slave raids intensified in the Guinea-Bissau region, Balanta reacted by adopting a settlement pattern that could better ensure the safety of members of independent *moranças*. Concentrating *moranças* into *tabancas*, Balanta fashioned institutions through which members of independent households could foster broad village identities and undertake large projects such as producing captives that could be exchanged for valuable imports, and cultivating new crops that could sustain dense populations.

The institutions through which Balanta organized their lives in this very violent period were fashioned during struggles that ensued among the individuals who formed *tabancas*. Thus they reflected tensions between old and young, and men and women. Community-based struggles resulted in *b'alante b'ndang* finding ways to shield young men from contact with "outsiders" while giving them incentives to stay in their natal communities and to perform tremendous amounts of labor. The same institutions encouraged women to make contacts with outsiders. They sometimes exploited these contacts to better their own lives as well as those of their families. For Balanta women, then, the period brought both new opportunities for trade and the real danger of being seized by raiders. For young men, it brought increased agricultural work, new military demands, and the promise that they would one day assume positions of authority in their egalitarian communities.

On the whole, the period saw revolutionary transformations in the daily lives of all Balanta. A new crop was adopted, population densities increased, and as we shall see in the next chapter, population sizes began to increase dramatically as a paddy rice monoculture brought tremendous surpluses to Balanta communities, surpluses that could be used to feed expanding numbers of people. Though the politically decentralized Balanta sat on the slaving frontiers of one of West Africa's largest predatory states, the seventeenth and eighteenth centuries were hardly a period of decay for Balanta society. Clearly many individuals found themselves in bondage, but Balanta society itself, and many of the communities that composed it, survived.

NOTES

1. See Diane Lima Handem, "O arroz ou a indentidade Balanta Brassa," *Soronda* 1 (1986): 55–67.

2. This information is from personal observations and informal conversations. For published sources, see J. D. Lea, Cornelius Hugo, and Carlos Rui Ribeiro, *Rice Production and Marketing in Guinea-Bissau,* report no. 118 (Washington, D.C.: U.S. Department of State, U.S. Agency for International Development, 1990); and Carlos Rui Ribeiro, "Arroz na mentalidade Balanta," *Boletim de Informação Sócio-Económica* 2 (1988): 1–11.

3. Interview with Bitar Nabidé, Thamba Nanghasen, and Cumé Nanghasen, Oko, February 18, 1995. Also interview with Saé Namghomdé, Cufar, March 3, 1995.

4. Assuming that "primitive" societies could only increase productive capacities by developing hierarchies, scholars have long held that the "development of rank and chieftainship becomes *pari passu* development of the productive force." See Marshall Marshall Sahlins, *Stone Age Economics* (Chicago: Aldine, 1972), 140. On "hydraulic societies," see Karl A. Wittfogel, *Oriental Despotism: A Comparative Study of Total Power* (New Haven, Conn.: Yale University Press, 1957), 18; Julian H. Steward, *Theory of Cultural Change* (Urbana: University of Illinois Press, 1955); William P. Mitchell, "The Hydraulic Hypothesis: A Reappraisal," *Current Anthropology* 14, no. 5 (1973): 532–534; R. A. L. H. Gunawardana, "Social Function and Political Power: A Case Study of State Formation in Irrigation Society," in *The Study of the State,* eds. Henri J. M. Claessen and Peter Skalník (The Hague: Mouton, 1981), 133–154; and Robert Adams, *The Evolution of Urban Society: Early Mesopotamia and Prehistoric Mexico* (Chicago: Aldine, 1966).

5. Albert van Dantzig, "Effects of the Atlantic Slave Trade on Some West African Societies," in *Forced Migration: The Impact of the Export Slave Trade on African Societies,* ed. Joseph E. Inikori (New York: Africana, 1982), 187–201. See also M. B. Gleave and R. M. Prothero, "Population Density and 'Slave Raiding': A Comment," *Journal of African History* 12, no. 2 (1971): 321–323; John K. Thornton, "Sexual Demography: The Impact of the Slave Trade on Family Structure," in *Women and Slavery in Africa,* eds. Claire C. Robertson and Martin A. Klein (Madison: University of Wisconsin Press, 1983), 41; and Joseph E. Inikori, introduction to Joseph E. Inikori, ed., *Forced Migration: The Impact of the Export Slave Trade on African Societies* (London: Hutchison University Press, 1982), 41–51.

6. Pier M. Larson, *History and Memory in the Age of Enslavement: Becoming Merina in Highland Madagascar, 1770–1822* (Portsmouth, N.H.: Heinemann, 2000), 218; Paul E. Lovejoy, *Transformations in Slavery: A History of Slavery in Africa* (Cambridge: Cambridge University Press, 1983), 34.

7. Martin Klein and Claire Robertson claim that "there is no reason to suspect that in precolonial times women did not perform most of the agricultural work." Martin A. Klein and Claire C. Robertson, "Women's Importance in African Slave Systems," Robertson and Klein, *Women and Slavery,* 9. David Eltis states, "Given the centrality of women in West African agriculture and textiles, the work of women was closer to the core of the African economy than was its English counterpart." David Eltis, *The Rise of African Slavery in the Americas* (Cambridge: Cambridge University Press, 2000), 92. See also Susan Herlin Broadhead "Slave Wives, Free Sisters: Bakongo Women and Slavery, c. 1700–1850," in Robertson and Klein, *Women and Slavery,* 171; Sandra Greene, *Gender, Ethnicity, and Social Change on the Upper Slave Coast: A History of the Anlo-Ewe* (Portsmouth, N.H.: Heinemann, 1996), 11; Larson, *History and Memory,* 131; and Thorton, "Sexual Demography," 44.

8. G. Ugo Nwokeji, "African Conceptions of Gender and the Slave Traffic," *William and Mary Quarterly* 58 (January 2001): 47–69.

9. See Chapter 2. D. G. Coursey and R. H. Booth show, "The cultivation of yams not only antedates European contact, but also the beginning of the use of iron tools in Africa." D. G. Coursey and R. H. Booth, "Root and Tuber Crops," in *Food Crops of the Lowland Tropics,* eds. C. L. A. Leakey and J. B. Willis (Oxford: Oxford University Press, 1977), 84. See also D. G. Coursey, *Yams: An Account of the Nature, Origins, Cultiva-*

tion, and Utilisation of the Useful Members of the Dioscoreaceae (London: Longman: 1967), 13.

10. Olga F. Linares, "Deferring to Trade in Slaves: The Jola of Casamance, Senegal, in Historical Perspective," *History in Africa* 14 (1987): 113–139; George E. Brooks, *Landlords and Strangers: Ecology, Society, and Trade in Western Africa, 1000–1630* (Boulder, Colo.: Westview Press, 1993), 87–89. Also see Chapter 2.

11. Interview with Alfrede Neves, Chiguna Clusse, and Bcolof Sukna, Patche Ialá, January 31, 1995.

12. Interview with Fô Kidum, Quinhaque, January 7, 1995.

13. Alberto Gomes Pimentel, "Circumscrição civil de Mansôa: Etnografia," *Boletim Official da Guiné Portuguesa* 50 (December 10, 1927), 4.

14. Avelino Teixeira da Mota, *Guiné portuguesa*, vol. 1 (Lisbon: Agência Geral do Ultramar, 1954), 208.

15. Olga F. Linares "Agriculture and Diola Society," in *African Food Production Systems: Cases and Theory*, ed. F. M. McLoughlin (Baltimore: Johns Hopkins University Press, 1970), 211; Olga F. Linares "From Tidal Swamp to Inland Valley: On the Social Organization of Wet Rice Cultivation Among the Diola of Senegal," *Africa* 51 (1981): 579; J. do Espírito Santo, "Notas sobre a cultura do arroz etre os balantas," *Boletim Cultural da Guiné Portuguesa* 4, no. 14 (April 1949): 197–233; Robert Martin Baum, *Shrines of the Slave Trade: Diola Religion and Society in Precolonial Senegambia* (Oxford: Oxford University Press, 1999), 30. Others put the average adult's annual rice consumption at between 180 and 365 kilograms. See Baum, *Shrines,* 197n. Whatever the case, paddy rice farmers tend to have high yields and surpluses. A survey of the scientific research conducted on yams and rice reveals that each of the crops offers certain biological advantages over the other. Coursey and Booth estimate that with the "simple" planting methods used by African subsistence yam farmers, yields are about 5–10 tons per hectare per crop. The yields for wetland rice appear to be lower: 1–3 tons per hectare according to R. Chabolin's estimates for West Africa and 1.5–3 tons per hectare according to António Castro's study of Guinea-Bissau. If wetland rice provides slightly lower yields than yams, it offers consumers more protein. Coursey writes that in Africa, "Rice is by far the most favoured competitor, and is, of course, nutritionally superior to yams." Coursey and Booth, "Root and Tuber Crops," 85; R. Chabolin, "Rice in West Africa," in Leakey and Willis, *Food Crops,* 9–10; António Castro, "Notas sobre algumas variedades de arroz em cultura na Guiné portuguesa," *Boletim Cultural da Guiné Portuguesa* 5, no. 19 (July 1950): 347–378; D. G. Coursey and P. H. Haynes, "Root Crops and Their Potential as Food in the Tropics," *World Crops* 22 (1970): 260–265. See also Coursey, *Yams,* 141–144.

16. Judith Carney writes that "mangrove rice is the highest-yielding crop in the West African rice region." Judith Carney, *Black Rice: The African Origins of Rice Cultivation in the Americas* (Cambridge: Harvard University Press, 2001), 65. See also Philip D. Curtin, *Economic Change in Precolonial Africa: Senegambia in the Era of the Slave Trade* (Madison: University of Wisconsin Press, 1975), 28–29.

17. See Coursey, *Yams,* 172–189.

18. Joseph Jerome Lauer, "Rice in the History of the Lower Gambia-Geba Area" (M.A. thesis, University of Wisconsin, 1969), 48. See also Carney, *Black Rice,* 43, 69, 72–73, 142–147, 154, 156, 159, 164.

19. Interview with Mam Nambatcha, Cufar, December 2, 1994. Also interview with N'Sar N'Tchala, Bera, April 5, 1995, on maize production in the Geba/Mansoa region.

20. Manuel Álvares, *Ethiopia Minor and a Geographical Account of the Province of Sierra Leone,* trans. P.E.H. Hair (Liverpool: University of Liverpool, Department of History, September 30, 1990), chap. 12.

21. See P.E.H. Hair's comments in André Donelha, *Descrição da Serra Leoa e dos rios De Guiné do Cabo Verde (1625),* ed. Avelino Teixeira da Mota, trans. P.E.H. Hair, Centro de Estudos de Cartografia Antiga no. 19 (Lisbon: Junta de Investigações Científicas do Ultramar, 1977), 180B, 209.

22. Álvares, *Ethiopia Minor,* chap. 13.

23. Sieur Michel Jajolet de La Courbe, *Premier voyage du Sieur de La Courbe fait a la coste de l'Afrique en 1685,* ed. Prosper Cultru (Paris: E. Champion, 1913), 208–209.

24. Lauer, "Rice," 28.

25. Walter Rodney, *A History of the Upper Guinea Coast, 1545 to 1800* (New York: Monthly Review Press, 1970), 21–22; Olga F. Linares, "Shell Middens of the Lower Casamance and Problems of Diola Protohistory," *West African Journal of Archaeology* 1 (1971): 22–54. Peter Mark argues that it was in the late seventeenth and early eighteenth centuries that Diola began to intensively farm paddy rice and to expand their populations. Peter Mark, *A Cultural, Economic, and Religious History of the Basse Casanance Since 1500* (Stuttgart: Franz Steiner Verlag Wiesbaden GMBH, 1985), 28.

26. J. B. Labat, *Nouvelle relation de l'Afrique occidentale* (Paris: Cavelier, 1728), 188.

27. Francisco de Lemos Coelho, *Description of the Coast of Guinea (1684),* trans. P.E.H. Hair (Liverpool: University of Liverpool, Department of History, 1985), chap. 4.

28. La Courbe, *Premier voyage,* 251.

29. Arquivo Histórico Ultramarino (AHU) (Lisbon, Portugal), Guiné, cx. 11, docs. 20, 43, 57.

30. Bernardino António Álvares de Andrade, *Planta da praça de Bissau e suas adjacentes,* ed. Damião Peres (Lisbon: Academia Portuguesa da História, 1952), 46.

31. Philip Beaver, *Africa Memoranda* (London: Dawsons of Pall Mall, 1968), 346.

32. Manuel António Martins, "Memória demonstrativa do estado actual das praças de Bissau, Cacheu e suas dependências em África, parte da história sobre sua fundação, com o plano de reforma mais acomodada às circunstâncias de Portugal," in "Os problemas de Bissau, Cacheu e suas dependências vistos em 1831 por Manuel António Martins," ed. J. Faro, *Boletim Cultural da Guiné Portuguesa* 50 (1958): 203–218.

33. José Conrado Carlos de Chelmicki, *Corografia Cabo Verdiana* (Lisbon: Typ. de L.C. da Cunha, 1841), 186.

34. Interview with Tchong Binhom and Wangna Sanhá, N'talod, January 25, 1995. Also interviews with N'Dafa Na Combé, Mato-Farroba, December 12, 1994; Tona Na Isna and Suna Na Isna, Cantoné, March 5, 1995; Tchuta Mbali, Patche Ialá, January 8, 1995; Frós Intchalá and Ndum Mhana, Ilonde, January 28, 1995; and Alfrede Neves, Chiguna Clusse,and Bcolof Sukna, Patche Ialá, January 31, 1995.

35. I have derived the vernacular names for rice from personal observations and informal interviews. For more on vernacular and scientific names of rice grown in Guinea-Bissau, see J. do Espírito Santo, *Nomes vernáculos de algumas plantas da Guiné portuguesa* (Lisbon: Junta de Investigações Científicas do Ultramar, 1963); and Castro, "Notas," 347–350.

36. Interview with Nhafede Sambe and Abna Dafa, Blimat, January 28, 1995.

37. A. J. Carpenter, "The History of Rice in Africa," in *Rice in Africa,* eds. I. W. Buddenhagen and G. J. Persley (New York: Academic Press, 1978), 4–5; Castro, "Notas," 347–350; Board on Science and Technology for International Development, *Lost Crops of Africa,* vol. 1, *Grains* (Washington, D.C.: National Academy Press, 1996), 21.

38. Ibid.

39. Interview with Mam Nambatcha, Cufar, March 3, 1995. Also interview with Tchong Binhom and Wangna Sanhá, N'Talod, January 25, 1995.

40. Linares, "From Tidal Swamp," 558–559.

41. Chelmicki, *Corografia,* 136.

42. Ibid.; José Joaquim Lopes de Lima, *Ensaios sobre a statistica das possessões portuguezas no Ultramar,* vol. 1, *Das ilhas de Cabo Verde e suas dependências* (Lisbon: Imprensa Nacional, 1844), 24.

43. Luiz Frederico de Barros, *Senegambia portugueza* (Lisbon: Mattos Mareira, 1878), 43.

44. AHU, Guiné, cx. 25, documents without dates, doc. 25 (references indicate that this document was written in the 1830s); Martins, "Memória," 207.

45. Information on Balanta rice production is taken from personal observations and informal interviews. For published material, see Santo, "Notas," 197–233; Pablo Sdersky, "As relações de trabalho numa sociedade de cultivadores de arroz: O caso dos Balantas de Tombali," *Soronda* 3 (1987): 21–38; Fernando R. Quintino, *Prática e utiensilagem agrícolas na Guiné* (Lisbon: Junta de Investigações Científicas do Ultramar, 1971); Handem, "O arroz," 55–67; and Ursula Funk, "Land Tenure, Agriculture, and Gender in Guinea-Bissau," in *Agriculture, Women, and Land: The African Experience,* ed. Jean Davison (Boulder, Colo.: Westview Press, 1988), 33–58.

46. Linares "Shell Middens," 26.

47. Sometimes lands are cleared of mangroves before the primary dike is built.

48. Agostinho Clode Suba et al., "As estructuras sociais balantas," *Bombolom* 1 (n.d.): 9.

49. See especially Baum's description of Diola rice farming in *Shrines,* 28–31.

50. See especially Funk, "Land Tenure," 43.

51. Carney, *Black Rice,* 111–113, 124–125.

52. See especially ibid., 64–65.

53. Ibid., 26–27, 52–53; Chelmicki, *Corografia,* 188. While in Gambia-area Mandinka communities, Francis Moore wrote that "the men work the corn ground and women and girls the rice ground." Francis Moore, "The Men Work the Corn Ground and Women and Girls the Rice Ground," *Travels into the Inland Parts of Africa* (London: Edward Cave, 1738), 127. And in 1841 Carlos de Chelmicki noted that interior Mandinka women did the digging for rice cultivation.

54. Funk, "Land Tenure," 43–44.

55. This is the reverse of what Claude Meillassoux sees as the typical pattern in Africa, in which men could sometimes replace women as laborers, but women "more often replaced men, even in the most painful tasks." He argues that female slaves were more valued in African than male slaves, because women performed most of the work in Africa. Claude Meillassoux, "Female Slavery," in Robertson and Klein, *Women and Slavery,* 55–56.

56. Funk, "Land Tenure," 46.

57. See, for example, Nwokeji, "African Conceptions," 47–67; Lovejoy, *Transformations,* 129–130; John K. Thornton, "The Slave Trade in Eighteenth Century Angola: Effects on Demographic Structures," *Canadian Journal of African Studies* 14, no. 3 (1980): 419–420, 423–424; and Thornton, "Sexual Demography," 39–46.

58. Larson, *History and Memory,* 124–131.

59. See Thornton, "Sexual Demography," 46.

60. Quoted in P.E.H. Hair and Avelino Teixeira da Mota, eds., *Jesuit Documents on the Guinea of Cape Verde and the Cape Verde Islands, 1585–1617* (Liverpool: University of Liverpool, Department of History, 1989), doc. 13.

61. Álvares, *Ethiopia Minor,* chap. 7.

62. Ibid., chap. 8.

63. Jean Mettas, "La traite portugaise en haute Guinée," *Journal of African History* 16, no. 3 (1975): 347–348. My own calculations, made from David Eltis, Stephen D. Behrendt, David Richardson, and Herbert S. Klein, eds., *The Trans-Atlantic Slave: A Database on CD-ROM* (Cambridge: Cambridge University Press, 1999), point to the same conclusion. Of the eleven ships whose months of departure are noted in the database, ten (91 percent) departed from Bissau or Cacheu between December and July over the period 1700 to 1839. Identification numbers: 31533, 9073, 9079, 9077, 7613, 2898, 3013, 2697, 11371, 2483, 30821.

64. AHU, Guiné, cx. 11–12.

65. André Álvares de Almada, *Tratado breve dos rios de Guiné,* trans. P.E.H. Hair (Liverpool: University of Liverpool, Department of History, 1984), 93.

66. Almada described these boats as "large," carrying "many people." Álvares wrote, "Canoes ride level with the water, but it is the habit of the Bijagos to raise [the sides] with two planks that we call false-sides, fitted on top, so that the canoes can ride deeper and carry more robbers and loot. A canoe normally carries 22–24 men, each rowing; and as well as the men it carries their weapons." Almada, *Tratado breve* (Hair's ed.), 97; Álvares, *Ethiopia Minor,* chap. 9.

67. Coelho, *Description,* chap. 7.

68. Almada, *Tratado breve* (Hair's ed.), 93.

69. Álvares, *Ethiopia Minor,* chap. 10.

70. Beaver, *Africa Memoranda,* 337–338.

71. Quoted in Thornton, "Sexual Demography," 44.

72. Nwokeji, "African Conceptions," 66.

6

POLITICAL, ECONOMIC, AND AGRICULTURAL PATTERNS IN THE NINETEENTH CENTURY

At the start of the nineteenth century, Balanta communities, like others in the Guinea-Bissau region, were producing wealth and reproducing themselves by growing wetland rice and raiding distant villages, isolated households, and merchant vessels for captives and material goods. In so doing, Balanta were responding to the demands of their own populations and an expanding Atlantic economic system. However, the demands of the Atlantic system would soon begin to shift. Europe and the United States were industrializing. As a result, attitudes about labor were changing. Espousing the virtues of free labor, capitalists attacked the institution of slavery. Further, in legislatures and churches and on factory floors and plantations, voices—of the free and enslaved—were increasingly raised against the inhumanity of a system that for several hundred years had forced the migration of millions of Africans to the Americas.

The slow death of slavery did not bring an end to the centuries-long relationship among West Africa, Europe, and the Americas. To the contrary, as the slave trade drew to a slow close, Europeans and Americans were increasingly attracted to Africa's shores. They went seeking "legitimate" or nonslave goods that would fuel industrial growth and feed the desires of a growing middle class. Among the items that they demanded from West Africa were increasing quantities of beeswax, palm oil, peanuts, rubber, ivory, and rice. As they had in the era of the Atlantic slave trade, local institutions influenced the economic decisions that Guinea-Bissau's coastal people made, shaping the manner in which they reacted to the pressures of an expanding and fickle Atlantic economy.

Scholars have long debated the effect that the end of the Atlantic slave trade had on African states and their structures o power.[1] Following Kenneth Dike, Anthony Hopkins proposed that the transi ion from slave to nonslave exports presented the leaders of African states with a "crisis of adaptation" rising "from a contradiction between past and present relations of production."[2] The notion that the nineteenth-century rise of a trade in "legitimate" goods brought revolutionary change to social and economic structures in Africa is contested by a handful of historians, who have also chosen states as their primary units of analysis. For example, in an examination of "West African trading states," Ralph Austen sees the transition from slave to palm oil production as "adaptation without revolution," states succeeding in maintaining their traditional institutions.[3] Similarly, Martin Lynn argues that the "trading institutions in brokering states survived the transition" from slaves to non-slave goods.[4]

By focusing on the production of "legitimate" goods in a decentralized region, this chapter offers a different look at the nineteenth century.[5] It is particularly concerned with the role of Balanta communities in producing and marketing paddy rice. In the nineteenth century, Balanta discovered new trading partners: Cape Verdean settlers, or *ponteiros,* who married into Balanta communities and linked Balanta with Atlantic merchants. Among the exports valued by those merchants was rice. Hence, to meet international as well as regional demands for a crop that they were very skilled at producing, Balanta expanded paddy rice production to the point that land became scarce. Conflicts ensued but did not result in powerful groups dominating weaker ones. Unable to meet their needs in the areas that they occupied, many Balanta uprooted themselves and moved to new lands. As they did, they maintained their decentralized political system and continued to organize themselves through institutions forged in the era of the Atlantic slave trade. The nineteenth century did not, then, present Balanta with a "crisis of adaptation." It presented them with opportunities that they managed effectively. By the start of the twentieth century, Balanta regions contained some of the densest populations on the Upper Guinea Coast and Balanta directed rice-production systems that were the envy of the Portuguese.

THE OFFICIAL PORTUGUESE PRESENCE IN GUINEA-BISSAU

As they had for centuries, most coastal people in Guinea-Bissau remained free from political control of interior state-based groups and would-be colonizers throughout the nineteenth century, and they did so despite Portuguese efforts to tighten any tenuous holds that they had in the region. In an attempt to shore up its position vis-à-vis France and Great Britain at the start of the century, Portugal designated Bissau and Cacheu as captaincies, thereby staking claims over ports from which its ships had long traded. After a series of administrative changes, an area dubbed *Guiné Portugueza* (Portuguese Guinea) was made a district of the governor-general of Cape Verde in 1836. A district governor resided in Bissau. He commanded detachments of soldiers stationed on the island and in Cacheu, Farim, Geba, and Ziguinchor. Other military posts were created later.[6] From these locations, the governor and other officials of Portugal's government attempted to enforce trade regulations. However, as R. J. Hammond makes clear, "The Portuguese dominions on the African mainland were quite limited in extent so far as direct sovereignty was concerned, whatever their claims might have been under the vaguer headings of suzerainty or sphere of influence."[7] Thus, official Portugal sat by and watched as Africans, Luso Africans, Cape Verdeans, and European merchants (*negociantes* or *comerciantes*) produced, traded, and transported an array of goods from coastal communities and entrepôts to regional ports.

At Bissau, the governor remained for the most part held up in the Praça de José de Bissau, which had been constructed by the Company of Grão Para e Maranhão.[8] This fort had strong 40-foot-high stone walls that formed a square, at the corners of which were four bulwarks, and all of this was surrounded by trenches. It was the only place in the region where Portuguese troops could feel a modicum of protection. However, life there was far from comfortable. By midcentury the fort had barracks for 200 soldiers, a church, a customs house, and a "very large store-house, built of stone and covered with tiles."[9] But as the governor pointed out, the troop quarters were "about to fall down and for this the better part of the soldiers live in grass huts." In the officers' quarters, it rained "like in the street."[10]

Further, though defended by walls, Portugal's state representatives were still at the mercy of their African neighbors. Troops needed to leave the fort for food and water, and when tensions flared between local Papel and their Portuguese guests, access to these things was sometimes denied. In 1818, when Governor Joaquim António Matos pointed two cannons at a Papel village near the fort, "the Papels forbade their wives to carry anything to the market of Bissao, so that the settlement was soon in a state of famine: the people were reduced to the necessity of eating all the cassada [cassava] which grew in the gardens of the inhabitants." Unable to settle this crisis by force, Matos sent his African wife to work out an agreement with the Papel king.[11] Decades later, the Portuguese had yet to improve their military position vis-à-vis local African communities. Francisco Travassos Valdez explained:

> A well which had formerly been sunk is now dry; the soldiers and inhabitants are therefore obliged to obtain water from the Fonte do Rey, or king's fountain, which is situated about a mile west of the town, on ground belonging to the natives; and when any disagreement occurs the latter immediately take possession of the fountain, and the Portuguese are obliged to fight for their daily supply.[12]

The state of other "fortresses" in Portuguese Guinea was even more deplorable. The military detachment at Cacheu was protected by little more than rotting wooden palisades, and at Geba, Farim, and Ziguinchor soldiers held up behind bastions made up of dirt mounds that turned to mud during the rainy season.[13]

Conditions being what they were, Portuguese Guinea was far from a choice post for anyone in Portugal's service. Thus, at the turn of the nineteenth century, the detachments stationed there were mainly composed of the dregs, or *degredados,* of the Portuguese army. They were convicts and undesirables who had been given what amounted in many cases to a death sentence—a post in West Africa. Though a small number of Portuguese soldiers survived, took native wives, profited as traders, and eventually returned to Portugal or lived out long lives on the coast, many were unable to adapt to the region's harsh environment. On the mosquito-infested shores, many died from malaria while others succumbed to dysentery or one of the myriad diseases that ran rampant due to poor sanitary conditions in the Portuguese "strongholds."

Over the course of the century, Portuguese troops were increasingly replaced with Guinean-born recruits.[14] Some of these men were black and others were of Luso African origin, the products of relationships between Portuguese soldiers and native women. Further, "incorrigible and thieving" Cape Verdeans were called upon for service.[15] Soldiers of all colors, lacking shoes and uniforms, "most of them . . . clothed in rags" and some nude, were paid with bars of iron, tobacco, or rum.[16] At times they received payment in paper bills, but these suffered "a discount of more than 50% in the shops."[17] Officers faired little better than recruits, the only difference being that they had "more wants, in consequence of the mode in which they have been brought up."[18]

Contemporary accounts paint a vivid picture of the life in Portuguese posts on the Upper Guinea Coast in the early nineteenth century. During an 1818 stopover in Geba, Gaspard Mollien described the tentativeness of the Portuguese position and the suffering of the Portuguese unfortunate enough to reside there:

> Geba is a village entirely of mud houses; there is no fort; some black soldiers cause respect to be paid to the government, which is supported by mildness rather than by actual force. Bounded on the south by a marshy river, and on the east by mountains, it is perhaps one of the most unhealthy spots on the face of the globe. I saw but three Europeans there, but their faces were so emaciated by the pernicious influence of the climate that they might have been taken for spectres returned from the tomb.[19]

And life in Bissau was equally bad. Having stayed in Bissau for six weeks in 1824, Jehudi Ashmun, an agent for the American Colonization Society in Liberia, said that one in ten of the Portuguese soldiers survived for a year in Bissau. The conditions he described were horrific: "Woe to the wretch that falls sick. He is carried off alive to death's ante-chamber—a building constructed of mud and stone, covered with thatch, floored with earth, and having neither bedstead, table, chair, stool nor blanket in it! I visited it last Sunday with the commandant of the place. About thirty miserables lay stretched on the ground, with nothing under them but a thin mat."[20]

Since the Portuguese government did not meet even their most basic needs, soldiers were at best insolent and at worst mutinous. British Captain W. F. W. Owen, who was charting the coast, reported that in May 1825 the garrison at Bissau "had mutinied, confined the governor, and put several of his officers to death." Apparently, Owen's arrival scared the mutineers; seventeen of them fled up the Rio Geba and a number were arrested.[21] Powerful local merchant Caetano Nozolini also played a part in putting down the rebellion. Disturbed by the thought of troops interfering with his commercial enterprise, he assembled a force of sixty Manjaco, who helped restore order.[22] This was not the last rebellion that the fort would face. In December 1839 the entire military corps in Bissau, with the exception of about seven soldiers, again mutinied, shooting an official, breaking into the prison and depository, and pointing artillery at a commander. This time peace was restored when the rebellious troops were given passage to Cape Verde and replaced by what Governor Honório Pereira Barreto sarcastically labeled "40 men called Soldiers."[23]

Holed up in a small fort, ill-clothed, and lacking sure access to the necessities of food and water, a small and sickly band of Portuguese administrators and mutinous troops hardly wielded influence over any part of Portuguese Guinea in the first three quarters of the nineteenth century. In the words of Governor Barreto, "Miserably, one could say that in these Possessions there is a Governor and Commanders but there is not a Government."[24] Official Portuguese could not dominate Africans politically or militarily, and they could not control regional trade. Mollien was perhaps not going far enough in portraying the weakness of the Portuguese position when he wrote, "There cannot be a milder government for the Negroes than that of the Portuguese." The blacks "are free to assume a perfect equality with Europeans."[25] Ashmun's critique of the Portuguese "power" in Bissau was even more stinging: "Let the pitiable pride which fancies the colour of the white man's skin, a certificate of his superiority written by the hand of the Creator, and legible to the most unlettered, make a voyage to Bissao. . . . Here a black man would resent the insult of being stigmatized a white. Our colour is here prima facie evidence of our contemptibleness."[26]

THE SLOW DEATH OF THE SLAVE TRADE

Though their official presence in the region was weak, the Portuguese government attempted to effect political and economic change by ending the slave trade and taxing the trade in "legitimate" goods. The year 1810 marked the signing of an Anglo-Portuguese treaty that prohibited the export of slaves from Guinea. Other legislation followed: in 1815 the trafficking of slaves north of the equator was prohibited; in 1817 the transporting of slaves aboard a Portuguese vessel was outlawed; and in 1836 the exportation of slaves from any Portuguese territory was abolished.[27] However, the trade of slaves from Guinea-Bissau did not end in 1810. Indeed, an "illegal" trade continued well into the century. Thus, a little less than a decade after the prohibition of slave exports from Guinea, Mollien could describe coastal Bijago and interior Fulani groups capturing people and selling them along side "legitimate" or nonslave goods at oceanside ports:

> The inhabitants of the Archipelago of the Bissagos visit Bissao for the purpose of selling rice and slaves. On their arrival at Bissao, these Negroes exclaim; "here is a vessel from the Bissagos!" and a market is immediately opened on the beach; they bring fruits the large size of which proves the fertility of the soil in their islands. . . . The Biafares bring ivory to Bissao; the Balantas, salt; the Mandingos, wax; the Poulas [Fula or Fulani], gold and slaves. Since Almamy of Fouta Diallon has threatened to make war upon the Mandingos, they have not allowed his subjects to pass through their territories, with a view to prevent all competition on their part. I saw three hundred and fifty slaves arrive in one month at the Portuguese establishments.[28]

Most of the export trade in slaves was controlled by powerful families in Cacheu and Bissau who claimed power with the dismantling of the Company of Grão Para e Maranhão at the end of the eighteenth century. Many of the founders of these families came from Cape Verde and others from Europe. Wherever they were from, the most successful settled in the region and took local African wives, integrating themselves into coastal communities as *lançados* had done for centuries. In Cacheu, the Pereira Barretos and Alvarengas, together with Tomás da Costa Ribeiro, emerged as the most powerful slavers, dominating the traffic in the northern part of the Guinea-Bissau region. On the Rio Geba and to the south, two rivals—Joaquim António de Matos and Caetano José Nozolini—competed for control of commerce. Linked through marriage to several local communities and eventually becoming the son-in-law of Cape Verdean governor António Pusich, Matos was well connected to dominate trade in the region in the 1810s and 1820s, and he continued to be an effective slaver into the 1830s.[29] Indeed, in 1834 British antislaving vessels stopped the *Felicidade,* finding 164 slaves aboard belonging to Matos.[30]

Throughout the 1830s, British vessels apprehended ships flying Portuguese colors and holding thousands of slaves traded under the watchful eyes of powerful local trading families.[31] Between 1835 and 1839 alone, antislaving ships patrolling the shores of Guinea-Bissau and Guinea-Conakry seized 3,989 slaves.[32] We can only speculate about how many vessels loaded with slave cargoes evaded British squadrons. A commission investigating the illegal trade concluded in 1841 that 2000 slaves were exported annually from Bissau to Cuba, which was experiencing an agricultural boom. Caetano Nozolini, the report stated, "has had the largest part of this trade and employs for this end on the Rio Nunes two European agents, beyond people of color employed in his service."[33] As late as 1849, the Portugal's Ministry of Foreign Affairs admitted that Bissau continued to be "frequented by ships that procured cargoes of slaves."[34] When the illegal seaboard trade from the region came to an end is impossible to say. René Pélissier figures it continued after Nozolini's death in 1850, probably tapering off through the remainder of the decade.[35] However, in 1863 a British antislaving vessel suspected that a ship called *Candinha,* which was owned by João Gomes Barboza Junior of Fogo, Cape Verde, was shipping slaves "from Bissau or Cacheu" to Havannah.[36] Further, in 1865 the Portuguese schooner *Bissau* was dispatched to investigate reports of Spanish slavers operating on the Rio Cacine.[37]

Traffickers prospered in the area for a number of reasons. First, the riverine coastal zone with its mangrove swamps was geographically ideal for illegal slaving since it provided many places for small vessels to hide. Second, jihads, or Muslim holy wars, launched by Fula polities just to the interior in the 1840s produced a steady flow of captives.[38] Third, Portugal's impotent presence in the region meant that it was in no position to put an end to illegal trading.[39] Finally, the ranks of the leadership in both Cacheu and Bissau were frequently staffed by Luso Africans, Cape Verdeans, and European settlers who had their own and their families' interests to defend, interests often rooted in the trafficking of slaves. The most important slavers in the region, Matos and Nozolini, both served stints as governor in Bissau, as did Honório Pereira Barreto of the powerful Barreto family. Barreto too was implicated in the illegaltrafficking of slaves. In 1839 the captain of a British vessel discovered that Barreto had title to three slaves who were on a detained ship.[40] Such accounts leave little doubt as to why the slave trade from the region flourished throughout the first half of the nineteenth century.

In addition to the export demand for Guinea-Bissau's slaves, there was also an internal market for them. Interior African states and coastal communities often put slaves to work producing "legitimate" goods for export or attempted to incorporate them into their communities as wives or soldiers.[41] Further, European, Cape Verdean, and Luso African merchants held large retinues of slaves on Bissau and Bolama and in several other coastal locations. Their labor included producing agricultural exports, loading and unloading cargo at ports, building boats, rowing canoes, cooking, cleaning, dressmaking, and performing a host of other tasks.[42] Among the largest holders of slaves in Guinea-Bissau were Nozolini and his influential Bijago wife, Mãe Aurélia. In the 1830s on the island of Bolama, they developed peanut plantations that utilized slave laborers. In 1838 the *Brisk,* a vessel that was part of the British antislavery squadron, seized 212 slaves from the couple's Ponta de Oeste plantation.[43] The Nozolini family also held hundreds of slaves on Bissau. They were engaged "in agriculture all over the island, in workshops and in the loading and unloading of peanuts," which was "the principle article of commerce" of the family's house.[44] João Marques Barros, too, controlled a large number of slave laborers on the island, possessing 197 in the 1850s. All told, 44 residents of Bissau owned more than 1,100 slaves. In Cacheu, other powerful families had large slave holdings. Some 1,085 slaves were held by 91 residents of Cacheu, Farim, and Ziguinchor. Honório Pereira Barreto owned 61, Roza Cavalho de Alvarenga 147, and Francisco Carvalho de Alvarenga 123.[45]

In addition to these, slaves were said to work across the region "in Portuguese *feitorias* that there profitably develop agriculture."[46] *Feitorias* (sometimes referred to as *pontas* when found on fertile "points" of riverside land) were agricultural production units, which European or Cape Verdean *comerciantes* and *negociantes* owned and from which they conducted commercial transactions with coastal people. *Feitoria* owners were instrumental in organizing slave exports from Guinea-Bissau in the first half of the nineteenth century.[47] However, as the nineteenth century progressed, *feitoria* owners increasingly found the pursuit of "legitimate" business to be profitable. Hence the volume of slave exports gradually tapered off as palm oil, peanut, rubber, coconut, and rice exports increased.

THE RISE OF THE TRADE IN "LEGITIMATE" GOODS

With *feitoria* and *ponta* owners as well as independent African producers embracing "legitimate" commerce, the end of the slave trade was not the most important change in the nineteenth century. Rather, the crucial change was other exports becoming more significant when compared to slaves.[48] Drawing on a dense body of French and British records, Philip Curtin takes pains to chart the changing nature of exports from the Senegambia region. Unfortunately, for Portuguese Guinea we do not have as dense a body of data upon which to base conclusions. Since the official Portuguese presence in the area was impotent, accurate export figures for the region are difficult to discern. Customs houses were unable to regulate or track trade.[49] Further, the official records that exist tend to combine figures for Cape Verde and Guinea-Bissau. However, as is evident from the findings of Philip Curtin, Paul Lovejoy and David Richardson, and other scholars, European demand for legitimate exports was rising dramatically toward the later half of the eighteenth and first

Figure 6.1 Ships trading at Bolama, late nineteenth century. From Élisée Reclus, *Africa and Its Inhabitants*, vol. 2 (London: H. Virtue, 1899), 187.

part of the nineteenth century.[50] This should have driven prices upward in the Guinea-Bissau region, as it did in Senegambia, the Bight of Biafra, and elsewhere.

An examination of the export figures that are available highlights the changing nature of commerce in Guinea Bissau. As we saw in Chapter 2, records of the Company of Grão Pará e Maranhão, a commercial house granted a monopoly on trade in the Guinea-Bissau region, reveal the vast importance of slave exports from 1755 to 1778. Slaves composed about 90 percent of the value of all exports from Guinea-Bissau's largest ports, Bissau and Cacheu. Beeswax was also exported, but it composed only about 10 percent of all exports for the period (see Table 2.6). A little over a century later, the components of the Guinea-Bissau region's export trade had completely changed. Peanuts had become the most valuable export, with other "legitimate" goods also bringing in considerable revenue (see Tables 6.1–6.2).

Though the available data do not allow us to calculate the volume of exports from year to year during the first three quarters of the nineteenth century, contemporary observers indicate that throughout much of this period the most important goods traded at Bissau were nonslave items. In 1841, José Conrad Carlos de Chelmicki wrote, "Bissau exports . . . rice, palm oil, beeswax, ivory, skins, timber, turtles and some gold in dust and rings."[51] This account conforms almost perfectly with Governor Honório Pereira Barreto's 1842 description of the commerce of Portuguese Guinea: "It consists of rice, beeswax, skins, some ivory, turtles, salt and a little gold."[52] Elsewhere, Barreto said that palm oil was among the most important exports from Bissau and Cacheu.[53] "These products," he continued, "are exported by English, French, and Americans of the United States, who purchase them with rum, gunpowder, tobacco, guns and other arms, iron in bars, beads, cotton products, and other merchandise."[54] These observations and the statistical data presented in Tables 6.1–6.2 make clear that communities of the Guinea-Bissau area helped feed an Atlantic appetite for palm oil, wax, skins, and rice in the first half of the nineteenth century and embraced peanut production in the second.

Table 6.1   Export Estimates for Portuguese Guinea, 1882

Peanuts	12,000 metric tons
Palm kernels	1,400 metric tons
Unmilled rice	1,000 metric tons
Skins	30,000
Copal gum	10,000 kilograms
Elastic gum	20,000 kilograms

Source: Ignácio de Gouveia, "Relatório," *BCGP* 7 (1952): 447.

Table 6.2   Value of Exports from Portuguese Guinea, 1879–1905

	Peanuts	Coconut	Rubber
1879–1880	240,000$000	28,000$000	3,500$000
1881–1885	134,000$000	40,200$000	16,000$000
1886–1890	77,400$000	72,000$000	37,000$000
1891–1895	66,000$000	42,000$000	90,000$000
1896–1900	32,000$000	66,500$000	195,000$000

Source: Alfredo Loureiro da Fonesca, *Guiné: Finanças e economia* (Lisbon: Typographia da Cooperativa Militar, 1910), 26–27.

THE PRODUCTION OF "LEGITIMATE" GOODS

Like many coastal people, Balanta joined in the production and marketing of legitimate exports. Having visited Bissau in 1844, J. M. de Sousa Monteiro left little doubt that small-scale farmers who lived near Bissau were among the most important producers in the Guinea-Bissau region. Arguing that the island of Rei, which sits in the middle of the Rio Geba, near Bissau, should host a Portuguese customs house, Monteiro wrote, "Its proximity to Bissau and to the countries of the Bissago, Balanta, Biafare and Corobal makes it very fitting as a general depot as much for the goods that they [merchants] intend for the interior trade as for the articles that they receive in exchange and that they intend to export."[55]

At about the same time, Governor Barreto noted the importance of the participation of coastal residents in the production of "legitimate" goods: "The internal commerce [of Portuguese Guinea] consists of rice, beeswax, hides, palm oil, turtles, everything amounting to a little more or less than 50:000$000 réis each year; and it is conducted with the savage Papels of the Island and others, with Berames, Balantas, Bujagós, Biafadas, Nalús, and Mandingas."[56] Barreto did not spell out exactly what he meant by "internal commerce." But since he addressed it while discussing the "Concelho de Bissau," which was composed of "Praça de Bissau, capital do Governo, Presidio de Geba, do ponto de Fá, da Ilha de Bolama, e do Ilheo de Rei," he was probably referring to all of the trade which occurred within the *ria,* or sunken coastline—that is, within Guinea-Bissau's politically decentralized coastal area.[57]

As it had been in the era of the Atlantic slave trade, Geba was still an important entrepôt. Emphasizing this, Valdez wrote:

Geba has a large market, where is exposed for sale a considerable assortment of various commodities, such as gold, ivory, hides, and other produce of the country—all of which are bartered for such articles as salt, glue, and European merchandise, which is transported in large canoes from Bissao, the trade of which place would be but inconsiderable were it not for that

of Geba. Any company trading with the natives living along the borders of
the rivers leading into the interior, if judiciously conducted, would realize
large profits, particularly in salt, glue, firearms, and gunpowder, the four
articles most in demand; for these they would obtain in barter the various
commodities brought . . . to the markets of Farim and Geba.[58]

Barreto figured that Geba was the largest trade center in Portuguese Guinea.
Its exports of beeswax, hides, ivory, and some gold exceeded 80:000$000 réis
annually.[59] But if we compare this estimate of the value of exports moving
from beyond the *ria* coastline's edge and through Geba to Barreto's rough
estimates of 50:000$000 réis for the value of "internal commerce," it is clear
that coastal people were major contributors to an economy geared toward the
production of nonslave items. That is, coastal people were producing, by very
rough estimate, about 38 percent of the value of the legitimate goods passing
through Bissau in the 1840s.

Coastal Africans marketed some of their products to Portuguese and Cape
Verdeans or their representatives who circulated in the interior or who had
established *feitorias* there. Many of these merchants visited Balanta villages.
"Any merchant who goes to be a guest in the house of a Balanta," one observer noted, "is sacred among them. There is nothing that they won't do for
the guest to make him comfortable."[60] Barreto said that "foreign" merchants—
estrangeiros—were often warmly welcomed in many coastal communities;
they actively competed in the Biafada, Papel, Balanta, and Mandinka
markets.[61]

Evidently, area farmers benefited from the competitive nature of coastal
trade. Valdez complained that there were "very many small rivers where
estrangeiros trade, and where they sell [imported] products for prices 50 percent lower than in our locations." Noting the lengths to which African producers were willing to go to get the best possible price for their wares, Valdez
said that "it is necessary also to state, so that no one is surprised, that a savage, in as much as he does not incur travel expenses, since he lives while on
the road from the products of nature or from what he brings with him, and
he makes himself a guest in any hut where he is welcome, walks hundreds of
leagues to obtain less expensive items."[62] Valdez also bemoaned the fact Portuguese were forced to pay high prices for exports since the "savages" who
visit "our *feitorias* on the Rios Geba, Curubal, and Cacheu wait eight and
many times fifteen days . . . to haggle over prices so as to obtain a very small
advantage." He concluded, "It is no wonder that they want to walk three or
four days more to reach the establishments of the neighboring *estrangeiros*."[63]

Emphasizing the continued importance of women in forging trade links
between Cape Verdean and Luso African merchants and local communities,
Valdez said:

> The native or coloured merchants generally conduct their trade by means of female agents, whom they select partly on account of their knowledge of the customs of the natives and their acquaintance with the people. They are very clever in managing stores; and, having friends and relations in the country, are very successful in their speculations. They are considered wives of those traders and are said to be very faithful to the interests of their husbands in every particular. Indeed, by their means some of their lords are said to become immensely rich.[64]

Perhaps recognizing the importance of such women merchants in the Bissau area, the Portuguese governor put forward legislation that was aimed at protecting those trading beyond the town's fortified center in the 1840s.[65] Other very powerful women traded from their own commercial houses within the protected walls of Bissau's fort. In 1861, Valdez listed eleven women among the most important merchants in Bissau. Some of these women had familial ties to powerful local families. Eugenia Nozolini and Leopoldina Demay were the daughters of Caetano Nozolini and Mãe Aurélia. Aiding Eugenia in business affairs was a contingent of over 100 slaves. Leopoldina Matos Spencer was the daughter of Joaquim António de Matos. In earlier years, Júlia da Silva Cardoso, Mãe Aurélia's aunt and a cousin of the chief of the island of Canhabaqe, was also an important Bissau-based merchant and had her own trading house.[66]

When less influential women from coastal communities visited Bissau to trade, they often went to the island's bustling market. During his 1844 journey to Bissau, Monteiro noted, "Here I saw a variety and abundance of products that came to the market, even though each one of these blacks brings very little."[67] Chelmicki made a similar observation: "From very far, Biafare, Balanta, Mandinga, and others carry a variety of trade items [to Bissau]."[68] Similarly, Valdez wrote, "There is a regular daily market held at Bissao, where there is a considerable sale of rice, salt, wax, palm-oil, and glue, supplied by the Ballantas, the islands Bussis, Jatta, and Caio, as well as by the Archipelago of the Bijagoz."[69]

If a number of the goods that Balanta and other coastal residents brought to Bissau were bound for export, other goods met the daily needs of the growing class of people dedicated not to farming but to trading and transporting commodities. The exact size of the merchant community in Bissau is difficult to pinpoint, but according to contemporary accounts, hundreds of people were involved "full time" in the town's trade in "legitimate" goods. Mollien, who visited Bissau in 1818, estimated its population at 2,000. Though we have no way of knowing what proportion of these people were fully engaged in the trade and transport sectors of the regional economy, we can be sure from Mollien's observation that Bissau possessed a growing urban class of "carpenters, caulkers, some masons, and blacksmiths" who built "boats of twenty tons of allotment" and did countless other jobs.[70] In the 1860s, Valdez provided a more detailed description of Bissau:

> In the fortress are the governor's quarters, barracks for 200 soldiers and their officers, the church, the custom-house, and very large store-houses, built of stone and covered with tiles. . . . A little to the west, outside the walls of the town, but under the protection of the guns, there is a village of about 300 cottages and huts, eight or nine of which are covered with tiles, and only four built of stone. These are the residences of Portuguese mercantile settlers, of some agents of English houses at the Gambia, and some French agents from Goree. The remainder of the population consists of Grumetes, or native Christians.[71]

Since ship crews, merchants, carpenters, caulkers, masons, blacksmiths, soldiers, and administrators were not involved in agricultural production, they had to obtain food from coastal people. Thus, with the tapering off of the slave trade, coastal residents increasingly visited Bissau to trade not only "legitimate" exports but also basic food crops.[72] And according to Januario Correia de Almeida's 1859 description, coastal groups produced large quantities of goods for Bissau's nonfarming community:

> Some of the movement that is noted in the population of Bissau results from the daily market that occurs on the *rua principal*. At this 400 to 600 savages, Papels, Balantas and Bijagos, compete regularly in trades among themselves and with the *grumetes* of the praça and other inhabitants. The sellers line themselves up squatted on the side of the street, preferring always the side of the sun, and they have in front of them the objects that they exhibit for sale, and these are usually fruits, milk, rice, palm oil and wine, chickens, eggs, pigs, vegetables, etc. The buyers, supplied with leaves of tobacco, bars of iron, knife blades, bands of cloth, rough cotton, gun powder, rum, etc., trade according to their needs passing from the market to the street.[73]

BALANTA PADDY RICE PRODUCTION AND TRADE

Though Balanta traded a variety of goods in the nineteenth century, their economy centered on the production and marketing of paddy rice. In Chapter 5, I examined the pre-nineteenth-century spread of *O. sativa* varieties of rice across Guinea-Bissau's coastal region, noting that *O. sativa* rices tend to be whiter in color than *O. glaberrima* varieties and that *O. sativa* varieties were therefore more attractive to Europeans. Because of its marketability, Cape Verdean merchant-planters, who settled in Guinea-Bissau in the eighteenth, nineteenth, and early twentieth centuries, encouraged the planting of the white *O. sativa.* Some Balanta narratives even link white rice to white or mulatto planters.[74]

Following in the footsteps of the men who had settled in Guinea and become *lançados* in the first centuries of Portuguese exploration, Cape Verdeans "threw themselves" into coastal societies. Some Balanta narratives recall the coming of these *babm hath,* white or mulatto settlers. "The first *babm hath* who settled in this zone," Tchong Bihom told me of the region around the Rio Mansoa, "procured land on which they resided. Thus, Londé settled in the area that [today] actually has his name. In N'talod [today called Boa Esperança] resided Nené, and in Quilatlê [Quinhamel] were Kimbito, Abuna, and Ricardo."[75] The Portuguese called these men *ponteiros* because they developed fertile *pontas* of land that had the advantage of offering easy access for cargo boats navigating many of Guinea-Bissau's meandering rivers.[76] According to Henrique Dias de Carvalho, a late-nineteenth-century observer, the *ponta* system had roots stretching deep into the past: "At the start of the eighteenth century, the sons of Cape Verde or colonists who from there came, obtained *Pontas,* and servitors of the sovereigns took care of the farming of the land according to their way. They established right away their dwellings and commercial houses, light structures, being commerce the manner to sustain themselves and to obtain more services and products from the interior sought for exportation."[77] Migrations reached their highpoint in the nineteenth century. Recurrent droughts (in the years 1831–1834, 1854–1856, and 1877–1879) and especially the great famine of 1863–1866 pushed many Cape Verdeans to the coast. At the same time, "legitimate" trade opportunities and a Portuguese program granting land concessions to those willing to develop trade pulled others.[78]

Few in number and far from urban centers, the position of the *ponteiros* vis-à-vis local populations was weak. Hence, they could not force locals to work for them. Rather, they negotiated labor contracts, principally with Balanta communities, and offered gifts to elders in exchange for protection.[79] It seems likely that the Balanta age-grade system lent itself to contractual arrangements. Today it is quite common for Balanta age grades to hire themselves out. When *moranças* need extra hands for burdensome tasks, they may contract age grades to work for them. Working in the paddies that belong to an individual *morança,* male age grades often prepare the soil for planting and transplant and harvest rice. These tasks may require more labor than individual *moranças,* particularly small ones, can muster with their own members. The *morança* that solicits the help of an age grade generally gives the grade a gift as a show of thanks. This gift may take the form of a pig or alcohol. The preferred alcoholic drink of young Balanta is *cana,* a rum made from the distilled juices of sugar cane. The use of *cana* as payment for the labors of age grades may in fact have begun on *pontas* in the eighteenth or nineteenth century. Indeed, the bulk of the agricultural efforts of *ponteiros* was dedicated to producing sugar cane, a crop that in Portuguese Guinea grew "marvelously."[80] On their islands, centuries of experience and experimentation made Cape Verdeans adept cane farmers and master *cana* makers. Assembling presses, which were used to extract juices from cane, and stills, *ponteiros* in Guinea-Bissau manufactured their potent drink so that they could pay laborers with it or exchange it for rice and myriad "legitimate" goods.

Cape Verdeans, then, sustained themselves by serving partly as planters and partly as traders. Isolated in the far reaches of Guinea-Bissau, *ponteiros* lived peacefully alongside and by the rules of their African hosts. Frequently taking African wives, they integrated themselves into and exploited existing social structures. "Men from Santiago, Maio, Brava and Santo Antão," António Carreira writes, "settled down there, many remaining forty or fifty years." For Cape Verdean immigrants, the period from the nineteenth through the early-twentieth century was favorable for their undertaking "since the peoples of the area then drank spirits. There were still many Soninke and Fula *bebedores* [drinkers] who only later were to become Muslims. So they were sure of a market."[81] Possessing *cana* as well as valued imported wares that they received from English and French commercial houses, Cape Verdean *ponteiros* were instrumental in encouraging Balanta to produce surpluses of rice for the export market. Into "the territories of the Balantas," a Portuguese administrator observed in 1867, *ponteiros* and *estrangeiros* "introduced from the Rio Mansoa an abundance of merchandise."[82] Along with *cana, ponteiros* traded guns, gunpowder, cloth, tobacco, iron, knives, and beads.[83] And for these goods, *ponteiros* demanded rice.[84]

"Balanta rice" was particularly valued on the Portuguese-administered islands of Cape Verde, where arid soils did not produce enough food crops to sustain the population. During nineteenth-century droughts, administrators in Bissau responded to desperate pleas from Cape Verde to ship "Balanta rice" to the island to stem "the crisis of hunger."[85] Cape Verdeans with connections in Balanta communities acted as middleman purchasers for the government, and they profited from the sales of their own stores. *Ponteiros* also encouraged Balanta to produce rice for the domestic market. In May 1867 the governor of Portuguese Guinea reported, "The greatest consumption of rice, that is bought in the Balanta territory, is on the Rio Grande and Bolama: the boats that come loaded with that product go there."[86] During this period, farmers in the Rio Grande area and Bolama were devoting considerable resources to peanut production. It is likely, then, that food-crop production had decreased around the Grande and on Bolama and that Balanta rice was being bought to meet farmers' nutritional needs.

Further, perhaps more than any other food crop, Balanta paddy rice was meeting the needs of the region's urban population. In his 1867 discussion of the rice trade in the "Balanta territory," a Portuguese observer noted that "the rice is the only sustenance of the [urban] black worker."[87] In 1876, officials in Bissau said that the Rio Mansoa, the banks of which were populated by Balanta, "supplies rice to the population of Bissau and Bolama."[88] Similarly in 1878, Balanta were said to be "harder workers than the Papel," so much so that "the trade of Bissau is sustained by them."[89] An 1883 report stated that the "republican" Balanta were "the hardest working tribe of Guinea, cultivating rice on a large scale and furnishing this precious foodstuff not only to the districts of that great region but also many other markets of Africa and Europe."[90] Later that decade, an administrator noted "frequent commercial relations" between Bissau and "coastal tribes, especially with Balanta who daily supply the market, carrying in grand quantity pigs, rice, corn, chickens, eggs, dried things, etc."[91] And in 1890, the governor wrote, "The Rio Geba is farmed on its right margin by Balanta, who cultivate almost exclusively rice, which supplies the market of Bissau, great quantities arriving for export."[92]

FISSION AND EXPANSION

As Balanta stepped up rice production for export and sale in domestic markets, Balanta populations were increasing. Though census figures do not exist for the nineteenth century, the slow death of the slave trade probably positively affected population growth. Further, Cape Verdean and Portuguese efforts to introduce new strains of rice—varieties of *O. sativa*—probably increased yields, providing sustenance for more people. Whatever the case, by 1890 the Balanta territories to the northeast of Bissau were burgeoning with people. That year, the governor of Guiné, Correia e Lança, wrote, "The margins of the Rios Mansôa and Gêba constitute the center of radiation of the rice culture in Portuguese Guinea and possess the greatest densities of population of the Colony."[93]

With populations increasing at the same time that production for domestic and export markets was on the rise, land, particularly in the fertile *bolanhas* of the Balanta "homeland," became scarce. Balanta reacted to this problem by splitting, or "fissioning," their communities. That is, some members left kin and neighbors to establish new communities elsewhere. When irresolvable conflicts over resources erupted, fissioning served as an outlet, relieving tensions that might have made community ties brittle. By fissioning communities, Balanta also kept their society politically decentralized. Powerful households could not dominate limited resources and subjugate others to their will, since the weaker could uproot themselves and find land for planting elsewhere. In fission, then, we find a crucial difference between decentralized and state-based societies. As Ronald Cohen explains, "States differ from nonstates in their capacity to withstand normal fissionable processes. . . . All other previous systems tend to breakup and send off budding and politically autonomous segments through time because one normal way of resolving conflicts or resource shortages is for groups within a polity to opt out and establish their own political entity elsewhere."[94]

Noting that there were numerous reasons for the nineteenth century Balanta expansions into new territories, Fona Benuma told me that communities divided "because of people's own wills and because others had greater force. For example, people moved [to new locations] to procure lands and *bolanhas* for cultivating when it was seen that *bolanhas* were insufficient in relation to the number of people." A lack of *bolanhas,* he continued, led to a proliferation of "inter-village wars that occurred in the northern zone [or the Balanta 'homeland' around the Mansoa and Geba]."[95] Complementing this statement, Alberto Gomes Pimentel, who compiled an "ethnography" of the Mansoa area in 1925, said that before the start of the twentieth century wars "over the *bolanhas*" were frequent in Balanta regions.[96]

If fissioning served to discourage any impetus toward political centralization (stronger *moranças* monopolizing resources and dominating weaker ones), the continued reliance on age-grade structures in long-established communities and in newly forming ones also prevented the development of political hierarchies. In the nineteenth century, then, European descriptions of the Balanta political structures mirrored those of the earlier times. For example, in 1841 Chelmicki noted, "The Balanta have kings but only in name, since each one governs and defends his own house as he can."[97] In 1890, Correia e Lança wrote, "The Balanta are a people who do not have a political organization, nor do they recognize kings nor chiefs of any sort. Each Balanta is the only chief of his family."[98] And at the turn of the century, Henrique Dias de Carvalho wrote, "The Balanta are the most democratic people of *Guiné:* They live in diverse populations independent among themselves; they do not have a political constitution and do not recognize chiefs of any sort. Each Balanta is solely the chief of his family, which conserves its autonomy."[99]

In a series of expansions dating from the late nineteenth century, Balanta populations first moved eastward along the Rio Mansoa and westward along the Rio Geba. These expansions caught the attention of Portuguese officials, who marveled at the industriousness of Balanta in new territories. Reflecting on his time as governor in the 1880s, Correia e Lança noted, "The Balanta made free use of a great deal of territory to the interior that they cultivate."[100] Further, in 1914 João Teixeira Pinto said, "The Balanta race is reproducing itself in an extraordinary manner and already the territory that they occupy does not suffice for them. Thus, to the east, they were infiltrating through

Mandinka territory and to the west through the Papel and Bramas. The rivers of Farim and Geba do not stop their expansion. They find themselves to the north in the region of Canja and to the south in Quinara."[101] And in 1917 Ernesto Vasconcellos wrote, "Since the territory of the Balanta is very populous and its agriculture is important, the Balanta felt the necessity to enlarge their sphere of action and rush into the territory of the Beafada."[102]

Balanta oral narratives provide further details as to how this expansion took place. Balanta say they frequently claimed new lands with support from European or Cape Verdean *ponteiros* or their African employees, who were known as *b'babm mon* or "white-blacks." For Balanta, *b'babm mon* are Africans who no longer practice "traditional" farming methods but make their living in very "European ways." Of Balanta migrations, Frós Intchalá told me, "Balanta migrated because of hunger and an insufficiency of *bolanhas* in the North [area around Rio Mansoa and Geba]. The people traveled with *b'babm mon* when they went to a locality, and they returned to tell other people that there was a location which was good for farming. Thus, people migrated."[103] That *ponteiros* assisted Balanta in migrating to new lands is also evidenced in the written record. Governor Correia e Lança, for example, noted that two *ponteiros* called on him "to ask in the name of a commission of Balantas" if he would concede to their moving "to the lands of Jabadá" on the south side of the Rio Geba "for the purpose of extending the cultivation of rice and peanuts." Fearing conflicts between the Biafada who occupied this region and Balanta settlers who would cultivate rice and *cana* for *ponteiros,* the governor refused this request, but he approved others.[104]

The *ponteiros* who assisted Balanta as they moved to new regions expected to turn a profit by advancing the settlers seed for their first crops and then demanding a full repayment with interest at harvest time. By official Portuguese accounts, the return that *ponteiros* demanded was substantial. It was, the Portuguese claimed, as much as 100 percent. Official accounts also state that *ponteiros* insisted that Balanta not deal with competitors when marketing the remainder of what they collected.[105] By the twentieth century, "official" descriptions of the *ponta* system painted a picture of the absolute exploitation of Balanta.[106]

Despite these accounts, there is good reason to believe that Balanta-*ponteiro* relations continued to be characterized by negotiation and compromise. Indeed, *ponteiros* had to be careful not to offend Balanta neighbors. When they did, harsh retaliation frequently came their way. For example, in 1885, Caetano Alberto da Costa, chief of the fort at Geba, reported that "repeated times Balanta sack the *feitorias* on the left side [of the river] forcing the owners to abandon them."[107] "The *pontas,*" James Cunningham explains, "were criticized for their practice of providing rice seedlings and tools to Balante [Balanta] at heavy rates of interest in return for trade goods. It is clear, however, that the relationship was not as simple or as straightforwardly exploitive as the Portuguese maintained, and the persistence and durability of the system raise doubts about such an analysis."[108] Cunningham figures that in the last quarter of the nineteenth century Portuguese officials depicted the system as exploitive because they disliked the fact that, when exporting rice, *ponteiros* frequently skirted Portuguese laws by avoiding the payment of export duties. In sum, the government was looking for a reason to institute tighter controls on the *ponta* system.

Of course, whether or not *ponteiros* paid taxes to the Portuguese government was of no concern to Balanta. As long as they had access to imported goods and *cana,* Balanta age grades were willing to hire themselves out to area *ponteiros*. And if these *ponteiros* could help poorer *moranças* relocate from densely populated regions to scarcely populated and fertile ones, Balanta were willing to fission communities and move, even if it meant that they would have to pay a price to do it.

CONCLUSION

The nineteenth century did not, then, present Balanta with a "crisis of adaptation." Rather, it presented opportunities for politically independent Balanta *moranças* to step up rice production and garner imports. At the start of the nineteenth century, Balanta already had institutions in place to meet increasing demands for rice. These institutions proved capable of responding to shifts in regional and global economic currents. Lacking powerful and broad-based rulers—lacking a centralized government—Balanta nonetheless cleared new lands, built new dikes, and harvested increasing amounts of rice, which they sold to Cape Verdean *ponteiros*. As Balanta moved to meet market demands, resources became scarce in the Balanta "homeland." However, since vast spans of virgin *bolanhas* were available nearby, Balanta averted a crisis of overproduction and resource scarcity by fissioning *tabancas*. Balanta populations increased and expanded across Guinea-Bissau.

As they did so, the bounty they produced caught the eye of one Portuguese official, who wrote, "The people of Guinea, above all the Balanta, who are the ones who produce the most rice, have a profound and perfect knowledge of its cultivation . . . farming the land very well by hand, doing the important work of irrigation and drainage, possessing diverse varieties of rice perfectly distinct, knowing very well which is most suited to the given conditions of the terrain, dampness, exposure, etc. As a consequence, they produce rice very much cheaper than European enterprises can produce it."[109] Though they had occupied a space on the slaving frontier of a powerful state in the centuries that had come before, Balanta had found ways to thrive, outproducing even European competition. Balanta communities continued to farm paddy rice and their populations continued to expand onto new territories well into the twentieth century.

NOTES

1. See especially Robin Law, "The Historiography of the Commercial Transition in Nineteenth-Century West Africa," in *African Historiography: Essays in Honor of Jacob Ade Ajayi,* ed. Toyin Falola (Harlow: Longman, 1993), 91–115.

2. Kenneth Dike, *Trade and Politics in the Niger Delta, 1830–1885* (Oxford: Clarendon Press, 1956). For an alternative view, see J. F. Ade Ajayi, "West African States at the Beginning of the Nineteenth Century," in *A Thousand Years of West African History,* eds. J. F. Ade Ajayi and Michael Crowder (London: Nelson, 1965), 248–261. Anthony G. Hopkins, *An Economic History of West Africa* (New York: Columbia University Press, 1973), 143.

3. Ralph A. Austen, "The Abolition of the Overseas Slave Trade: A Distorted Theme in West African History," *Journal of the Historical Society of Nigeria* 5 (June 1970): 257–274. See also Julian Clarke, "Households and the Political Economy of Small-Scale Cash Production in South-West Nigeria," *Africa* 51 (1981): 807–823; and Elisée Soumonni, "Slave and Palm Oil Trades in Dahomey, 1818–1858," in *From Slave Trade to "Legitimate" Commerce,* ed. Robin Law (Cambridge: Cambridge University Press, 1995), 78–90.

4. Martin Lynn, "The West African Palm Oil Trade in the Nineteenth Century and the 'Crisis of Adaptation,'" in Law, *From Slave Trade to "Legitimate" Commerce,* 57–77.

5. To be sure, in decentralized regions, "merchant elites" played a critical role in the transition from slave to legitimate exports. This was especially true in the transportation sector; commoners sometimes relied on well-organized merchant communities to move goods to ports. And it was also true of the production sector. In studies of the Rio Grande region of Guinea-Bissau, Joye Bowman examines the role of European, Luso African, and Senegalese traders in establishing *feitorias,* from which they shipped great quantities of peanuts from about 1840 to 1890. She points out that migrant Manjaco met the labor needs of *feitorias.* In general, however, her work is one-sided, exploring the role that Europeans and Creoles played in organizing trade, but ignoring the fact that African small holders across Guinea-Bissau were producing crops for export. Joye L. Bowman, "'Legitimate Commerce' and Peanut Production in Portuguese Guinea, 1840s–1880s," *Journal of African History* 28, no. 1 (1987): 87–106.

6. Avelino Teixeira da Mota, *Guiné portuguesa,* vol. 2 (Lisbon: Agência Geral do Ultramar, 1954), 43–44.

7. R. J. Hammond. *Portugal and Africa* (Stanford: Stanford University Press, 1966), 37.

8. Gaspard Mollien, *Travels in the Interior of Africa to the Sources of the Senegal and Gambia Performed by the Command of the French Government in the Year 1818,* ed. T. E. Bowdich (London: Frank Cass, 1967), 131–132; Mota, *Guiné portuguesa,* 27.

9. Francisco Travassos Valdez, *Six Years of a Traveller's Life in Western Africa* (London: Hurst and Blackett, 1861), 238.

10. Honório Pereira Barreto, "Memória sobre o estado actual de Senegambia portugueza, causas de sua decadencia, e meios de a fazer prosperar" (Lisbon: Typ. da

Viuva Coelho 1843), reprinted in Jaime Walter, *Honório Pereira Barreto* (Lisbon: Centro de Estodos da Guiné Portuguesa, 1947), 15.

11. Mollien, *Travels,* 336–337.

12. Valdez, *Six Years,* 238.

13. George E. Brooks, "A Nhara of the Guinea-Bissau Region: Mãe Aurélia Correia," in *Women and Slavery in Africa,* eds. Claire C. Robertson and Martin A. Klein (Madison: University of Wisconsin Press, 1983), 304–305.

14. Mollien, *Travels,* 334; Jehudi Ashmum, "Bissao," *Africa Repository and Colonial Journal* 3 (1967): 73–78.

15. Barreto, "Memória," 12.

16. Brooks, "A Nhara," 305–306; Christiano José de Senna Barcellos, *Subsidios para a história de Cabo Verde e Guiné,* vol. 3 (Lisbon: Academia Real das Sciencias, 1899–1913), 96–97, 158; Mollien, *Travels,* 335; Barreto, "Memória," 12.

17. Barcellos, *Subsidios,* vol. 5, 3.

18. Mollien, *Travels,* 335.

19. Ibid.

20. Quoted in Brooks, "A Nhara," 306.

21. W.F.W. Owen, *Narrative of Voyages to Explore the Shores of Africa, Arabia, and Madagascar,* vol. 1 (London: Richard Bentley, 1833), 259–260.

22. Barcellos, *Subsidios,* vol. 3, 349–350, and vol. 4, 72.

23. Barreto, "Memória," 40–41. Problems at the fort compelled officials to seek a better location to house soldiers and mercantile establishments. However, since they could not challenge local rulers, their plans were thwarted. Valdez, *Six Years,* 239.

24. Barreto, "Memória," 9.

25. Mollien, *Travels,* 336.

26. Ashmun, "Bissao," 76.

27. René Pélissier, *História da Guiné: Portugueses e Africanos na Senegâmbia, 1841–1936,* vol. 1 (Lisbon: Imprensa Univerisitária, 1989), 43–44.

28. Mollien, *Travels,* 336.

29. Joel Frederico Silveira, "Guiné," in *O Império Africano 1825–1890,* eds. Valentim Alexandre and Jill Dias (Lisbon: Editorial Estampa, 1998), 221–223; Brooks, "A Nhara," 310–315; Mollien, *Travels,* 337. Before his marriage to Pusich's daughter, Matos had an African wife, perhaps of Papel descent.

30. António Carreira, *O tráfico de escravos nos rios de Guiné e ilhas de Cabo Verde (1810–1850): Subsídios para o seu estudo* (Lisbon: Junta de Investigações Científicas do Ultramar, 1981), 42.

31. Arquivo Histórico Nacional (AHN) (Praia, Cape Verde), SGG A1/A1.10/cx. 72–73.

32. Some sources put the figure at 3,825. Carreira, *O tráfico,* 39–42.

33. Ibid., 42. Slaves also went to Cape Verde. José Conrado Carlos de Chelmicki, *Corografia Cabo Verdiana,* vol. 2 (Lisbon: Typ. de L.C. da Cunha, 1841), 63.

34. Silveira, "Guiné," 245.

35. Pélissier, *História,* 45.

36. Arquivo Histórico Ultramarino (AHU) (Lisbon, Portugal), Cabo Verde, SENMU/DGU/RG/001/cx. 91, doc. 199. In 1856, the governor-general of Cape Verde authorized the governor of Portuguese Guiné to subject the chiefs in the Tombali and Cacine to Portuguese authority to end "the traffic of slaves that has been conducted at those points." AHU, Cabo Verde, SENMU/DGU/RG/001/cx. 91, doc. 428, pasta 21.

37. AHU, Cabo Verde, SENMU/DGU/RG/001/cx. 91, doc. 87.

38. Gervase Clarence-Smith, *The Third Portuguese Empire, 1825–1975* (Manchester: Manchester University Press, 1985), 42. On the nineteenth-century export of slave exports from Guinea-Bissau, see Carreira, *O tráfico*, 45. See also James Duffy, *Portuguese Africa* (Cambridge: Harvard University Press, 1959), 144.

39. One statistic illustrates this perfectly. From 1800 to 1880, there were more than forty captain-majors and governors (different titles being used in different periods) representing Portuguese interests in Bissau. During the same period, Cacheu's leadership was not much more stable or enduring. Note that from 1836 to 1879, Cape Verde was the administrative capital of Portuguese Guinea. In 1879, the coastal colony became an autonomous province.

40. Carreira, *O tráfico*, 42.

41. The internal trafficking of slaves continued into the twentieth century.

42. See the jobs specified in AHU, AUL, GG, Lv. 0036, "Livro dos escravosdo concelho de Bissau e ilheu do Rei," 1856.

43. Brooks, "A Nhara." See also Barcellos, *Subsidios,* vol. 4, 253.

44. The 1856 census lists 432 slaves in Bissau owned by Nozolini Junior and Company. AHU, AUL, GG, Lv. 0036, "Livro dos escravosdo"; Januario Correia de Almeida, *Uma mez na Guiné* (Lisbon: Typographia Universal, 1859), 18; Francisco Travassos Valdez, *Africa occidental: Noticias e considerações,* vol. 1I (Lisbon: Imprensa Nacional, 1864), 307–308.

45. Collecção de Livors da Guiné, book 35, "Provinçia de Cabo Verde, Districto da Guiné, Concelho de Cacheu, Livro 1, de Registro d'Escravos," 1856.

46. Almeida, *Um mez na Guiné,* 60.

47. Brooks, "A Nhara." See also Almeida, *Um mez na Guiné,* 18.

48. Philip D. Curtin, *Economic Change in Precolonial Africa: Senegambia in the Era of the Slave Trade* (Madison: University of Wisconsin Press, 1975), 196; Y. Pearson, "States and Peoples of Senegambia and Upper Guinea," in *General History of Africa,* vol. 6, *Africa in the Nineteenth Century Until the 1880s,* ed. J. F. Ade Ajaye (Oxford: Heinemann, 1989), 636–638.

49. In 1861, Valdez said that "the most recent returns" for the commerce of Bissau dated from the first quarter of 1853. He emphasized that all figures were misleading, since imports were undervalued by custom houses ("the real value must be considered three times the stated"). He also noted problems with making projections for the year based on one quarter. Valdez, *Six Years,* 259–260.

50. Paul E. Lovejoy and David Richardson, "The West African Palm Oil Trade in the Nineteenth Century and the 'Crisis of Adaptation,'" in Law, *From Slave Trade to "Legitimate" Commerce,* 48. See also Pearson, "States and Peoples," 638.

51. Chelmicki, *Corografia,* vol. 4, 290; Valdez, *Africa occidental,* 252; J. M. de Souza Monteiro, *Diccionario geográfico das provincias e possessões portuguezas no Ultramar* (Lisbon: Typographia Lisbonense, 1850), 159. Monteiro put the total value of exports from Bissau at 120,000 réis annually, "more or less."

52. Barreto, "Memória," 8. See also José Joaquim Lopes de Lima, *Ensaios sobre a statistica das possessões portuguezas no Ultramar,* vol. 1, *Das ilhas de Cabo Verde e suas dependências* (Lisbon: Imprensa Nacional, 1844), 24–29. Monteiro put the value of imports at 100,000 réis annually. Monteiro, *Diccionario geográfico,* 159.

53. Barreto, "Memória," 16, 22.

54. Ibid., 8.

55. J. M. de Sousa Monteiro, "Estudos sobre a Guiné de Cabo Verde," *O Panorama* 10 (1853): 148–149.

56. Barreto, "Memória," 1–48.

57. Ibid., 14–17.

58. Valdez, *Six Years,* 241–242.

59. Barreto, "Memória," 17.

60. Francisco Antonio Marques Geraldes, "Guiné portugueza, communicação á sociedade de geographia sobre esta provincia e suas condições actuaes," *Boletim da Sociedade de Geografia de Lisboa* ser. 7a, no. 8 (1887): 517.

61. Ibid.

62. Valdez, *Africa occidental,* 344–345.

63. Ibid., 345.

64. Valdez, *Six Years,* 217.

65. Philip J. Havik, "Women and Trade in the Guinea-Bissau Region," *Stvdia* 52 (1994): 94.

66. Valdez, *Africa occidental,* 352–353; AHU, AUL, GG, Lv. 0010, "Livro dos escravosdo concelho de Bissau e ilheu do Rei," 1856; Havik, "Women and Trade," 107.

67. Monteiro, "Estudos sobre a Guiné," 128.

68. Chelmicki, *Corografia,* vol. 1, 122.

69. Valdez, *Six Years,* 240.

70. Mollien, *Travels,* 339.

71. Valdez, *Six Years,* 238–239.

72. Monteiro, "Estudos sobre a Guiné, 128. They also traded "exotic" souvenirs— "different live animals, like parrakeet, monkeys with mugs like dogs, and others which have white faces and are called *fidalgos,* lizards, etc."

73. Almeida, *Uma mez na Guiné,* 16. See also Valdez, *Africa occidental,* 313; and Chelmicki, *Corografia,* vol. 1, 122–125. Coastal residents also conducted considerable trade at Bandim, a Papel-controlled port near Bissau. Monteiro, "Estudos sobre a Guiné," 149.

74. Interviews with Alfrede Neves, Chiguna Clusse, and Bcolof Sukna, Patche Ialá, January 31, 1995; and Quemade N'dami and Armando Dias, N'tatelai, February 2, 1995.

75. Interview with Tchong Binhom and Wangna Sanhá, N'talod, January 25, 1995.

76. See, for example, Henrique Augusto Dias de Carvalho, *Guiné: Apontamentos inéditos* (Lisbon: Agência Geral das Colónias, Divisão de Pubicações e Biblioteca, 1944), 140–141. See also Rosemarry E. Galli and Jocelyn Jones, *Guinea-Bissau: Politics, Economics, and Society* (London: Frances Pinter, 1987), 28, 54; and Joye Bowman Hawkins, "Conflict, Interaction, and Change in Guinea-Bissau: Fulbe Expansion and Its Impact, 1850–1900" (Ph.D. diss., University of California–Los Angeles, 1980), 162–163.

77. Carvalho, *Guiné,* 148–149; also Joaquim da Graça Correia e Lança, *Relatório da provincia da Guiné portugueza: Referido ao anno economico de 1888–1889* (Lisbon: Imprensa Nacional, 1890), 19.

78. James Cunningham, "The Colonial Period in Guiné," *Tarikh* 6 (1980): 39; Galli and Jones, *Guinea-Bissau,* 28; António Carreira, *The People of the Cape Verde Islands: Exploitation and Emigration,* trans. Christopher Fyfe (London: C. Hurst, 1982), 55.

79. Cunningham, "The Colonial Period," 39.

80. Correia e Lança, *Relatório,* 19; Galli and Jones, *Guinea-Bissau,* 28. See also Carvalho, *Guiné,* 117–118.

81. Carreira, *The People,* 55–56. See also Galli and Jones, *Guinea-Bissau,* 28.

82. AHN, SGG Al/A6.9/cx. 348.

83. Carvalho, *Guiné,* 171.

84. Galli and Jones, *Guinea-Bissau,* 44.

85. For example, requests were made in 1846 (AHN, SGG, A1, cx. 347, doc. 67). In 1855, Portuguese officials bought 3,417 alqueires of rice for the island of S. Nicholau, 8,090 arrobas of unhusked rice for Praia, and 3,550 arrobas of husked yellow rice for other parts of Cape Verde (Barcellos, *Subsidios,* vol. 6, 60). Further requests were made in 1856 (AHN, SGG Al/A2.22, docs. 29, 61, 95). Other droughts occurred in 1832 and 1856. During each of these, rice was shipped from Bissau to the islands (AHU, Cabo Verde, SENMU/DGU/RG/001/cx. 73, pasta 21). See also documents from 1875 (AHN, SGG, Al/A6.9, cx. 350) and Lima, *Ensaios,* 24.

86. AHU, SGG Al/A6.9/cx. 348.

87. Ibid.

88. AHU, SGG, Al/A6.9/cx. 351.

89. Barros, *Senegambia portugueza,* 80.

90. A. J. Socrates da Costa, "Provincia da Guiné portugueza," *Boletim da Sociedade de Geografia de Lisboa* ser. 4a, no. 2 (1883): 106–107.

91. Francisco Teixeira da Silva, *Relatório do governo da provincia da Guiné portugueza com referencia a 1887–1888* (Lisbon: Typographia Minerva Central, 1889), 41.

92. Correia e Lança, *Relatório,* chap. 1.

93. Ibid.

94. Ronald Cohen, "Evolution, Fission, and the Early State," in *The Study of the State,* eds. Henri J. M. Claessen and Peter Skalník (The Hague: Mouton, 1981), 94–95. See also Jean Ensminger, *Making a Market: The Insitutional Transformation of an African Society* (Cambridge: Cambridge University Press, 1992), 146–147; and Robert W. Harms, *River of Wealth, River of Sorrow: The Central Zaire Basin in the Era of the Slave and Ivory Trade, 1500–1891* (New Haven, Conn.: Yale University Press, 1981), 118–125.

95. Interview with Fona Benuma, Encheia, January 13, 1995.

96. Alberto Gomes Pimentel, "Circumscrição civil de Mansôa: Etnografia," *Boletim Official da Guiné Portugueza* 50 (December 10, 1927): 1–26.

97. Chelmicki, *Corografia,* vol. 2, 343.

98. Correia e Lança, *Relatório,* 50.

99. Carvalho, *Guiné,* 76.

100. Correia e Lança, *Relatório,* 51.

101. João Teixeira Pinto, *Teixeira Pinto: A ocupação militar da Guiné* (Lisbon: Divisão de Publicações e Biblioteca, 1936), 127.

102. Ernesto J. de C. e Vasconcellos, *Guiné portuguesa: Estudo elementar de geografia física, económica e politica* (Lisbon: Tip. da Cooperativa Militar, 1917). Oral narratives support the conclusion that growing populations and increased crop production were important factors in Balanta expansions from the region of the Mansoa and Geba. Interview with Alfrede Neves, Chiguna Clusse, and Bcolof Sukna, Patche Ialá, January 31, 1995.

103. Interview with Frós Intchalá and Ndum Mhana, Ilonde, January 28, 1995.

104. Correia e Lança, *Relatório,* 51.

105. *Boletim da Sociedade de Geografia de Lisboa* ser. 23, no. 11 (November 1905): 400.

106. Rosemary E. Galli, "Capitalist Agriculture and the Colonial State in Portuguese Guinea, 1926–1974," *African Economic History* 23 (1995), 55.

107. Quoted in Silva, *Relatório,* 48.

108. Cunningham, "The Colonial Period," 39. See also AHN, SGG A1/16.7/cx. 348.

109. Armando Corezão, *Boletim da Sociedade de Geografia de Lisboa* ser. 43a, nos. 7–9 (July–September 1925): 139.

CONCLUSION

In this book I have used two lenses, one wide and one narrow, to examine interactions among coastal farmers of the politically decentralized Guinea-Bissau area, an interior state's military, and Atlantic merchants from 1400 to 1900. Drawing on evidence found in European archives and local African vernaculars, I have shown that in the era of the Atlantic slave trade, decentralized societies were not necessarily passive victims of predatory state-based neighbors. Though they did not possess great armies, most decentralized societies discovered ways to defend themselves and to engage with the market. Further, I have argued that within the communities that composed decentralized societies, the changes that accompanied the rise of the Atlantic slave trade were not determined by "outside" forces. Rather, they grew from negotiations among "insiders" who sought to defend themselves and to exploit a shifting array of opportunities. Communities were contentious places. Within them, young and old and men and women struggled to determine how work was allocated, resources were utilized, and trade was conducted.

Through a wide-angle lens I have explored how coastal people responded to the intensification of slaving in the Guinea-Bissau region after the mid-sixteenth century. Living on the frontiers of one of West Africa's leading slave-producing states, Kaabu, they sought ways to defend themselves from predatory armies. Hence, households uprooted themselves from difficult-to-defend upland regions and settled in isolated, marshy, and riverine coastal zones. These areas provided natural hiding places for small groups and barriers that inhibited the movement of armies. Here coastal residents adopted new architectural designs for houses so slave raiders would have a difficult time snatching victims, and they concentrated houses into fortified villages.

Though defensive settlements often kept would-be attackers at bay, the actions of coastal people should not be seen as mindfully revolutionary strategies against the slave trade itself. The aims of coastal dwellers were much more immediate: the protection of kin and communities. Moreover, those who feared attack by slaving armies one day, often became slave producers themselves the next, making captives for what were considered both "legitimate" and "illegitimate" reasons. Some coastal slavers operated illegitimately by capturing and selling the vulnerable in order to enrich themselves personally through the accumulation of cloth, beads, alcohol, tobacco, and other Atlantic imports. Thus, small bandit outposts formed in a variety of places, preying on whomever they could catch off-guard, and individuals within communities sometimes "illegally" kidnapped children or duped unsuspecting travelers. But in many instances, coastal people accepted the enslavement and sale of certain people as legitimate. To defend themselves, communities in the Guinea-Bissau area needed weapons. Since European guns were cumbersome, inaccurate, and difficult to repair, coastal people preferred iron or iron-tipped spears, swords, arrows, and knives. Lacking iron of their own, they engaged in the slave trade in order to obtain this precious metal from Atlantic merchants. They produced captives by convicting those deemed socially deviant and criminal to sale and by organizing young men into raiding parties who struck distant strangers. Hence, one of the cruel ironies of the slave trade in Guinea-Bissau was that in order to obtain the iron necessary to defend themselves, coastal people captured and sold those in their midst.

They orchestrated the sale of captives by "wedding" themselves to the Atlantic market. That is, coastal communities and Atlantic merchants forged lasting commercial ties with one another by working through the predominant African mode of social and economic interaction—the extended family. Thus women became the nexus of coastal-Atlantic exchange as foreign male merchants married locals, creating familial bonds with their kin, who were the potential suppliers of exports.

Shifting the focus from broad regional interactions among societies and merchants, I have used a tighter lens to peer deeply into Balanta communities, examining interactions among men and women and youths and elders. Like others in the Guinea-Bissau area, Balanta concentrated their households, or *moranças,* into defensive villages, or *tabancas,* to combat the threat presented by slave raiders. Living side by side in *tabancas,* Balanta sought to restructure local institutions so that they could normalize interactions with one another, ensure a strong defense, and carry out large-scale work projects. However, the nature of community institutions was contentious. Through their dominance of three institutions—age grades, councils of elders, and marriages—older men gained some power over women and youths and directed them to produce resources for sustenance and sale. Older men sent young male age grades to raid distant communities for the purpose of producing captives. Because these raiding parties were relatively small, they did not generally have the physical force necessary to subdue large numbers of strong men and therefore targeted females and children, who were either traded for iron or integrated into Balanta communities. Further, in the late seventeenth and eighteenth centuries, older Balanta men organized male age grades into large work groups for undertaking a new and labor-intensive agricultural pursuit—the production of paddy rice.

Since paddy farming became centered on young males, the period saw the masculinization of agricultural labor. But young males did not perform the bulk of fieldwork without some concessions from older men. If elders' demands became too great, young men could leave their communities to seek employment with area merchants or they could form bandit communities who preyed on the weak. Hence, to retain their sons, older men offered them an incentive: work in paddies now and assume the right to sit on powerful councils of elders in the future. At the same time, older men limited young males' opportunities by denying them contact with outsiders. Older men did this by relying on women to forge bonds with area merchants who demanded slaves and rice for iron. This strategy had an unforeseen consequence: women gained more freedom of mobility, some taking advantage of connections with area merchants to enrich themselves personally and to wrench themselves free from the demands of patriarchal communities.

Though the manner in which Balanta organized *tabancas* was the result of negotiations and compromises among community insiders, Balanta communities were generally able to defend themselves against threatening raiders and to provide food for growing numbers of people. By the nineteenth century, Balanta were producing increasing volumes of paddy rice for both domestic consumption and export and their populations were among the densest on the Upper Guinea Coast. The slave trade did not, then, decimate communities of the Guinea-Bissau area. It presented great challenges to them. Coastal people met these by planting rice and harvesting slaves.

This book has focused on a region where the responses of people were unique in that they were shaped by very local circumstances and very particular struggles. However, because the Atlantic economic system presented people living in other decentralized areas with a similar range of challenges and opportunities, broad patterns of change across Africa resemble those in Guinea-Bissau. The task of identifying those patterns will be best accomplished only after scholars have undertaken more studies of the precolonial period. From the work that has been done, a number of tentative conclusions can be drawn. Specifically, in politically decentralized places, people often responded to the rise of the Atlantic slave trade by relocating and fortifying communities; by linking these communities to trade networks through marriages; and by producing and trading captives, a high proportion of whom were women and children.

First, when politically decentralized societies were threatened with the violence associated with slaving, members often relocated to easy-to-defend locations and fortified compact settlements. As in Guinea-Bissau, people in other places concentrated in areas that offered natural protections from slave raiders. For example, Kabre retreated to the mountains of northern Togo in an attempt to escape the armies of the powerful states of Ashanti and Dahomey, which staged predatory raids onto their frontiers.[1] In the coastal zones of Benin, people built stilt villages over waterways. In north central Africa, plain dwellers, who were vulnerable to powerful warlords in the late nineteenth and early twentieth centuries, took refuge in outcroppings of rocks that were riddled with crevasses and caves.[2] In the middle belt of Nigeria, pagans threatened by Muslim slave raiders "withdrew into large upland areas such as the Jos Plateau, where they sought refuge both in the broken country of the plateau edge and on the high plateau."[3] And in the Chad basin, Kimre "withdrew to the secure heights of their cotton-trees," frequently leaving their Bagirmi attackers "at a loss to know what to do in the face of such a situation. Hundreds of armed men standing around . . . without the courage to risk an attack."[4]

Where the landscape provided few natural defenses from slave raiders, many members of decentralized societies chose to concentrate in walled settlements.[5] The great warrior Samori was kept at bay by the walls of Sikasso for fifteen months in 1888 and 1889, and at Ntentu, a wall 3 meters high protected inhabitants until a persistent Samori finally broke the community's will.[6] Similarly, in West Africa's Sahel, Samo villagers constructed thick-sided *banco* houses that were connected to one another so that they offered no openings to attack. "Neighboring groups," French observers stated in the late nineteenth century, "while coveting the region, were not able to reduce the solid earthen villages of the Samo."[7] In the middle belt of Nigeria people concentrated populations and used walls and ditches to keep predators at bay. Here the towns of Wushishi, Kontagora, and Abuja were formed by people who had had "little centralized government" but recognized the need to unite against raiders.[8] Chamba also built walled settlements when they had to venture onto plains to cultivate crops, and some Igbo used walls to protect communities in southeast Nigeria.[9]

Second, across Africa's politically decentralized regions in the era of the Atlantic slave trade, people found ways to engage with broad markets and to gain access to valuable Atlantic imports. Not possessing the same broad institutions that regulated exchange and ensured safe trade routes in state-based societies, the members of decentralized societies often linked communities to the outside world through marriages. That is, they forged bonds with merchants by integrating them into the most important social, political, and economic unit—the extended family. Hence women became critical links between communities and larger economies. As in Guinea-Bissau, in politically decentralized stretches of the Congo River male merchants took wives "from great distances" and relied on marriage "to facilitate trade and to increase profits." Since local men were less likely to harm merchants who had married into their families, marriages helped ensure the safety of those who plied the river, moving commerce and purchasing slaves.[10] Similarly, in Igbo and

Ibibio areas of southeast Nigeria, the "protector a trader could depend on was an in-law, so it was not unusual for trading contacts to lead to marriage between the trader and a woman from his host's family."[11] And in politically decentralized Anlo-Ewe areas of the Slave Coast, the wealthy trading family of Gbodzo established itself when a foreign merchant called Tettega married Kpetsimine, who was the daughter of Amegashi Akofi, a wealthy local slave producer at Woe. "This union, which ultimately led to the birth of Gbodzo [and] secured for Amagashi Akofi an additional buyer for his slaves; and it is likely that through his wife Kpetsimine, a member of the Nygbla religious order, Tettega obtained access to the young women whom this order had begun to sell to the slave traders."[12]

Third, in other decentralized regions people produced and traded slaves, and they did so for reasons considered both "legitimate" (as when slave production brought imports needed for the good of the whole) and "illegitimate" (as when slave production brought imports used solely for personal gain). For example, on the Congo River, as in Guinea-Bissau, Bobangi communities often approved of the sale of "people who caused trouble . . . by committing one of a wide variety of offenses, including adultery, stealing, fighting, and witchcraft," and they organized raids to produce captives who could be traded for valued imports. However, "small gangs" of young men also acted outside the moral bounds of communities by enriching themselves through the kidnapping of women and children.[13] Similarly, Igbo and Ibibio villagers organized "legitimate" raids and conducted judicial proceedings, generating captives whom they traded for weapons and iron, which had great use in warfare and agriculture.[14] However, kidnappers also "illegally" harvested large numbers of slaves, principally children, whom they sold to get money for purchasing private titles or other riches.[15] This point is best illustrated in the narrative of Olaudah Equiano, who was made captive in the region. The son of respected slave-owning parents, Equiano himself was kidnapped and sold to merchants at the coast:

> But, alas! Ere long it was my fate to be thus attacked, and to be carried off, when none of the grown people were nigh. One day, when all our people were gone out to their works as usual, and only I and my dear sister were left to mind the house, two men and a woman got over our walls, and in a moment seized us both; and without giving us time to cry out, or make resistance, they stopped our mouths, tied our hands, and ran off with us into the nearest wood.[16]

Montagnards in northern Cameroon also produced slaves by staging kidnappings and raids that resembled "feuds" between lineages.[17]

Finally, how decentralized societies produced slaves often meant that the gender and age ratios of the captive populations they sold for export were different from those leaving state-based regions. Where small-scale raids and kidnappings were the most common means of generating captives, slavers typically avoided seizing dangerous men, targeting easier-to-transport women and children. Hence, like their Portuguese counterparts in coastal Guinea-Bissau, French officials in the area of present-day Burkina-Faso noted that "the Samo custom, adopted as well by the Marka of the region," was to kidnap women.[18] Similarly, British observers in East Africa said that Lango raids produced "large numbers of women and children" captives.[19] Further, a high proportion of child captives were shipped from the Cameroon grassfields because young men, operating individually or in small clandestine groups, encouraged the trade by swiping and selling children to finance marriages that did not meet their fathers' approval.[20] And in Igboland young warriors acted much like Balanta in killing men "as a matter of honor" and seizing women and children, who were easier to subdue and transport over long distances.[21]

From Balanta areas, the relatively high proportion of female-slave exports can also be attributed to the fact that women played a relatively insignificant role in paddy rice production. Hence female slaves were not desired as laborers. This was also the case among Igbo. When looked at as a whole, the Atlantic slave trade took about twice as many males as females from Africa, but from the Igbo-dominated Bight of Biafra, about the same proportion of male and female slaves were exported during certain periods. As in Guinea-Bissau, in the Bight the nature of African warfare coupled with the role of women in agricultural production shaped the decisions captors made about whom to retain and whom to export. Igbo yam production centered on male labor, so women slaves were not utilized in fields. Hence Igbo incorporated some female captives into communities as wives but sold many to Atlantic merchants.[22] Further work on the precolonial gendered division of labor in other decentralized societies will inevitably yield more fruitful comparisons and perhaps change our views of the nature of precolonial African labor.

Though most people living on the dangerous frontiers of powerful predatory states did not aim to bring revolutionary changes to the Atlantic economy, the strategies they pursued may have had revolutionary consequences. Decentralized societies certainly forced large state-based slaving armies to go greater and greater distances in their quest for captives, thereby increasing the cost of slaving. Further, since predatory states relied on the sale of some captives and labor of others to provide the wealth necessary to sustain militaries, the actions of decentralized societies destabilized states themselves. At times, the strategies of decentralized societies may also have increased the cost of slaves sold for export, causing periodic shocks that rippled through the entire Atlantic system.[23] In addition, the manner in which decentralized societies produced and traded captives affected the gender and age composition of slave populations entering the Atlantic and arriving on American plantations.

The slave trade was a terrible tragedy for those caught up in it. However, the states that produced the bulk of the exports from Africa did not "decimate" all of the societies on their frontiers. People living outside states and in politically decentralized regions responded to the violence of the Atlantic slave trade by carefully considering the options available to them. The decisions they made shaped their own lives and the nature of the slave trade itself.

NOTES

1. Charles Piot, "Of Slaves and the Gift: Kabre Sale of Kin During the Era of the Slave Trade," *Journal of African History* 37, no. 1 (1996): 33–34.

2. Denis D. Cordell, "The Myth of Inevitability and Invincibility: Resistance to Slavers and the Slave Trade in Central Africa in the Late Nineteenth and Early Twentieth Centuries," paper presented at the conference "Fighting Back: African Strategies Against the Slave Trade," Rutgers University, February 16–17, 2001.

3. M. B. Gleave and R. M. Prothero, "Population Density and 'Slave Raiding': A Comment," *Journal of African History* 12, no. 2 (1971): 321.

4. Gustav Nachtigal, *Sahel and Sudan,* trans. Allan G. B. Fisher and Humphery J. Fisher (London: C. Hurst, 1987), 340–343.

5. For more on how war shaped African architecture, see Thierno Mouctar Bah, *Architecture militaire traditionnelle et poliorcétique dans le Soudan occidental du XVIIe à la fin du XIXe siècle* (Yaounde: Editions Cle, 1985). For a narrative of populations concentrating in reaction to the violence associated with slaving, see George Schwab, *Tribes of the Liberian Hinterland,* papers of the Peabody Museum of American Archaeology and Ethnology, Harvard University, vol. 31 (Cambridge: Peabody Museum, 1947), 29.

6. Martin A. Klein, "The Slave Trade and Decentralized Societies," *Journal of African History* 42, no. 1 (2000): 53–55.

7. Andrew Hubbell, "A View of the Slave Trade from the Margin: Souroudougou in the Late Nineteenth-Century Slave Trade of the Niger Bend," *Journal of African History* 42, no. 1 (2000): 32.

8. Michael Mason, "Population Density and 'Slave Raiding': The Case of the Middle Belt of Nigeria," *Journal of African History* 10, no. 4 (1969): 553; Gleave and Prothero, "Population Density," 320–321.

9. Richard Fardon, *Raiders and Refugees: Trends in Chamba Political Development, 1750–1950* (Washington, D.C.: Smithsonian Institution Press, 1988), chap. 5; Klein, "The Slave Trade and Decentralized Societies." For another example of walls protecting communities from attack, see M.D.D. Newitt, "The Portuguese on the Zambezi: An Historical Interpretation of the Prazo," *Journal of African History* 10, no. 1 (1969): 81. Newitt describes fortifications or "aringas" around the Zambezi in the nineteenth century.

10. Robert W. Harms, *River of Wealth, River of Sorrow: The Central Zaire Basin in the Era of the Slave and Ivory Trade, 1500–1891* (New Haven, Conn.: Yale University Press, 1981), 80–81.

11. Ibid., 98.

12. Sandra Greene, *Gender, Ethnicity, and Social Change on the Upper Slave Coast: A History of the Anlo-Ewe* (Portsmouth, N.H.: Heinemann, 1996), 71–75.

13. Ibid.

14. David Northrup, *Trade Without Rulers: Pre-Colonial Economic Development in South-Eastern Nigeria* (Oxford: Clarendon Press, 1978), 69, 167.

15. Ibid., 76. J. N. Oriji argues that, among Ngwa, most slaves were produced by kidnappers, since judicial structures were weak. J. N. Oriji, "A History of the Ngwa People: Social and Economic Developments in an Igbo Clan from the Thirteenth to the Twentieth Centuries" (Ph.D. thesis, State University of New Jersey, 1977), 50–53, 130–136, 189–206. Similarly, Andrew Hubbell reports the "'illegal' seizure and slave of persons (banditry) was increasingly practiced by groups of young men" in the politically decentralized Souroudougou. Hubbell, "A View," 38.

16. Olaudah Equiano, *The Interesting Narrative and Other Writings* (New York: Penguin Books, 1995), 47.

17. Scott MacEachern, "Selling the Iron for Their Shackles: Wandala Montagnard Interactions in Northern Cameroon," *Journal of African History* 34, no. 2 (1993): 257.

18. Andrew Hubbell, "Patronage and Predation: A Social History of Colonial Chieftaincies in a Chiefless Region—Souroudougou (Burkina Faso), 1850–1946" (Ph.D. diss., Stanford University, 1997), 112–113.

19. John Tosh, *Clan Leaders and Colonial Chiefs: The Political History of an East African Stateless Society, c. 1800–1939* (Oxford: Clarendon Press, 1978), 86.

20. Jean-Pierre Warnier, "Traite sans raids au Cameroun," *Cahiers d'Études Africaines* 113, 29–1 (1989): 5–32; Klein, "The Slave Trade and Decentralized Societies," 60.

21. G. Ugo Nwokeji, "African Conceptions of Gender and the Slave Traffic," *William and Mary Quarterly* 58, no. 1 (January 2001): 62. Marcia Wright has assembled some moving personal narratives by children and women captured and kidnapped by slavers in East Africa. See Marcia Wright, *Strategies of Slaves and Women: Life-Stories from East/Central Africa* (New York: Lilian Barber, 1993).

22. Ibid., esp. 55–61.

23. See Patrick Manning, "Contours of Slavery and Social Change in Africa," *American Historical Review* 88 (October 1983): 844–845.

APPENDIX 1:
BISSAU SLAVE CENSUS
OF 1856

GUINEA-BISSAU'S COASTAL ZONE

Table A1.1   Numbers and Percentages of Males and Females Who Originated in Guinea-Bissau's Coastal Zone in the Bissau Slave Census of 1856

Ethnic Group	Total in Census	Males	%	Females	%
Balanta	18	4	0.22	14	0.78
Banyun	5	3	0.60	2	0.40
Biafada	35	19	0.54	16	0.46
Bijago	183	78	0.43	105	0.57
Brame	30	10	0.33	20	0.67
Papel	10	7	0.70	3	0.30
Cassanga	1	0	0.00	1	1.00
Floup	10	6	0.60	4	0.40
Manjaco	12	7	0.58	5	0.42
Total	304	134	0.44	170	0.56

Source: AHU, AUL, GG, Lv. 0010, "Livro dos escravos do concelho de Bissau e ilheu do Rei," 1856.

INTERIOR OF THE UPPER GUINEA COAST

Table A1.2 Numbers and Percentages of Males and Females Who Originated in the Interior of the Upper Guinea Coast in the Bissau Slave Census of 1856

Ethnic Group	Total in Census	Males	%	Females	%
Bambara	5	2	0.40	3	0.60
Fula	74	57	0.77	17	0.23
Futa Fula	23	20	0.87	3	0.13
Jalonke	1	1	1.00	0	0.00
Mandinka	154	119	0.77	35	0.23
Kissi	3	2	0.67	1	0.33
Tilibonca	186	112	0.60	74	0.40
Wasulunke	26	16	0.62	10	0.38
Total	472	329	0.70	143	0.30

Source: AHU, AUL, GG, Lv. 0010, "Livro dos escravos do concelho de Bissau e ilheu do Rei," 1856.

SENEGAL, GUINEA, AND SIERRA LEONE'S COASTAL ZONES

Table A1.3 Numbers and Percentages of Males and Females Who Originated in Guinea and Sierra Leone's Coastal Zones in the Bissau Slave Census of 1856

Ethnic Group	Total in Census	Males	%	Females	%
Nalu	29	18	0.62	11	0.38
Sape	10	6	0.60	4	0.40
Sosso	9	7	0.78	2	0.22
Temne	1	0	0.00	1	1.00
Toma	42	27	0.64	15	0.36
Total	91	58	0.64	33	0.36

Source: AHU, AUL, GG, Lv. 0010, "Livro dos escravos do concelho de Bissau e ilheu do Rei," 1856.

BORN IN CAPTIVITY OR ETHNICITY NOT LISTED

Table A1.4 Numbers and Percentages of Males and Females Born in Captivity or Whose Ethnicity Was Not Listed in the Bissau Slave Census of 1856

Ethnic Group	Total in Census	Males	%	Females	%
Bissau	139	71	0.51	68	0.49
Boa Esperança	4	2	0.50	2	0.50
Bolama	50	27	0.54	23	0.46
Cacheu	2	2	1.00	0	0.00
Corubal	1	1	1.00	0	0.00
Galinhas	9	5	0.56	4	0.44
Geba	31	15	0.48	16	0.52
Mato Grande	1	1	1.00	0	0.00
Reinuno	1	1	1.00	0	0.00
Rio Grande	1	0	0.00	1	1.00
No information	1	1	1.00	0	0.00
Total	240	126	0.52	114	0.48

Source: AHU, AUL, GG, Lv. 0010, "Livro dos escravos do concelho de Bissau e ilheu do Rei," 1856.

APPENDIX 2:
CAPE VERDE SLAVE CENSUS
OF 1856

GUINEA-BISSAU'S COASTAL ZONE

Table A2.1 Numbers and Percentages of Males and Females Who Originated in Guinea-Bissau's Coastal Zone in the Cape Verde Slave Census of 1856

Ethnic Group	Total in Census	Males	%	Females	%
Balanta	17	8	0.47	9	0.53
Banyun	4	3	0.75	1	0.25
Biafada	3	1	0.33	2	0.67
Bijago	18	12	0.67	6	0.33
Brame	1	0	0.00	1	1.00
Floup	9	5	0.56	4	0.44
Manjaco	5	4	0.80	1	0.20
Papel	3	1	0.33	2	0.67
Total	60	34	0.57	26	0.43

Source: António Carreira, *Cabo Verde: Formação e extinção de uma sociedade escravocrata (1460–1878)* (Praia, Cape Verde: Instituto Caboverdeano de Livro, 1983), 428.

INTERIOR OF THE UPPER GUINEA COAST

Table A2.2   Numbers and Percentages of Males and Females Who Originated in the Interior of the Upper Guinea Coast and Senegambia in the Cape Verde Slave Census of 1856

Ethnic Group	Total in Census	Males	%	Females	%
Assolum	2	1	0.50	1	0.50
Bambara	4	3	0.75	1	0.25
Fula	19	18	0.95	1	0.05
Mandinka/Soninka	34	27	0.79	7	0.21
Tilibonca	4	2	0.50	2	0.50
Kissi	4	3	0.75	1	0.25
Total	67	54	0.81	13	0.19

Source: António Carreira, *Cabo Verde: Formação e extinção de uma sociedade escravocrata (1460–1878)* (Praia, Cape Verde: Instituto Caboverdeano de Livro, 1983), 428.

SENEGAL, GUINEA, AND SIERRA LEONE'S COASTAL ZONES

Table A2.3   Numbers and Percentages of Males and Females Who Originated in Guinea and Sierra Leone's Coastal Zones in the Cape Verde Slave Census of 1856

Ethnic Group	Total in Census	Males	%	Females	%
Nalu	1	1	1.0	0	0.0
Surua	1	1	1.0	0	0.0
Wolof	1	1	1.0	0	0.0
Total	3	3	1.0	0	0.0

Source: António Carreira, *Cabo Verde: Formação e extinção de uma sociedade escravocrata (1460–1878)* (Praia, Cape Verde: Instituto Caboverdeano de Livro, 1983), 428.

APPENDIX 3:
CACHEU SLAVE CENSUS
OF 1856

GUINEA-BISSAU'S COASTAL ZONE

Table A3.1 Numbers and Percentages of Males and Females Who Originated in Guinea-Bissau's Coastal Zone in the Cacheu Slave Census of 1856

Ethnic Group	Total in Census	Males	%	Females	%
Balanta	58	15	0.26	43	0.74
Banyun	115	46	0.40	69	0.60
Biafada	2	1	0.50	1	0.50
Bijago	25	10	0.40	15	0.60
Brame	48	16	0.33	32	0.67
Papel	12	6	0.50	6	0.50
Cassanga	19	9	0.47	10	0.53
Floup	199	79	0.40	120	0.60
Baoite	1	1	1.00	0	0.00
Total	479	183	0.38	296	0.62

Source: AHU, AUL, GG, Lv. 0035, "Livro dos escravos do concelho de Cacheu, Farim e Ziguichor," 1856.

INTERIOR OF THE UPPER GUINEA COAST

Table A3.2 Numbers and Percentages of Males and Females Who Originated in the Interior of the Upper Guinea Coast in the Cacheu Slave Census of 1856

Ethnic Group	Total in Census	Males	%	Females	%
Fula	11	3	0.27	8	0.73
Futa Fula	6	3	0.40	3	0.60
Mandinka	74	36	0.49	38	0.51
Tilibonca	39	19	0.49	20	0.51
Mouro	1	1	1.00	0	0.00
Total	131	62	0.47	69	0.53

Source: AHU, AUL, GG, Lv. 0035, "Livro dos escravos do concelho de Cacheu, Farim e Ziguichor," 1856.

SENEGAL, GUINEA, AND SIERRA LEONE'S COASTAL ZONES

Table A3.3 Numbers and Percentages of Males and Females Who Originated in Guinea and Sierra Leone's Coastal Zones in the Cacheu Slave Census of 1856

Ethnic Group	Total in Census	Males	%	Females	%
Nalu	4	4	1.00	0	0.00
Sape	1	0	0.00	1	1.00
Wolof	2	0	0.00	2	1.00
Gore	1	0	0.00	1	1.00
Total	8	4	0.50	4	0.50

Source: AHU, AUL, GG, Lv. 0035, "Livro dos escravos do concelho de Cacheu, Farim e Ziguichor," 1856.

BORN IN CAPTIVITY OR ETHNICITY NOT IDENTIFIABLE

Table A3.4 Numbers and Percentages of Males and Females Born in Captivity or Whose Ethnicity Was Not Identifiable in the Cacheu Slave Census of 1856

Ethnic Group	Total in Census	Males	%	Females	%
Bissau	8	2	0.25	6	0.75
Cacheu	257	108	0.42	149	0.58
Farim	49	21	0.43	28	0.57
Zeguinchor	148	58	0.39	90	0.61
Not identifiable	5	3	0.60	2	0.40
Total	467	192	0.41	275	0.59

Source: AHU, AUL, GG, Lv. 0035, "Livro dos escravos do concelho de Cacheu, Farim e Ziguichor," 1856.

APPENDIX 4:
BISSAU, CAPE VERDE, AND CACHEU SLAVE CENSUSES OF 1856 COMBINED

GUINEA-BISSAU'S COASTAL ZONE

Table A4.1   Numbers and Percentages of Males and Females Who Originated in Guinea-Bissau's Coastal Zone in the Bissau, Cape Verde, and Cacheu Slave Censuses of 1856

Ethnic Group	Total in Census	Males	%	Females	%
Balanta	93	27	0.29	66	0.71
Banyun	124	52	0.42	72	0.58
Biafada	40	21	0.53	19	0.47
Bijago	226	100	0.44	126	0.56
Brame	79	26	0.33	53	0.67
Papel	25	14	0.56	11	0.44
Cassanga	20	9	0.45	11	0.55
Floup	218	90	0.41	128	0.59
Manjaco	17	11	0.65	6	0.35
Baoite	1	1	1.00	0	0.00
Total	843	351	0.42	492	0.58

Source: AHU, AUL, GG, Lv. 0035, "Livro dos escravos do concelho de Cacheu, Farim e Ziguichor," 1856; AHU, AUL, GG, Lv. 0010, "Livro dos escravos do concelho de Bissau e ilheu do Rei," 1856; and António Carreira, *Cabo Verde: Formação e extinção de uma sociedade escravocrata (1460–1878)* (Praia, Cape Verde: Instituto Caboverdeano de Livro, 1983), 428.

INTERIOR OF THE UPPER GUINEA COAST

Table A4.2 Numbers and Percentages of Males and Females Who Originated in the Interior of the Upper Guinea Coast in the Bissau, Cape Verde, and Cacheu Slave Censuses of 1856

Ethnic Group	Total in Census	Males	%	Females	%
Bambara	9	5	0.56	4	0.44
Fula	104	78	0.75	26	0.25
Futa Fula	29	23	0.79	6	0.21
Jalonke	1	1	1.00	0	0.00
Mandinka	262	182	0.69	80	0.31
Kissi	7	5	0.71	2	0.29
Tilibonca	229	133	0.58	96	0.42
Wasulunke	26	16	0.62	10	0.38
Assolum	2	1	0.50	1	0.50
Mouro	1	1	1.00	0	0.00
Total	670	445	0.66	225	0.34

Source: AHU, AUL, GG, Lv. 0035, "Livro dos escravos do concelho de Cacheu, Farim e Ziguichor," 1856; AHU, AUL, GG, Lv. 0010, "Livro dos escravos do concelho de Bissau e ilheu do Rei," 1856; and António Carreira, *Cabo Verde: Formação e extinção de uma sociedade escravocrata (1460–1878)* (Praia, Cape Verde: Instituto Caboverdeano de Livro, 1983), 428.

SENEGAL, GUINEA, AND SIERRA LEONE'S COASTAL ZONES

Table A4.3 Numbers and Percentages of Males and Females Who Originated in Guinea and Sierra Leone's Coastal Zones in the Bissau, Cape Verde, and Cacheu Slave Censuses of 1856

Ethnic Group	Total in Census	Males	%	Females	%
Nalu	34	23	0.68	11	0.32
Sape	11	6	0.55	5	0.45
Sosso	9	7	0.78	2	0.22
Temne	1	0	0	1	1
Toma	42	27	0.64	15	0.36
Surua	1	1	1	0	0
Wolof	3	1	0.33	2	0.67
Gore	1	0	0	1	1
Total	102	65	0.64	37	0.36

Source: AHU, AUL, GG, Lv. 0035, "Livro dos escravos do concelho de Cacheu, Farim e Ziguichor," 1856; AHU, AUL, GG, Lv. 0010, "Livro dos escravos do concelho de Bissau e ilheu do Rei," 1856; and António Carreira, *Cabo Verde: Formação e extinção de uma sociedade escravocrata (1460–1878)* (Praia, Cape Verde: Instituto Caboverdeano de Livro, 1983), 428.

BORN IN CAPTIVITY OR ETHNICITY NOT LISTED

Table A4.4 Numbers and Percentages of Males and Females Born in Captivity or Whose Ethnicity Was Not Listed or Identifiable in the Bissau, Cape Verde, and Cacheu Slave Censuses of 1856

Ethnic Group	Total in Census	Males	%	Females	%
Bissau	147	73	0.50	74	0.50
Boa Esperança	4	2	0.50	2	0.50
Bolama	50	27	0.54	23	0.46
Cacheu	259	110	0.42	149	0.58
Corubal	1	1	1.00	0	0.00
Galinhas	9	5	0.56	4	0.44
Geba	31	15	0.48	16	0.52
Mato Grande	1	1	1.00	0	0.00
Reinuno	1	1	1.00	0	0.00
Rio Grande	1	0	0.00	1	1.00
Farim	49	21	0.43	28	0.57
Zeguinchor	148	58	0.39	90	0.61
Not identifiable	5	3	0.60	2	0.40
No information	1	1	1.00	0	0.00
Total	707	318	0.45	389	0.55

Source: AHU, AUL, GG, Lv. 0035, "Livro dos escravos do concelho de Cacheu, Farim e Ziguichor," 1856; AHU, AUL, GG, Lv. 0010, "Livro dos escravos do concelho de Bissau e ilheu do Rei," 1856; and António Carreira, *Cabo Verde: Formação e extinção de uma sociedade escravocrata (1460–1878)* (Praia, Cape Verde: Instituto Caboverdeano de Livro, 1983), 428.

APPENDIX 5:
SLAVE EXPORTS FROM THE
GUINEA-BISSAU REGION

Table A5.1 Ships Whose Logs Reveal Numbers of Males and Females Aboard, 1700–1840

Unique Identity Number	Principal Port of Slave Purchase	Principal Port of Disembarkation	Year of Departure from Last Slaving Port	Men at First Port of Purchase	Women at First Port of Purchase	Boys at First Port of Purchase	Girls at First Port of Purchase	Imputed Numbers of Males (Dis)-Embarked[a]	Imputed Numbers of Females (Dis)-Embarked[a]	Imputed Numbers of Children Embarked[a]	Proportion of Males (Dis)-Embarked[a]	Proportion of Children (Dis)-Embarked[a]	Total Slaves (Dis)-Embarked with Sex Identified[a]
11371	Cacheu/Bijago	Captured	1700	30	15	9	6	39	21	15	0.65	0.25	60
9061	Bissau	Maranhao	1759	0	0	0	0	123	55	0	0.69	0	178
9064	Bissau	Maranhao	1761	106	19	23	14	129	33	37	0.80	0.23	162
9065	Bissau	Maranhao	1762	83	54	29	26	112	80	55	0.58	0.29	192
9066	Cacheu	Maranhao	1762	65	33	26	17	91	50	43	0.65	0.31	141
9067	Bissau	Maranhao	1763	0	0	0	0	54	123	0	0.69	0	177
9069	Bissau/Cacheu	Maranhao	1764	101	40	12	5	113	45	17	0.72	0.11	158
9070	Bissau	Maranhao	1765	175	0	1	0	176	0	1	1.00	0.01	176
31533	Bissau	Cap Francais	1766	0	0	0	0	62	53	55	0.53	0.48	115
9071	Cacheu	Maranhao	1766	59	53	15	11	74	64	26	0.54	0.19	138
9072	Cacheu	Maranhao	1767	77	35	22	26	99	61	48	0.62	0.30	160
9073	Bissau	Para	1774	91	62	40	28	131	90	68	0.59	0.31	221
9074	Cacheu	Maranhao	1774	125	28	12	13	137	41	25	0.77	0.14	178
9079	Bissau	Para	1775	74	60	34	32	108	92	66	0.54	0.33	200
9077	Bissau	Para	1775	59	63	14	10	73	73	24	0.50	0.16	146
7613	Bissau	S. Leone	1817	135	53	0	0	135	53	81	0.72	0.30	188
2898	Bissau	S. Leone	1822	70	40	26	30	96	70	56	0.58	0.34	166
3013	Cacheu	S. Leone	1829	115	51	26	28	141	79	54	0.64	0.25	220
1213	Cacheu	Bahamas	1831	0	0	0	0	88	69	23	0.56	0.15	157
1860	Bissau	Jamaica	1839	0	0	0	0	119	55	37	0.68	0.21	174
2697	Bissau	Jamaica	1840	0	0	0	0	229	50	0	0.82	0	279
Total				1,365	606	289	246	2,329	1,257	731	0.65	0.20	3586

Note: a. Where figures for embarkation were not available, figures for disembarkation have been used.

Source: David Eltis, Stephen D. Behrendt, David Richardson, and Herbert S. Klein, eds., *The Trans-Atlantic Slave Trade: A Database on CD-ROM* (Cambridge: Cambridge University Press, 1999).

GLOSSARY OF FOREIGN TERMS AND MEASUREMENTS

alante ndang (Graça): Respected male elder; a male head of a household; a recognized rank in the Balanta age-grade system that is typically attained by males in their late twenties or early thirties, depending on the region. Once they attain this rank, men gain the right to sit on councils of elders and to make decisions for their communities.

anin ndang (Graça): Respected female elder.

arroba (Portuguese): Unit of weight, about 15 kilograms.

babm hath (Graça): Whites or mulattos.

b'anin b'ndang (Graça): Plural of *anin ndang*.

b'lante b'ndang (Graça): Plural of *alante ndang*.

b'kindeu (Graça): Plural of *kindeu*.

blufos (Graça): Youths or uncircumcised males.

b'minde (Graça): Word used by Balanta to refer to Muslims to the east of coastal Guinea-Bissau.

bolanha (Creole): Lowland area where rice is grown. In Graça, *thambe*.

bombolom (Graça/Creole): "Talking drum." A drum fashioned from a hollowed-out section of log that Balanta use to communicate over long distances.

b'ostemoré (Graça): Plural of *ostemoré*.

cana (Creole): Distilled spirit made from the extracts of sugar cane.

Note: Graça is the Balanta language. It has no accepted written form, so I have provided phonetic spellings. Guinean Creole (or simply Creole or Crioulo) is the language spoken by most people in Guinea-Bissau. It developed in the era of the Atlantic slave trade as a language of commerce.

chôro (Creole): Funeral.

comerciante (Portuguese): Trader or merchant.

Crioulo (Creole): Guinean Creole. Also a Luso African or mixed-race person.

escravo (Portuguese): Slave.

estrangeiro (Portuguese): Foreigner.

fanado (Creole): Male circumcision ceremony.

feitorias (Portuguese): Agricultural production units that European or Cape Verdean merchants owned and from which they conducted commercial transactions with coastal people.

gampisas (Creole or Biafada): bandit communities.

gentios (Portuguese): Savages or pagans.

grumetes (Creole/Portuguese): From the Portuguese for "cabin boy." Africans who worked for coastal traders.

hala (Graça): God.

irã (Creole): A local god.

kebinde (Graça): The Balanta plow or fulcrum shovel. Long wooden shovel-type instrument used to prepare fields.

kindeu (Graça): "The hunting of people." A raid with the purpose of taking captives.

lançados (Creole/Portuguese): From the Portuguese *lançar,* or "to throw." Portuguese and Cape Verdeans who either threw themselves or who were thrown onto the coast to live out their lives, typically as traders.

limbi prato (Creole): "Plate licker." An insult (e.g., "In the commercial center, he was so poor that he had to become a *limbi prato.*").

malageta (Creole/Portuguese): Chili pepper.

malu or *maale* (Graça): Rice.

malu mon (Graça): See *n'contu.*

milho (Creole/Portuguese/Graça): maize or grain, sometimes sorghum or millet.

morança (Creole): Household.

n'contu (Graça): A dark rice that is indigenous to Africa. The scientific name is *Oryza glaberrima.* Also *malu mon.*

negociante (Portuguese): Merchant or businessperson.

n'haye (Graça): Last of the youth age grades. After this grade, young males become *b'lante b'ndang*.

ostemoré (Graça): a raid.

pmusee bele (Graça): See *limbi prato*.

pontas (Portuguese): Farms begun on "points" of land along the Guinea-Bissau region's rivers.

ponteiros (Portuguese): The owners of *pontas*.

praça (Portuguese): Commercial center or fort where trade was conducted.

quintal (Portuguese): A unit of measurement equal to 100 kilograms or 220.46 pounds.

réis (Portuguese): Portuguese currency of account in the eighteenth century. 1,000 réis is written 1$000, with the dollar sign marking the thousands.

ria (Portuguese): Estuary, inlet or sunken. The Upper Guinea Coast is characterized by its "sunken" coastline. Geologic activity submerged it, allowing ocean waters to flood considerable distances inland with the coming of the tides.

tabanca (Creole): A village or a collection of *moranças*. The word is derived from a Mane word for "entrenchments."

tangomaos (Creole/Portuguese): Portuguese and Cape Verdean outcasts who settled on the Upper Guinea Coast to become traders. Generally, the word has negative connotations.

thambe (Graça): See *bolanha*.

BIBLIOGRAPHY

ORAL INTERVIEWS

I conducted most of these interviews in Graça, the Balanta language, and some in Crioulo (Guinean Creole). I recorded all of them on cassette tape. Carlos Intigue and Agostinho Clode Suba Nania assisted with interviews and transcription. Since Graça has no written form, we translated the interviews into Portuguese while transcribing them. I gave the transcriptions and recordings to the Arquivo Histórico do Instituto Nacional de Estudos e Pesquisa (INEP) in Bissau. Unfortunately, large portions of INEP's holdings were lost when the archive was bombed and looted several years ago. I plan to make new copies available to INEP as soon as its directors are in a position to accept materials. Interviews are listed alphabetically by first name.

Adelino Bidenga Sanha. Quinhaque, January 7, 1995.
Alfrede Neves, Chiguna Clusse, and Bcolof Sukna. Patch Ialá, January 31, 1995.
Ana Na Tchuda and N'Simba Na Diana. Mato-Farroba, December 6, 1996.
Alberto Saná Mané, Atitia Camará, Lamine Mané, and N'fath Biai. Begeue, July 12, 2000.
Aussé NaFanda. Cantoné, March 5, 1995.
Baiem NaAda. Cufar, March 12, 1995.
Basca Fonre, Pam Bighate, Bwasat Basca, and Bian Bekle. Nhacra, January 1, 1995.
Batcha Bedocua, Barbosa Indani, João Imbali, Sobré Betura, and Agostinho Elsabai. Binar, July 15, 2000.
Bínha Nambana. Cantoné, March 5, 1995.
Binhang Thambe and N'Cutcha Nanumna. Anhede, January 7, 1995.
Biselha Na Pirana. Cufar, March 2, 1995.
Bisi Binhaga and José Gomes. Cafa, January 31, 1995.
Bitar Nabidé, Thamba Nanghasen, and Cumé Nanghasen. Oko, February 18, 1995.
Cabi Na Tambá. Mato-Farroba, December 6, 1996.
Canhe Na Diana. Mato-Farroba, December 6, 1996.
Ceredu Mané, Aliu Mané, Ussumane Mané, Nababú Mané, Bullé Camará, Landim Mané, Mamba Mané, Idrissa Mané, Suleimane Mané, Albino Mané, and Sambai Mané. Caraban, July 12, 2000.

Cubumba Sangê, Bletê, and Chefe Lima. N'Tin, April 5, 1995.

Cul NaMbatu. Cantoné, March 5, 1995.

Estanislau Correia Landim. João Landim, February 222, 1995.

Fduk Nam Ialá. Cantoné, March 5, 1995.

Fô Kidum. Quinhaque, January 7, 1995.

Fona Benuma. Encheia, January 13, 1995.

Frós Intchalá and Ndum Mhana. Ilonde, January 28, 1995.

Funi Quiyangue. Bera, April 5, 1995.

Iamta Na Nfad. Cufar, March 12, 1995.

Inguessa Nhasse. Oko, February 2, 1995.

Inrani Natsuné. Oko, February 18, 1995.

Isnaba Nambatcha. Cufar, March 3, 1995.

João Bafã. Patch Ialá, January 8, 1995.

Mada NaBikinthunde and Filif NaBininthunde. Oko, February 25, 1995.

Mada NaBikinthunde, Filif NaBininthunde, Madate NaFunda, and Mbunde Ntchcala. Oko,
    February 18, 1995.

Mam Bicura. Oko, February 25, 1995.

Mam Nambatcha. Cufar: December 2, 1994; March 3, 1995.

Mande Nathokn, Nthala Kilinque Nancade, and Tempo Kiluthe Nakilike. Nhoma, January
    25, 1995.

Mariano Martinho Natidai. N'Fotot or Quidet, July 15, 2000.

M'Bak MBana. Ntcheretê, April 5, 1995.

Mbunh Nanful. Mato-Farroba, December 6, 1994.

Mode N'ghasse and Pam N'ghasse. G'Bucra, January 25, 1995.

N'Dafa Na Combé. Mato-Farroba, December 12, 1994.

N'dai Na Barna. Cantoné, March 10, 1995.

N'kathaba Nathoken. Oko, February 25, 1995.

N'Raba Na Bedanh and Imbunh Na Bedanh. Cufar, December 18, 1995.

N'Sar N'Tchala. Bera, April 5, 1995.

N'Tchala Boda. Nhamad, April 5, 1995.

N'tera Siga. Patch Ialá, January 25, 1995.

N'tokde Nanatche. Anhede, January 7, 1995.

Ndami Nafanda. Oko, February 25, 1995.

Ndiba Ntchala. Patch Ialá, January 8, 1995.

Ngwetan Sanha. Quinhaque, January 7, 1995.

Nhafede Sambe and Abna Dafa. Blimat, January 28, 1995.

Nquissa Ba Mbali. Nhacra, January 25, 1995.

Quemade N'dami and Armando Dias. N'tatelai, February 2, 1995.

Quidama Kabi and Buetman Bidam. Oko, February 18, 1995.

Saé Namghomdé. Cufar, March 3, 1995.

Sami Nandingue. Oko, February 18, 1995.

Sanhá NaBecamba. Cantoné, March 5, 1995.

Sidu Nakiluth. Oko, February 18, 1995.

Tchong Binhom and Wangna Sanhá. N'talod, January 25, 1995.

Tchuta Mbali. Patch Ialá, January 8, 1995.

Tona Na Isna and Suna Na Isna. Cantoné, March 5, 1995.

Virginia da Silva. Ntalai, February 2, 1995.

ARCHIVES

Bissau, Guinea-Bissau: Arquivos Históricos do Instituto Nacional de Estudos e Pesquisa (INEP).
Dakar, Senegal: Archives Nationales de Sénégal (ANS).
Lisbon, Portugal: Arquivo Histórico Ultramarino (AHU); Arquivo Nacional da Torre do Tombo (ANTT).
Praia, Cape Verde: Arquivo Histórico Nacional (AHN).

PUBLISHED AND UNPUBLISHED SOURCES

Adams, Robert. *The Evolution of Urban Society: Early Mesopotamia and Prehistoric Mexico.* Chicago: Aldine, 1966.
Ajayi, J. F. Ade. "West Africa in the Anti-Slave Trade Era." In *The Cambridge History of Africa.* Vol. 5, *From 1790 to 1870.* Edited by J. F. Ade Ajayi and B. O. Oloruntimehin. Cambridge: Cambridge University Press, 1976, 200–221.
———. "West African States at the Beginning of the Nineteenth Century." In *A Thousand Years of West African History.* Edited by J. F. Ade Ajayi and Michael Crowder. London: Nelson, 1965, 253–267.
Akinjogbin, I. A. *Dahomey and Its Neighbors, 1708–1818.* Cambridge: Cambridge University Press, 1967.
Almada, André Álvares de. *Tratado breve dos rios de Guiné.* Translated by P.E.H. Hair. Liverpool: University of Liverpool, Department of History, 1984.
———. *Tratado breve dos rios de Guiné do Cabo Verde dês do Rio de Sanagá até os Baixios de Santa Ana de todas as nações que há na dita costa e de seus costumes, armas, trajos, juramentos, guerras, ano 1594.* Edited by António Brásio. Lisbon: Editorial LIAM, 1964.
Almeida, Januario Correia de. *Uma mez na Guiné.* Lisbon: Typographia Universal, 1859.
Álvares, Manuel. *Ethiopia Minor and a Geographical Account of the Province of Sierra Leone.* Translated by P.E.H. Hair. Liverpool: University of Liverpool, Department of History, September 30, 1990.
Andrade, António Alberto de. "Benardino Álvares de Adrade, um 'Guineense' esquecido." *Boletim Cultural da Guiné Portuguesa* 98 (1970): 190–195.
Andrade, Bernardino António Álvares de. *Planta da praça de Bissau e suas adjacentes.* Edited by Damião Peres. Lisbon: Academia Portuguesa da História, 1952.
Anguiano, Mateo de. *Misiones Capuchinas en África.* Madrid: Instituto Santo Toribio de Mogrovejo, 1950.
Ashmun, Jehudi. "Bissao." *African Repository and Colonial Journal* 3 (1967): 73–78.
Austen, Ralph A. "The Abolition of the Overseas Slave Trade: A Distorted Theme in West African History." *Journal of the Historical Society of Nigeria* 5 (June 1970): 257–274.
———. "The Slave Trade as History and Memory: Confrontations of Slaving Voyage Documents and Communal Traditions." *William and Mary Quarterly* 58, no. 1 (January 2001): 229–247.
Azurara, Gomes Eannes de. *The Chronicle of the Discovery and Conquest of Guinea.* Translated by Charles Raymond Beazely and Edgar Prestage. London: Hakluyt Society, 1899.

Bah, Thierno Mouctar. *Architecture militaire traditionnelle et poliorcétique dans le Soudan occidental du XVIIe à la fin du XIXe siècle.* Yaounde: Editions Cle, 1985.

Barcellos, Christiano José de Senna. *Subsidios para a história de Cabo Verde e Guiné.* 7 vols. Lisbon: Academia Real das Sciencias, 1899–1913.

Barreto, Honório Pereira. "Memória sobre o estado actual de Senegambia portugueza, causas de sua decadencia, e meios de a fazer prosperar." Lisbon: Typ. da Viuva Coelho, 1843. Reprinted in Jaime Walter. *Honório Pereira Barreto.* Lisbon: Centro de Estodos da Guiné Portuguesa, 1947.

Barreto, João. *História da Guiné, 1418–1918.* Lisbon: J. Barreto, 1938.

Barros, Luiz Frederico de. *Senegambia portugueza.* Lisbon: Mattos Mareira, 1878.

Barros, Philip de. "Iron Metallurgy: Sociocultural Context." In *Ancient African Metallurgy: The Sociocultural Context.* Edited by Joseph O. Vogel. Walnut Creek, Calif.: Altamira Press, 2000, 147–198.

———. "Ironworking in Its Cultural Context." In *Encyclopedia of Precolonial Africa, Archaeology, History, Languages, Cultures, and Environments.* Edited by Joseph O. Vogel. Walnut Creek: Altamira Press, 1996, 135–148.

Barry, Boubacar. *Senegambia and the Atlantic Slave Trade.* Cambridge: Cambridge University Press, 1998.

Baum, Robert Martin. *Shrines of the Slave Trade: Diola Religion and Society in Precolonial Senegambia.* Oxford: Oxford University Press, 1999.

Beaver, Philip. *African Memoranda.* London: Dawsons of Pall Mall, 1968.

Bella, L. de Sousa. "Apontamentos sôbre a língua dos Balantas de Jabadá." *Boletim Cultural da Guiné Portuguesa* 1 (October 1946): 729–766.

Berger, Iris. *Religion and Resistance: East African Kingdoms in the Precolonial Period.* Tervuren, Belgium: Musee Royal de l'Afrique Centrale, 1981.

Bertrand-Bocandé, M. "Notes sur la Guinée portugaise ou Sénégambie méridionale." *Bulletin de la Société de Géographie* 3, nos. 11–12 (1849): 265–350, 392, 57–93.

Boahen, A. Adu. "New Trends and Process in Africa in the Nineteenth Century." In *General History of Africa.* Vol. 6, *Africa in the Nineteenth Century Until the 1880s.* Edited by J. F. Ade Ajayi. Heinemann International: Oxford, 1989, 40–63.

Board on Science and Technology for International Development. *Lost Crops of Africa.* Vol. 1, *Grains.* Washington, D.C.: National Academy Press, 1996.

Bohannan, Paul. "The Migration and Expansion of the Tiv." *Africa* 24 (January 1954): 2–16.

Boulègue, Jean. *Les Luso-Africains de Sénégambie.* Lisbon: Instituto de Investigação Cinetífica Tropical, 1989.

Bowman, Joye L. "'Legitimate Commerce' and Peanut Production in Portuguese Guinea, 1840s–1880s." *Journal of African History* 28, no. 1 (1987): 87–106.

———. *Ominous Transition: Commerce and Colonial Expansion in the Senegambia and Guinea, 1857–1919.* Brookfield, Vt.: Avebury, 1997.

Bowman Hawkins, Joye. "Conflict, Interaction, and Change in Guinea-Bissau: Fulbe Expansion and Its Impact, 1850–1900." Ph.D. diss., University of California–Los Angeles, 1980.

Bowser, Frederick P. *The African Slave in Colonial Peru, 1524–1650.* Stanford: Stanford University Press, 1974.

Brantley, Cynthia. "Geroncratic Government: Age-Sets in Pre-Colonial Giriama." *Africa* 48 (1978): 249–264.

Brásio, António. *Monumenta Missionaria Africana.* Ser. 2a. Lisbon: Agência Geral do Ultramar, 1958.

Bravman, Bill. *Making Ethnic Ways: Communities and Their Transformations in Taita, Kenya, 1800–1950.* Portsmouth, N.H.: Heinemann, 1998.

Broadhead, Susan Herlin. "Slave Wives, Free Sisters: Bakongo Women and Slavery, c. 1700–1850." In *Women and Slavery in Africa.* Edited by Claire C. Robertson and Martin A. Klein. Madison: University of Wisconsin Press, 1983, 160–184.

Brooks, George E. *Kola Trade and State Building: Upper Guinea Coast and Senegambia, Fifteenth–Seventeenth Centuries.* Boston University African Studies Center Working Papers no. 38. Boston: Boston University Press, 1980.

———. *Landlords and Strangers: Ecology, Society, and Trade in Western Africa, 1000–1630.* Boulder, Colo.: Westview Press, 1993.

———. "A Nhara of the Guinea-Bissau Region: Mãe Aurélia Correia." In *Women and Slavery in Africa.* Edited by Claire C. Robertson and Martin A. Klein. Madison: University of Wisconsin Press, 1983, 295–319.

———. *Perspectives on Luso-African Commerce and Settlement in the Gambia and Guinea-Bissau Region, Sixteenth–Nineteenth Centuries.* Boston University African Studies Center Working Papers no. 24. Boston: Boston University Press, 1980.

———. "The *Signares* of Saint-Louis and Gorée: Women Entrepreneurs in Eighteenth-Century Senegal." In *Women in Africa: Studies in Social and Economic Change.* Edited by Nancy J. Hafkin and Edna G. Bay. Stanford: Stanford University Press, 1976, 19–44.

Buddenhagen, I. W. "Rice Ecosystems in Africa." In *Rice in Africa.* Edited by I. W. Buddenhagen and G. J. Persley. New York: Academic Press, 1978, 11–27.

Bühnen, Stephan. "Ethnic Origins of Peruvian Slaves (1548–1650): Figures for the Upper Guinea Coast." *Paideuma* 39 (1993): 57–110.

Bull, Benjamim Pinto. *O Crioulo da Guiné-Bissau: Filosophia e sabedoria.* Bissau: Arquivo Histórico do Instituto Nacional de Estudos e Pesquisa, 1989.

Cação, S. F. "Letters to the King, Recommending Conquest of the Bissagos Islands." In *Jesuit Documents on the Guinea of Cape Verde and the Cape Verde Islands, 1585–1617.* Edited by P.E.H. Hair and Avelino Teixeira da Mota. Liverpool: University of Liverpool, Department of History, 1989, doc. 24.

Carneiro, Robert. "The Chiefdom: Precursor of the State." In *The Transition to Statehood in the New World.* Edited by Grant D. Jones and Robert R. Dantz. Cambridge: Cambridge University Press, 1981.

———. "A Theory of the Origin of the State." *Science* 169 (August 1970): 733–738.

Carney, Judith. *Black Rice: The African Origins of Rice Cultivation in the Americas.* Cambridge: Harvard University Press, 2001.

Carpenter, A. J. "The History of Rice in Africa." In *Rice in Africa.* Edited by I. W. Buddenhagen and G. J. Persley. New York: Academic Press, 1978, 3–10.

Carreira, António. "As companhias pombalinas." *Boletim Cultural da Guiné Portuguesa* 13, nos. 91–92 (1968): 310–334.

———. *As companhias pombalinas de navegação comércio e tráfico de escravos entre Africana e o nordeste Brasileiro.* Bissau: Centro de Estudos da Guiné Portuguesa, 1969.

———. *As Companhias pombalinas de navegação comércio e tráfico de escravos entre Africana e o nordeste Brasileiro.* Lisbon: Editorial Presença, 1982.

————. *Cabo Verde: Formação e extinção de uma sociedade escravocrata (1460–1878).* Praia, Cape Verde: Instituto Caboverdeano de Livro, 1983.

————. *Mandingas da Guiné portuguesa.* Publicação Comemerativa do Centenário de Descoberta da Guiné no. 4. Bissau: Centro de Estudos da Guiné Portuguesa, 1947.

————. *O tráfico de escravos nos rios de Guiné e ilhas de Cabo Verde (1810–1850): Subsídios para o seu estudo.* Lisbon: Junta de Investigações Científicas do Ultramar, 1981.

————. "Organização social e ecónomica dos povos da Guiné portuguesa." *Boletim Cultural da Guiné Portuguesa* 16 (1961): 641–736.

————. *Os portuguêses nos rios de Guiné (1500–1900).* Lisbon: António Carreira, 1984.

————. *Panaria Cabo-Verdiano-Guineense: Aspectos históricos e sócio-economicos.* Lisbon: Junta de Investigações Científicas do Ultramar, 1968.

————. *The People of the Cape Verde Islands: Exploitation and Emigration.* Translated by Christopher Fyfe. London: C. Hurst, 1982.

Carreira, António, and A. Martins de Meireles. "Quelques notes sur les mouvements migratories des populations de la province portugaise da Ginée." *Bulletin de l'IFAN* 22 (1960): 379–392.

Carvalho, Clara. "Ritos de poder e a recriação da tradição, os régulos manjaco da Guiné-Bissau." Ph.d. diss., Instituto Superior de Ciências do Trabalho e da Empresa, 1998.

Carvalho, Henrique Augusto Dias de. *Guiné: Apontamentos inéditos.* Lisbon: Agência Geral das Colónias, Divisão de Pubicações e Biblioteca, 1944.

Carvalho, J. P. Garcia de. "Nota sobre a distribuição e história das população do posto de Begand." *Boletim Cultural da Guiné Portuguesa* 4 (April 1949): 308–318.

Castro, António. "Notas sobre algumas variedades de arroz em cultura na Guiné portuguesa." *Boletim Cultural da Guiné Portuguesa* 5, no. 19 (July 1950): 347–378.

Caughan, James. "Mafakur: A Limbic Institution of the Margi." In *Slavery in Africa: Historical and Anthropological Perspectives.* Edited by Suzanne Miers and Igor Kopytoff. Madison: University of Wisconsin Press, 1977, 85–103.

Chabolin, R. "Rice in West Africa." In *Food Crops of the Lowland Tropics.* Edited by C. L. A. Leakey and J. B. Willis. Oxford: Oxford University Press, 1977, 7–26.

Chelmicki, José Conrado Carlos de. *Corografia Cabo Verdiana.* Lisbon: Typ. de L.C. da Cunha, 1841.

Cissoko, Sékéné Mody. "De l'organisation polituque du Kaabu." *Éthiopiques* 28 (October 1981): 195–206.

Claessen, Henri J. M., and Peter Skalník. "The Early State: Models and Reality." In *The Early State.* Edited by Henri J. M. Claessen and Peter Skalník. The Hague: Mouton, 1978, 637–650.

————. "The Early State: Theories and Hypotheses." In *The Early State.* Edited by Henri J. M. Claessen and Peter Skalník. The Hague: Mouton, 1978, 3–30.

Clarence-Smith, Gervase. *The Third Portuguese Empire, 1825–1975.* Manchester: Manchester University Press, 1985.

Clarke, Julian. "Households and the Political Economy of Small-Scale Cash Production in South-West Nigeria." *Africa* 51 (1981): 807–823.

Coelho, Francisco de Lemos. "Descrição da costa da Guiné desde o Cabo Verde athe Serra Lioa com todas as ilhas e rios que os Brancos Navegam." In *Duas descrições seiscentistas da Guiné.* Edited by Damião Peres. Lisbon: Academia Portuguesa da História, 1953, 3–88.

————. *Description of the Coast of Guinea (1684)*. Translated by P.E.H. Hair. Liverpool: University of Liverpool, Department of History, 1985.

Cohen, David William. "Doing Social History from *Pim*'s Doorway." In *Reliving the Past*. Edited by Olivier Zunz. Chaple Hill: University of North Carolina Press, 1985, 191–235.

————. *The Historical Tradition of Busoga, Mukama, and Kintu*. Oxford: Clarendon Press, 1972.

Cohen, Ronald. "Evolution, Fission, and the Early State." In *The Study of the State*. Edited by Henri J. M. Claessen and Peter Skalník. The Hague: Mouton, 1981, 87–116.

Colson, Elizabeth. *The Plateau Tonga of Northern Rhodesia (Zambia): Social and Religious Studies*. Manchester: University of Zambia, Institute for Social Research, 1970.

Cordell, Denis D. "The Myth of Inevitability and Invincibility: Resistance to Slavers and the Slave Trade in Central Africa in the Late Nineteenth and Early Twentieth Centuries." Paper presented at the conference "Fighting Back: African Strategies Against the Slave Trade," Rutgers University, February 16–17, 2001.

Correia e Lança, Joaquim da Graça. *Relatorio da provincia da Guiné portugueza: Referido ao anno economico de 1888–1889*. Lisbon: Imprensa Nacional, 1890.

Coursey, D. G. *Yams: An Account of the Nature, Origins, Cultivation and Utilisation of the Useful Members of the Dioscoreaceae*. London: Longman, 1967.

Coursey, D. G., and R. H. Booth. "Root and Tuber Crops." In *Food Crops of the Lowland Tropics*. Edited by C. L. A. Leakey and J. B. Willis. Oxford: Oxford University Press, 1977, 75–96.

Coursey, D. G., and P. H. Haynes. "Root Crops and Their Potential as Food in the Tropics." *World Crops* 22 (1970): 260–265.

Crowley, Eve Lakshmi. "Contracts with the Spirits: Religion, Asylum, and Ethnic Identity in the Cacheu Region of Guinea-Bissau." Ph.D. diss., Yale University, 1990.

Cunningham, James. "The Colonial Period in Guiné." *Tarikh* 6 (1980): 31–45.

Curtin, Philip D. "Africa North of the Forest in the Early Islamic Age." In *African History: From Earliest Times to Independence*. 2nd ed. Edited by Philip Curtin et al. London: Longman, 1995, 64–100.

————. *The Atlantic Slave Trade: A Census*. Madison: University of Wisconsin Press, 1969.

————. *Cross-Cultural Trade in World History*. Cambridge: Cambridge University Press, 1984.

————. *Economic Change in Precolonial Africa: Senegambia in the Era of the Slave Trade*. Madison: University of Wisconsin Press, 1975.

————. *The Rise and Fall of the Plantation Complex*. Cambridge: Cambridge University Press, 1990.

Davidson, Basil. *Black Mother: The Years of the African Slave Trade*. Boston: Little, Brown, 1961.

Davies, Kenneth Gordon. *Royal Africa Company*. London: Longman, 1957.

Dike, Kenneth. *Trade and Politics in the Niger Delta, 1830–1885*. Oxford: Clarendon Press, 1956.

Dinis, A. J. Dias. "As tribos da Guiné portuguesa na história." In *Congresso comemorativo do quinto centenário do descobrimento da Guiné*. Lisbon: Sociedade de Geografia de Lisboa, 1946, 241–271.

Donelha, André. *Descrição da Serra Leoa e dos rios de Guiné do Cabo Verde (1625)*.

Edited by Avelino Teixeira da Mota. Translated by P.E.H. Hair. Centro de Estudos de Cartografia Antiga no. 19. Lisbon: Junta de Investigações Científicas do Ultramar, 1977.

Duffy, James. *Portuguese Africa.* Cambridge: Harvard University Press, 1959.

Dupré, M.C. "Pour une histoire des productions: La métalurgie du fer chez les Téké—Ngungulu, Tio, Tsaayi." *Cahiers del'ORSTOM, Série Sciences Humaines* 18 (1981–1982): 195–223.

Elbl, Ivana. "The Portuguese Trade with West Africa, 1440–1521." Ph.D. diss., University of Totonto, 1986.

———. "The Volume of the Early Atlantic Slave Trade, 1450–1521." *Journal of African History* 38, no. 1 (1997): 31–75.

Eltis, David. *The Rise of African Slavery in the Americas.* Cambridge: Cambridge University Press, 2000.

———. "The Volume, Age/Sex Ratios, and African Impact of the Slave Trade: Some Refinements of Paul Lovejoy's Review of the Literature." *Journal of African History* 31, no. 3 (1990): 485–492.

———. "The Volume and Structure of the Transatlantic Slave Trade: A Reassessment." *William and Mary Quarterly* 58 (January 2001): 17–45.

Eltis, David, Stephen D. Behrendt, David Richardson, and Herbert S. Klein, eds. *The Trans-Atlantic Slave: A Database on CD-ROM.* Cambridge: Cambridge University Press, 1999.

Eltis, David, and Stanley L. Engerman. "Fluctuations in Sex and Age Ratios in the Transatlantic Slave Trade, 1663–1864." *Economic History Review* 46, no. 2 (1993): 308–323.

———. "Was the Slave Trade Dominated by Men?" *Journal of Interdisciplinary History* 23, no. 2 (Autumn 1992): 237–257.

Eltis, David, and David Richardson. "West Africa and the Transatlantic Slave Trade: New Evidence of Long-Run Trends." *Slavery and Abolition* 18, no. 1 (1997): 16–35.

Ensminger, Jean. *Making a Market: The Insitutional Transformation of an African Society.* Cambridge: Cambridge University Press, 1992.

Equiano, Olaudah. *The Interesting Narrative and Other Writings.* New York: Penguin Books, 1995.

Evans-Pritchard, E. E. *The Nuer.* Oxford: Clarendon Press, 1940.

———. "The Nuer of the Southern Sudan." In *African Political Systems.* Edited by Meyer Fortes and E. E. Evans-Pritchard. London: Oxford University Press, 1940, 272–296.

Fage, J. D. "Slavery and the Slave Trade in the Context of West African History." *Journal of African History* 10, no. 3 (1969): 393–404.

———. "Some Notes on a Scheme for the Investigation of Oral Tradition in the Northern Territories of the Gold Coast." *Journal of the Historical Society of Nigeria* 1, no. 1 (1956): 15–19.

Fardon, Richard. *Raiders and Refugees: Trends in Chamba Political Development, 1750–1950.* Washington, D.C.: Smithsonian Institution Press, 1988.

Faro, André de. "Relaçam (1663–4)." In *André de Faro's Missionary Journey to Sierra Leone in 1663–1664.* Translated by P.E.H. Hair. Occasional Paper no. 5. Sierra Leone: University of Sierra Leone, Institute of African Studies, 1982.

Faro, J. "A aclamação de D. João IV na Guiné." *Boletim Cultural da Guiné Portuguesa* 13, no. 52 (1958): 490–515.

Feierman, Steven. "African Histories and the Dissolution of World History." In *Africa and the Disciplines: The Contributions of Research in Africa to the Social Sciences and Humanities.* Edited by Robert H. Bates and others. Chicago: University of Chicago Press, 1993, 167–212.

———. "A Century of Ironies in East Africa." In *African History.* Edited by Philip Curtin et al. New York: Longman, 1995, 352–376.

Fonesca, Alfredo Loureiro da. *Guiné: Finanças e Economia.* Lisbon: Typographia da Cooperativa Militar, 1910.

Forrest, Joshua B. *Lineages of State Fragility: Rural Civil Society in Guinea-Bissau.* Athens, Ohio: Ohio University Press, 2003.

Fortes, Meyer. *The Dynamics of Clanship Among the Tallensi.* London: Oxford University Press, 1945.

Funk, Ursala. "Labor, Economic Power, and Gender: Coping with Food Shortage in Guinea-Bissau." In *The Political Economy of African Famine.* Edited by R. E. Downs, Donna O. Kerner, and Stephen P. Reyna. Philadelphia: Gordon and Breach Science, 1991, 205–226.

———. "Land Tenure, Agriculture, and Gender in Guinea-Bissau." In *Agriculture, Women, and Land: The African Experience.* Editied by Jean Davison. Boulder, Colo.: Westview Press, 1988, 33–59.

Furedi, Frank. *The Mau Mau War in Perspective.* Athens, Ohio: Ohio University Press, 1989.

Galli, Rosemary E. "Capitalist Agriculture and the Colonial State in Portuguese Guinea, 1926–1974." *African Economic History* 23 (1995), 51–78.

Galli, Rosemary E., and Jocelyn Jones. *Guinea-Bissau: Politics, Economics, and Society.* London: Frances Pinter, 1987.

Geraldes, Francisco Antonio Marques. "Guiné portugueza, communicação á sociedade de geographia sobre esta provincia e suas condições actuaes." *Boletim da Sociedade de Geografia de Lisboa* ser. 7a, no. 8 (1887): 517–518.

Giesing, Cornélia. "Agricultura e resistência na história dos Balanta-Begaa." *Soronda* 16 (July 1993): 125–177.

Glassman, Jonathon. *Feasts and Riot: Revelry, Rebellion, and Popular Consciousness on the Swahili Coast, 1856–1888.* Portsmouth, N.H.: Heinemann, 1995.

Gleave, M. B., and R. M. Prothero, "Population Density and 'Slave Raiding': A Comment." *Journal of African History* 12, no. 2 (1971): 321–323.

Gluckman, Max. *Custom and Conflict in Africa.* Oxford: Basil Blackwell, 1960.

Greene, Sandra. *Gender, Ethnicity, and Social Change on the Upper Slave Coast: A History of the Anlo-Ewe.* Portsmouth, N.H.: Heinemann, 1996.

Gouveia, Ignácio de. "Relatório." *Boletim Cultural da Guiné Portuguesa* 7 (1952): 432–456.

Grist, D. H. *Rice.* New York: Longman, Green, 1953.

Gunawardana, R. A. L. H. "Social Function and Political Power: A Case Study of State Formation in Irrigation Society." In *The Study of the State.* Edited by Henri J. M. Claessen and Peter Skalník. The Hague: Mouton, 1981, 133–154.

———. "O arroz ou a indentidade Balanta Brassa." *Soronda* 1 (1986): 55–67.

Hair, P.E.H. "The Enslavement of Koelle's Informants," *Journal of African History* 6, no. 2 (1965): 193–203.

Hair, P.E.H., Adam Jones, and Robin Law, eds. *Barbot on Guinea: The Writing of Jean Barbot on West Africa, 1678–1712.* London: Hakluyt Society, 1992.

Hair, P.E.H., and Avelino Teixeira da Mota, eds. *Jesuit Documents on the Guinea of Cape*

Verde and the Cape Verde Islands, 1585–1617. Liverpool: University of Liverpool, Department of History, 1989.

Hammond, R. J. *Portugal and Africa*. Stanford: Stanford University Press, 1966.

Handem, Diane Lima. *Nature et fonctionnement du pouvoir chez les Balanta Brassa*. Bissau: Arquivo Histórico do Instituto Nacional de Estudos e Pesquisa, 1986.

Harlan, Jack R. "Wild-Grass Seed Harvesting in the Sahara and Sub-Sahara of Africa." In *Foraging and Farming*. Edited by David R. Harris and Godon C. Hillman. London: Unwin Hyman, 1989, 79–98.

Harms, Robert W. *The Diligent: A Voyage Through the Worlds of the Slave Trade*. New York: Basic Books, 2002.

———. *River of Wealth, River of Sorrow: The Central Zaire Basin in the Era of the Slave and Ivory Trade, 1500–1891*. New Haven, Conn.: Yale University Press, 1981.

Harries, Patrick. *Work, Culture, and Identity: Migrant Laborers in Mozambique and South Africa, c. 1860–1910*. Portsmouth, N.H.: Heinemann, 1994.

Havik, Philip J. "Female Entrepreneurship in a Changing Environment: Gender, Kinship, and Trade in the Guinea Bissau Region." In *Negotiation and Social Space: A Gendered Analysis of Changing Kin and Security Networks in South Asia and Sub-Saharan Africa*. Edited by Carl Risseeuw and Kamala Ganesh. London: Sage, 1998, 205–225.

———. "Women and Trade in the Guinea-Bissau Region." *Stvdia* 52 (1994): 83–120.

Hawthorne, Walter. "The Interior Past of an Acephalous Society: Institutional Change Among the Balanta of Guinea-Bissau, c. 1400–1950." Ph.D. diss., Stanford University, 1999.

———. "Migrations and Statelessness: The Expansion of the Balanta of Guinea-Bissau, 1900–1950." In *Migrations anciennes et peuplement actuel des côtes guinéennes*. Edited by Gérald Gaillard. Paris: L'Harmattan, 2000, 139–150.

———. "Nourishing a Stateless Society During the Slave Trade: The Rise of Balanta Paddy-Rice production in Guinea-Bissau." *Journal of African History* 42, no. 1 (2000): 1–24.

———. "The Production of Slaves Where There Was No State: The Guinea-Bissau Region, 1450–1815." *Slavery and Abolition* 20, no. 2 (August 1999): 97–124.

———. "The Strategies of the Decentralized: Defending Communities from Slave Raiders in Coastal Guinea-Bissau, 1450–1815." In *Fighting Back: African Strategies Against the Slave Trade*. Edited by Sylviane A. Diouf. Athens, Ohio: Ohio University Press, forthcoming.

Hechter, Michael, Karl-Dieter Opp, and Reinhard Wippler, eds. *Social Institutions: Their Emergence, Maintenance, and Effects*. New York: Walter de Gruyter, 1990.

Hodgson, Dorthy L., and Sheryl A. McCurdy, eds. *"Wicked" Women and the Reconfiguration of Gender in Africa*. Portsmouth, N.H.: Heinemann, 2001.

Hopkins, Anthony G. *An Economic History of West Africa*. New York: Columbia University Press, 1973.

Horton, Robin. "Stateless Societies in the History of West Africa." In *History of West Africa*. Vol. 1. Edited by J. F. A. Ajayi and M. Crowder. London: Longman, 1976, 78–119.

Hubbell, Andrew. "Patronage and Predation: A Social History of Colonial Chieftaincies in a Chiefless Region—Souroudougou (Burkina Faso), 1850–1946." Ph.D. diss., Stanford University, 1997.

————. "A View of the Slave Trade from the Margin: Souroudougou in the Late Nine-teenth-Century Slave Trade of the Niger Bend." *Journal of African History* 42, no. 1 (2000): 25–47.

Inácio, Pedro. "Relatorio." In "A Guiné—ou Senegâmbia portuguesa—no tempo do Governador Pedro Inácio de Gouveia." Edited by Fausto Duarte. *Boletim Cultural da Guiné Portuguesa* 26 (1952): 403–434.

Inikori, Joseph E., ed. *Forced Migration: The Impact of the Export Slave Trade on African Societies.* London: Hutchison University Press, 1982.

————. "The Import of Firearms into West Africa, 1750–1807: A Quantitative Analysis." *Journal of African History* 18, no. 3 (1977): 339–368.

Isaacman, Allen F. *Mozambique: The Africanization of a European Institution—The Zambesi Prazos, 1750–1902.* Madison: University of Wisconsin Press, 1972.

Jobson, Richard. *The Golden Trade.* London: Nicholas Okes, 1623.

Johnson, Allen W., and Timothy Earle. *The Evolution of Human Societies: From Foraging Group to Agrarian State.* Stanford: Stanford University Press, 1987.

Kanogo, Tabitha. *Squatters and the Roots of Mau Mau.* Athens, Ohio: Ohio University Press, 1987.

Keim, Curtis A. "Women in Slavery Among the Mangbetu, c. 1800–1910." In *Women and Slavery in Africa.* Edited by Claire C. Robertson and Martin A. Klein. Portsmouth, N.H.: Heinemann, 1997, 144–159.

Klein, Martin A. "Ethnic Pluralism and Homogeneity in the Western Sudan: Saalum, Segu, Wasulu." *Mande Studies* 1 (1999): 113–119.

————. "The Impact of the Atlantic Slave Trade on the Societies of the Western Sudan." In *The Atlantic Slave Trade: Effects on Economies, Societies, and Peoples in Africa, the Americas, and Europe.* Edited by Joseph E. Inikori and Stanley L. Engerman. Durham: Duke University Press, 1992, 25–48.

————. "The Impact of the Atlantic Slave Trade on the Societies of Western Sudan." *Social Science History* 14, no. 2 (1990): 231–253.

————. *Islam and Imperialism in Senegal: Sine-Saloum, 1847–1914.* Edinburgh: Edinburgh University Press, 1968.

————. "The Slave Trade and Decentralized Societies." *Journal of African History* 42, no. 1 (2000): 49–65.

————. "Slavery, the Slave Trade, and Legitimate Commerce in Late Nineteenth Century Africa." *Etudes d'Histoire Africaine* 2 (1971): 5–28.

————. *Slavery and Colonial Rule in French West Africa.* Cambridge: Cambridge University Press, 1998.

————. "Social and Economic Factors in the Muslim Revolution in Senegambia." *Journal of African History* 13, no. 3 (1972): 419–441.

————. "Studying the History of Those Who Would Rather Forget: Oral History and the Experience of Slavery." *History in Africa* 16 (1989): 209–217.

Klein, Martin A., and Paul E. Lovejoy. "Slavery in West Africa." In *The Uncommon Market: Essays in the Economic History of the Atlantic Slave Trade.* Edited by H. A. Gemery and J. S. Hogendorn. New York: Academic Press, 1979, 181–212.

Klein, Martin A., and Claire C. Robertson. "Women's Importance in African Slave Systems." In *Women and Slavery in Africa.* Edited by Claire C. Robertson and Martin A. Klein. Portsmouth, N.H.: Heinemann, 1997, 3–28.

Kopytoff, Igor, and Suzanne Miers. "African 'Slavery' as an Institution of Marginality." In *Slavery in Africa: Historical and Anthropological Perspectives*. Edited by Igor Kopytoff and Suzanne Miers. Madison: University of Wisconsin Press, 1977.

La Courbe, Sieur Michel Jajolet de. *Premier voyage du Sieur de la Courbe fait à la coste de l'Afrique en 1685*. Edited by Prosper Cultru. Paris: E. Champion, 1913.

Labat, J. B. *Nouvelle relation de l'Afrique occidentale*. Paris: Cavelier, 1728.

Lance, James Merriman. "Seeking the Political Kingdom: British Colonial Impositions and African Manipulations in the Northern Territories of the Gold Coast Colony." Ph.D. diss., Stanford University, 1995.

Larson, Pier M. *History and Memory in the Age of Enslavement: Becoming Merina in Highland Madagascar, 1770–1822*. Portsmouth, N.H.: Heinemann, 2000.

Lauer, Joseph Jerome. "Rice in the History of the lower Gambia-Geba Area." M.A. thesis, University of Wisconsin, 1969.

Law, Robin. "The Historiography of the Commercial Transition in Nineteenth-Century West Africa." In *African Historiography: Essays in Honor of Jacob Ade Ajayi*. Edited by Toyin Falola. Harlow: Longman, 1993, 91–115.

———. *The Oyo Empire, c. 1600–1836: A West African Imperialism in the Era of the Atlantic Slave Trade*. Oxford: Oxford University Press, 1977.

———. *The Slave Coast of West Africa, 1550–1750*. Oxford: Oxford University Press, 1991.

———. "Slave-Raiders and Middlemen, Monopolists and Free-Traders: The Supply of Slaves for the Atlantic Trade in Dahomey, c. 1715–1850." *Journal of African History* 30, no. 1 (1989): 45–68.

Lea, J. D., Cornelius Hugo, and Carlos Rui Ribeiro. *Rice Production and Marketing in Guinea-Bissau*. Washington, D.C.: U.S. Department of State, U.S. Agency for International Development, 1990.

Lima, José Joaquim Lopes de. *Ensaios sobre a statistica das possessões portuguezas no Ultramar*. Vol. 1, *Das ilhas de Cabo Verde e suas dependências*. Lisbon: Imprensa Nacional, 1844.

Linares, Olga F. "Agriculture and Diola Society." In *African Food Production Systems: Cases and Theory*. Edited by F. M. McLoughlin. Baltimore: Johns Hopkins University Press, 1970.

———. "Deferring to Trade in Slaves: the Jola of Casamance, Senegal, in Historical Perspective." *History in Africa* 14 (1987): 113–139.

———. "From Tidal Swamp to Inland Valley: On the Social Organization of Wet Rice Cultivation Among the Diola of Senegal." *Africa* 51 (1981): 557–595.

———. "Shell Middens of the Lower Casamance and Problems of Diola Protohistory." *West African Journal of Archaeology* 1 (1971): 22–54.

Lobban, Richard A., Jr. *Cape Verde: Crioulo Colony to Independent Nation*. Boulder, Colo.: Westview Press, 1995.

———. *Historical Dictionary of the Republics of Guinea-Bissau and Cape Verde*. Metuchen, N.J.: Londres, 1979.

Lockhart, James. *Spanish Peru, 1532–1560: A Colonial Society*. Madison: University of Wisconsin Press, 1968.

Lopes, Carlos. *Kaabunké, espaço, território e poder na Guiné-Bissau, Gâmbia e Casamance pré-coloniais*. Lisbon: Comissão Nacional para as Comemorações dos Descobrimentos Portugueses, 1999.

————, ed. *Mansas, escravos, grumetes e gentio: Cacheu na encruzilhada de civilizações.* Bissau: Arquivo Histórico do Instituto Nacional de Estudos e Pesquisa, 1993.

Lovejoy, Paul E. "The Impact of the Atlantic Slave Trade on Africa: A Review of the Literature." *Journal of African History* 30, no. 3 (1989): 365–394.

————. *Transformations in Slavery: A History of Slavery in Africa.* Cambridge: Cambridge University Press, 1983.

Lovejoy, Paul E., and Jan S. Hogendorn. "Slave Marketing in West Africa." In *The Uncommon Market: Essays in the Economic History of the Atlantic Slave Trade.* Edited by H. A. Gemery and J. S. Hogendorn. New York: Academic Press, 1979, 213–232.

Lovejoy, Paul E., and David Richardson. "Competing Markets for Male and Female Slaves: Prices in the Interior of West Africa, 1750–1850." *International Journal of African Historical Studies* 28, no. 2 (1995): 261–293.

————. "The West African Palm Oil Trade in the Nineteenth Century and the 'Crisis of Adaptation.'" In *From Slave Trade to "Legitimate" Commerce.* Edited by Robin Law. Cambridge: Cambridge University Press, 1995, 32–56.

Luttrell, Anthony. "Slavery and Slaving in the Portuguese Atlantic (to About 1500)." In *The Transatlantic Slave Trade From West Africa.* Edinburgh: University of Edinburgh, Center of African Studies, 1965, 61–79.

Lynn, Martin. "The West African Palm Oil Trade in the Nineteenth Century and the 'Crisis of Adaptation.'" In *From Slave Trade to "Legitimate" Commerce.* Edited by Robin Law. Cambridge: Cambridge University Press, 1995, 57–77.

Ly-tall, M.. "The Decline of the Mali Empire." In *General History of Africa.* Vol. 4, *Africa from the Twelfth to the Sixteenth Century.* Edited by D. T. Niane. London: Heinemann, 1984, 172–186.

MacCormack, Carol P. "Wono: Institutionalized Dependence in Sherbro Descent Groups." In *Slavery in Africa: Historical and Anthropological Perspectives.* Edited by Suzanne Miers and Igor Kopytoff. Madison: University of Wisconsin Press, 1977, 181–204.

MacEachern, Scott. "Selling the Iron for Their Shackles: Wandala Montagnard Interactions in Northern Cameroon." *Journal of African History* 34, no. 2 (1993): 247–270.

Mané, Mamadou. "Contribuition á l'histoire du Kaabu, des origins au XIXe siécle." *Bulletin de l'I.F.A.N.* 40, ser. B, no. 1 (January 1978): 87–159.

Manning, Patrick. "Contours of Slavery and Social Change in Africa." *American Historical Review* 88, no. 4 (October 1983): 835–857.

————. *Slavery and African Life: Occidental, Oriental, and African Slave Trades.* Cambridge: Cambridge University Press, 1990.

Mark, Peter. "Constructing Identity: Sixteenth- and Seventeenth-Century Architecture in the Gambia-Geba Region and the Articulation of Luso-African Ethnicity," *History in Africa* 22 (1995): 307–327.

————. *A Cultural, Economic, and Religious History of the Basse Casanance Since 1500.* Stuttgart: Franz Steiner Verlag Wiesbaden GMBH, 1985.

————. "The Evolution of 'Portuguese' Identity: Luso-Africans on the Upper Guinea Coast from the Sixteenth to the Early Nineteenth Century." *Journal of African History* 40, no. 2 (1999): 173–191.

———. "'Portuguese' Architecture and Luso-African Identity in Senegambia and Guinea, 1730–1890." *History in Africa* 23 (1996): 179–196.

———. *"Portuguese" Style and Luso-African Identity: Precolonial Senegambia, Sixteenth–Nineteenth Centuries*. Bloomington: Indiana University Press, 2002.

Martin, Susan. "Slaves, Igbo Women, and Palm Oil in the Nineteenth Century." In *From Slave Trade to "Legitimate" Commerce: The Commercial Transition in Nineteenth-Century West Africa*. Edited by Robin Law. Cambridge: Cambridge University Press, 1995, 57–78.

Martins, Manuel António. "Memória demonstrativa do estado actual das praças de Bissau, Cacheu e suas dependências em África, parte da história sobre sua fundação, com o plano de reforma mais acomodada às circunstâncias de Portugal." In "Os problemas de Bissau, Cacheu e suas dependências vistos em 1831 por Manuel António Martins," edited by Jorge Faro, *Boletim Cultural da Guiné Portuguesa* 50 (1958): 203–218.

Mason, Michael. "Population Density and 'Slave Raiding': The Case of the Middle Belt of Nigeria." *Journal of African History* 10, no. 4 (1969): 551–564.

Mbilinyi, Marjorie. "Runaway Wives in Colonial Tanganyika: Forced Labour and Forced Marriage in Colonial Rungwe District, 1919–1961." *International Journal of Sociology of Law* 16, no. 1 (1988): 1–29.

McIntosh, Robert J. *The Peoples of the Middle Niger*. Oxford: Blackwell, 1988.

Meillassoux, Claude. *The Anthropology of Slavery: The Womb of Iron and Gold*. Translated by Alide Dasnois. Chicago: University of Chicago Press, 1991.

———. "The Economy in Agricultural Self-Sustaining Societies: A Preliminary Analysis." In *Relations of Production: Marxist Approaches to Economic Anthropology*. Edited by D. Sheldon. London: Frank Cass, 1978, 127–156.

———. "Female Slavery." In *Women and Slavery in Africa*. Edited by Claire C. Robertson and Martin A. Klein. Portsmouth, N.H.: Heinemann, 1997, 49–66.

Mendy, Peter Karibe. *Colonialismo português em África: A tradição de resistência na Guiné-Bissau (1879–1959)*. Bissau: Arquivo Histórico do Instituto Nacional de Estudos e Pesquisa, 1991.

Menezes, Vítor Hugo de. "Ethnografia, Manjacos e Brames, povoadores da circunscrição civil da Costa de Baixo." *Boletim Oficial da Colónia da Guiné* no. 3, apenso (Jan., 3 1928), 1–23.

———. "Respota ao questionário de inquérito sôbre as raças da Guiné e seus cárácteres étnicos, formulado pelo governo da colónia em portoria provincial no. 70, de 12 Abril de 1927." *Boletim Oficial da Colónia da Guiné* no. 3, apenso (January 21, 1928).

Mettas, Jean. "La traite portugaise en haute Guinée." *Journal of African History* 16, no. 3 (1975): 343–363.

Miers, Suzanne, and Igor Kopytoff, eds. *Slavery in Africa: Historical and Anthropological Perspectives*. Madison: University of Wisconsin Press, 1977.

Miller, Joseph C. *Way of Death: Merchant Capitalism and the Angolan Slave Trade, 1730–1830*. Madison: University of Wisconsin Press, 1988.

Mitchell, William P. "The Hydraulic Hypothesis: A Reappraisal." *Current Anthropology* 14, no. 5 (1973): 532–534.

Mollien, Gaspard. *Travels in the Interior of Africa to the Sources of the Senegal and Gambia Performed by the Command of the French Government in the Year 1818*. Edited by T. E. Bowdich. London: Frank Cass, 1967.

Monteiro, J. M. de Souza. *Diccionario geográfico das provincias e possessões portuguezas no Ultramar*. Lisbon: Typographia Lisbonense, 1850.

―――. "Estudos sobre a Guiné de Cabo Verde." *O Panorama* 10 (1853): 20 ff.

Moore, Francis. *Travels into the Inland Parts of Africa*. London: Edward Cave, 1738.

Moraes e Castro, Armando Augusto Gonçalves de. *Annuario da provincia da Guiné do anno de 1925*. Bolama: Imprensa Nacional, 1925.

Mota, Avelino Teixeira da. "A agricultura dos Brames e Balantas vista através da fotografia aérea." *Boletim Cultural da Guiné Portuguesa* 5 (1950): 131–172.

―――. *A habitação indígena na Guiné portuguesa*. Bissau: Centro de Estudos da Guiné Portuguesa, 1948.

―――. *Guiné portuguesa*. Lisbon: Agência Geral do Ultramar, 1954.

―――. *Some Aspects of Portuguese Colonisation and Sea Trade in West Africa in the Fifteenth and Sixteenth Centuries*. Bloomington: Indiana University Press, 1978.

―――. *Topónimos de origem portuguesa na costa ocidental de África*. Bissau: Centro de Estudos da Guiné Portuguesa, 1950.

―――, ed. *As viagens do Bispo D. Frei Vitoriano Portuense à Guiné e a cristianização dos reis de Bissau*. Lisbon: Junta de Investigações Científicas do Ultramar, 1974.

Nachtigal, Gustav. *Sahel and Sudan*. Translated by Allan G. B. Fisher and Humphery J. Fisher. London: C. Hurst, 1987.

Nayar, N. M. "Origin and Cytogenetics of Rice." *Advances in Genetics* 17 (1974): 153–292.

Newbury, David. "Africanists' Historical Studies in the United States: Metamorphosis or Metastasis?" In *African Historiographies: What History for Which Africans?* Edited by Bogumil Jewsiewicki and David Newbury. Beverly Hills: Sage, 1986, 151–164.

Newitt, M. D. D. "The Portuguese on the Zambezi: An Historical Interpretation of the Prazo." *Journal of African History* 10, no. 1 (1969): 67–85.

Niane, D. T. "Mali and the Second Mandingo Expansion." In *General History of Africa*. Vol. 4, *Africa from the Twelfth to the Sixteenth Century*. Edited by D. T. Niane. London: Heinemann, 1984, 117–171.

North, Douglas C. *Institutions, Institutional Change, and Economic Performance*. Cambridge: Cambridge University Press, 1990.

Northrup, David. *Trade Without Rulers: Pre-Colonial Economic Development in South-Eastern Nigeria*. Oxford: Clarendon Press, 1978.

Nwokeji, G. Ugo. "African Conceptions of Gender and the Slave Traffic." *William and Mary Quarterly* 58, no. 1 (January 2001): 47–69.

Oliveira, E. J. da Costa. "Guiné portugueza." *Boletim da Sociedade de Geografia de Lisboa* (1888–1889): 307.

―――. *Viagem á Guiné*. Lisbon: Imprensa Nacional, 1890.

Oriji, J. N. "A History of the Ngwa People: Social and Economic Developments in an Igbo Clan from the Thirteenth to the Twentieth Centuries." Ph.D. thesis, State University of New Jersey, 1977.

Owen, W. F. W. *Narrative of Voyages to Explore the Shores of Africa, Arabia, and Madagascar*. London: Richard Bentley, 1833.

Pavy, David. "The Provenience of Colombian Negroes." *Journal of Negro History* 52, no. 1 (January 1967): 35–80.

Pearson, Y. "The Coastal Peoples: From Casamace to the Ivory Coast Lagoons." In *Gen-*

eral History of Africa. Vol. 4, *Africa from the Twelfth to the Sixteenth Century.* Edited by D. T. Niane. London: Heinemann, 1984, 301–323.

———. "States and Peoples of Senegambia and Upper Guinea." In *General History of Africa.* Vol. 6, *Africa in the Nineteenth Century Until the 1880s.* Edited by J. F. Ade Ajaye. Oxford: Heinemann, 1989, 636–661.

Peires, J. B. *The Dead Will Arises: Nongqawuse and the Great Xhosa Cattle-Killing Movement of 1856–7.* Bloomington: Indiana University Press, 1989.

Pélissier, René. *História da Guiné: Portugueses e Africanos na Senegâmbia, 1841–1936.* Lisbon: Imprensa Univerisitária, 1989.

———. *Les paysans du Sénégal: Les civilisations agraires du Cayor à la Casamonace.* Saint-Yrieix: Imprimerie Fabrègue, 1966.

Pereira, Carlos. *La Guinée portuguaise.* Lisbon: Editora Limitada 1914.

Pereira, Duarte Pacheco. "Esmeraldo de situ orbis." In *Os mais antigos roteiros da Guiné.* Edited by Damião Peres. Lisbon: Academia Portuguesa da História, 1952, 69–144.

Pimentel, Alberto Gomes. "Circumscrição civil de Mansôa: Etnografia." *Boletim Official da Guiné Portuguesa* 50 (December 10, 1927): 1–26.

Pinto, Françoise Latour da Veiga, and António Carreira. "Portuguese Participation in the Slave Trade: Opposing Forces, Trends of Opinion Within Portuguese Society— Effects on Portugal's Socio-Economic Development." In *The African Slave Trade from the Fifteenth to the Nineteenth Century.* Paris: UNESCO, 1979, 119–149.

Pinto, João Teixeira. *Teixeira Pinto: A ocupação militar da Guiné.* Lisbon: Divisão de Publicações e Biblioteca, 1936.

Piot, Charles. "Of Slaves and the Gift: Kabre Sale of Kin During the Era of the Slave Trade." *Journal of African History* 37, no. 1 (1996): 31–49.

Portères, Roland. "African Cereals: Eleusine, Fonio, Black Fonio, Teff, Brachiaria, Paspalum, Pennisetum, and African Rice." In *Origins of African Plant Domestication.* Edited by Jack R. Harlan et al. Paris: Mouton, 1976, 409–452.

———. "Berceaux agricoles primaires sur le continent africain." *Journal of African History* 3, no. 2 (1962): 195–210.

———. "Les appelations des céréales en Afrique." *Journal d'Agriculture Tropicale et de Botanique* 5–6 (1958–1959).

———. "Taxonomie agrobotanique des riz cultivés." *Journal d'Agriculture Tropicale et de Botanique* 3 (1956): 341 ff.

———. "Vieilles agricultures africaines avant le XVIe siecle." *L'Agranomie Tropicale* 5 (1950): 489–507.

Quintino, Fernando R. *Algumas notas sobre a gramática balanta.* Bissau: Centro de Estudos da Guiné, 1951.

———. *Conhecimento da língua balanta através da sua estrutura.* Bissau: Centro de Estudos da Guiné, 1961.

———. *Prática e utiensilagem agrícolas na Guiné.* Lisbon: Junta de Investigações Científicas do Ultramar, 1971.

———. "Serão os balantas negros sudaneses? Cronologia e âmbito das viagens portu- guesas de descoberta na África ocidental, de 1445 a 1462." *Boletim Cultural da Guiné Portuguesa* (April 1947): 299–314.

Rasmussen, Susan J. "The Slave Narrative in Life History and Myth, and Problems of Ethnographic Representation of the Tuareg Cultural Predicament." *Ethnohistory* 46 (1999): 67–108.

Ribeiro, Carlos Rui. "Arroz na mentalidade Balanta." *Boletim de Inforação Sócio-econica* 2 (1988): 1–11.

Richards, W. A. "The Import of Firearms into West Africa in the Eighteenth Century." *Journal of African History* 21, no. 1 (1980): 43–59.

Roberts, Andrew. "Portuguese Africa." In *The Cambridge History of Africa*. Vol. 7, *From 1905–1940*. Edited by A. D. Robterts. Cambridge: Cambridge University Press, 1986, 494–536.

Roberts, Richard L. "Linkages and Multiplier Effects in the Ecologically Specialized Trade of Precolonial West Africa." *Cahiers d'Études Africaines* 20, nos. 77–78 (1980): 135–148.

———. "Production and Reproduction of Warrior States: Segu Bambara and Segu Tokolor, c. 1712–1890," *International Journal of African Historical Studies* 13, no. 3 (1980): 389–419.

———. *Warriors, Merchants, and Slaves*. Stanford: Stanford University Press, 1987.

Robertson, Claire C., and Martin A. Klein, eds. *Women and Slavery in Africa*. Madison: University of Wisconsin Press, 1983.

Robinson, David. *Holy War of Umar Tal: The Western Sudan in the Mid–Nineteenth Century*. Oxford: Clarendon Press, 1985.

———. "The Islamic Revolution in Futa Toro." *International Journal of African Historical Studies* 8, no. 2 (1975): 185–221.

Rodney, Walter. "The Guinea Coast." In *The Cambridge History of Africa*. Vol. 4, *From c. 1600 to c. 1790*. Edited by Richard Gray. Cambridge: Cambridge University Press, 1975, 223–324.

———. *A History of the Upper Guinea Coast, 1545 to 1800*. New York: Monthly Review Press, 1970.

———. *How Europe Underdeveloped Africa*. Washington, D.C.: Howard University Press, 1982.

———. "Jihad and Social Revolution in Futa Djalon in the Eighteenth Century." *Journal of the Historical Society of Nigeria* 4 (June 1968): 269–284.

———. "Portuguese Attempts at Monopoly on the Upper Guinea Coast, 1580–1650." *Journal of African History* 6, no. 3 (1965): 307–322.

———. "Slavery and Other Forms of Social Oppression on the Upper Guinea Coast in the Context of the Atlantic Slave Trade," *Journal of African History* 7, no. 3 (1966): 431–447.

Roper, H. R. Trevor. "The Rise of Christian Europe." *The Listener* 70 (1963): 871.

Sahlins, Marshall. "Patterns of Marital Alliance." In *Tribesmen*. Edited by Marshall Sahlins. Englewood Cliffs, N.J.: Prentice Hall, 1968, 56–63.

———. "The Segmentary Lineage: An Organization of Predatory Expansion" *American Anthropologist* 63, no. 2 (1961): 322–345.

———. *Stone Age Economics*. Chicago: Aldine, 1972.

Samb, Amar. "L'islam et le Ngabou." *Éthiopiques* 28 (October 1981): 116–123.

Sandoval, Alonso de. *Natvraleza, policia, sagrada i profana, costvmbres i ritos, disciplina i catechismo evangelico de todos etiopes*. Seville: Francisco de Lira, 1627.

Santo, J. do Espírito. *Nomes vernáculos de algumas plantas da Guiné portuguesa*. Lisbon: Junta de Investigações Científicas do Ultramar, 1963.

———. "Notas sobre a cultura do arroz etre os balantas." *Boletim Cultural da Guiné Portuguesa* 4 (April 1949): 197–233.

Schmidt, Elizabeth. *Peasants, Traders, and Wives: Shona Women in the History of Zimbabwe, 1870–1939.* Portsmouth, N.H.: Heineman, 1992.

Schoenmakers, Hans. "Old Men and New State Structures in Guinea Bissau." *Journal of Legal Pluralism and Unofficial Law* nos. 25–26 (1987): 99–138.

Schwab, George. *Tribes of the Liberian Hinterland.* Papers of the Peabody Museum of American Archaeology and Ethnology, Harvard University, vol. 31. Cambridge: Peabody Museum, 1947.

Sdersky, Pablo. "As relações de trabalho numa sociedade de cultivadores de arroz: O caso dos Balantas de Tombali." *Soronda* 3 (1987): 21–38.

Searing, James F. *West African Slavery and Atlantic Commerce: The Senegal River Valley, 1700–1860.* Cambridge: Cambridge University Press, 1993.

Silva, Arthur Augusto da. "Apontamentos sobre as populações Oeste-Africanas segundo os autores portuguese dos séculos XVI e XVII." *Boletim Cultural da Guiné Portuguesa* 16 (1959): 373–406.

Silva, Francisco Teixeira da. *Relatorio do governo da provincia da Guiné portugueza com referencia a 1887–1888.* Lisbon: Typographia Minerva Central, 1889.

Silva, Maria da Graça Garcia Nolasco da. "Subsídios para o estudo dos 'lançados' na Guiné." *Boletim Cultural da Guiné Portuguesa* 25, nos. 97–100 (1970): 25 ff.

Silveira, Joel Frederico. "Guiné." In *O Império Africano 1825–1890.* Edited by Valentim Alexandre and Jill Dias. Lisbon: Editorial Estampa, 1998, 211–268.

Socrates da Costa, A. J. "Provincia da Guiné portugueza." *Boletim da Sociedade de Geografia de Lisboa* ser. 4a, no. 2 (1883): 106–107.

Soumonni, Elisée. "Slave and Palm Oil Trades in Dahomey, 1818–1858." In *From Slave Trade to "Legitimate" Commerce.* Edited by Robin Law. Cambridge: Cambridge University Press, 1995, 78–90.

Steward, Julian H. *Theory of Cultural Change.* Urbana: University of Illinois Press, 1955.

Stroble, Margaret. *Muslim Women in Mombasa: 1890–1975.* New Haven, Conn.: Yale University Press, 1979.

Suba, Agostinho Clode, et al. "As estructuras sociais balantas." *Bombolom* 1 (n.d.).

Tardieu, Jean-Pierre. "Origins of the Slaves in the Lima Region in Peru (Sixteenth and Seventeenth Centuries)." In *From Chains to Bonds: The Slave Trade Revisited.* Edited by Doudou Diène. Paris: UNESCO, 2001, 43–54.

Taylor, Michael. *Community, Anarchy, Liberty.* Cambridge: Cambridge University Press, 1982.

Thomas, R., and R. Bean, "The Fishers of Men: The Profits of the Slave Trade." *Journal of Economic History* 34 (September 1974): 885–904.

Thornton, John K. *Africa and Africans in the Making of the Atlantic World, 1400–1680.* Cambridge: Cambridge University Press, 1992.

———. *The Kongolese Saint Anthony: Dona Beatriz Kimpa Vita and the Antonian Movement, 1684–1706.* Cambridge: Cambridge University Press, 1998.

———. "Sexual Demography: The Impact of the Slave Trade on Family Structure." In *Women and Slavery in Africa.* Edited by Claire C. Robertson and Martin A. Klein. Madison: University of Wisconsin Press, 1983, 39–48.

———. "The Slave Trade in Eighteenth Century Angola: Effects on Demographic Structures." *Canadian Journal of African Studies* 14, no. 3 (1980): 417–427.

Tosh, John. *Clan Leaders and Colonial Chiefs: The Political History of an East African Stateless Society, c. 1800–1939.* Oxford: Clarendon Press, 1978.

Valdez, Francisco Travassos. *Africa occidental: Noticias e considerações.* Lisbon: Imprensa Nacional, 1864.

———. *Six Years of a Traveller's Life in Western Africa.* London: Hurst and Blackett, 1861.

van Allen, Judith. "'Aba Riots' or Igbo 'Women's War'? Ideology, Stratification, and the Invisibility of Women." In *Women in Africa: Studies in Social and Economic Change.* Edited by Nancy J. Hafkin and Edna G. Bay. Stanford: Stanford University Press, 1976, 59–86.

van Dantzig, Albert. "Effects of the Atlantic Slave Trade on Some West African Societies." In *Forced Migration: The Impact of the Export Slave Trade on African Societies.* Edited by Joseph E. Inikori. New York: Africana, 1982, 187–201.

Vansina, Jan. *Living with Africa.* Madison: University of Wisconsin Press, 1994.

———. *Oral Tradition: A Study in Historical Methodology.* Chicago: Aldine, 1965.

———. *Oral Tradition as History.* Madison: University of Wisconsin Press, 1985.

———. *Paths in the Rainforests: Toward a History of Political Tradition in Equatorial Africa.* Madison: University of Wisconsin Press, 1990.

Vansina, J., R. Mauny, and L. V. Thomas. *The Historian in Tropical Africa: Studies Presented and Discussed at the Fourth International African Seminar at the University of Dakar, Senegal, 1961.* London: Oxford University Press, 1964.

Vasconcellos, Ernesto J. de C. e. *Guiné portuguesa: Estudo elementar de geografia física, económica e politica.* Lisbon: Tip. da Cooperativa Militar, 1917.

Verger, Pierre. *Trade Relations Between the Bight of Benin and Bahia from the Seventeenth to the Nineteenth Century.* Ibadan, Nigeria: Ibadan University Press, 1976.

Vogel, Joseph O., ed. *Ancient African Metallurgy: The Sociocultural Context.* Walnut Creek, Calif.: Altamira Press, 2000.

———, ed. *Encyclopedia of Precolonial Africa, Archaeology, History, Languages, Cultures, and Environments.* Walnut Creek, Calif.: Altamira Press, 1996.

Warnier, Jean-Pierre. "Traite sans raids au Cameroun." *Cahiers d'Études Africaines* 113, 29–1 (1989): 5–32.

Webb, James. *Desert Frontier, Ecological Change, and Economic Change Along the Western Sahel, 1600–1850.* Madison: University of Wisconsin Press, 1995.

Weiskel, Timothy. *French Colonial Rule and the Baule Peoples: Resistance and Collaboration, 1889–1911.* Oxford: Clarendon Press, 1980.

White, Luise. *The Comforts of Home: Prostitution in Colonial Nairobi.* Chicago: University of Chicago Press, 1990.

Wilks, Ivor. "The Mossi and Akan States." In *History of West Africa.* Vol. 1. Edited by J. F. Ade Ajayi and Michael Crowder. New York: Columbia University Press, 1972, 344–386.

Willis, John Ralph. "Jihad Di-Sabil Allah: Its Doctrinal Basis in Islam and Some Aspects of Its Evolution in Nineteenth-Century West Africa." *Journal of African History* 8, no. 3 (1967): 395–415.

Wilson, W. W. *Outline of the Balanta Language.* London: University School of Oriental and African Studies, 1961.

Wittfogel, Karl A. *Oriental Despotism: A Comparative Study of Total Power.* New Haven, Conn.: Yale University Press, 1957.

Wondji, C. "The States and Cultures of the Upper Guinea Coast." In *General History of*

Africa. Vol. 5, *Africa from the Sixteenth Century to the Eighteenth Century.* Edited by B. A. Ogot. London: Heinemann, 1992, 368–398.

Wright, Donald R. *The Early History of Niumi: Settlement and Foundation of a Mandinka State on the Gambia River.* Athens, Ohio.: Ohio University, Center for International Studies 1977.

———. *The World and a Very Small Place in Africa.* Armonk, N.Y.: M. E. Sharpe, 1997.

Wright, Marcia. *Strategies of Slaves and Women: Life-Stories from East/Central Africa.* New York: Lilian Barber, 1993.

———. "Women in Peril: A Commentary on the Life Stories of Captives in Nineteenth Century East-Central Africa." *African Social Research* 20 (1975): 800–819.

Zurara, Gomes Eanes de. *Chrónica de Guiné.* Edited by José de Bragança. Lisbon: Biblioteca Histórica, n.d.

INDEX

About the Author

WALTER HAWTHORNE is Assistant Professor of History at Ohio University, Athens, Ohio.